NEWARK PUBLIC LIBRARY
DISCARDED
5 2125 300850379

D1257637

ballet

Donated in Memory
of
Betty Falstick
by the
Newark Tuesday Club
NEWARK PUBLIC
LIBRARY Connect. Explore. Imagine.

ballet

THE DEFINITIVE ILLUSTRATED STORY

NEWARK PUBLIC LIBRARY
121 HIGH ST.
NEWARK, NY 14513

Senior Editor Victoria Heyworth-Dunne
Senior Art Editor Jane Ewart
Editors Chauney Dunford, Anna Fischel, Kathryn Hennessy, Zoë Rutland
US Editor Megan Douglass
Designers Stephen Bere, Mark Cavanagh
Managing Editor Gareth Jones
Senior Managing Art Editor Lee Griffiths
Picture Researcher Sarah Smithies
Jacket Designer Surabhi Wadhwa-Gandhi
Jacket Editor Amelia Collins
Jacket Design Development Manager Sophia MTT
Pre-production Producer Jacqueline Street-Elkayam
Senior Producer Mandy Inness
Publisher Liz Wheeler
Art Director Karen Self
Publishing Director Jonathan Metcalf

DK India

Senior Managing Art Editor Arunesh Talapatra
Managing Art Editor Sudakshina Basu
Senior Art Editor Chhaya Sajwan
Project Art Editor Rupanki Arora Kaushik
Art Editors Meenal Goel, Devika Khosla
Production Manager Pankaj Sharma
Pre-production Manager Balwant Singh
Senior DTP Designers Harish Aggarwal, Neeraj Bhatia
DTP Designers Dheeraj Singh, Vikram Singh
Jacket Designer Suhita Dharamjit
Jackets Editorial Coordinator Priyanka Sharma
Managing Jacket Editor Saloni Singh
Picture Research Manager Taiyaba Khatoon
Senior Picture Researcher Sumedha Chopra
Picture Researcher Rituraj Singh

With thanks to The Royal Ballet for their help and guidance in the making of this book.

First American Edition 2018
Published in the United States by DK Publishing
345 Hudson Street, New York, New York, 10014

Copyright © 2018 Dorling Kindersley Limited
DK, a Division of Penguin Random House LLC
18 19 20 21 22 10 9 8 7 6 5 4 3 2 1
001-306013-Sep/2018

All rights reserved. Without limiting the rights under the copyright reserved above, no part of this publication may be reproduced, stored in or introduced into a retrieval system, or transmitted, in any form, or by any means (electronic, mechanical, photocopying, recording, or otherwise), without the prior written permission of the copyright owner.
Published in Great Britain by Dorling Kindersley Limited
A catalog record for this book is available from the Library of Congress.

ISBN 978-1-4654-7478-0
Printed and bound in China

A WORLD OF IDEAS:
SEE ALL THERE IS TO KNOW
www.dk.com

Contents

ROMANTIC BALLET (1830–1860) 40

CLASSICAL BALLET (1860–1905) 76

MODERN BALLET (1905–1945) 140

The very essence of ballet is poetic, deriving from dreams rather than from reality.

THEOPHILE GAUTIER, WRITER

CONSULTANT

Viviana Durante is considered to be one of the greatest, most dramatic ballerinas of her generation. Born in Rome, she trained at The Royal Ballet School and became principal dancer at The Royal Ballet at the age of 21. She was also prima ballerina with American Ballet Theatre, Teatro alla Scala, and Japan's K-Ballet. Viviana holds a Diploma of Dance Teaching from The Royal Ballet School and a Diploma in Dance Teaching and Learning from Trinity College, London. She coaches and teaches internationally.

CONTRIBUTORS

Sheila Dickie trained with The Royal Ballet School. After she stopped performing, she ran her own dance school for 15 years. She was also Education Officer at Sadler's Wells Theatre and a dance history lecturer at Birkbeck, University of London and the Royal Academy of Dance.

David Mead is editor of SeeingDance.com and is a frequent contributor to magazines, including *Dancing Times*. He also wrote chapters for *ReOrienting Taiwan's Modern Dance* and *Dance, Access and Inclusion: Perspectives on Dance, Young People and Change*. David lectures and choreographs, working largely with vocational schools in Taiwan.

Caroline Hamilton is an Australian-born historian and writer based in the UK. She is a specialist in early 20th-century ballet and the evolution of dance costume. Caroline writes for a wide range of dance magazines and publications, and was a researcher for *Anna Pavlova: Twentieth Century Ballerina*.

Jessica Teague is a dance journalist and researcher, contributing regularly to international dance publications. Trained at the School of American Ballet, Jessica danced professionally with the Pacific Northwest Ballet, Dutch National Ballet, and Royal Ballet of Flanders. She also holds an MA in Cultural Policy and a BA in Art History and Criticism.

Antonia Barron trained as a dancer in Australia by the diaspora of the Pavlova and the Ballet Russe de Monte Carlo ballet companies. A published author and journalist, she was a feature writer for an Australian newspaper chain for 14 years. She is now a ballet teacher as well as a writer.

Esther Ripley worked for many years as a journalist, education magazine editor, book reviewer, and short-story competition judge. She writes on a range of cultural subjects, especially ballet and contemporary dance.

Yuka Maeno is a freelance writer with a keen interest in ballet and dance. After winning the First Word Journalism Award in 2009, she entered the publishing industry and has since contributed to various publications in the UK and Japan.

Foreword

Ballet has been—and always will be—my passion as well as my career, and I honestly cannot imagine a life without it. I began dancing in a garage in Rome at the age of six and have danced nearly every day since.

One of my greatest pleasures is sharing the joy of ballet with others, whether through coaching new talent at The Royal Ballet, directing productions for my company, or now through this wonderful book. In these pages you will find the whole story of ballet in one beautiful package, and it is a vital part of all ballet lovers' libraries.

This is the first illustrated history showcasing many of the famous ballets and productions that have thrilled audiences across the world, offering you the opportunity to experience the essential works from the beginnings of ballet to today. It will help you gain a deeper appreciation of the best-known ballets, like *The Sleeping Beauty* and *Giselle*, and also the lesser-known ones, like *Chroma* and *Bella Figura*.

As you follow the art of ballet through five centuries, you will learn about its remarkable evolution from Marie Taglioni's time, when dancing en pointe first became fashionable, to today when choreographers are creating ever more daring and challenging work. Charting changes in taste, this book reveals the political and societal as well as the individual influences that made ballet what it is today. You will read about the colorful and dramatic lives of the leading ballet personalities, accompanied by exquisite photographs and illustrations that take us straight into their worlds. Ballet is a collaboration, and here you will find profiles of the most important choreographers—all former dancers—and composers, as well as the dancers themselves and the characters they bring to life.

Ballet has only risen in popularity and importance since I first started dancing. I am often struck by how personal and unique each audience member's experience of a single performance can be, and how this response can take place on an emotional, intellectual, spiritual, or even a physical level. Ballet allows us to connect with our inner being through the power of movement and the sound of music. Ballet is about the raw humanity of Anastasia's plight contrasted with Clara's childlike joy and wonder in *The Nutcracker*: it has the power to entertain, delight, challenge, and shock, and it is continually evolving.

I hope you will enjoy reading this book and gazing at the images as much as I have, reliving scenes from your favorite ballets. As the audience of ballet continues to broaden through live cinema screenings, I am so excited about the newest generation of ballet lovers. I cannot wait to see what the future brings in terms of new interpretations, works, and dancers. I feel immensely privileged to have been given the gift of ballet, and to be able to share that gift with you.

Viviana Durante

1

BEGINNINGS OF BALLET

(1550–1830)

Beginnings of ballet 1550–1830

Ballet as it is known today can be traced back to the early 16th century. In 1533, Catherine de' Medici of Italy married Henri II of France—they were both just 14—but it was an unhappy union. Politically and emotionally sidelined by Henri, Catherine indulged in her love of arts, and introduced aspects of Italian court life to the French court. At the time, the monarchy was held in little regard in France, and Catherine believed that court entertainment, with implied messages and motifs, could be used to help reassert the monarchy's authority over the nobility.

Italian musician and composer Balthasar de Beaujoyeulx was engaged by the French court in 1555 as a servant, where he revealed a talent for staging informal court celebrations. Having made a name for himself, in 1581 he was commissioned by Catherine's daughter-in-law, Marguerite de Vaudémont, to create *Ballet Comique de la Reine* in celebration of her marriage to the Duke of Joyeuse. The resulting five-and-a-half-hour work is credited with being the first ballet to combine choreography with a narrative—the style becoming known as ballet de cour (court ballet).

Ballets de cour thrived for the next century as court entertainment in France, and became a powerful tool, in which political and allegorical messages could be woven. However, it was under the reign of Louis XIV that ballet really began to flourish. In 1653, at the age of 14, Louis XIV appeared in the 12-hour spectacle *Ballet de la nuit* as the god Apollo, and would be forever immortalized as the Sun King.

In 1661, Louis XIV founded the Académie Royale de Danse. Led by 13 prominent ballet masters, the academy standardized and codified practices in court dance. Just eight years later, the Académie Royale de Musique, also known as the Opéra, was established, which incorporated singers, musicians, and dancers from the Académie Royale de Danse. It was here that ballet dancer and teacher Pierre Beauchamp first defined the five positions of the feet—the first thing that every ballet dancer is taught to this day. As ballet became more organized and structured, it developed into a profession—one no longer only staged in aristocratic courts but in theaters for paying audiences.

Ballet continued to thrive in France, but remained largely a male-dominated field. In the 18th century, ballet d'action emerged, which relied solely on movement and mime to convey and progress the ballet's story. It was also during this century that other great centers for ballet began to appear in Copenhagen, St. Petersburg, Moscow, and Milan—but Paris would remain the center for ballet innovation until the second half of the 19th century.

Ballet Comique de la Reine

First performed: October 15, 1581 ▪ Venue: Salle du Petit-Bourbon, Louvre, Paris ▪ Choreography: Balthasar de Beaujoyeulx ▪ Music: Collaboration including Lambert de Beaulieu and Jacques Salmon ▪ Story: Nicolas Filleul de la Chesnaye (the king's poet)

With its structured choreography and written narrative, *Ballet Comique de la Reine* is often cited as the first true ballet. This lengthy work was created to celebrate the wedding of Marguerite de Lorraine to the Duc de Joyeuse. Following recent civil wars in France, the originators hoped that the scale of the extravaganza would spell out the monarchy's power to the court audience.

STORY LINE

The work told the Greek myth of Odysseus's escape from Circe, and contained many allegorical figures that would have been recognizable to courtiers at the time. It included three ballets within it, which both furthered and enhanced the narrative.

The first ballet This was a dance for 12 naiads (water nymphs) and their pages.

The grand ballet Naiads and dryads (wood nymphs) performed this.

The final grand ballet This contained planned, specific, geometric choreography, using shapes and patterns to create interesting moves with a particular meaning.

Afterward, the spectators were invited to join the performers at a grand ball.

While previous ballets de cour (court ballets) included dance sections that were purely decorative, Beaujoyeulx wove a coherent choreographic story into the spectacle. However, unlike ballets of today, the work still combined sung and spoken sections with musical interludes as well as dance.

Beaujoyeulx described his choreography as "a geometrical arrangement of several persons dancing together, to the diverse harmonies of numerous instruments." *Ballet Comique de la Reine* is the first ballet of which there is a libretto (printed account), published in 1582. This libretto was seen in courts across Europe, and hugely influenced the development of ballets de cour.

◀ **Valois tapestry of the wedding**
The ballet was one of 17 entertainments, including tournaments, a horse ballet, fireworks, and poetry that celebrated the wedding, and were commemorated in a series of tapestries. This tapestry shows courtiers in the palace garden.

▲ **Three sirens from *Ballet Comique de la Reine***
Wearing matching costumes with their legs hidden behind a watery stage set, the sirens, who in Greek myth lured sailors to destruction with their sweet song, warned courtiers of the dangers of straying from the path of loyalty to the monarchy.

Italian style comes to France

When Catherine de' Medici of Italy married Henri II of France in 1533, she brought many styles of pageantry and entertainment from the Italian court to France, including a type of court dance. Catherine was a huge lover of dance and, in 1555, she sent for her Italian ballet master, Balthasar de Beaujoyeulx, who came to Paris. Catherine became known for her lavish court spectacles, and was skilled at including symbolism that had political significance, designed to bring plotting courtiers into line.

In 1581, Catherine's daughter-in-law Louise, married to Henri III of France, commissioned Beaujoyeulx to create *Ballet Comique de la Reine* to celebrate her sister's marriage. The ballet was on a grand—and lengthy—scale. It began at 10 pm and lasted five and a half hours. It was performed in a large hall with no proscenium arch or separate stage area as seen today. The audience were therefore immersed in the action. The dancers were not professionals, but members of the court, nobility, and royalty.

At the end of the ballet, selected guests were presented with symbolic emblems. Louise gave Henri III a disk with the emblem of a dolphin—a play on the word *dauphin* (meaning "heir apparent" as well as "dolphin").

▲ **Integrated stage and audience**
Members of the audience were seated on three sides on the same level as the performers, or on a balcony. The performance space was divided, with sorceress Circe's palace and garden at the back.

BEGINNINGS OF BALLET

The earliest dance notation dates from the mid-15th century in Italy. Wealthy families in the various Italian states sponsored dancing masters, who created court dances and extravaganzas for them. For instance, Domenico de Piacenza wrote down the dances he created for the d'Este family in Ferrara in about 1460, and it is manuscripts such as these that are the beginnings of ballet. When Florentine Catherine de' Medici married the future Henri II of France in 1533 she took her love of art with her, and introduced the spectacular performances and musical events of Italy to her husband's court. A century on, Louis XIV, himself a talented dancer, inaugurated an academy for dance in 1666. His dancing masters Jean-Baptiste Lully (like Catherine, born in Florence) and Pierre Beauchamp taught there. Beauchamp defined the five positions in ballet and devised a notation system. Raoul-Auger Feuillet published notated dances in 1700, probably using Beauchamp's system, and his written works helped to develop ballet.

With dance academies, professionals were needed. Only men were admitted initially, followed by women in the late 17th century. Soon, a balletic technique emerged. Steps became more intricate and difficult so that only trained dancers could perform them.

The new technique required costume reform. Women still wore heeled shoes, but their skirts were shortened so that audiences could see their footwork. By the 18th century, dancers abandoned masks and heavy costumes in favor of lighter clothes. Around 1820, female dancers discarded heeled slippers and began experimenting with pointe work to portray the lightness of the Romantic ballerina.

> [Dance] became, apart from anything else, a fine excuse for dressing up.
>
> CLIVE BARNES, DANCE CRITIC, 1999

◀ ***The Wedding Ball*, 1604**
Martin Pepyn's painting shows the wedding couple leading a procession of guests in the kind of courtly dances that took place before Louis XIV set up a professional academy.

Ballet de la nuit

First performed: February 23, 1653 ▪ Venue: Salle du Petit-Bourbon, Louvre, Paris ▪ Choreography: Clément and others ▪ Music: Jean-Baptiste Boësset, Jean de Cambefort, Michel Lambert, Jean-Baptiste Lully, and others ▪ Story: Isaac de Bensérade

During the 17th century, ballets de cour (court ballets) flourished, and were performed by royalty, nobility, and foreign dignitaries. While much of the footwork of these early ballets is recognizable today, ballets de cour contained no large jumps or turns, which developed later. *Ballet de la nuit* was a huge, opulent spectacle representing the four watches of the night in real time.

STORY LINE

The ballet is in four acts, with 43 separate dances symbolizing the 12 hours of the night between sunset and sunrise.

Act I 6–9 o'clock—the activities at the end of the day, on the theme of sunset.

Act II 9 o'clock to midnight—the entertainment of the evening.

Act III Midnight to 3 o'clock—the fantasies, freedoms, and horrors of the night.

Act IV 3 o'clock to sunrise—the activities of the dawn.

Between 1648 and 1653, there was a series of civil wars in France, sparked by a resistance toward the growing power of the monarchy. Cardinal Mazarin, first minister and advisor to the young king Louis XIV, understood the strength of court spectacle, notably ballet, as a political tool. He therefore commissioned *Ballet de la nuit* after the defeat of the rebels in 1653 to promote Louis XIV as an absolute monarch and figure of authority.

Night of majestic display

Ballet de la nuit spanned 12 hours, and it was performed in real time. It contained allegorical figures and song, music, and drama, as well as dancing. Act I included huntsmen and shepherds returning from work, alongside gypsies, knife-grinders, lamp-lighters, and dancers dressed as lamps. Robbers prepared for their nighttime misdeeds and fraudulent beggars revealed their tricks.

Act II featured the evening delights of a ball, a ballet within the ballet, and a comedy. The third act centered on the tale of the moon and her love for the shepherd Endymion (a Greek myth), which caused her to leave the heavens and create an eclipse. With darkness came chaos. Witches, demons, magicians, and sorcerers appeared, and thieves tried to loot a burning house from which cats and monkeys fled. The final act showed money counterfeiters packing up and blacksmiths beginning work. Aurora, the dawn, arrived with her attendants, the 12 Hours, and the sun god Apollo arose, chasing out the evils of the night. Honor, Grace, Love, Riches, Victory, Fame, and Peace accompanied him. The young king played the role of Apollo, and so the legendary Sun King was born, which became the enduring image of Louis XIV for centuries.

The ballet had at least 100 performers in over 150 different roles. These dancers were a mix of nobility and courtiers, professional dancers, actors, acrobats, and children. James Stuart, Duke of York—later to be King James II—appeared as a Transient Patriot and Honor. The ballet was so successful that it was repeated seven times that year.

In a modern take, David Bintley created *The King Dances*, inspired by Baroque dance, *Ballet de la nuit,* and Louis XIV. It premiered in 2015.

◀ **Le Roi Soleil (the Sun King)**
Louis XIV was only 14 when he donned the costume of the Roman god of the sun, Apollo. He was said to be an excellent dancer.

▶ **The king presents a flourish**
The image of the boy king personifying the rising sun in the magnificent setting of the Petit-Bourbon theater in Paris symbolized the power of the monarchy and the hope for a new France.

▶ **Scenery design of sunset**
This backdrop of a seashore with the sun dipping below the horizon was used for the first entrée of the first watch of the night in Act I.

PARIS OPERA BALLET

The oldest ballet company in the world was created in 1669, when Louis XIV was on the throne. Reflecting the formality of the Sun King's court, dancing was elegant but stiff. Even today, the terminology used at the Paris Opéra Ballet dates back to Louis XIV's court. Dancers are called *coryphées* (leading members of the corps de ballet), *sujets* and *grands sujets* (soloists), and *étoiles* (stars). The tradition of *Le Grand Défilé*—a hierarchical file on stage of the entire ballet company from the youngest student to the *étoiles*—still takes place at the Palais Garnier, where Paris Opéra Ballet usually performs.

The groundbreaking role of the Paris Opéra Ballet was apparent from the start. The company was the first to use professional ballerinas—before then, young men took the female parts. Nearly a century later, director Jean-Georges Noverre (1776–1781) had radical ideas, such as changing the awkward panier costumes and disposing of masks to make dancing look more natural. Despite often being frustrated by conservative governors, the Paris Opéra Ballet led the way for other European courts, which hired French-trained dancers and choreographers to shape their own ballet companies.

Many of the greatest ballets, ballet masters, and dancers are linked with Paris Opéra Ballet. Romantic ballet was born with the company's productions of *La Sylphide* (1832) and *Giselle* (1841). In 1929, Serge Lifar was invited to direct the company. He gave dancers much greater freedom of movement and expression. Rudolf Nureyev directed from 1983 to 1990, commissioning new works, reviving old ones, and encouraging new stars such as Sylvie Guillem. And in the 21st century, Paris Opéra Ballet has traveled so far from its male-dominated roots that it has a female director, Aurélie Dupont, appointed in 2016.

> For me, it's about finding the right balance between the company's illustrious past and its future at the epicenter of French innovation.
>
> DIRECTOR AURELIE DUPONT, 2016

Behind the scenes of *The Nutcracker*, 2016 ▶
Marion Barbeau and Stéphane Bullion of the Paris Opéra Ballet practice their lifts backstage for the 2016 production of *The Nutcracker*, directed by Dmitri Tcherniakov. The production was staged at Palais Garnier, the company's Paris venue.

Jean-Baptiste Lully

Composer, instrumentalist, and dancer ▪ 1632–1687

Although he is best known as a composer of Baroque music, Italian-born Jean-Baptiste Lully was also a strong advocate of dance, both as a profession and a serious art form. He collaborated with playwright and actor Jean-Baptiste Molière and choreographer Pierre Beauchamp to invent a new art form, which culminated in *Le Bourgeois gentilhomme* (1670). As director of the Académie Royale de Musique in Paris, he introduced female dancers to the stage.

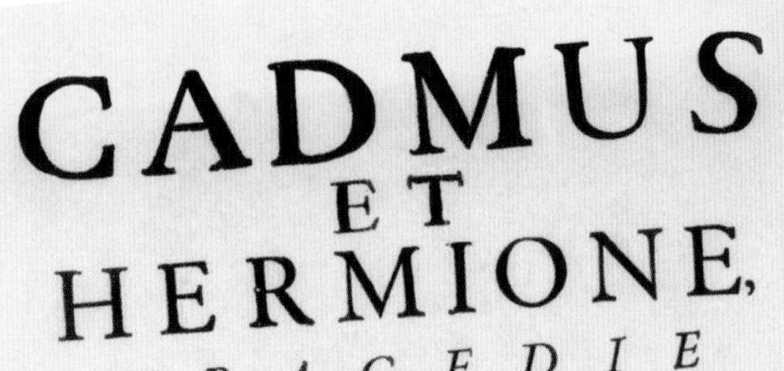

CADMUS
ET
HERMIONE,
TRAGEDIE
MISE EN MUSIQUE
Par Monſieur DE LULLY, Ecuyer-Conſeiller-Secretaire du Roy, Maiſon, Couronne de France & de ſes Finances, & Sur-Intendant de la Muſique de Sa Majeſté;
REPRÉSENTÉE POUR LA PREMIERE FOIS,
devant le Roy, à Saint-Germain-en-Laye, en l'Année 1674.
PARTITION générale, imprimée pour la premiere fois.

DE L'IMPRIMERIE
De J-B-CHRISTOPHE BALLARD, ſeul Imprimeur du Roy pour la Muſique, à Paris, ruë Saint Jean de Beauvais, au Mont-Parnaſſe.
M. DCC XIX.
Avec Privilege de Sa Majeſté.

▲ ***Cadmus et Hermione***
One of Lully's best-known operas and one of the first to use French rather than Italian, this is the first of Lully's tragedies set to music. A king, Cadmus, falls for Hermione, daughter of Venus and Mars.

Jean-Baptiste Lully was born Giovanni Battista Lulli in Florence, Italy, in 1632. The son of a miller, little is known about his early life. It is thought that the French Duke of Guise discovered Lully in Florence in the mid-1640s, amusing crowds during Mardi Gras festivities with his clowning and guitar skills. The Duke brought him back to France where Lully was employed as a *garçon de chambre* (chamber boy) to Mademoiselle de Montpensier, cousin to Louis XIV.

By 1653, his skills in dancing, clowning, and playing the violin had attracted the attention of the young French king. In the same year, Lully performed alongside the king in the ballet de cour (court dance) *Ballet de la nuit*—a spectacular production which lasted 12 hours.

Keeping the king happy

Lully joined the service of Louis XIV, and his talents as a dancer and composer soon made him indispensable. He became the king's composer of dance music, as well as the director of the king's personal violin orchestra, and by 1662 he had complete control over music at court.

Lully's composition also had an effect on the style of court dance and ballets de cour. Previously, slow and stately movements had been the norm, but Lully introduced lively and more rapid rhythms. These, in turn, influenced steps and choreography. From 1664, he began to collaborate with Molière and Beauchamp. Together they devised the new art form of comédie-ballet, which mixed spoken-word plays with music and dance. They created 10 works, including the masterpiece *Le Bourgeois gentilhomme*. Both Lully and the king often performed in the productions.

Music and dancing

In 1672, Lully was appointed director of the Académie Royale de Musique, also known as the Opéra. Established three years earlier, this institution brought together singers, musicians, and dancers to create and promote French opera (as opposed to Italian opera). As director, Lully produced a new work almost every year, and is credited as the "Father of French Opera." In 1673, his work *Cadmus et Hermione* premiered, introducing a new style of French opera known as tragédie en musique.

The Opéra also provided the first public stage for ballet, which had before only been staged at court or private events. Ballet quickly became an integral component of operas and a professional art form in its own right, and by the 19th century, it had its own repertoire at the Opéra, separate from the operatic performances held there.

Under Lully's directorship, women were permitted to perform, and took on roles that had previously been filled by men. In 1681, Lully staged the work *Le Triomphe de l'amour*, which featured dancer Mademoiselle de Lafontaine. This was the first time a female dancer had been showcased in this way, and paved the way for the development of ballerinas. The legacy of Lully's first professional ballet dancers endures, and his company— the oldest professional ballet company in the world—continues, now known as the Paris Opéra Ballet.

> The prince of French musicians … Lully entertained the king infinitely, by his music, by the way he performed it …

TITON DU TILLET, BIOGRAPHER, 1732

▲ ***Ballet de la nuit***
Beginning at sunset and ending with sunrise, this lavish ballet de cour featured various mythological figures. A gifted dancer and violinist, Lully performed alongside Louis XIV in this courtly dance.

KEY WORKS

Dancer: *Ballet royal d'Alcidiane*, 1658 • *Le Mariage forcé*, 1664 • *Ballet de la naissance de Vénus*, 1665 *Le Bourgeois gentilhomme*, 1670 • *Le Triomphe de l'amour*, 1681 • *Armide*, 1686

TIMELINE

- **November 29, 1632** Born Giovanni Battista Lulli in Florence, Italy, the son of a miller.
- **1640s** Moves to France, probably with the help of the Duke of Guise, and begins working for Mademoiselle de Montpensier, the Duke's niece.
- **1652** Dismissed from de Montpensier's string ensemble for composing risqué pieces.
- **1653** Dances alongside the French king, Louis XIV, in the epic ballet, *Ballet de la nuit*.
- **1661** Receives his *lettres de nationalisation* and becomes a French subject, changing his name to the French form, Jean-Baptiste Lully.

JEAN-BAPTISTE LULLY'S OPERA *ARMIDE*—ACT IV, SCENE 1

- **May 1661** Becomes superintendent and composer of music of the King's Bedchamber.
- **July 1662** Marries Madeleine Lambert, daughter of renowned French dancer, singer, and composer Michel Lambert.
- **1662** Is promoted to master of music of the King's Bedchamber, which brings him into regular contact with the king.
- **1664** Begins to collaborate with the playwright Molière and the choreographer Pierre Beauchamp on 10 comédie-ballets.
- **1672** Becomes director of the Académie Royale de Musique, and remains in this post for 15 years.
- **1681** Receives his *lettres de noblesse*, formally investing him with the status of a French nobleman.
- **March 22, 1687** Dies from the effects of gangrene after injuring his toe with his long conducting staff during a rehearsal. He had refused to have his foot amputated, for fear of being unable to dance.

Le Bourgeois gentilhomme

First performed: October 14, 1660 ▪ Venue: Château de Chambord, Loir-et-Cher ▪ Choreography: Pierre Beauchamp ▪ Music: Jean-Baptiste Lully
Story: Jean-Baptiste Molière

A political and social satire, *Le Bourgeois gentilhomme*—a comédie-ballet—was one of Louis XIV's favorite pieces of entertainment, despite the fact that it poked fun at the social climbing and foibles endemic in 17th-century society and in his own court. Contemporary foreign affairs and interests were also reflected in the work's references to the Ottoman Empire.

STORY LINE

Le Bourgeois gentilhomme follows the ambitions of a pretentious member of the middle classes—Monsieur Jourdain—as he tries to gain acceptance into the aristocracy. Monsieur Jourdain attempts to elevate his status by learning dancing, fencing, music, and philosophy, but frustrates his teachers with his incompetence. When his daughter, Lucille, falls in love with a middle-class suitor, Cleonte, Jourdain refuses to accept him. The young couple decide to deceive Jourdain by disguising Cleonte as the Sultan of Turkey. Jourdain is fooled and happily agrees to his daughter marrying into a foreign noble family, where he will also be ennobled.

The ninth collaboration between Jean-Baptiste Molière and Jean-Baptiste Lully, *Le Bourgeois gentilhomme* formalized the genre of the comédie-ballet. A product of the court of Louis XIV, this type of entertainment gave equal weight to music, comedy, dance, and song. It had been enjoyed at court fêtes, often featuring the king and his courtiers as performers. The king's only involvement in this more professional production was to suggest the comic subject matter for the central musical episode—the recent visit of a haughty Turkish emissary to the French court, which had not been a success. As well as poking fun at the Turkish delegation, Molière satirized the social climbing and extreme manners that prevailed at Louis' court. While all courtiers were expected to be proficient in dancing, fencing, and horsemanship, the lead character of *Le Bourgeois gentilhomme*, middle-class Monsieur Jourdain, is incapable. The title of the piece is an oxymoron—a "gentleman" was by definition an aristocrat and could not be "bourgeois." Monsieur Jourdain is repeatedly humiliated in his attempts to advance his status, and becomes a victim of his own ambitions when he is deceived by his daughter and her bourgeois suitor. At the first performance of this ballet, Molière took the role of Monsieur Jourdain and Lully danced the role of the Mufti (an Islamic law expert).

From court to stage

Ten years after its first performance, on November 23, 1670, the ballet was given the first of many public performances at the Palais-Royal in Paris. In 1912, Max Reinhardt directed a German adaptation of the play with music by Richard Strauss. Strauss's music was then used by George Balanchine when he created a balletic interpretation of the play for Les Ballets Russes de Monte Carlo in 1932.

Balanchine went on to create a second rendition in 1944, for the Ballet Russe de Monte Carlo, and a third version in 1979 for New York City Opera. His last revival starred Rudolf Nureyev in the lead role and included variations to the choreography with help from Jerome Robbins and Peter Martins.

International reinterpretation
The National Drama Company of Korea perform *Le Bourgeois gentilhomme* in France in 2006. The Baroque music was rearranged for traditional Korean instruments.

L'Europe galante

First performed: October 24, 1697 ▪ Venue: Salle du Palais-Royal, Paris ▪ Choreography: Louis Guillaume Pécour ▪ Music: André Campra
Story: Antoine Houdar de la Motte

Signaling a new alliance between the arts of dance and music, this work is widely credited with establishing the genre of opéra-ballet. Comprising a number of independent scenes linked by a common theme, the piece featured no speaking, and instead used sung exchanges and arias interspersed with dances and processions to create striking visual tableaux.

▲ **Love in a Turkish seraglio**
In Scene 4, Zuliman the Sultan's new favorite, Zayde, and his old lover, Roxane, vie for the Sultan's affections. Roxane is banished from court by the Sultan after nearly stabbing Zayde out of jealousy.

The first dramatic work of church composer André Campra, *L'Europe galante* was initially attributed to his brother Joseph for fear that Campra would lose his post as music master at Notre Dame. The work's great success, however, established Campra as a much celebrated stage composer and lyricist, and enhanced the reputation of the already honored choreographer Louis Pécour.

Comprising a prologue, four scenes linked by the theme of love, and a brief epilogue, *L'Europe galante* takes the audience on an evocative European voyage using popular French and Italian musical styles. Prevailing cultural stereotypes and caricatures were used to add further color and drama.

A French pastoral idyll is conjured in Scene 1, featuring a fickle and indiscreet shepherd. Faithful, romantic caballeros serenade their loves in a Spanish square in Scene 2, while violence and jealousy divides lovers at a dramatic masked Venetian ball in Scene 3. The Turkish seraglio (harem) in Scene 4 portrays a passionate power game in a suitably exotic setting.

Political allegory

The underlying theme of this ballet—the victory of love over discord—referenced contemporary events. The Treaty of Rijswijk (September 1697) had just ended the Nine Years' War, ushering in a new period of harmony and enabling the marriage of the Duc de Bourgogne (Louis XIV's grandson) to Marie Adélaïde de Savoie. Performed at the time of the wedding festivities, *L'Europe galante* represented hopes for peace after the enmity of war. It promoted the idea of diplomacy and international harmony, and also presented a lighter style of musical entertainment that chimed with the mood of a newly optimistic audience.

STORY LINE

Two goddesses, Love (Venus) and Discord (sometimes called Enmity), argue that each rules the world. To settle the dispute, they travel through Europe to observe how courtship is conducted in different countries. They journey to France, Spain, Italy, and Turkey, where stories of love are played out. Despite elements of tragedy in each of the scenes, the epilogue concludes that love is ultimately the winner, resolving the argument.

L'Europe galante enjoyed enduring popularity after its first successful run, and was restaged repeatedly until 1775. In 1997, on the 300th anniversary of the ballet, dance company Istanbul Baroque, led by artistic director Leyla Pinar, staged the work at Istanbul's Dolmabahçe Palace, and then at Brussels' Printemps Baroque du Sablon Festival later the same year.

▼ **Turkish costume sketch**
Louis-René Boquet designed an exotic costume for the fourth scene, to be worn in the 1766 production of *L'Europe galante*.

Pierre Beauchamp

Dancer, choreographer, and composer ▪ 1631/36–1705

Sometimes described as "the father of ballet masters," Beauchamp was a successful choreographer, composer, and dancing master in the court of Louis XIV. He was highly influential in the development and codification of French Baroque dance, and paved the way for the creation of ballet in the form that we recognize today. Beauchamp was also one of the first to create a system of notation using written symbols, and defined the five positions of the feet that are still fundamental to ballet.

▲ **Comédie-ballet in five acts**
First performed on January 17, 1671, *Psyche* was characteristic of the spectacles commissioned by Louis XIV. It was written by Molière and choreographed by Beauchamp to a score by Lully.

Trained in dance and the violin from an early age, Beauchamp made his stage debut in 1648 in the court ballet *Le Dérèglement des passions*. He went on to appear in many ballets de cour (court ballets) with the young Louis XIV, to whom he taught dancing for over 20 years.

Beauchamp was noted for his technique, and is thought to have been one of the first male dancers to perform the tour en l'air (turn in the air). This virtuoso step consists of a single or double turn in the air, beginning and ending in the fifth position. It is still performed by male dancers today.

Creative collaborations

Beauchamp was appointed as the first *intendant des ballets de roi* in 1661, a royal position that saw him staging court ballets—often hugely elaborate spectacles—for the king. He collaborated with composer Jean-Baptiste Lully, and also worked as both a composer and choreographer with playwright and actor Jean-Baptiste Molière.

Beauchamp, Lully, and Molière frequently worked together, creating popular works such as *Le Bourgeois gentilhomme*. Together they were instrumental in shaping the evolution of comédie-ballet, which mixed spoken word plays with music and dance.

In 1661, Louis XIV also founded the Royal Academy of Dance, which is thought to be the first dance institution in the Western world. Its aim was to establish standards in the world of dance, and to codify the existing court and character dances. Louis XIV put this task in the hands of 13 ballet masters.

The academy also created examinations for dance teachers—those who passed were issued with a certificate that qualified them to teach. Although he is likely to have been associated with the academy much earlier, Beauchamp was made its director in 1680. The institution ran for more than 100 years before finally closing during the French Revolution of 1789.

Ballet steps

A further step in the formation of French ballet came in 1669, when the Royal Academy of Music—also known as Académie d'Opéra or the Opéra—was founded in Paris. This institution brought together singers, musicians, and the ballet company of the Royal Academy of Dance to create and promote French opera, in which ballet was integral.

Joining the Opéra as ballet master in 1672, Beauchamp worked there until the death of its director, Lully, in 1687. After retiring, Beauchamp worked as court choreographer until his death in 1705.

Beauchamp is credited by Pierre Rameau, a French dancing master, as being the first person to codify—if not actually invent—the five standard positions of the feet into a form of steps that is still used today. While there has been an increase in the amount of turnout from the hip in these steps, they have remained essentially unchanged since Beauchamp's time. As the fundamental positions of ballet, which begin and end all movements, they have become the first steps to be taught in ballet classes today around the world.

They [Beauchamp and Lully] have carried these pieces to a higher degree of perfection than anyone will ever attain …

FRANÇOIS RAGUENET, 18TH-CENTURY HISTORIAN AND MUSICOLOGIST

▲ ***Le Bourgeois gentilhomme*, 1979**
Beauchamp first choreographed this work, based on Molière's play, in 1670. George Balanchine's interpretation, created for Rudolf Nureyev 300 years later, still included the five steps that Beauchamp would have been familiar with.

KEY WORKS

Dancer: *Le Dérèglement des passions*, 1648
Choreographer: *Les Fâcheux*, 1661 • *Le Mariage forcé*, 1664 • *Le Bourgeois gentilhomme*, 1670 • *Alceste*, 1674
Le Triomphe de l'amour, 1681

TIMELINE

- **1631/36** Born in Versailles, France, into a family of musicians and dance masters to the royal family, and baptized on October 30.
- **January 23, 1648** Makes his stage debut in *Le Dérèglement des passions*.
- **1660** Dances in Cavalli's opera *Xerse* in a gala celebrating the marriage of Louis XIV and Princess Maria Theresa of Spain.
- **1664** Principal choreographer for the Troupe de Roi, the drama company of actor and playwright Molière, a distant cousin.
- **March 19, 1671** Robert Cambert's *Pomone* debuts, with choreography by Beauchamp.

LES FACHEUX, 1661, CHOREOGRAPHED BY BEAUCHAMP

- **1672** Appointed ballet master at the Royal Academy of Music, Paris.
- **1680** Becomes director of the Royal Academy of Dance, and begins devising a notation system for the instruction of dance steps, commissioned by Louis XIV.
- **1681** Choreographs *Le Triomphe de l'amour*, the first ballet in which female professional dancers perform in public.
- **1687** Retires from the Opéra after the death of his friend Jean-Baptiste Lully, and becomes Louis XIV's court choreographer.
- **1700** Choreographer and publisher Raoul-Auger Feuillet publishes *Chorégraphie, ou l'Art de d'Ecrire la Danse*, a detailed description of Beauchamp's dance notation.
- **1704** Sues Feuillet for plagiarism of his notation, but loses the case. The system becomes known as Beauchamp-Feuillet notation, and remains in use for decades.
- **February 1705** Dies in Paris, France.

BALLET D'ACTION

In the early 18th century, dances were often inserted into plays between the acts to give the actors time to change costumes, but they had no story and no connection with the plays. At the Theatre Royal, Drury Lane, however, John Weaver was devising dances that told stories through mime and movement. This was the basis of ballet d'action—changing the form of dances by adding a dramatic narrative. Weaver's first really successful work was *The Loves of Mars and Venus* in 1715. Mars was danced by the great Louis Dupré. Another French star, Marie Sallé, saw Weaver's work, which influenced her own choreography, particularly her ballet, *Pygmalion*.

Jean-Georges Noverre, who trained in Paris and was taught by both Dupré and Sallé, is most often associated with this genre of dance because of his book *Letters on Dancing*. He aimed to have a harmonious balance of drama, dance, music, and design. However, after the publication of his book, Noverre was accused of plagiarism by Gaspero Angiolini, who cited his ballet teacher in Vienna, Franz Hilverding, as the rightful originator of this work. Hilverding and Angiolini were the other major exponents of ballet d'action. Nevertheless, Noverre managed to choreograph many more memorable works than those of his detractors. Encyclopedist Denis Diderot called him "le génie," and predicted that he would save dance from falling into obscurity. He was right—in the theater, new movements spread quickly, and the notion of ballet d'action was no exception, delighting dancers and audiences alike.

> A ballet is a picture, or rather a series of pictures connected one with the other by the plot.
>
> JEAN-GEORGES NOVERRE

Marie Sallé in action, 1732 ▶
Rococo artist Nicolas Lancret painted this portrait of the dancer Marie Sallé dancing in a woodland setting graced with a classical temple.

Gaétan Vestris

Dancer and choreographer ▪ 1729–1808

For a period of some 60 years, the Vestris family, headed by Gaétan, dominated the ballet world and the Paris Opéra. Many dancers at the Opéra were Italian-born, and Gaétan Vestris was the most famous—and conceited—of them all, often referred to as *Le Dieu de la Danse* ("The God of Dance"), a title of which he appeared to approve. He and his dynasty were pivotal in the development and promotion of the male dancer, and his influence is still evident today.

▶ **In performance**
Gaétan Vestris dances in the ballet-pantomime *Ninette à la cour*, a comedy in three acts with verse and dance, first performed in 1755 in Paris.

Gaetano Apolline Baldassarre Vestris was born into a theatrical family in Florence in 1729 (though some sources say 1728). In the mid-1740s, he and his family moved to Paris, gallicizing his name to Gaétan. The young Gaétan had studied dance in Italy, and in Paris he continued his training with influential ballet master Louis Dupré at the Royal Academy in Paris.

In the late 1740s, Gaétan made his debut at the Paris Opéra. His brother Angiolo and sister Thérèse were also dancers there. Thérèse remained at the Opéra until the mid-1760s, while Angiolo had a successful career in Stuttgart.

In 1751, Gaétan was appointed premier danseur (first male dancer) at the Paris Opéra. He became hugely popular as a dancer, and was one of the first to dispense with a mask, relying instead on facial expression and mime. Over the next 30 years, Gaétan danced the lead in more than 70 operas and ballets.

Narrative ballet

In 1761, Gaétan was appointed co-choreographer of the Paris Opéra, and from 1770 to 1776 he was chief choreographer. In this role, he introduced the ballet d'action to the Paris Opéra. Ballet d'action was a form of ballet that emerged in the mid-18th century, largely influenced by the choreographer Jean-George Noverre, with whom Gaétan and his brother Angiolo had danced in Stuttgart. It relied solely on the movement and mime of the dancers to convey the ballet's story and move the plot forward.

In 1760, Gaétan had a son by his lover, the French ballerina, Marie Allard. Their son, Auguste Vestris (Marie-Jean-Augustin Vestris), would later be considered one of the greatest dancers of his time, and would also come to be called "The God of Dance." In the early 1780s, Gaétan and Auguste appeared together at the King's Theatre in London. Their performances caused such a sensation that parliament took a recess so that members could go to see the father and son dance.

Gaétan performed at the Paris Opéra until 1782. After this time he continued to teach, laying down the French style and method of teaching ballet.

Coaching son and grandson

Gaétan's son Auguste trained with his father, making his first appearance in the divertissement *La Cinquantaine* in 1772, at the age of only 12. His formal debut at the Opéra took place in 1776. Auguste had a completely different style from his father. He was short and athletic, and pioneered many virtuoso steps. When Auguste retired from the stage and began teaching, August Bournonville was one of the pupils that he influenced, and some of his steps can still be seen today in Danish Bournonville work.

Auguste's own son, Auguste-Armand Vestris, also became a dancer, training with his grandfather before making his debut at the Paris Opéra in 1800 (at which it is thought Gaétan also danced). Gaétan died in September 1808.

KEY WORKS

Soloist, *Daphnis et Alcimadure* (opera), 1754
Endymion, *Les Surprises de l'amour* (opera-ballet), 1757 • Jason, *Médée et Jason*, 1763 • Pluto, *Orefeo ed Euridice*, 1763 • Choreographer: *Iphigénie en Aulide* (opera), 1774

There are but three great men in Europe—the king of Prussia, Voltaire, and me.

GAETAN VESTRIS

▲ **Italian duo**
Gaétan Vestris and fellow Italian Teresa Fogliazzi Angiolini dance in a Tyrolean ballet at the Paris Opéra c.1755 in this engraving by Nicolaus von Heideloff.

TIMELINE

- **April 18, 1729** Born Gaetano Apolline Baldassarre Vestris in Florence, Italy, second child of Tommaso Vestris, and brother of Thérèse and Angiolo, both of whom also become ballet dancers.
- **1748** Joins the Paris Opéra ballet school, studying under Louis Dupré, and becomes premier danseur three years later.
- **1754–1755** Dances in Turin and Berlin.
- **March 27, 1760** Has a son, Auguste (Marie-Jean-Augustin), with his lover, the ballerina Marie Allard.
- **1761** Appointed co-choreographer at the Paris Opéra, with Jean Dauberval.
- **1770** Becomes ballet master at the Paris Opéra.
- **1772** Oversees Auguste's performance debut at the age of 12 in *La Cinquantaine*.
- **1776** Continues to teach Auguste, who makes a formal debut at the Opéra and becomes premier danseur two years later.
- **Early 1780s** Dances together with his son Auguste at the King's Theatre, London, to rapturous reviews.

GAETAN'S SON AUGUSTE VESTRIS, ALSO A FAMOUS DANCER

- **1782** Retires from performing at the Paris Opéra, instead turning to teach the French style of ballet he had created.
- **1788** His grandson Auguste-Armand—son of Auguste—is born, and also grows to be a talented dancer and choreographer.
- **1792** In Stuttgart, marries the German ballerina Anna Friedrike Heinel, mother of his second son, Adolphe, who had been born a year earlier.
- **1800** At the age of 71, witnesses his grandson Auguste-Armand's stage debut.
- **September 23, 1808** Dies in Paris.

BOLSHOI BALLET

Russia's leading ballet company, renowned for its sumptuous stagings of 19th-century classics, is also one of the world's oldest. The Bolshoi ("big") Ballet was formed in 1776, and its school, now known as the Moscow State Academy of Choreography, started three years earlier and can trace its origins to a Moscow orphanage. The company originally performed at the Petrovsky Theater, on the site of the present Bolshoi Theater, which was opened in 1825. By 1850, there were 150 dancers in the Bolshoi performing works that included folk dancing, comedy, pantomime, and drama.

In the early 20th century, the Bolshoi began to shape its unique identity. Under Alexander Gorsky's direction from 1900 to 1924, the company developed an intense and dramatic style characterized by bold leaps, especially for male dancers. The Communist regime encouraged a genre of social realism, which portrayed the Communist ideals in works such as *The Red Poppy* (1927) and *The Fountain of Bakhchisatai* (1934). After World War II, the Bolshoi returned to what it did best with a production of *Cinderella*. When Galina Ulanova was transferred from St. Petersburg in 1944, and created the role of Juliet, it marked a new era for the company, which was joined by legendary dancers such as Nikolai Fadeyechev, Maya Plisetskaya, and Raisa Struchkova.

By the 1960s, the Bolshoi was one of the foremost ballet companies, especially with Yuri Grigorovich (of *Spartacus* fame) as chief choreographer from 1964. He defined the spectacular work of the company with virtuoso dancers such as Natalia Bessmertnova and Vladimir Vasiliev. The 21st century brought in more Bolshoi superheroes, such as Ivan Vasiliev (no relation), dubbed "the boy who can fly."

> Every company has its style, and that's what makes the Bolshoi so impressive: their attack on jumps … their attack on choreography.
>
> DAVID HALLBERG, FORMER BOLSHOI PRINCIPAL DANCER

Behind the scenes of *Swan Lake*, 2013 ▶
The Bolshoi Ballet tour internationally—this performance is in Minsk, Belarus—with their lavish productions of traditional favorites such as *Swan Lake*, written for the company

Les Indes galantes

First performed: August 23, 1735 ▪ Venue: Palais-Royal, Paris ▪ Choreography: Michel Blondy ▪ Music: Jean-Philippe Rameau ▪ Story: Louis Fuzelier

This opera-ballet—a genre that had begun in the 1690s, and which mixed both art forms in a performance—was inspired by an event in 1725. French settlers in North America sent Chief Agapit Chicagou of the Mitchigamea (a Native American leader) and five other chiefs to visit Louis XV in Paris. The chiefs performed three ceremonial dances, moving Jean-Philippe Rameau to compose his rondeau (sung verse) *Les Sauvages.*

STORY LINE

The first performance This consisted of a prologue and two acts and received a lukewarm reception. A third act, *Les Fleurs* ("The Flowers"), was introduced at the third performance. It included cross-dressing for the hero, but this did nothing to increase the opera-ballet's popularity.

Expanded work In March 1736, the work was extended. It now consisted of a prologue and four acts on the theme of love in far-off lands, entitled *Le Turc généreux* ("The Generous Turk"), *Les Incas du Pérou* ("The Incas of Peru"), a revised *Les Fleurs*, and *Les Sauvages* ("The Savages"). This version proved extremely popular and was performed 185 times up until 1761.

Ten years after writing *Les Sauvages*, Jean-Philippe Rameau—who excelled in creating music for the opera-ballet form—set *Les Indes galantes* to music. Its four exotic stories from four corners of the world, complete with love triangles, infidelity, virtue rewarded, and erupting volcanoes, took the audience to foreign regions and gave Rameau's admirers cause for celebration.

The costumes by Jean-Baptiste Martin were equally exotic. His Chinese outfits for men and women inspired many designs in the chinoiserie style, which became popular in the 18th century.

▲ **Title page of the score**
The Académie Royale de Musique, Paris, staged the first performance of *Les Indes galantes*. Later, extended versions met a more positive reception.

Marie Sallé, ballet star

The dancers included Louis Dupré and the legendary Marie Sallé. Sallé danced in the first performance and was probably responsible for the choreography in the popular 1736 version of the third act, *Les Fleurs*. She was a famous dancer in both Paris and London and was remarkable at the time for being independent, with no patron to help her financially. As a child, she danced with her brother and became well known in London, working for theater manager John Rich at Lincoln's Inn Field Theatre and later at Covent Garden Theatre. London's flourishing ballet scene gave her the freedom to choreograph her own works such as *Pygmalion*, in which she wore a Greek-style flowing costume, sandals, and loose hair. Her dramatic acting skills made her popular with audiences and Handel wrote music for her to perform in some of his operas. When she returned to Paris to perform in *Les Indes galantes* she was at the height of her fame. Professional dancers like Sallé performed difficult jumps, turns, and balances as well as courtly dance arrangements.

◀ **Chinese-inspired costumes**
Designer Jean-Baptiste Martin made this hand-colored engraving of the costume for the Chinese man, a role incorporated as a divertissement in *Les Indes galantes*.

20th-century revivals

In 1925, a version of *Les Fleurs* was presented at the Opéra-Comique in Paris with new orchestration by Paul Dukas. A full version of *Les Indes galantes* was staged at the Palais Garnier on June 18, 1952. It also used the Dukas orchestration, but Henri Busser supplemented the other acts. The production was directed by Maurice Lehmann and, like the original, it was notable for its lavish staging. The choreography was rearranged in a collaborative effort: Albert Aveline for the first act, Serge Lifar the second and fourth, and Harald Lander the third. The opera-ballet stood the test of time, and audiences had enjoyed 236 performances by September 1961.

Médée et Jason

First performed: February 11, 1763 ▪ Venue: Stuttgart Opera House ▪ Choreography and story: Jean-Georges Noverre ▪ Music: Joseph Rodolphe

Originally created as a 35-minute interlude between the acts of Jommelli's opera *Didone Abbandonate*, this ballet did not provide any light relief but told the grim story of Jason and Medea, using a form of pantomime that dated back to ancient Rome. One evening, when the lead singer was indisposed, the ballet was performed alone to great acclaim—and so *Médée et Jason* helped ballet to develop as an independent art form.

Jean-Georges Noverre was hired as ballet master to the newly founded court ballet in Stuttgart by the wealthy Charles Eugene, Duke of Württemberg, in 1760. This post allowed him to develop his new ideas on ballets d'action (ballets with a plot) and to employ the best dancers. *Médée et Jason* was one of several works he produced in Stuttgart in the 1760s, all with expressive gestures to describe the story.

Noverre choreographed the mime scenes—the pantomime elements—to match the music for dramatic effect. He had seen the actor David Garrick in London, and was influenced by his style (although it would appear melodramatic and plodding to modern audiences). By discarding the masks that had to be worn at the Paris Opéra, Noverre was able to show expressions on the dancers' faces.

Original cast and later versions

The star-studded cast included Gaétan Vestris as Jason and his brother, Angiolo, as Creon. In 1767, Vestris arranged his own version of the ballet and performed it in Paris before the king (taking all the credit for Noverre's work, as Noverre himself had done when he ignored others' contributions to the concept of ballet d'action). The work became very popular and was performed in London. In 1805, Pierre Gardel revived the ballet in Paris.

Médée et Jason was the first ballet d'action to be seen in Paris and it changed the way ballets were devised. Later ballet choreographers such as Dauberval and Gardel used less stylized mime, but it was Noverre who initiated narrative.

▲ **Medea the sorceress**
Holding a wand in her right hand, Medea extends her left hand in an imperious gesture to mime the dramatic plot of the ballet.

STORY LINE

Médée et Jason was based on the Greek myth of Jason's rejection of his wife, Medea. The ambitious Jason wishes to marry Creusa, the daughter of King Creon, to reclaim the crown of Corinth which is rightfully his. Medea is so filled with jealousy and rage that she sends a poisoned cloak to Creusa which kills her. Medea then kills both of her children.

Not everyone approved of such high drama. Writing 20 years after the first production, essayist Marie-Joseph Chenier wrote: "I dislike seeing the children of Jason whose throats have been cut in the course of a dance by their dancing mother, to die in time to music under her rhythmic blows."

▶ **Story of love, betrayal, and tragedy**
Gaétan Vestris played the role of Jason and English dancer Mademoiselle Nency danced Medea in the original production, which so terrified the audience that some of its members reportedly fainted or fled.

LA SCALA THEATER BALLET

Milan's world-famous classical ballet company was inaugurated in 1778, but its origins go back two centuries before that to the Renaissance courts of Italy and the first glimmerings of ballet technique. Among La Scala's many illustrious directors, it boasts Carlo Blasis, who codified classical ballet technique in 1820, and Enrico Cecchetti, who was ballet master for the Ballets Russes, devised the Italian Cecchetti system, and who taught at La Scala from 1925 until his death in 1928.

In the sumptuous Teatro alla Scala opera house, La Scala performs traditional favorites such as *Swan Lake*, *Le Corsaire*, and *La Bayadère* as well as modern works like Jiří Kylián's *Petite Mort*. La Scala Theater Ballet also tours extensively in Italy and abroad, reaching a wider audience.

In 1813, the affiliated dance academy, now called Accademia Teatro alla Scala, was founded. It accepts students from the age of 11, where they undertake a rigorous program of dance and academic studies. Luminaries such as Carla Fracci, Alessandra Ferri, and Roberto Bolle have come through the school. Graduate students find places in companies worldwide including La Scala Theater Ballet itself.

> See you at La Scala, they say.
>
> STENDHAL, FRENCH NOVELIST, 1817

Carla Fracci on La Scala's stage ▶
The audience applauds ballerina Carla Fracci and throws flowers at her feet as tokens of appreciation. The Italian dancer is revered for her interpretations of Romantic ballets, such as *La Sylphide* and *Giselle*.

ROMANTIC BALLET

(1830–1860)

Romantic ballet 1830–1860

As the Industrial Revolution gathered pace, the early 19th century saw huge and rapid advances in technology and commerce. It also brought unsettling social changes for many in Europe, inspiring an idealized notion of the past and an interest in spirituality, which became known as Romanticism. As a cultural movement, Romanticism encompassed literature, music, and art. In ballet, the years of Romanticism proved to be the most significant period in the development of the art form so far, and marked the arrival of many of its defining features.

One of the groundbreaking developments of the period was the rise of the ballerina. While ballet had traditionally been the preserve of male dancers, female performers now took center stage, where their grace and femininity added a new dimension. Starting in Paris, and spreading across Europe, many ballerinas became celebrities with cultlike followings.

Romanticism embraced spirituality and all things supernatural, and these were soon seen in ballet. The first work to include such elements was a scene in the grand opera (lavish operas that featured dancing), *Robert le Diable*. Opening at Paris Opéra in 1831, ballerina Marie Taglioni and a chorus of ballet dancers dressed in white tutus appeared as the ghosts of nuns. This grand opera became an instant hit, and as the first appearance of ballet blanc—a ballet or scene from a ballet in which the ballerinas wear traditional white costumes, and usually populated by otherworldly spirits and fairies—it had considerable influence.

The ghostly white act was the catalyst for Filippo Taglioni's genre-defining masterpiece, *La Sylphide*, which premiered the following year. As the first ballet to feature pointe work—dancing on tiptoes—as an integral component of the choreography, and the first where ballerinas were seen in long white tutus, the ballet catapulted ballerina Marie Taglioni into the public eye. She was not alone. Another ballerina whose career was propelled to new heights by a ghostly role was Carlotta Grisi for her performance in Jean Coralli's and Jules Perrot's *Giselle*. A spectral tale of thwarted love and vengeance, it is the archetypal ballet blanc, and is widely regarded to be the icon of the Romantic period.

While Romanticism may have turned its back on the changing world, ballet benefited from the ever-advancing technologies of the early 19th century. Elaborate lighting and staging reached its peak during this period in Mazilier's sea-faring work, *Le Corsaire*. Culminating in a dramatic shipwreck scene, the ballet impressed audiences, including Napoleon III, with its wizardry, as well as its dancing.

La Sylphide

First performed: March 12, 1832 ▪ Venue: Salle Le Peletier, Paris ▪ Choreography: Taglioni ▪ Music: Jean-Madeleine Schneitzhöffer ▪ Story: Adolphe Nourrit

Choreographed by Filippo Taglioni, *La Sylphide* is credited with inspiring the Romantic era of ballet, and as the first ballet in which dancing en pointe was used to enhance the choreography and the aesthetic quality of the performance. It established the reputation of Filippo's daughter, the romantic and ethereal ballerina, Marie Taglioni, whose white silk tutu—shortened to show off her footwork—became the model for a classical ballet costume.

STORY LINE

Act I A Scottish Manor House On the morning of his wedding to Effie, James wakes up to see a tantalizing sylph before him. When the wedding festivities begin, the sylph reappears and James, unable to resist, follows her into the forest. Effie is left brokenhearted.

Act II A Forest Glade The sylph and her sisters fill the forest and dance for James, who tries in vain to catch the sylph. Madge, an old witch/sorceress, gives James a scarf that will bind the sylph to him. When he places the scarf around her shoulders, her wings fall off and she dies. The wedding procession of Effie and her husband is seen in the background, while the sylph is carried away by her sisters. James collapses lifeless, and Madge triumphs.

◀ **Marie Taglioni** This lithograph depicts Taglioni in her defining role as the sylph in 1832.

For this ballet, Adolphe Nourrit, an operatic tenor and patron of the arts, was inspired by Charles Nodier's novel *Tribly, ou le lutin d'Argail* ("The Elf of Argyll"), published in 1822. It told the story of a male elf who lures a Highland fisherman's wife away from her husband, and Nourrit thought that with some alteration it would make an ideal plot for a ballet. Ideas of the supernatural were widespread at the time, as alluring as the seemingly exotic setting of Scotland described so thrillingly in Walter Scott's best-selling novels.

Nourrit took his idea to ballet master, Filippo Taglioni, who saw its potential as a vehicle for his daughter, Marie Taglioni. Filippo commissioned Jean-Madeleine Schneitzhöffer to write the music, and the ballet premiered in March 1832, with Marie Taglioni as the sylph and Joseph Mazilier as James. Employing theatrical techniques, such as flying harnesses so that the sylphs appeared to fly and modern gaslight to simulate moonlight, *La Sylphide* proved highly popular and was performed across Europe, including in London, Milan, and St. Petersburg.

Later versions

In 1834, Danish choreographer and dancer August Bournonville visited Paris and saw Taglioni perform *La Sylphide.* Bournonville was inspired by this work, and set about creating his own version in Copenhagen. He commissioned a new score from Norwegian composer Herman Løvenskiold, and created the choreography himself. Bournonville remained faithful to the plot and style of Filippo Taglioni's original work, but elevated the role of James, creating a dancing role equal to that of the sylph. He also decided that James, danced by himself, and the sylph by Lucile Grahn, should be unable to touch, conveying through dance the tantalizing nature of their attraction. Premiering in 1836 at The Royal Theater, Copenhagen, this version is still regularly staged, making it the oldest ballet performed today.

By the 1860s, Taglioni's version of *La Sylphide* ceased to be performed and was largely forgotten. Over a century later, in 1972, it was carefully reconstructed by choreographer Pierre Lacotte using original notes, drawings, and archival material. It is now part of the repertoire of the Paris Opéra.

La Sylphide was reworked again in 1994 as *Highland Fling* by innovative choreographer Matthew Bourne. He set the magical fairy world in the contrasting setting of the mean streets of Glasgow.

▶ **Popular review** This engraving from *The Exquisite* magazine, 1842, shows Marie Taglioni as the sylph and her younger brother Paul dancing as James.

▶ **Family performance** This 1832 oil painting by François Gabriel Guillaume shows Paul and Marie Taglioni in the lead roles of *La Sylphide.*

NEWARK PUBLIC LIBRARY
121 HIGH ST.

Marie Taglioni

Dancer and choreographer ▪ 1804–1884

Born with a rounded back and shoulders, Marie Taglioni may initially have seemed an unlikely ballet dancer. Indeed one former teacher is said to have asked, "Will that little hunchback ever learn to dance?" However, with utter determination and dedicated training from her choreographer father, she did, and went on to become one of the most celebrated ballerinas of her age. She even revolutionized ballet through her artistic use of dancing en pointe.

▲ **Venetian grandeur**
This 19th-century painting by Carlo Ferrari (1813–1871) depicts Marie Taglioni boarding a gondola in front of a palace in Venice.

The daughter of Italian dancer, choreographer, and ballet master Filippo Taglioni and Swedish ballet dancer Sophie Karsten, Marie Taglioni studied ballet from a young age. Despite being dismissed by one teacher due to her curved shoulders, in her mid-teens Taglioni joined her father to study dance in Vienna, where he was ballet master at the Court Opera. There, he took over his daughter's training, and for two years she trained six hours a day, six days a week.

Redefining the ballerina

Taglioni made her debut in Vienna in 1822, in *La reception d'une jeune nymphe à la cour de Terpsichore*, choreographed by her father. For the next five years she danced in Vienna, Munich, and Stuttgart before her Paris Opéra debut in 1827.

In 1832, Taglioni was cast in her father's ballet *La Sylphide*, which would not only redefine ballet but also the role of the female dancer. Through her light and graceful style, Taglioni became the archetypal ballerina. She was the first to move while en pointe—previous dancers had only posed in the position.

Such was her resulting fame that her hairstyle became the height of fashion, dolls were made in her image, and products bore her name. Queen Victoria even named a racehorse after her.

During the mid-1830s, ballet critics sparked a rivalry between Taglioni and fellow dancer Fanny Elssler. Paris audiences divided into either pro-Marie or pro-Fanny camps. In contrast with the ethereal Taglioni, Elssler was described as an "earthbound," voluptuous dancer. The press described Taglioni as a "Christian" dancer because of her chaste style, whereas Elssler was a "Pagan."

Taglioni accepted a contract in 1837 to perform with the Imperial Ballet at the Mariinsky Theater, St. Petersburg—and it was here that she reached the height of her career. After her last performance there in 1842, a group of her fans allegedly purchased a pair of her pointe shoes, cooked them, and served them in special sauce. Another tale from this time states that on a trip to Europe, Taglioni's party was stopped by bandits who simply wanted to see her dance.

In 1845, Taglioni was cast in the *Pas de quatre*, choreographed by Jules Perrot, at Her Majesty's Theatre, London, and danced alongside Carlotta Grisi, Lucile Grahn, and Fanny Cerrito—at the time the most famous ballerinas in the world.

Away from the stage

After retiring from the stage in 1847, Taglioni spent time in Italy before she moved to Paris and became the inspectrice de la danse at the Paris Opéra Ballet, where she established a new system of dance examinations.

The only ballet choreographed by Taglioni, *Le Papillon*, premiered in 1860. She created it for her protégée, Emma Livry, who died in 1863 when her ballet costume caught fire on stage.

In the 1870s Taglioni moved to London and taught society women and children to dance—including the future Queen Mary, who reportedly boasted that Taglioni had taught her to curtsy.

KEY WORKS

Dancer: Naiad, *La Belle au bois dormant*, 1829
Title role, *La Sylphide*, 1832 • Title role, *La Fille du Danube*, 1836 • Title role, *La Gitana*, 1838
Pas de quatre, 1845

Taglioni danced beautifully and looked lovely … I was very much amused.

PRINCESS VICTORIA (LATER QUEEN VICTORIA) IN HER PERSONAL JOURNAL, JULY 1833

▲ **Striking a pose**
Taglioni, shown here in 1850, used her elegant movements to conceal her curved back and shoulders. Although she danced en pointe, her shoes were just satin slippers with darning at the toe.

TIMELINE

- **April 23, 1804** Born in Stockholm, Sweden, into a family of professional dancers, chief among whom is her father Filippo, a celebrated Italian ballet master.
- **1805** Following her father's appointment as ballet master in Vienna, Marie is raised by her mother in Paris, first learning ballet under Jean-François Coulon.
- **June 1822** Debuts in Vienna, dancing in *La reception d'une jeune nymphe à la cour de Terpsichore*, choreographed by her father to music by Rossini.
- **1826** Creates the title role in *Danina*, which debuts in Stuttgart.

TAGLIONI WITH SIGNOR GUERRA IN *L'OMBRE* (1840)

- **1827** Makes her first appearance at the Paris Opéra, dancing in *Le Sicilien* to great acclaim.
- **1832** Appears in the first performance of her father's *La Sylphide*, in the title role. Marries Comte Auguste Gilbert de Voisins in London—they separate three years later.
- **1843** Creates the title role in *La Péri*, staged by her father at La Scala in Milan.
- **1845** Appears as one of the four lead dancers in Jules Perrot's *Pas de quatre* at Her Majesty's Theatre, London.
- **1847** Makes her last appearance on stage in *The Judgment of Paris*, retiring to Blevio on Lake Como, Italy.
- **1857** Moves to France to take up the position of dance examiner at the Paris Opéra.
- **April 22, 1884** Dies at her son's home in Marseille, France.

Giselle

First performed: June 28, 1841 ▪ Venue: Théâtre de l'Académie Royale de Musique, Paris ▪ Choreography: Jean Coralli and Jules Perrot
Music: Adolphe Adam with additional music by Friedrich Burgmüller, Ludwig Minkus, and Cesare Pugni ▪ Story: Théophile Gautier and Vernoy de Saint-Georges

The archetypal Romantic ballet, *Giselle* is a ghostly tale of thwarted affection, deceit, revenge, and the power of love. This genre was hugely popular with audiences at the time and Carlotta Grisi shot to fame when she danced the lead role in the first production. While the ballet has been reworked many times since, and a number of versions exist, *Giselle* continues to be popular today and is performed around the globe.

IN CONTEXT

From the early 1800s to the end of the century, a widespread fascination with the supernatural developed across Europe and the US. Tales of ghostly figures and events became commonplace, and the pseudo-sciences of mesmerism and spiritualism found favor—and followers. It was a time of rapid and extensive social change, brought about by industrialization, scientific discovery, and renewed Christian fervor, and many people started to question the world around them. In the arts, Gothicism replaced Romanticism—from architecture to painting—and novels such as Mary Shelley's *Frankenstein* (1818) and the works of Edgar Allan Poe became essential reading. With its vengeful wilis, *Giselle* found a ready audience.

Such was the popularity of Filippo Taglioni's *La Sylphide* that Parisian audiences were eager for something new that would fulfill their love of the supernatural. Poet, writer, and critic Théophile Gautier was inspired to write the scenario for *Giselle* after reading Heinrich Heine's *De l'Allemagne*, in which the spirits of brides who had died before their weddings lured men into the forest, forcing them to dance until their deaths. Gautier was also influenced by Victor Hugo's poem "Fantômes," in which a young woman dances herself to death.

Gautier approached librettist Vernoy de Saint-Georges to help develop the plot, and the result was readily accepted by the Paris Opéra. Adolphe Adam created the music and Jean Coralli the choreography, and, while not originally credited for it, Jules Perrot choreographed Giselle's variations (solos).

▲ **Advertising poster, 1841**
This French poster illustrates Carlotta Grisi in *Giselle*, featuring scenes from the ballet, and from the operas *La Juive* and *Les Hugenottes*.

Originally entitled *Giselle ou Les Wilis*, the ballet premiered with Carlotta Grisi as Giselle, Lucien Petipa as Albrecht, and Adèle Dumilâtre as the queen of the wilis, spirits of dead brides.

▼ **Mikhailovsky Ballet, 2014**
Dancers of the Mikhailovsky Ballet rehearse Act I of *Giselle*, staged by Nikita Dolgushin at the David H. Koch Theater in New York.

> The greatest success of a ballet at the Opéra since *La Sylphide*.
>
> THEOPHILE GAUTIER

Yumiko Takeshima (1970–)

Born in Japan in 1970, Yumiko Takeshima joined the San Francisco Ballet School, aged 14. She went on to dance with many leading companies around the world, while also pursuing her interest in designing dance wear. In 2008, Takeshima created the title role in choreographer David Dawson's production of *Giselle* at the Semperoper in Dresden, Germany—Takeshima also designed the costumes. She last danced as Giselle in 2014, before retiring from ballet in order to focus on designing costumes and dance wear.

Early revisions

In 1848, Jules Perrot staged a version of *Giselle* for the Imperial Theater, assisted by Marius Petipa. In turn, Petipa created his own version in 1884, revised in 1903 with Anna Pavlova as Giselle. Petipa did away with the flying harnesses that had been used in earlier productions, incorporated additional music, and created Giselle's variation in Act I as it is known today.

In 1910, Sergei Diaghilev decided to stage a production of *Giselle* for the Paris season of the Ballets Russes. It was presented during the same season as *The Firebird*, *Schéhérazade*, and *Le Carnaval*. Although Tamara Karsavina as Giselle and Vaslav Nijinsky as Albrecht received high acclaim in their roles, Parisian audiences found the ballet itself outdated compared to the new exotic ballets such as *Schéhérazade* choreographed by Michel Fokine and the designs of Léon Bakst.

At The Royal Ballet

When Nicholas Sergeyev, the former régisseur of the Imperial Ballet, fled Russia after the Russian Revolution, he took with him the notations (written records of choreography) for many ballets, including *Giselle*. He first staged the work in the UK for the Camargo Society in 1932 with Olga Spessivtseva as Giselle and Anton Dolin as Albrecht. In 1934, Sergeyev staged *Giselle* for the Vic-Wells Ballet. For this production, Alicia Markova danced Giselle and Dolin played the role of Albrecht again.

In 1985, Peter Wright staged his version of *Giselle* with exquisite designs by John Macfarlane. It was revived in 1988 with French ballerina Sylvie Guillem as Giselle and Rudolf Nureyev as Albrecht. Wright's version of *Giselle* remains a staple of The Royal Ballet's repertoire.

New directions

The English National Ballet has staged two starkly different versions of *Giselle*. The first was produced for the company in 1971 by Mary Skeaping, who had learned the ballet as a member of Anna Pavlova's company. In 2016, a second production of the ballet entered the company's repertoire, choreographed by Akram Khan. For this version, for which Khan commissioned a new score, the ballet was reimagined in a dystopian world with Giselle as a member of a community of migrant garment factory workers, or "outcasts." The wilis in Act II took the form of the ghosts of these factory workers. The ballet received high critical acclaim.

◀ **Premiere role**
Alicia Markova at the 1934 premiere of *Giselle* at the Vic-Wells Ballet, London. Partnered by Anton Dolin as Albrecht, Markova was acclaimed for the lightness of her performance.

STORY LINE Giselle

Giselle is a peasant girl in love with Loys who, unbeknownst to her, is Duke Albrecht in disguise. When a hunting party stops at Giselle's cottage for refreshments, Albrecht's fiancé Bathilde is with them, and his deception is revealed. This betrayal causes Giselle to go mad with grief, and she dances herself to death. Act II takes place in the forest by Giselle's grave where the wilis rise and welcome Giselle as one of them. Myrtha, the queen, and her wilis capture men and make them dance until death. They set their sights on Albrecht, who has come to visit Giselle's grave, but Giselle protects him. The wilis vanish and Albrecht is left alone.

KARSAVINA AND NIJINSKY AS GISELLE AND ALBRECHT, 1911

ACT I

HILARION'S ARRIVAL, THE ROYAL BALLET, LONDON, 2016

PLOT OVERVIEW

Act I opens outside Giselle's cottage.

Hilarion, who loves Giselle, arrives at the cottage. He sees Albrecht with his squire, and watches him disguise himself as Loys.

Giselle and Albrecht dance. She then plays "He loves me, he loves me not" with a daisy. Hilarion tries to warn Giselle not to put her faith in Albrecht, but she ignores him.

The villagers return from the harvest. Giselle's mother Berthe warns her about the legend of the wilis, and reminds her that she has a weak heart.

The royal party arrives at the cottage, including Bathilde, who befriends Giselle and gives her a necklace.

Hilarion discovers Albrecht's hidden sword, revealing his true identity. Giselle shows Albrecht her necklace.

THE DANCES

Giselle's entrance—she dances happily and mimes that she heard a knock at the door.

Albrecht and Giselle dance a pas de deux together.

Giselle dances with her friends; she asks Albrecht to dance with her.

The peasant pas de deux is danced to music composed by Friedrich Burgmüller.

Giselle performs a beautiful variation for the group.

ISSAC HERNANDEZ AS ALBRECHT ARRIVES AT GISELLE'S COTTAGE DRESSED AS LOYS, ENGLISH NATIONAL BALLET, 2017

GISELLE ADMIRES BATHILDE'S BEAUTY, UNAWARE THAT SHE IS BETROTHED TO ALBRECHT, LOS ANGELES BALLET COMPANY, 2015

MARIANELA NUNEZ PERFORMS A SOLO AS GISELLE, THE ROYAL BALLET, 2009

GISELLE DANCES HERSELF TO DEATH, MIKHAILOVSKY BALLET, DAVID H. KOCH THEATER, NEW YORK, 2014

HILARION IS KILLED BY THE WILIS, HUNGARIAN NATIONAL BALLET, STATE OPERA HOUSE, 2011

Hilarion reveals Albrecht's identity to Giselle, but she does not believe him. The hunting party returns and Bathilde acknowledges that Albrecht is her fiancé. Giselle, heartbroken and mad with grief, dances herself to death.

Giselle dances the famous mad scene with her hair loose.

ACT II

Act II opens in the forest at Giselle's grave.

Hilarion visits Giselle's grave. The wilis appear and frighten him away.

Myrtha performs a solo.

The wilis appear from each side of the stage and dance together.

Myrtha raises Giselle as a wili. Albrecht arrives at Giselle's grave and dances with her spirit before she flees, with him in pursuit. The wilis attack Hilarion.

Hilarion is forced to dance and is then drowned by the wilis.

Myrtha orders Albrecht to dance and for Giselle to dance, too. The pair dance together. Albrecht begins to tire, and it seems that he will dance to his death, but Giselle defies the wilis and saves him.

Giselle and Albrecht dance a pas de deux together.

Dawn finally breaks and the wilis are powerless. Giselle slowly disappears and Albrecht is left alone.

Albrecht dances a dynamic variation.

In some versions, instead of dancing herself to death, Giselle either kills herself with Albrecht's sword or dies because of her weak heart.

KRISZTIA KEVEHAZI AS GISELLE RISES FROM THE GRAVE AS A WILI, HUNGARIAN NATIONAL BALLET, 2011

NATALIA OSIPOVA AS GISELLE AND MATTHEW GOLDING AS ALBRECHT, THE ROYAL BALLET, 2016

The Royal Ballet, 2011
In this production of Peter Wright's ballet, the ghostly wilis approach Giselle's grave before she is raised as a wili by Myrtha.

Adolphe Adam

Composer ▪ 1803–1856

While French composer Adolphe Adam wrote music for a range of art forms, his most popular work remains his score for the ballet *Giselle*. He gave each of the main characters a theme tune, which subtly varied with their mood and situation, so helping to tell the story through the music. He also composed the score for *Le Corsaire*, described by one critic as "some of the prettiest and most animated music that Adolphe Adam has ever composed."

▲ **Scene from *Giselle***
Natalya Bessmertnova dances Giselle and Mikhail Lavrovsky dances Albrecht in a production staged at the State Academic Bolshoi Theater of the USSR in 1963. Adam created a signature tune to express the duo's love for each other.

Born into a musical family, Adolphe Charles Adam began improvising musical compositions from a young age. While his father was a well-known composer and professor at the Paris Conservatoire, he was against his son following in his footsteps, and so the teenage boy studied and composed in secret. When Adam was 17, his father finally relented, reluctantly allowing him to study music and composition at the Paris Conservatoire.

From opera to ballet

Adam worked for several years as an organist, but also composed songs for vaudeville theater (a genre of variety entertainment). In 1826, he met librettist Eugène Scribe on tour in Geneva, and they began to collaborate on several comic operas. Adam's first one-act opera, *Pierre et Cathérine*, premiered in 1829 at the Opéra-Comique in Paris.

Adam spent the early 1830s in London before returning to Paris in 1833. The following year he wrote *La Chalet*, which is widely considered to be the first true French operetta (a short opera, usually light and humorous).

In 1836, Adam made his Paris Opéra debut with his composition for the ballet, *La Fille du Danube*. Marie Taglioni danced the principal role. While it received mixed reviews in Paris, when it transferred to London in 1837, *The Times* gave it an enthusiastic write-up, concluding: "There can be no doubt that it will have, as it deserves to have, a long run."

Thematic score for *Giselle*

Adam's most famous work was his composition for the ballet *Giselle* (1841). Théophile Gautier and Vernoy de Saint-Georges developed the libretto for the ballet, based on the Slavic myth of the wilis. These are the spirits of brides who have died before their wedding, that rise at night, forcing men to dance to their death. Adam was approached to create the score. He is said to have composed the ballet in just three weeks (although some sources claim it took him only one week).

The music for *Giselle* was completely different from any previously written ballet scores. It is significant for Adam's use of leitmotifs (recurring themes). They served as an audible reminder to the audience of certain characters and themes. There are leitmotifs associated with Giselle, Albrecht, and Hilarion.

Gautier's original libretto stated that the wilis were each from different countries, and initially Adam composed music for each in their own national style. As the ballet developed, this idea was dropped, but some of the original musical compositions were retained. For example, wili Moyna and wili Zulma—attendants to Myrtha, the Queen of the wilis—each dance to their own theme. Moyna was originally intended as an odalisque (a Turkish slave or dancing girl), and Zulma was a bayadère (Hindu dancing girl). Moreover, the French wilis dance to a typical French minuet and the German wilis dance to a Bavarian waltz.

Adam's other works

Over the course of his career, Adam worked in four distinct styles: grand opera, ballet, comic opera, and incidental music (for plays). He also wrote pianoforte pieces, church music, and songs.

Adam composed the music to 14 ballets in total, for companies in Paris,

> Adam's music is superior to the usual run of ballet music, it abounds in tunes and orchestral effects.

THEOPHILE GAUTIER, FRENCH POET, JOURNALIST, AND ART CRITIC

▲ **Stage set design for *Le Corsaire***
Anatolij Fjorodowitsch Gelzer designed this stage set in 1888 for Act II, which takes place in the secret cave of the pirates. Adolphe Adam composed a spirited score to suit the action.

Berlin, St. Petersburg, and London. However, only *Giselle* and *Le Corsaire*, his final score, composed in 1856, have survived. Contemporary critics of *La Jolie Fille de Gand* praised the originality of Adam's score, while the audience of *La Filleule des fées* particularly enjoyed a flute variation that Marie Taglioni danced to at the premiere in Paris in 1849.

In the late 1840s, Adam invested in a new opera house in Paris, which left him in financial ruin. From 1849 until his death seven years later, he taught composition at the Paris Conservatoire while also writing his own music.

KEY WORKS

La Fille du Danube, 1836 • *L'Écumeur des mer*, 1840 *Giselle*, 1841 • *La Jolie Fille de Gand*, 1842 • *Le Diable à quatre*, 1845 • *Griseldis ou les cinq senses*, 1848 • *La Filleule des fées*, 1849 • *Orfa*, 1852 • *Le Corsaire*, 1856

TIMELINE

- **July 24, 1803** Born in Paris, the son of composer Jean-Louis Adam.
- **1821** Enters the Paris Conservatoire, studying organ, composition, and counterpoint under leading operatic composer François-Adrien Boieldieu.
- **July 26, 1830** His first ballet score, *La Chatte blanche* (composed with Casimir Gide), debuts at the New Theater in Paris.
- **1830** Moves to London after the July Revolution in Paris results in the overthrow of the reigning monarch, Charles X. Continues to compose while in the UK, creating works including *His First Campaign*.
- **1833** Returns to Paris permanently.
- **1836** His ballet score for *La Fille du Danube* debuts at the Paris Opéra.
- **June 28, 1841** His masterpiece, *Giselle*, premieres at the Paris Opéra, with Carlotta Grisi in the title role.
- **1842** Follows the success of *Giselle* by composing *La Jolie Fille de Gand* at the Paris Opéra, in which the heroine spurns a nobleman in favor of her true love.
- **1848** Incurs heavy losses after borrowing large sums to open a new opera venue, the Opéra-National, in Paris. The venture fails due to the French Revolution of 1848.
- **1849** Becomes professor of composition at the Paris Conservatoire, largely to clear his debts.
- **1849** Writes the score for *La Filleule des fées* at the Paris Opéra.
- **May 3, 1856** Dies in his sleep in Paris, just four days after the premiere of his operetta *Les Pantins de Violette*.

CANTIQUE DE NOËL (1847) PROGRAM

ENTER THE BALLERINA

The word "ballerina" comes from the Italian name for female dancer. The first ballerinas emerged in France—Marie-Thérèse Subligny was première danseuse at the Paris Opéra and, when she performed in London in 1699, was the first ballerina English audiences had ever seen. Françoise Prévost succeeded Subligny, and her performance in *Les Horaces* in 1708 is said to have made her audience weep. She retired in 1730.

The second generation, led by Prévost's students Marie Camargo and Marie Sallé, shortened their skirts to reveal their intricate steps. These two dancers, who debuted in the 1720s, became stars of the Paris Opéra and a great rivalry grew up between them. Camargo performed difficult technical feats while Sallé, also a great technician, was a highly expressive dancer and daring choreographer.

In the 1700s, ballerinas began removing the heels from their shoes to make it easier to jump. With the ethereal quality required for Romantic ballets, female dancers started experimenting with holding poses on their toes. This led to pointe work, which every ballet dancer since then has performed. Marie Taglioni is the best known of these pioneers, but her pointe shoes were just flat slippers with some darning around the toes. Brief rises to pointe were all that were possible, and sometimes ballerinas were suspended on wires so their toes could skim the floor.

With the literal rise of the ballerina by the mid-19th century, male dancers declined in importance to the extent that women took some men's roles en travestie (in disguise, wearing male attire). The arrival of Anna Pavlova raised the profile of ballerinas even higher, while the many stars of the Ballets Russes and the ballet companies it inspired brought celebrity status to the most brilliant dancers of both sexes.

> And then you have the classical ballerinas—they're like sopranos. Applied to the dance.
>
> NINETTE DE VALOIS, CHOREOGRAPHER

◀ ***La Péri*, 1843**
Jean Coralli choreographed this ballet for his favorite ballerina, Carlotta Grisi. As in many engravings of ballerinas of the Romantic period of ballet, she appears to be weightless, floating on the tip of one toe.

Carlotta Grisi

Dancer ▪ 1819–1899

Born into a famous Italian theatrical family, Carlotta Grisi (Caronna Adele Josephine Marie Grisi) is best known for her lead role in *Giselle*, which opened in Paris in 1841. This role brought her critical acclaim for her ability to dance in two celebrated styles—with the earthy vivacity of Fanny Elssler, and with the ethereality of Marie Taglioni—and helped her to join them as one of the most renowned dancers of their day. Grisi went on to dance many roles in London, Paris, and St. Petersburg.

▲ **London debut**
This drawing from *The Illustrated London News*, June 1846, depicts Carlotta Grisi performing in the new ballet, *Paquita*, at Drury Lane Theatre, London.

Initially training at La Scala ballet school in Milan, Carlotta Grisi left early to work with a touring opera to earn money for the family. By 1834, aged just 14, she was dancing with a ballet company in Naples, where she met French dancer and choreographer Jules Perrot. Taken by Grisi's talent, he trained her himself, and they danced together at engagements in Vienna and London. While they never married, they had a child together, and Grisi sometimes performed under the name Madame Perrot.

Paris debut

In 1840 in Paris, Grisi and Perrot received acclaim for their performances in *Le Zingaro*, a comedy opera-ballet in which Grisi allegedly sang as well as danced. Due to this success, Perrot hoped to negotiate his way back into the Paris Opéra, having left previously over a dispute, but only Grisi was hired.

The following year, Théophile Gautier developed the libretto of *Giselle* specifically with Grisi in mind. The ballet was created by Jean Coralli but it was Perrot who choreographed all of Giselle's solos for Grisi—although he did not receive credit for this at the time. Act I required dramatic acting to portray firstly the light-hearted Giselle, then her demise into madness. Act II portrays Giselle as a ghostly, other-worldly spirit. The ballet established her reputation as one of the great ballerinas.

Gautier became a close friend of Grisi, writing the ballet *La Péri* for her in 1843, also choreographed by Jean Coralli. It had music by Friedrich Burgmüller, and an in-vogue theme of the supernatural. Grisi portrayed Péri, a Persian spirit who appears to the wealthy Sultan Achmet (danced by Lucien Petipa), who then falls in love with her. To test his love, she takes the form of an escaped slave and Achmet is killed (or imprisoned) for not returning her to her master. The ballet ends with Péri and Achmet entering heaven. One of the most striking moments of the ballet was a leap, choreographed by Coralli, in which Grisi jumped from a 6 ft (2 m) high platform into the arms of Petipa.

Of Grisi's performance, Gautier later wrote, "Carlotta danced with a perfection, lightness, and boldness, and a chaste and refined seductiveness, which place her in the front rank between Elssler and Taglioni …."

Grisi in London

Throughout the 1840s, Grisi also performed as ballerina at Her Majesty's Theatre, London, which, from the early 1830s until the late 1840s, was the home of the city's Romantic ballet. The theater's resident company was widely respected, and attracted many other guest ballerinas, including Fanny Elssler, Marie Taglioni, Lucile Grahn, and Fanny Cerrito. In 1845, Perrot choreographed *Pas de quatre* for four of these great ballerinas: Taglioni, Grahn, Cerrito, and Grisi.

While in London, Grisi danced in *Giselle* and *Le Diable à quatre*, and created roles in Perrot's ballet *La Esmeralda* (1844), and Paul Taglioni's *Electra* (1849) and *Les Métamorphoses* (1850). However, by the late 1840s, the appetite for ballet had declined in London and artists were forced to look elsewhere. Grisi traveled to St. Petersburg and spent her last years as a dancer with the Imperial Theater, where Petipa was ballet master.

Who is Giselle? Giselle is Carlotta Grisi, a charming girl with blue eyes …

THÉOPHILE GAUTIER, IN A PRIVATE LETTER, 1841

▲ **Defining role**
This 19th-century engraving shows Carlotta Grisi as Giselle in Act II of the ballet. Here, the spirit of Giselle has been raised from the dead by the ghostly and vengeful wilis.

KEY WORKS

Title role, *Giselle*, 1841 • Title role, *La Péri*, 1843 • *Pas de quatre*, 1845 • Title role, *Paquita*, 1846 • Ysaure, *La Filleule des fées*, 1849 • *Les Métamorphoses*, 1850 • *Gazelda*, 1853

TIMELINE

- **June 28, 1819** Born into a renowned Italian theatrical family in Vižinada, Istria, now part of Croatia.

- **1829** Joins the corps de ballet at La Scala ballet school in Milan, aged 10.

- **1834** Joins the touring company of the San Carlo Theater, Naples, and comes to the attention of Jules Perrot.

- **1836** Dances *Le Rossignol* in London with her dance partner, choreographer, and lover Jules Perrot.

- **1841** Joins the Paris Opéra, making her debut in Donizetti's *La Favorita*.

CARLOTTA GRISI DANCES CESARE PUGNI'S *OPERA POLKA* WITH JULES PERROT

- **June 28, 1841** Becomes an overnight star after playing the title role in *Giselle*—her first full-length ballet. The name "Carlotta Grisi" becomes synonymous with *Giselle*.

- **1845** Appears at Her Majesty's Theatre in London as part of a celebrated quartet of ballerinas in Perrot's *Pas de quatre*.

- **1850** Dances at the Imperial Ballet in St. Petersburg. Her first major role—that of Giselle—is not received positively, but she soon becomes prima ballerina.

- **1851** Appears in *The Naiad and the Fisherman*, the first of a series of new works created for her by Perrot, followed by *The War of the Women*, and *Gazelda*.

- **1853/1854** Makes her final appearance onstage in Warsaw. After giving birth to her second daughter, she retires in St-Jean, Geneva, with her family.

- **May 29, 1899** Dies aged 80 in Geneva, Switzerland.

Napoli

First performed: March 29, 1842 ▪ Venue: Royal Theater, Copenhagen ▪ Choreography and story: August Bournonville ▪ Music: Holger Simon Paulli, Edvard Helsted, Niels Wilhelm Gade, Hans Christian Lumbye

One of Denmark's most popular ballets, this light-hearted work was inspired by Bournonville's time in France and Italy, and combines the romance of the French style of ballet with colorful characters and folk dance. An instant hit, at the premiere there was said to have been "a gaiety throughout the whole house which could waken the dead." Despite its frivolity, *Napoli* is nonetheless a moral tale of Christian virtue over temptation, themes rarely explored in ballet.

STORY LINE

Act I The Market Engaged to the fisherman Gennaro, Teresina is washed overboard from his boat during a storm. Fra Ambrosio tells Gennaro to search the sea, and gives him an image of the Madonna for protection.

Act II Blue Grotto Rescued by naiads, Teresina is taken to the grotto of the sea sprite, Golfo, who turns her into a naiad. Gennaro finds Teresina, but she does not recognize him. Gennaro prays to the Madonna, Teresina becomes human again, and Golfo is defeated.

Act III Wedding The couple returns, but the villagers believe Gennaro is touched by evil. Reassured that Teresina was rescued by the power of the Madonna, they all celebrate.

In 1841, dancer, choreographer, and artistic director of the Royal Danish Ballet, August Bournonville, addressed the Danish king directly from the stage during a heated moment in a performance, in order to resolve a dispute. The king was not amused by his impertinence, and Bournonville was placed under temporary house arrest and given unpaid leave from the theater.

Finding inspiration

During his suspension, Bournonville traveled to Italy, where he was greatly inspired by the vibrant culture and local people of Naples. He also went to France, and it was during a stagecoach journey from Paris to Dunkirk that Bournonville drew on his recent experiences and created the lively tune for the tarantella that then inspired *Napoli*.

While Bournonville was influenced by the romanticism and mystery of the French style of ballet, unlike French ballets which focused on the ballerina, Bournonville's work contained challenging roles for male dancers.

In the premiere of *Napoli*, in 1842, Bournonville himself took the role of Gennaro, and the ballerina Caroline Fjeldsted danced as Teresina. The ballet proved hugely popular, not only for its dancing but also for its stagecraft. When Teresina was transformed into a naiad, and later back to a woman, her costume changed onstage as if by magic, although in reality it was via an ingenious method using fishing line and a trapdoor.

Act III became particularly famous for its pas de six (a dance for two men and four women) and the joyful tarantella that comes at the end of the ballet. This act is also often performed in isolation—as a stand-alone work.

Royal Danish Ballet revivals

Outside of Denmark, *Napoli* has been adjusted various times. The choreography for Act I and III has remained little changed in Denmark, but Act II has often been altered to comply with changing styles and techniques. The extensive mime sections, for example, have been both removed and reinstated.

In 1992, to celebrate the 150th anniversary of *Napoli*'s premiere, the ballet was revised for the Royal Danish Ballet by choreographer Dinna Bjørn, with new choreography for Act II. More recently, in 2009, a new production was created by Nikolaj Hübbe and Sorella Englund, which moved the action to 1950s Naples.

▼ **French revival**
French dancers Florence Clerc and Charles Jude perform as Teresina and Gennaro in *Napoli* for the Paris Opéra Ballet in 1985.

▶ **National treasure**
Lis Jeppesen dances as Teresina for the Royal Danish Ballet in 1981. The company has performed *Napoli* over 700 times.

Paquita

First performed: April 1, 1846 ▪ Venue: Salle Le Peletier, Paris ▪ Choreography: Joseph Mazilier ▪ Music: Edouard Deldevez ▪ Story: Paul Foucher and Mazilier

This two-act ballet set in Spain during the Napoleonic Wars relates the love story of a French officer and a Spanish gypsy. *Paquita* has the most famous example of a grand pas classique and, throughout the 20th century, it was known for this showpiece dance, performed separately from the ballet narrative. Recently, however, the full-length ballet has been revived for the Bavarian State Ballet.

STORY LINE

Act I The ballet begins with a memorial for Count d'Hervilly. Present are d'Hervilly's nephew Lucien, a French officer, and Spanish governor Don Lopez de Mendoza. Some gypsies arrive, and Lucien falls in love with lead dancer Paquita. The gypsy chief Iñigo wants Paquita for himself and plots with Don Lopez to kill Lucien, but Paquita saves him.

Act II In safety at the house of the French commander, it is discovered that the gypsies abducted Paquita as a child, and she is the lost daughter of Count d'Hervilly. Paquita and Lucien marry.

▼ **English National Ballet, 2017**
Isabelle Brouwers and Emilio Pavan perform the stand-alone grand pas classique from *Paquita* at Sadler's Wells Theatre, London.

The Paris Opéra premiered with leading lights Carlotta Grisi as Paquita and Lucien Petipa (brother of Marius) as Lucien d'Hervilly. A year later, in 1847, the ballet debuted in St. Petersburg. It was the first full-length work to be staged by Marius Petipa, and he starred as Lucien while Yelena Andreyanova was Paquita. Petipa revived the ballet with new choreography in 1881, adding music by Ludwig Minkus and the famed pas de trois and grand pas classique into the Act II celebrations.

Classic show dances

The ballet fell from the repertoire but Petipa's additional dances survived. The grand pas classique (sometimes just called the grand pas) is a Spanish-themed ensemble of Paquita and Lucien, six female first soloists, and eight female second soloists. If included in productions, the pas de trois is for one male and two female dancers.

Anna Pavlova performed the grand pas classique with her company, and introduced it to Western Europe. Many choreographers, including George Balanchine, Alexandra Danilova, Galina Samsova, and Natalia Makarova, also staged the dance, which is viewed as a perfect example of Russian imperial choreography.

Revivals and reconstructions

In 1964, Rudolph Nureyev staged *Paquita*'s grand pas classique for a gala in aid of the Royal Academy of Dance. Margot Fonteyn partnered him, supported by soloists and students from The Royal Ballet and The Royal Ballet School. Nureyev also put on the work for La Scala in Milan, the Vienna State Opera Ballet, and American Ballet Theatre. French choreographer Pierre Lacotte staged his own version of the two-act ballet for the Paris Opéra Ballet in 2001, reinstating Mazilier's original mime sequences as well as Petipa's additions. Russian choreographer Alexei Ratmansky and dance historian Doug Fullington also delved into the past. They used the Stepanov notations (written choreographic records housed at Harvard University) for Petipa's *Paquita* to create a reconstruction of Petipa's final version. The ballet had its world premiere at the National Theater in Munich in 2014.

▶ **Bolshoi Ballet, 2010**
Natalia Osipova dances as Paquita at the Royal Opera House, London, in a triple bill with *Petrushka* and *Russian Seasons*.

▼ **Petipa's revival, 1881**
Ekaterina Vazem, Petipa's favorite Russian dancer, portrayed the title role in his restaged *Paquita*. He choreographed the grand pas classique for her.

Pas de quatre

First performed: July 12, 1845 ▪ Venue: Her Majesty's Theatre ▪ Choreography: Jules Perrot ▪ Music: Cesare Pugni ▪ Story: Benjamin Lumley and Jules Perrot

In 1845, Benjamin Lumley, the director of Her Majesty's Theatre, London, had the idea of showcasing the talents of the four most famous ballerinas of the day. The resulting ballet was an overnight sensation, with even Queen Victoria and Prince Albert attending a performance. Although *Pas de quatre* was performed just four times with the original cast, it has continued to enchant ballerinas and audiences ever since.

STORY LINE

A divertissement in one act, although *Pas de quatre* has no story, it is the epitome of a Romantic ballet with its delicate, light movements. The four ballerinas danced together at the beginning and end, as well as each performing her own variation. Each solo was choreographed to display the ballerina's best features. The dancers performed in age order—Lucile Grahn first, followed by Carlotta Grisi, and then Fanny Cerrito—with Taglioni, the oldest, taking the coveted last solo.

Jules Perrot brought together the celebrated dancers Marie Taglioni, Carlotta Grisi, and Fanny Cerrito in *Pas de quatre.* Fanny Elssler had also been asked but declined, so Danish ballerina Lucile Grahn took the fourth role instead.

Among the unanimously rapturous reviews, the newspaper *The Era* wrote on August 24, 1845, that if Elssler had also been present "to form the quintet," we would have "died of excess of dancing" and "yet the *Pas de quatre* shook one's soul to its very centre." While it was a miracle that Perrot convinced four of the biggest ballerinas of the time to dance together, they only performed the ballet four times.

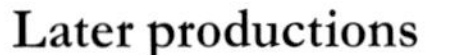

Later productions

In 1936, a group of collaborators from the Markova-Dolin Company gathered at Anton Dolin's London studio, discussing ideas for a new ballet. One of them suggested a work based on A.E. Chalon's print of *Pas de quatre* (Dolin had a copy on his wall). Keith Lester arranged the choreography, and dance historian Cyril Beaumont traced a copy of Pugni's piano score for the piece, which Leighton Lucas was able to orchestrate. Their *Pas de quatre* premiered that same year.

In 1941, Ballet Theatre (now American Ballet Theatre) asked Anton Dolin to restage the work. Dolin wrote to Lester for his choreographic notes, but the story goes that they were detained by War Customs authorities, as they were thought to be a coded message. Dolin therefore created his own choreography for the piece. The ballet premiered with ballerinas Nana Gollner, Alicia Alonso, Nina Stroganova, and Katherine Sergava.

◄ **The original lineup**
While nothing remains of Jules Perrot's original choreography, a sense of the romance of the work is captured in this lithograph of the original four ballerinas by Alfred Edward Chalon.

▲ **De Cuevas Ballet, 1954**
Chilean-born impresario George de Cuevas put together another star-studded production of *Pas de quatre* at London's Stoll Theatre, featuring Alicia Markova, Rosella Hightower, Denise Bourgeois, and Jacqueline Moreau.

Dolin staged the work for the Ballet Russe de Monte Carlo in 1946, and in the late 1940s ballerinas Nathalie Krassovska, Mia Slavenska, Alexandra Danilova, and Alicia Markova took the four roles. This was to become an iconic role for Markova (who had danced it earlier with Ballet Theatre). Dolin later recalled of this casting that "never have four dancers worked so magnificently together in an attempt to give us an idea of one of the greatest occasions in the whole history of ballet." Markova also danced in George de Cuevas's production in the 1950s.

Pas de quatre remains in the repertoire of many companies. Notably, the ballet features in the repertory of all-male comic Les Ballets Trockadero de Monte Carlo—with a rather different flavor from the original that Queen Victoria enjoyed.

Le Conservatoire

First performed: May 6, 1849 • Venue: Royal Danish Theater, Copenhagen • Choreography and story: Bournonville • Music: Holger Simon Paulli

Set in a ballet school in Paris and interwoven with a comic romance, *Le Conservatoire* is a memoir of Danish choreographer August Bournonville's training with Auguste Vestris in the 1820s. The ballet class in Act I is based on Bournonville's comprehensive notes on Vestris's teaching method, in the French style of mime and dance. As a director of the Royal Danish Ballet, Bournonville strove to make dancing a respectable profession in Denmark.

The ballet class begins and ends with the dancers performing a full plié and features all the dancers wearing practice clothes from the 1820s. It exemplifies Romantic ballet, with the dancers displaying poise and delicacy as they go from simple steps to more complex moves, such as pirouettes and pas de trois, which all demand control. Bournonville showcases ballet in its purest form, but also uses the plot to evoke comedy, especially in Act II when the pupils pretend to be marriage candidates to trick the inspector at their school.

One-act version

The complete ballet was performed from 1849 until 1934. After that, it disappeared from the repertoire, deemed to be old-fashioned. However, in 1941, *Le Conservatoire* was revised as a one-act piece featuring the ballet-class scene only. The Australian Ballet became the first company outside Scandinavia to stage the one-act version of *Le Conservatoire*, produced by former soloist of the Royal Danish Ballet Poul Gnatt in 1965. The company included the ballet in touring lecture demonstrations, and as part of their general repertoire.

The one-act version also remained in the Danish repertoire until 1995, when the Royal Danish Ballet revived the complete work. The reconstruction was created by Kirsten Ralov, Niels Bjørn Larsen (both of whom danced in the 1933 production), and Dinna Bjørn, a teacher and choreographer, and the international authority on the Bournonville style.

STORY LINE

Act I Set in the 1820s, the ballet portrays the daily life and intrigues of a Parisian ballet academy. The main action takes the form of a ballet class, presented on stage in the style of French ballet master Auguste Vestris.

Act II The humorous plot concerns Monsieur Dufour, the pompous inspector of the ballet school, who writes a matrimonial advertisement in the newspaper. The pupils of the school disguise themselves as potential candidates in an attempt to trick Monsieur Dufour, but eventually he marries his faithful housekeeper Mademoiselle Bonjour.

▼ **Royal Danish Ballet, 2010**
Le Conservatoire is one of the finest examples of Bournonville's technique and choreography and it brought the French style to Scandinavia.

Jules Perrot

Dancer and choreographer • 1810–1892

At the height of his career, in the 1840s, Jules Joseph Perrot was dancing the role of Albrecht in the premiere of *Giselle*, as well as developing a unique style as a choreographer. His ballets, which included the celebrated *Pas de quatre* and *La Esmeralda*, were noted for their fast-paced choreography and his way of using this pace to carry the action and story forward. With poetic sensitivity, Perrot often contrasted and combined unusual dances and dramatic mimed scenes.

▲ ***La Esmeralda*'s tambourine dance**
The fame of Perrot's ballet endures in this exciting solo that Esmeralda dances—played here by Matilda Kschessinska at the Mariinsky Theater, St. Petersburg, in 1899. Ballerinas still choose to perform this bravura piece at galas and competitions today.

Even as a child, young Jules Perrot was dancing professionally, performing first as an acrobat and clown with a traveling circus. At the age of 13, he moved to Paris alone, where he worked in a French style of variety called boulevard theater. During this time, Perrot refined his classical ballet technique, training with famed male dancer Auguste Vestris.

The male Taglioni

In 1830, Perrot made his ballet debut at the Paris Opéra. He was one of the few male dancers to achieve critical acclaim during the Romantic period, an era of ballet that was dominated by female ballerinas. He became a regular partner of Marie Taglioni, and was even referred to in the press as the "male Taglioni."

After several successful years, Perrot left the Paris Opéra over a contract dispute. Allegedly, the management would not agree to pay Perrot an equal salary to the top ballerinas. He went to Naples, where he met the young Carlotta Grisi. They toured the cities of Munich, Vienna, Milan, and Lyon. A couple both on stage and off, they had a daughter in 1837, but never married. It was at this time that Perrot made his initial forays into choreography, creating his first major work—*La Nymphe et le papillon*—for Vienna Kärntnertortheater in 1836. He also choreographed all of Grisi's solos for *Giselle*, although he was uncredited.

By 1840, Perrot was well known, both as a choreographer and principal dancer. He was employed as principal ballet master at Her Majesty's Theatre, London, from about 1842 to 1848. These were his most significant years as a choreographer. In 1844, Perrot created the ballet *La Esmeralda*, based on Victor Hugo's book *The Hunchback of Notre Dame*. The ballet was set to the music of Cesare Pugni (the resident composer at Her Majesty's Theatre) and opened in London. It was later reworked by fellow-countryman Marius Petipa. This ballet has largely faded from the classical canon, surviving in full only in the repertoire of several Eastern European ballet companies.

Perrot's most famous work was *Pas de quatre* (1845), devised for the four great ballerinas of the day—Taglioni, Grisi, Fanny Cerrito, and Lucile Grahn. In London, Perrot also created the ballets *Ondine* (1843), *L'Aurore* (1843), *Caterina ou La Fille du bandit* (1846), *Le Jugement de Paris* (1848), and *Les Quatre Saisons* (1848).

Russia and romance

In 1848, Perrot worked as choreographer at La Scala, Milan, where he created *Faust* for ballerina Fanny Elssler. That year, Perrot and Elssler toured to St. Petersburg and the Imperial Theater. He decided to stay, and was appointed dancer and later ballet master at the Imperial Ballet, a post he held until 1858.

During this period, Perrot staged many ballets. He produced expanded versions of *La Esmeralda* and *Caterina ou La Fille du bandit*, and a series of major new works, including *The Naiad and the Fisherman* (1851), *The War of the Women* (1852), and *Gazelda* (1853), all for Grisi as lead ballerina, and *Armida* (1855) for Cerrito. Perrot was assisted at the Imperial Theater by Marius Petipa.

In Russia, Perrot—no longer with Grisi—met and married dancer Capitoline Samovskaya with whom he had two children. In 1860, Perrot and his wife returned to France where he continued to teach until his death.

> ... quiet agility, perfect rhythm, and easy grace ... Perrot the aerial, Perrot the sylph, Perrot the male Taglioni.

CRITIC THEOPHILE GAUTIER, IN A REVIEW OF *LE ZINGARO* CONTRIBUTED TO THE *PRESSE*, MARCH 2, 1840

▲ **Immortalized in paint**
French Impressionist artist Edgar Degas depicted Jules Perrot conducting a class of dancers in *The Ballet Class* (1875). The imaginary scene features around 24 women and is set in a rehearsal room in the old Paris Opéra.

KEY WORKS

Choreographer: *Le Nymphe et le papillon*, 1836 • *Der Kobold*, 1836 • *Giselle*, 1841 • *La Esmeralda*, 1844 • *Pas de quatre*, 1845 • *La Filleule des fées*, 1849 • *Armida*, 1855

TIMELINE

- **August 18, 1810** Born in Lyon, France.
- **1818** Gives his first performance at the Lyon Grand Theater.
- **1823** After mastering the comic, acrobatic style of Charles-François Mazurier, joins the Théâtre de la Gaîté.
- **1826** Moves to the more upmarket Théâtre de la Porte-St-Martin, Paris.
- **1830** Debuts as a dancer at the Paris Opéra, becoming the company's lead male dancer and partnering Marie Taglioni.
- **1834** Meets Carlotta Grisi in Naples, later choreographing his first major works for her—*Das Stelldichein* and *Der Kobold*.
- **1842** Joins Her Majesty's Theatre, London, as assistant to André Deshayes, taking over as ballet master the next year.
- **1843** While in London, produces major works including *Ondine* (1843) for Grisi, *Le Délire d'un peintre* (1843) for Fanny Elssler, *La Esmeralda* (1844) for Fanny Cerrito, and *Éoline* (1845) for Lucile Grahn.
- **1848** Creates *Faust* for Elssler at La Scala, Milan, and dances part of Mephistopheles.
- **1849** Stages *La Filleule des fées* at the Paris Opéra, then joins the Imperial Ballet, St. Petersburg, as dancer and choreographer, becoming ballet master in 1851.
- **1855** Creates *Armida*, his final new work for the Imperial Ballet.
- **1860** Returns to France with his wife Capitoline Samovskaya and family.
- **1864** Retires from staging ballets following an unsuccessful season in Milan.
- **August 24, 1892** Dies in the French seaside resort of Paramé, Britanny.

POSTER FOR *LA ESMERALDA* (1844)

LIGHTING THE SCENE

Lighting for theater, and specifically dance, has changed dramatically over the centuries. The first stage performances were illuminated by candles or oil lamps and reflectors, which created indistinct and rather eerie spectacles. By the mid-1850s, gas lighting was becoming more common, and lighting rigs were beginning to assume an order that is recognized today. Footlights (across the front of the stage at ground level), border lights (horizontal strip lights placed between each border, such as two curtains), and wing lights (vertical strip lights hung between stage wings) were normal practice, and gave an overall and more adequate illumination.

While gas lighting could produce a great sense of atmosphere through dimming effects, gas lights with inadequate guards alongside costumes made of highly flammable material were responsible for some tragic accidents. Emma Livry, one of the last great ballerinas of the Romantic era, died a few months after sustaining burn injuries when her tulle skirts caught fire during a stage rehearsal in 1862. Following this, gas lights were redesigned with inverted flames and wet blankets were kept in the wings for safety.

In the late 20th century, advances saw stage lighting become more sophisticated and direction-specific. Clever illumination began to lessen the need for, and to a degree replace, elaborate painted sets and intricate costumes. Today, the absence of scenery flats means that the entire stage can be filled without interruption. Dramatic effect is now easily achieved by a complex range of computer-programmed lighting cues, robotic lamps, and projections.

> Gas lighting … [lifted] the ballerina into a position of supremacy on the stage.
>
> HELEN THOMAS, *DANCE, MODERNITY, AND CULTURE*, 2003

◀ **Illuminating *Lest We Forget***
In Liam Scarlett's *No Man's Land*, one of a three-part ballet called *Lest We Forget* commemorating World War I, strong background lighting links the furthest soldier and munitions workers. Fellow-soldiers trudge rhythmically along planks into the shadowed foreground.

Le Corsaire

First performed: January 23, 1856 ▪ Venue: Théâtre Impérial de l'Opéra, Paris ▪ Choreography: Joseph Mazilier ▪ Music: Adolphe Adam
Story: Vernoy de Saint-Georges and Joseph Mazilier

The Emperor Napoleon III himself went to the opening performance of *Le Corsaire* in Paris, and his empress said she had never seen anything so beautiful and moving. Since Mazilier's first production, Petipa and others have recreated both choreography and score for this tale of pirates and derring-do. The result is still a triumph today.

IN CONTEXT

Like many great ballets, *Le Corsaire* has had a complex evolution. In 1856, Joseph Mazilier created the work for the Paris Opéra. He based the story on the 1814 poem "The Corsair" by Lord Byron, which had previously inspired two ballets—one in Milan in the 1820s, and a second in London in 1837. Mazilier (who had danced James in the premiere of *La Sylphide* in 1832) worked with Vernoy de Saint-Georges (who had been the librettist for *Giselle*) on streamlining the plot for *Le Corsaire*. Adolphe Adam composed the score. It was his last work, as he died shortly afterward.

Two years later, in 1858, Jules Perrot, assisted by Marius Petipa, staged *Le Corsaire* for the Imperial Ballet of St. Petersburg. Ekaterina Friedburg danced the role of Medora and Marius Petipa himself the part of Conrad.

From the very first night, the swashbuckling *Le Corsaire* proved highly popular, and it has gone on to be performed as far away from France as the US and Hong Kong. In the first production, Carolina Rosati danced the role of Medora alongside her fellow Italian, Domenico Segarelli, who created the part of Conrad. Initially, Conrad was purely a mimed role and it was not until the 1870s in Russia that it evolved into dance.

Le Corsaire relied on the state-of-the-art prowess of the Paris Opéra's technical department to create the final thrilling shipwreck scene. An eyewitness recalled, "The opera stage seemed to have taken on suddenly the vast proportion of the open sea … it was reality in all its grandiose horror." It still makes an arresting sight in productions today.

▲ **Birbanto, renegade pirate**
Yonah Acosta takes a leap as Birbanto, betrayer of his friend the pirate leader Conrad. *Le Corsaire* contains especially strong roles for male dancers.

In contrast to the flashy pyrotechnics and piratical leaps, Act II has a silky-smooth adagio duet for Medora and Conrad and Act III, after Petipa's revisions, includes *Le Jardin animé*—a dream scene of dancing flowers creating arches and avenues, set to sweet music by Léo Delibes. Petipa reworked *Le Corsaire*, and current versions are based on his 1899 ballet.

Into the 21st century

Le Corsaire remained popular in Russia throughout the 20th century. In 1931 and 1936, the Mariinsky Ballet (renamed the Kirov during Soviet times) restaged

Miyako Yoshida (1965–)

Noted for her classical style, Japanese ballerina Miyako Yoshida danced the pas de deux from *Le Corsaire* as a gala number with Tetsuya Kumakawa at London's Royal Opera House in 1996. A year earlier, she had transferred from Birmingham Royal Ballet to The Royal Ballet, where she stayed until 2010. Yoshida came to the UK in 1983 and became well-tuned to the English style, dancing the lead in Frederick Ashton ballets such as *Cinderella*, *La fille mal gardée*, and *Ondine*. Among her many starring performances, however, Yoshida is perhaps most associated with the role of Sugar Plum Fairy in *The Nutcracker*.

the work with the help of Agrippina Vaganova (an influential teacher who developed the Vaganova ballet method). Choreographer Pyotr Gusev staged *Le Corsaire* for the Mikhailovsky Ballet (a St. Petersburg–based company) in 1955. Today, the Mariinsky Ballet continues to perform this version, which is divested of almost all of Adam's original score.

In 1973, Kirov ballet master Konstantin Sergeyev created a version of *Le Corsaire* based on Petipa's 1899 staging of the ballet. The Bolshoi Ballet revived this in 1992. Meanwhile, Canadian ballerina Anna-Marie Holmes, having studied in Russia and been the first North American invited to dance with the Kirov, was inspired to stage many of the Russian classics. In 1997, she created *Le Corsaire* for the Boston Ballet, based on the Bolshoi's revival of the Sergeyev version after Petipa. Holmes has restaged this production worldwide, and today it is the best-known version. English National Ballet engaged Holmes to direct *Le Corsaire* in 2013. It premiered at the London Coliseum with Alina Cojocaru and Vadim Muntagirov in the lead roles.

Spectacular pas de deux

The *Le Corsaire* pas de deux is one of the most famous in the classical repertoire today, although it was not in the original ballet. This pas de deux is often seen at ballet galas and competitions, and consists of an adagio, male variation, female variation, and coda between Medora and the slave, Ali. The original ballet had instead a pas de trois in Act II and included a third character, Conrad. Many full-length productions still perform this pas de trois version.

While Vaganova is credited with creating the structure of the pas de deux, it was Georgian dancer Vakhtang Chabukiani (who performed with the Kirov) who is said to have produced the virtuoso choreography that we know today.

Rudolph Nureyev, partnered by Margot Fonteyn, introduced the *Le Corsaire* pas de deux to Western Europe in 1962. This style of bravura dancing was instantly popular with London audiences, and remained Nureyev's party piece throughout his long career.

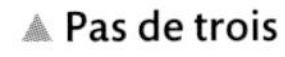

▲ **Pas de trois**
Vadim Muntagirov as Conrad lifts his beloved Medora (Alina Cojocaru), in a pas de trois with Junor Souza as Ali the slave.

◀ **Stage design, 1914**
Konstantin Alekseyevich Korovin made this oil painting of a set design for the Mariinsky Theater's *Le Corsaire*.

> *Le Corsaire* is a romp, packed to the gills with pirates, daft plotting, and virtuoso dancing.
>
> *THE INDEPENDENT*, 2016

STORY LINE Le Corsaire

Le Corsaire begins in a marketplace where Lankendem is selling his slave girls. Conrad arrives with his band of pirates. He sees and falls in love with Lankendem's ward, Medora, but the Pasha buys her. Conrad, his friend Birbanto, and his corsairs (pirates) kidnap Medora, the slave girls, and Lankendem. Now in the pirates' lair, a struggle reveals Birbanto to be a traitor, and Lankendem takes Medora away to the Pasha's palace. Conrad and his corsairs enter in disguise and steal the slave girls, including Medora, who tells him that Birbanto is a traitor. Conrad shoots him. The group escapes to the corsairs' ship, but a storm wrecks it—Conrad and Medora survive.

CONRAD, THE LEAD PIRATE, FALLS IN LOVE WITH MEDORA

ACT I

PLOT OVERVIEW

Act I takes place in a crowded bazaar. The slave trader Lankendem is preparing to sell his slave girls at the busy market. The corsairs appear, led by Conrad with his friend Birbanto and his slave Ali. Medora enters and throws Conrad a rose.

Lankendem pulls Medora away. The Pasha, governor of the citadel, arrives to buy some slave girls.

The Pasha rejects the three slave girls who dance for him. Lankendem then brings out the beautiful Gulnare.

The Pasha agrees to buy Gulnare, but then sees Medora and wants her, too. Lankendem and the Pasha haggle, but eventually settle on a price for Medora. They leave.

Conrad and his slave Ali make plans. They raid the village with the pirates and kidnap Medora, the slave girls, and Lankendem.

THE DANCES

Conrad performs a virtuoso solo, then dances with the rose. He and Medora dance together.

PROGRAM FOR 1844 VERSION BASED ON BYRON'S POEM

Three slave girls dance the pas de trois des odalisques.

Gulnare dances the pas d'esclave with Lankendem.

Medora dances for the crowd, teasing the Pasha.

The corsairs and Birbanto perform a folk dance.

PAS DE TROIS DES ODALISQUES

THE PASHA CHOOSES SLAVES, ELDAR ALIEV'S PRODUCTION AT THE PRIMORYE STAGE OF THE MARIINSKY THEATER, VLADIVOSTOK, 2016

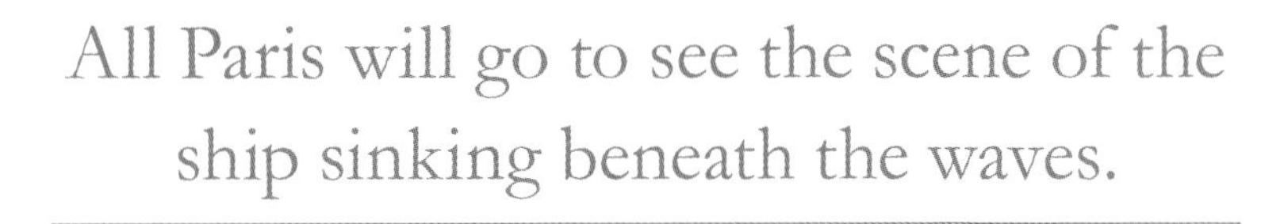

All Paris will go to see the scene of the ship sinking beneath the waves.

LA FRANCE MUSICALE, 1856

ALINA COJOCARU AS MEDORA AND VADIM MUNTAGIROV AS CONRAD, 2013

ACT II

Act II is set in the pirates' secret cave. Medora begs Conrad to free the slave girls. He agrees, despite the other pirates' protests. A fight breaks out between Conrad and Birbanto. Birbanto and Lankendem devise a plot against Conrad.

The dynamic pas de trois of Medora, Conrad, and Ali the slave is full of virtuoso steps.

Conrad and Medora dance a beautiful pas de deux. The smooth legato dancing contrasts with the fiery pas de trois.

MEDORA AND CONRAD, PAS DE DEUX

While Conrad is asleep, Lankendem snatches Medora away. When he awakes, Birbanto lies about what has happened and falsely swears his loyalty.

ACT III

The slave girls and Gulnare dance for the Pasha, and then Gulnare performs a beautiful solo.

Act III starts in the Pasha's palace. Lankendem arrives with Medora. Delighted, the Pasha buys her and celebrates by smoking opium. He dreams of a fantasy garden.

Le Jardin animé, a fantasy ballet in a garden, ensues. A corps de ballet of dancers en pointe performs with flowers and garlands.

Medora and Gulnare also dance.

The Pasha wakes up when Conrad and his corsairs arrive. They are disguised (as pilgrims in some productions; as entertainers in others).

The slave girls dance.

YEKATERINA GELTSER AS MEDORA AND VASILY TIKHOMIROV AS CONRAD, 1912

Conrad reveals his true self and rescues Medora. Medora recognizes Birbanto and exposes him as a traitor. Conrad shoots him. Conrad, Medora, Ali, and the corsairs flee to their ship. A storm breaks and the ship is wrecked. As the storm clears, Medora and Conrad are visible, alive and safe.

Conrad and Medora escape to the ship.

JUNOR SOUZA (ALI), ERINA TAKAHASHI (GULNARE), ALINA COJOCARU (MEDORA), AND VADIM MUNTAGIROV (CONRAD) AT SEA, 2013

Bolshoi Ballet, 2016
Choreographer Alexei Ratmansky restaged *Le Corsaire* with theatrical flair in scenes such as this piratical sword dance.

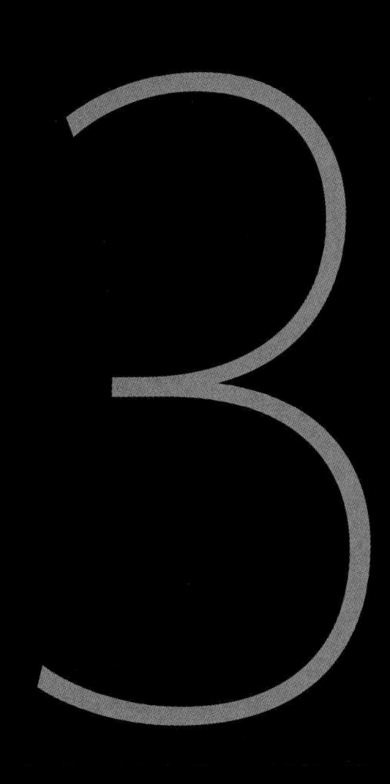

CLASSICAL BALLET

(1860–1905)

Classical ballet 1860–1905

The second half of the 19th century saw the popularity of ballet slowly decline in Western Europe, but rise in Russia. Sensing the shift of allegiances, and drawn to the security of employment in the Imperial Theaters, many dancers, choreographers, and composers moved to Russia. Although several key ballets still emerged in Paris during this time, such as Louis Mérante's *Sylvia* (1876), it was those created during this "golden age" of Russian ballet that proved to be the most influential and enduring—many are still performed around the world today.

Just as ballet's center of gravity shifted, so, too, did its themes and styles of choreography. Fairy tales, folk stories, and myths came to form the basis for elaborate story ballets such as *Swan Lake* (1877), while many other ballets of this period, including *Coppélia* (1870), featured national and traditional European-inspired group dances and divertissements to showcase the talents of multiple dancers. Productions also became more extravagant, with elaborate costumes, staging, and lighting, brought about as technological advances continued to find their way into theaters.

As ballet flourished in Russia, many of those who had moved there from the West became household names. These included French-born choreographers Marius Petipa and Jules Perrot, who, between them, produced some of the world's best-known ballets; and Italian ballerina Pierina Legnani, who found fame after performing in *Cinderella* at the Imperial Theater in 1893. Russia did not rely solely on imported talent, however, as it was already home to some of ballet's leading lights. Alongside innumerable acclaimed dancers and choreographers, one name stands out—Pyotr Ilyich Tchaikovsky. As the composer of the scores of the most famous ballets in the classical repertoire, *The Sleeping Beauty* (1890), *The Nutcracker* (1892), and *Swan Lake* (1895), his influence on ballet was profound and long-lasting.

This period in Russia also saw several developments in ballet choreography, including the revival of the male role, which reintroduced a level of muscularity and robustness to performances, rarely seen in the earlier Romantic ballets. The era also saw the rise of the grand pas de deux as a dramatic finale, introduced by Petipa as a way of displaying the technique of the lead dancers. This has since become a ballet staple.

In addition to producing some of ballet's best-known classical works, Russian ballet of this period inspired and trained the country's next generation of dancers and choreographers. It was this generation, and its dancers such as Anna Pavlova and Vaslav Nijinsky, who would go on to disseminate their country's classical ballets around the globe.

Don Quixote

First performed: December 26, 1869 ▪ Venue: Imperial Bolshoi Theater, Moscow ▪ Choreography: Marius Petipa ▪ Music: Ludwig Minkus ▪ Story: Cervantes

The flamboyant *Don Quixote* is loosely based on the Spanish novel *Don Quixote de la Mancha* by Miguel de Cervantes and was the first collaboration between Marius Petipa and Ludwig Minkus. Despite the ballet's complex evolution, Petipa's show-stopping classical dances, ending in a spectacular pas de deux at the wedding finale, remain largely unchanged and highlight his skill in creating works with wide, enduring appeal.

IN CONTEXT

Petipa's *Don Quixote* was not the first use of Cervantes' story for ballet. Several works were based on the book in the 18th century, and in 1801 the ballet *Les Noces de Gamache* premiered at the Paris Opéra. Choreographed by Louis Milon, it focused on the characters of Basilio and Kitri. While Petipa's *Don Quixote* was successful when it first appeared, it was Alexander Gorsky's 1902 revival of the ballet that became the basis for ensuing productions.

This ballet was first shown in Moscow, with comedy and character dancing to appeal to the Muscovite audience. Two years later, Petipa reworked *Don Quixote* more formally for a St. Petersburg audience, with the two lead female parts, Kitri and Dulcinea, as a dual role. Petipa's original *Don Quixote* contained many bravura elements that still make for some of the most popular passages in ballet today, including the flying leaps for Kitri in Act I and the overhead lifts, huge jumps, and fan-snapping variation in the grand pas de deux in Act III, a favorite of gala performances. Despite the positive reception, in 1902, the management of the Imperial Ballet, St. Petersburg, asked Alexander Gorsky to restage the work.

▼ **Mariinsky Ballet, 2017**
Viktoria Tereshkina as Kitri and Kimin Kim as Basilio dance a Spanish-style duet in the lively town square amid the admiring onlookers, who cheer them on with fans and flourishes.

▲ **Russian artist's stage design**
This oil painting of a stage set for *Don Quixote* was painted in 1940 by Ryndin Vadim Fyodorovich and is on public display in Moscow.

Gorsky's revival reworked the ballet into three acts, and created the Dream of the Dryads scene in the form danced today. In Petipa's version, Don Quixote fought off various monsters, including a giant spider and its web; after this, the garden of Dulcinea was revealed. Gorsky altered the symmetry of many of the group and corps de ballet scenes, instead giving the individual dancers their own character.

Popular revivals and revisions

Anna Pavlova and her company brought *Don Quixote* to Europe in a condensed version, put on in London in 1924. The ballet became an audience favorite when Rudolph Nureyev staged his version for the Vienna State Opera Ballet in 1966. Nureyev, who had performed the ballet with the Kirov, in Moscow, devised choreography based on the Petipa-Gorsky version. He made the role of Basilio a vehicle for his own virtuoso dancing. He then revived *Don Quixote* in 1970 for The Australian Ballet, in which Lucette Aldous danced the role of Kitri. In 1972, Nureyev directed a film version of the ballet with Australian dancer-choreographer and actor Robert Helpmann. It was filmed in an aircraft hangar in Melbourne and released in 1973. The film was a huge success and was screened around the globe.

Meanwhile, George Balanchine had brought the ballet to the US, creating his version of *Don Quixote* in 1965 for the New York City Ballet. The ballet bore little resemblance to the Petipa-Gorsky version, and used new music by Nicolas Nabokov. Balanchine's muse Suzanne Farrell danced the role of Dulcinea, and Balanchine himself appeared several times in the title role. The ballet focused on Don Quixote's search for Dulcinea, his ideal woman, reflecting Balanchine's own quest for the perfect muse. It was only performed until the 1970s, but in 2005 it was reconstructed by Farrell for her company, The Suzanne Farrell Ballet.

Mikhail Baryshnikov staged his own version of *Don Quixote* for American Ballet Theatre in 1978. Like Nureyev, Baryshnikov developed the role of Basilio for his own talents. His comic version of the ballet remains a favorite today.

In the UK, Ninette de Valois staged the first production of *Don Quixote* for what is now The Royal Ballet in 1950. Most recently, Carlos Acosta brought Spanish passion and exoticism to his 2013 interpretation.

> I danced and played the castanets no worse than the best dancers of Andalusia.
>
> MARIUS PETIPA, WHO LOVED SPANISH DANCE

Natalia Osipova (1986–)

Russian dancer Natalia Osipova had only been a member of the Bolshoi Ballet's corps de ballet for a year when she made her debut as Kitri in *Don Quixote* in 2005. The role launched her career as a soloist, earning her further critical acclaim for her "electric vitality" and "airy bravura" during the Bolshoi's tour to London in 2006. She has appeared as a guest artist in companies across the world and is a principal at The Royal Ballet, which she joined in 2013.

▲ **Anna Pavlova**
In 1924, Pavlova danced Kitri in an abridged version of the ballet at the Royal Opera House, London.

STORY LINE Don Quixote

Don Quixote sets out on a quest with his squire Sancho Panza to find Dulcinea, the woman of his dreams. In a market square, Kitri (daughter of the innkeeper Lorenzo), who is in love with the barber Basilio, learns that her father has agreed she should marry the nobleman, Gamache. Upon seeing Kitri, Don Quixote believes he has found Dulcinea. Kitri and Basilio sneak away to a gypsy camp, where Don Quixote attacks a windmill in the belief that he is protecting Dulcinea. Dazed, he envisions a garden of dryads. Meanwhile, Lorenzo forces Kitri to accept the attentions of Gamache. Basilio and Kitri contrive to trick her father into agreeing they can marry.

MATADOR DANCE, MIKHAILOVSKY BALLET OF ST. PETERSBURG, 2014

ACT I

PLOT OVERVIEW

In the prologue, Don Quixote has a vision of a beautiful woman, Dulcinea. He embarks on his adventures with Sancho. The ballet itself opens onto a lively town square full of action and Spanish-inspired dance. Kitri makes a dramatic entrance. After her solo dance, Basilio enters with a guitar.

DON QUIXOTE AND SANCHO IN NINETTE DE VALOIS' SADLER'S WELLS BALLET, 1950

Lorenzo separates the couple and will not agree to their marriage. The foppish Gamache enters and expresses his wish to marry Kitri. The Spanish peasant men and women dance, normally with tambourines.

A group of matadors arrives, accompanied by bullfighter Espada and his partner, street dancer Mercedes. The matadors dance, led by Espada. Mercedes joins them.

Don Quixote and Sancho enter the village. Don Quixote sees Kitri and believes she is Dulcinea. Basilio whisks her aside and they continue to dance together.

THE DANCES

Kitri performs a Spanish-style solo with a fan.

Basilio and Kitri dance together, teasing one another as the music gets faster.

KITRI AND BASILIO IN RUDOLPH NUREYEV'S VERSION, PARIS OPERA BALLET, 1981

GROUP DANCE WITH TAMBOURINES AND DAGGERS, BOLSHOI BALLET, LONDON, 2016

ACT II, SCENE 1, WITH WINDMILLS IN THE BACKGROUND, THE ROYAL BALLET, 2013

Do you see yonder, friend Sancho, 30 or 40 hulking giants? I intend to do battle with them and slay them.

DON QUIXOTE, TAKING ON WINDMILLS IN CERVANTES' NOVEL

ACT II

Scene 1 takes place in a gypsy camp. Kitri and Basilio, who have sneaked away, dance together. The gypsies demand to know who they are. Don Quixote and Sancho arrive. The wind increases and sails on the windmill behind begin to turn. Believing it is a giant, and trying to protect Dulcinea-Kitri, Don Quixote fights the windmill.

In Scene 2, Don Quixote dreams of a garden of dryads and Kitri as Dulcinea. Gamache and Lorenzo arrive looking for Kitri and wake Don Quixote, who gives them false directions.

Scene 3, in a village square, is action-packed. The crowd tries to hide Kitri, but Lorenzo makes Kitri accept Gamache. Basilio fakes his suicide and Lorenzo relents. The couple are free to marry.

Basilio dances a solo, often with a tambourine. Kitri joins him.

The gypsies may dance, too.

Sometimes a puppet show or play is performed.

The Dream of the Dryads is a beautiful scene with a corps de ballet of female dancers, often en pointe, and wearing tutus. Don Quixote dances with them.

ACT III

The wedding festivities of Basilio and Kitri take place in the village square. The villagers celebrate and the couples dance.

DON QUIXOTE (CHRISTOPHER SAUNDERS) AND SANCHO PANZA (PHILIP MOSLEY)

Basilio and Kitri perform a grand pas de deux.

The whole group dances in celebration.

The happiness of the couple spreads to general merriment.

Don Quixote sees a vision of Dulcinea and leaves on a new adventure.

DREAM OF THE DRYADS LED BY OLGA SPINOVA, BOLSHOI BALLET, 2014

WEDDING SCENE, CARLOS ACOSTA'S ROYAL BALLET PRODUCTION, 2013

Kitri realizes Basilio's suicide is a deception and begs to be married to the "corpse." When Lorenzo agrees, Basilio bounces back to life.

Bolshoi Ballet, London, 2006
Natalia Osipova delights as Kitri, watched by the corps de ballet as villagers, during a dress rehearsal at the Royal Opera House.

Coppélia

First performed May 25, 1870 ▪ Venue: Salle Louvois, Paris ▪ Choreography: Arthur Saint-Léon ▪ Music: Léo Delibes ▪ Story: Saint-Léon and Charles Nuitter

An enduringly popular ballet of dolls and human mischief-making, *Coppélia* marked a turning point in the art form in Paris. Instead of a tragic plot with ethereal characters manipulated by the supernatural, this is a light-hearted comedy of village folk. Its new style of choreography included clockwork dances and set the trend for incorporating European national and character dances into the action.

STORY LINE

Act I Dr. Coppélius, an eccentric inventor, puts a lifelike doll in the window of his house, and Franz becomes infatuated with it. Franz's betrothed, Swanilda, is jealous of his interest. Upon finding Coppélius's door key, Swanilda and her friends determine to meet the figure.

Act II Swanilda and friends enter the house and discover that the figure is a doll, Coppélia. Coppélius returns and chases the girls out, except Swanilda who hides and puts on the doll's clothes. Coppélius spots Franz outside, beckons him in, and drugs him in order to transfer his soul to Coppélia. Swanilda, dressed as the doll, pretends to come to life. In the confusion, she and Franz escape.

Act III After an argument about damages due to Coppélius, Swanilda and Franz marry.

◄ **Early loss, 1870**
Swanilda was first danced by Italian ballerina Giuseppina Bozzacchi. Weakened by a lack of food during the Siege of Paris, she died of smallpox the same year on her 17th birthday.

The director of the Paris Opéra commissioned librettist Charles Nuitter and choreographer Arthur Saint-Léon to create a new work in 1870. The story for the resulting ballet, *Coppélia*, was based on an adaptation of E.T.A. Hoffmann's story *Der Sandmann* ("The Sandman").

The ballet premiered at the Salle Louvois theater in 1870, the last to do so before it was closed during the Siege of Paris. At that time, the role of the male dancer had been dispensed with almost completely in France, and instead male parts were danced by women—en travesti (dressed as men). At *Coppélia's* premiere, Franz was danced by ballerina Eugénie Fiocre. The role continued to be performed by women at the Paris Opéra until the 1950s.

The innovations in *Coppélia* made Saint-Léon famous. He dispensed with the sylphs, wilis, otherworldly figures, and tragic endings formerly so common. Its first act also included several national dances, such as the Hungarian *Czárdás* and Polish Mazurka.

Coppélia goes global

In 1884, Petipa rechoreographed *Coppélia* for the Imperial Ballet. The role of Franz was danced by a man, and Petipa added a variation (solo) to Act I and an Act III pas de deux. In doing so, he established the basis for the grand pas de deux (adagio, male and female variations plus a coda) now seen in most ballets.

In 1933, *Coppélia* was produced by Nicholas Sergeyev, former régisseur of the Imperial Ballet, for the Vic-Wells Ballet in London, with Ninette de Valois dancing as Swanilda. The Royal Ballet continues to perform *Coppélia* today, based on de Valois' 1954 version, with designs by Osbert Lancaster.

The San Francisco Opera Ballet staged *Coppélia* in 1939 with choreography by William Christensen. It was the company's first full-length production, and the first full-length production by an American choreographer. However, the most widely performed version in the US today is based on George Balanchine's 1974 production for the New York City Ballet. Balanchine, assisted by ballerina Alexandra Danilova, rechoreographed parts of Act I and all of Act III.

▲ **Balanchine's choreography**
New York City Ballet's Mikhail Baryshnikov and Patricia McBride take the lead as Franz and Swanilda in this 1978 production of *Coppélia*.

► **English National Ballet, 2014**
Choreographed by Ronald Hynd after Petipa, this production featured Shiori Kase as Swanilda, and Yonah Acosta as Franz.

MARIINSKY BALLET

Called the Mariinsky Ballet at home in St. Petersburg, this company uses the name Kirov Ballet for touring outside Russia. It was started in 1738 by Empress Anna Ivanova, when she opened a school in the attic of the Winter Palace for 12 girls, daughters of palace staff. As there were no boys, ballet was introduced into the naval cadet school so that the girls would have dancing partners. From these small beginnings grew the Imperial Ballet, as the Mariinsky Ballet was called in Czarist Russia. Performances took place at the Mariinsky Theater in St. Petersburg.

With the onset of the Franco-Prussian War in the late 19th-century, French ballet slipped into decline, with few works produced or performed. The Russian Czars revived the ballet scene, importing the best dancers and teachers from France and Italy. These included the talented Franz Hilverding, Gasparo Angiolini, and Charles Didelot, all interested in developing the ballet d'action style of dance with a flowing narrative.

The Mariinsky Ballet is famous for the ballets created there as well as for its virtuoso dancers. Jules Perrot, made ballet master there in 1851, choreographed *Giselle* and *La Esmeralda*, teaching the company the importance of artistry, not just technique. He was followed by Arthur St. Léon of *Coppélia* fame. Marius Petipa went to Russia as a dancer in 1847 and, in 1869, became chief choreographer. He created the classical repertoire of over 60 ballets including *Swan Lake*, *The Sleeping Beauty*, and *The Nutcracker.*

The legacy survives today—the finest training from the Mariinsky Ballet's school, the Vaganova Academy, has produced some of the greatest classical dancers in the world, including Galina Ulanova, Yuri Soloviev, Alla Sizova, Alla Osipenko, Rudolf Nureyev, Mikhail Baryshnikov, and Irina Kolpakova.

> I created a ballet company of which everyone said: St. Petersburg has the greatest ballet in Europe.
>
> MARIUS PETIPA, 1907

Mariinsky Theater, St. Petersburg ▶
The plush interior makes a fitting setting for the classical ballets that Russian dancers perform so well, recalling the imperial splendor of the days of the czars.

Sylvia

First performed: June 14, 1876 ▪ Venue: Palais Garnier ▪ Choreography: Louis Mérante ▪ Music: Léo Delibes ▪ Story: Jules Barbier and the Baron de Reinach

Like *Coppélia*, this ballet broke free from French Romantic conventions of the female lead being an ethereal sylph. *Sylvia* is constructed around the strong title role of a huntress, which allows a ballerina to show all facets of her technique. Like many of the major ballets from the past, *Sylvia* has fallen in and out of favor and been through several reimaginings.

IN CONTEXT

In its checkered career, *Sylvia* met a second lukewarm response at the start of the 20th century. In 1900, a lavish production of *Sylvia* to be directed by Sergei Diaghilev (not yet the impresario of the Ballets Russes) was planned for the upcoming season of the Imperial Ballet, St. Petersburg. With his pugnacious nature, Diaghilev argued with the management, and the production was canceled. This was the end of Diaghilev's association with the Imperial Theater.

The production of *Sylvia* was rescheduled and presented in 1901. Lev Ivanov and Pavel Gerdt choreographed the ballet, and the cast included the great prima ballerina Olga Preobrajenska as Sylvia. Once again, the ballet met with mixed reviews, and soon fell from the repertoire.

The original production, entitled *Sylvia, ou la Nymphe de Diane* ("Sylvia, or Diana's Nymph") was the first ballet to be shown in the newly completed Palais Garnier in Paris. Jules Barbier and the Baron de Reinach devised the classical libretto by adapting the court play *Aminta,* written by Torquato Tasso in the late 16th century. Based on several strands of classical mythology, the ballet begins outside the shrine of Eros, god of love, and ends at the temple of Diana, goddess of hunting. *Sylvia* received a mixed reception, as was the case with further early 20th-century productions.

▶ Original program, 1876
In the center is a photograph of Rita Sangalli, who played Sylvia in the original production, set to Léo Delibes's music.

Léo Delibes's score, however, received much admiration, not least from Tchaikovsky. The great Russian composer later wrote that: "Never before has there been a ballet with such grace, such melodic and rhythmic richness, such superlative scoring," and, "If I had known this music earlier, I would not have written *Swan Lake*."

The magic of Ashton and Fonteyn

Fifty years after a semi-successful Russian revival at the turn of the century, the fortune of *Sylvia* changed for the better.

▼ Frederick Ashton revival, 1952
In the best-known production, Alexander Grant as Eros, here disguised in a cloak, revives the wounded Aminta, played by Michael Somes.

Mark Morris (1956-)

Founder of the Mark Morris Dance Group and best known for his modern-dance choreography, American Mark Morris updated *Sylvia* in 2004. For this production, he brought *Sylvia* into the 21st century while remaining true to the traditions of classical ballet and the story itself. Instead of the expected irreverence, he gave psychological depth—both serious and witty—to the conventional characters of the chaste nymph, love-struck shepherd, and evil hunter with arm-sweeping gestures, kicks, and recoils, and choreographed different styles of dancing in each act in order to show the plot's progress.

▶ **Paris Opéra Ballet, 2005**
John Neumeier recast the ballet, giving it a neoclassical purity matched by the chilly austerity of Yannis Kokkos's sets.

In 1952, Frederick Ashton revived and rechoreographed the work. He had been thinking about creating a ballet to Delibes's score for several years. The work was Ashton's second full-length ballet, and he intended it for ballerina Margot Fonteyn. Critic Clive Barnes wrote, after seeing Fonteyn in the role: "It gives us Fonteyn triumphant, Fonteyn bewildered, Fonteyn exotic, Fonteyn pathetic, Fonteyn in excelsis." The ballet lost popularity without Fonteyn as the lead, and was reworked into a one-act piece before finally being dropped yet again from the repertoire.

The whole ballet is a garland presented to the ballerina by her choreographer.

CLIVE BARNES, ON FREDERICK ASHTON'S *SYLVIA* OF 1952

***Sylvia* lives on**
A very different version of *Sylvia* emerged in 1997, choreographed by John Neumeier for the Paris Opéra Ballet and Hamburg Ballet. This version placed the ballet in a modern setting, but with classical statuary, and did not use the original libretto, instead looking at Tasso's play for inspiration.

In 2004, the ballet was reconstructed by répétiteur (a coach in existing repertoire) and former dancer Christopher Newton for The Royal Ballet. The ballet premiered with athletic ballerina Darcey Bussell in the title role, partnered by British dancer Jonathan Cope. This revival gave the ballet a new lease on life. While remaining in the repertoire of The Royal Ballet, it has since been produced by a range of companies including Staatsballett Berlin; American Ballet Theatre; and Mariinsky Ballet, St. Petersburg.

The same year The Royal Ballet put on their revival, in 2004, San Francisco Ballet premiered their own production of *Sylvia*. This was to be the first time that a US company produced the full ballet. Contemporary choreographer Mark Morris was invited to create the choreography based on the original 1876 production. Morris stayed close to Mérante's original intentions and style. As Morris said, "I'm using the score and libretto exactly as they're built."

STORY LINE Sylvia

In Ashton's version, Aminta, a shepherd, is in love with the nymph Sylvia. Arriving back from a hunt, Sylvia rejects him and shoots an arrow at the statue of Eros, but Aminta protects the god and it pierces him. Eros retaliates and shoots Sylvia—who falls in love with Aminta. Orion has been watching and takes his chance to kidnap Sylvia. In Orion's cave, Sylvia gets her captor drunk in order to escape, finally leaving with the help of Eros. In the final act, Aminta and Sylvia are reunited, but Orion finds them. Sylvia seeks the protection of Diana, who kills Orion but will not bless the couple's union. Eros intervenes once more and reminds Diana that she, too, once loved a shepherd.

THE GOATS DANCE A PAS DE DEUX, THE ROYAL BALLET, 2010

ACT I

PLOT OVERVIEW

Act I starts with a woodland dance. Aminta hides as Sylvia and her nymphs return from their hunt. One of the nymphs finds Aminta and he pleads his love for Sylvia. Angry at Eros, the god of love, Sylvia and her nymphs aim at his statue, but Aminta steps in front of the arrow.

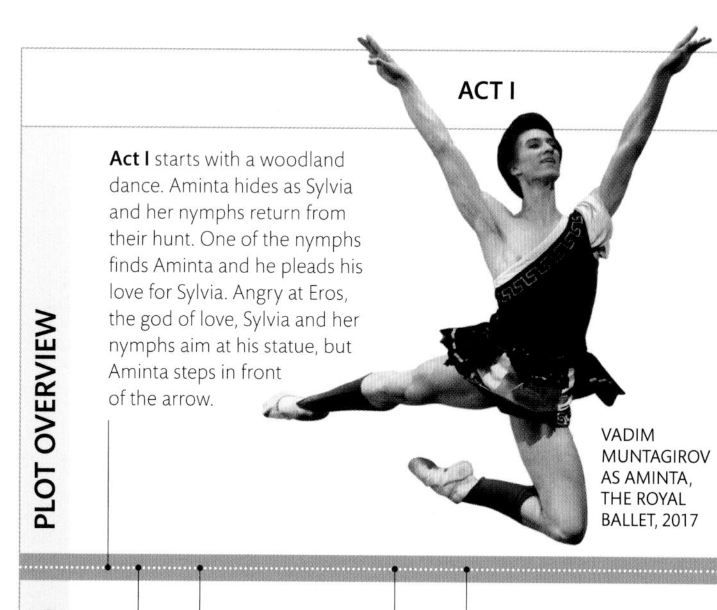
VADIM MUNTAGIROV AS AMINTA, THE ROYAL BALLET, 2017

Eros shoots Sylvia, and the arrow makes her fall in love with Aminta. Orion, who has been secretly watching, enters and kidnaps Sylvia. Eros in disguise revives Aminta, who finds Sylvia's bow and leaves to look for her.

THE DANCES

The ballet opens with a group of woodland creatures dancing before the shrine of Eros.

Aminta dances a solo.

Sylvia and her attendant nymphs perform a spirited dance with their bows and arrows.

Orion dances a solo with large jumps and turns.

Sylvia performs a passionate solo of love and longing.

ACT II

PLOT OVERVIEW

In Act II, in Orion's island cave, his concubines and slaves tempt Sylvia with fine gowns, silk, and jewels. She casts them aside and instead cherishes the arrow that pierced her heart. Orion takes the arrow. Angry and upset, Sylvia has an idea to escape Orion by getting him drunk.

Orion, the concubines, and slaves all fall asleep drunk. Sylvia calls to Eros for help and he appears. The scene transforms, and a magical boat appears. Sylvia sees a vision of Aminta and leaves with Eros.

THE DANCES

Orion's slaves dance a comic pas de deux.

Sylvia dances seductively while filling Orion's wine glass. They dance together, then Sylvia performs a solo.

MARGOT FONTEYN (SYLVIA) AND ALEXANDER GRANT (EROS), 1952

DELIBES'S SCORE FOR *SYLVIA*

LAUREN CUTHBERTSON AS SYLVIA AND THOMAS WHITEHEAD AS ORION, THE ROYAL BALLET, 2010

Boy loves girl, girl captured by bad man, girl restored to boy by God.

FREDERICK ASHTON SUMS UP THE PLOT OF *SYLVIA*

LEON BAKST'S COSTUME DESIGN FOR SYLVIA, 1901

ACT III

DIANA KEEPS LOVERS AMINTA AND SYLVIA APART

Act III is set outside the temple of Diana. Festivities are underway in honor of Bacchus, god of wine. Aminta enters, looking for Sylvia and interrupting the celebrations. Eros arrives in his boat with Sylvia.

The whole party dances.

Sylvia returns by boat with Eros.

Eros and the nymphs dance.

Sylvia and Aminta each dance a solo.

The sacrificial goats dance a comic pas de deux.

Sylvia and Aminta dance a grand pas de deux, which begins with Aminta entering, carrying Sylvia high above him.

Orion enters, wanting Sylvia back. He fights Aminta. Sylvia hides inside the temple of Diana. The goddess herself appears. She shoots Orion and demands that Sylvia come out.

Everyone celebrates.

KENTA KURA AS EROS AND MARIANELA NUNEZ AS SYLVIA, 2010

Diana will not bless the union of Sylvia and Aminta until Eros reminds her that she, too, once loved a shepherd. She relents, and the whole party celebrates.

ZENAIDA YANOWSKY AS SYLVIA AND DAVID MAKHATELI AS AMINTA, THE ROYAL BALLET, 2008

Paris Opéra Ballet, 2002
Delphine Moussin as the hunter goddess Diana (center) dances with Eleonora Abbagnato in the title role and other nymphs in John Neumeier's contemporary take on *Sylvia*.

Marius Petipa

Dancer and choreographer ▪ 1818–1910

Regarded as the "father of classical ballet," Marius Petipa laid the foundations for classical ballet in the 19th and 20th centuries. During his 60-year career, he breathed new life into the art form through his introduction of the dramatic use of the corps de ballet, and through his renowned choreographies, including *The Sleeping Beauty*, *The Nutcracker*, and *Swan Lake*, which still hold vital positions in the repertoires of major ballet companies across the globe more than 100 years after he created them.

▲ **Marius Petipa in the ballet *Giselle***
This 19th-century print portrays Petipa performing a pas de deux in the role of Albrecht from *Giselle* in 1842. As choreographer at the Imperial Ballet, he first restaged the work in 1884.

Petipa was born in France in 1818 to Victorine Grasseau, an actress, and Jean Petipa, a well-known ballet master and choreographer. From a young age, Marius and his older brother, Lucien, were encouraged to follow in their father's footsteps, and Jean began to teach Marius when he was seven years old. The young Petipa initially disliked dancing, but his gift was evident. He made his debut in Nantes, France, aged nine, in his father's production of *La Dansomanie*.

In 1834, the family moved to Bordeaux, where Jean became ballet master at the Ballet du Grand Théâtre and Petipa trained with the famous Auguste Vestris. At 20, Petipa was made principal dancer at the Ballet de Nantes, where he also produced his early choreographies, before joining his father on a tour of the US the following year. After the tour, Petipa joined Lucien at the Paris Opéra, and partnered with the great Carlotta Grisi for his Parisian debut.

A fortunate affair

In 1841, Petipa returned to Bordeaux, where he was appointed principal dancer at the Grand Théâtre. Here he spent three years dancing lead roles and choreographing many successful works, before becoming principal dancer at the King's Theater, Madrid. It was during this time that Petipa became absorbed with Spanish national dance, which influenced many of the major ballets that he later developed.

Following a love affair with the wife of a Marquis, Petipa was forced to flee Spain. In May 1847, he arrived in St. Petersburg, where the Imperial Ballet was looking for a new principal dancer. Petipa made his acclaimed debut a few months later in the first Russian production of Joseph Mazilier's *Paquita*, which he staged with fellow dancer Frédéric Malevergne.

Petipa's breakthrough

Petipa continued to dance and stage works at the Imperial Ballet, and his breakthrough as a choreographer came in 1862 with his *La Fille du pharaon*. He was made chief choreographer in 1869, the same year he created *Don Quixote*, followed by *La Bayadère* in 1877.

As a choreographer, Petipa's invention of the climactic grand pas de deux allowed lead dancers to showcase their technique. Never before had the audience seen the corps de ballet deliver such elaborately choreographed spectacles. Petipa gave precise instructions to dancers and composers, and famously collaborated with Tchaikovsky in creating the music for *The Sleeping Beauty*, which he choreographed in 1890, and also for two further ballets *The Nutcracker* (1892) and *Swan Lake* (1895), which he created with Lev Ivanov.

In 1901, Vladimir Telyakovsky was appointed director at the Imperial Ballet. Believing Petipa's style to be outdated, he did everything he could to overthrow him, even inviting Alexander Gorsky to restage *Don Quixote*. During these years, Petipa trained Anna Pavlova, while continuing to fight Telyakovsky. However, after the unfortunate failure of his ballet *The Magic Mirror*, Petipa retired in 1903 at the age of 85.

KEY WORKS

Choreographer: *La Fille du pharaon*, 1862 • *Don Quixote*, 1869 • *La Bayadère*, 1877 • *The Sleeping Beauty*, 1890 • *The Nutcracker*, 1892 • *Swan Lake*, 1895 • *Le Corsaire*, 1899 • *Raymonda*, 1898

▲ **The last dance**
Petipa danced the part of Ta-Hor in his romantic fantasy *La Fille du pharaon* in 1862, his last role before becoming a ballet master.

TIMELINE

- **March 11, 1818** Born Victor Marius Alphonse Petipa in Marseilles, France, to actress Victorine Grasseau, and dancer and choreographer Jean Petipa.
- **1825** Begins learning ballet alongside his older brother, Lucien, from his father.
- **1827** Debuts in Nantes, France, in his father's production of *La Dansomanie*.
- **1834** Moves to Bordeaux and begins training with dancer Auguste Vestris.

SCENE FROM SWAN LAKE IN 1895, CHOREOGRAPHED BY PETIPA

- **1838** Becomes principal dancer at the Théâtre Nantes at the age of 20.
- **1839** Joins his father on a tour of the US, dancing in the first ever ballet performed in the country—Jean Coralli's *La Tarentule*.
- **1841** Appointed principal dancer at the Grand Théâtre in Bordeaux.
- **1844** Appointed principal dancer at the King's Theater in Madrid, Spain. He flees the country two years later following a love affair with the wife of a Marquis.
- **1847** Joins the Imperial Ballet in St. Petersburg, becoming a principal dancer and ballet master.
- **1862** Gains critical acclaim for his choreography of *La Fille du pharaon*.
- **1869** Appointed chief choreographer of the Imperial Ballet, creating *Don Quixote* the same year.
- **1890** Choreographs *The Sleeping Beauty*, followed by *The Nutcracker* two years later.
- **1898** Choreographs *Raymonda*, his last great ballet, featuring his muse, Pierina Legnani, in the lead role.
- **1903** Retires from the Imperial Ballet.
- **July 14, 1910** Dies in Gurzuf, Ukraine, aged 92.

PALAIS GARNIER

For its sheer size, majesty, opulence, and dazzling decorative detail, the Palais Garnier in the heart of Paris is often compared to the Palace of Versailles. Its architecture is a mixture of Second Empire and Beaux Arts styles, recalling the classical and Baroque splendor of earlier times. The building was commissioned by Napoléon III, who died two years before its inauguration on January 5, 1875. The Avenue de l'Opéra, which leads from the Louvre in a straight line to the Palais Garnier, was left unplanted with trees, to give an uninterrupted view of the imposing exterior, a symbol of emperor Napoléon III's power. Sculptures on the facade pay homage to many eminent musicians and artistes.

Building had already begun on this new opera house when the Salle Le Peletier, the temporary home of the opera, was destroyed by fire in 1873. The new building soon became known as the Palais Garnier after its architect, Charles Garnier. Since 1989, the opera has usually been staged at the Opéra Bastille, while the Paris Opéra Ballet, the oldest ballet company in the world, performs mainly at the Palais Garnier.

Entering the Palais Garnier is a theatrical experience in itself. The Grand Escalier (staircase) is set within a vault 33yd (30m) high, built of colored marbles. The auditorium, awash with red velvet, gold, and bronze, boasts the largest stage in Europe and seats nearly 2,000. It was designed for the audience to be seen as well as see. The ceiling was painted by early modernist Marc Chagall, centering on a 7-ton (6.3-tonne) crystal and bronze chandelier, the inspiration for the chandelier drop in Gaston Leroux's novel *The Phantom of the Opera*.

> The spectators themselves become actors and perform, directed by the creative force of Garnier.
>
> GERARD FONTAINE, *CHARLES GARNIER'S OPERA*, 2000

Grand Escalier ▶
At the top of the imposing stairway, two female statues bearing torches greet visitors to the Palais Garnier. The double staircase then leads to foyers decorated with frescoes and gilding.

AMPHITHEATRE
BAIGNOIRES · ORCHESTRE
ORCHESTRE

La Bayadère

First performed: January 23, 1877 ▪ Venue: Mariinsky Theater, St. Petersburg ▪ Choreography: Petipa ▪ Music: Ludwig Minkus ▪ Story: Sergei Khudekov

Set in the royal India of the past, *La Bayadère* tells the story of the doomed love between the young warrior, Solor, and the beautiful bayadère (temple dancer), Nikiya. The ballet is Marius Petipa at his most exotic. It was created especially for the benefit performance of Ekaterina Vazem, most famous for later being Anna Pavlova's teacher. Lev Ivanov, then premier danseur of the Imperial Theaters, danced Solor. *La Bayadère* was an immediate success.

IN CONTEXT

La Bayadère presents a particular view of India that would make the story and characters accessible to 19th-century Russian eyes. While Petipa's choreography contains various elements that hint at the ballet's setting, it is not a representation of Indian culture and never was. Not once does his choreography stray from classical technique, and while Minkus's score contains melodies that suggest the Orient, it varies little from the usual lightly orchestrated polkas, adagios, and waltzes.

The ballet has changed much over the years with music and choreography being added and moved around. Most significant is the omission from Russian productions of Act III, in which the temple is destroyed, a tradition that Fyodor Lopukhov started in 1920.

This Eastern-flavored ballet provides powerful moments for all the main characters, and it was the role of Nikiya that shot Anna Pavlova to fame when she first danced it in 1902. It was also the final role she danced with the Imperial Ballet in 1914 before she left Russia for good.

La Bayadère contains one of the most mesmerizing scenes in ballet, the Kingdom of the Shades, seen in an opium-induced dream, in which a procession of ballerinas in white tutus and veils dance in unison across a moonlit stage. Petipa staged this scene as a grand pas classique, devoid of any dramatic action. The simple, academic choreography is probably his most celebrated. The entrance, in which 48 ballerinas make their way down a long winding ramp repeating the same combination, was inspired by Gustav Doré's illustrations for Dante's Paradiso from *The Divine Comedy*. The entrance is not technically complex—the challenge lies in maintaining the unison of the whole. One mistake and the effect is spoiled. Today's usual rocky Himalayan setting comes from Petipa's 1900 staging, when he also increased the number of dancers from the previous 32.

The ballet also features a bronze idol, who comes to life in a stunning solo. This demanding male variation is relatively recent, created by Nikolai

▼ **Entire cast, Mariinsky Theater, 1900**
The cast is dressed in designer Orest Allegri's costumes for Act II. Mathilde Kschessinska in the principal role of Nikiya is in the center, left.

Bollywood reimagining
The Australian Ballet perform Stanton Welch's opulent revival of *La Bayadère* at the Sydney Opera House in 2014.

Zubkovsky in 1948. The music is by Minkus but taken from Petipa's 1874 revival of Marie Taglioni's ballet, *Le Papillon* (1860). It is a waltz in 5/4 time, a signature used by 19th-century composers to portray "the exotic" because it was an unconventional timing.

Out of Russia

Although regularly performed within Russia and the former Soviet Union throughout the 20th century, none of *La Bayadère* was seen outside Russia until 1961, when the Teatro Municipal danced the Kingdom of the Shades in Rio de Janeiro. The Kirov Ballet put on the entire ballet at the Palais Garnier in Paris later that year. It was danced in London on the same tour and quickly won recognition. Two years later, in 1963, Rudolf Nureyev staged *La Bayadère* for The Royal Ballet.

Nearly 20 years on, Natalia Markova introduced the complete ballet to the US in a 1980 production for American Ballet Theatre. She derived her version from Vladimir Ponomarev and Vakhtang Chabukiani's 1941 revival for the Kirov Ballet, which is what Russian productions today are based on.

Ponomarev and Chabukiani followed Fyodor Lopukhov's 1920s version, which omitted Act III and instead reunited Solor and Nikiya in a short epilogue at the end of Act II. Possible explanations for leaving out the temple despoiling scene in Act III include lack of funds for a replacement set if it was ruined in each performance, and a lack of technicians to make the destruction work. It has also been suggested that the Soviet regime would not allow the inclusion of a scene where Hindu gods destroy a temple.

While Markova deviated from Petipa's choreography and libretto, she reinstated his final act. She choreographed it herself, and John Lanchbery rearranged and reorchestrated Minkus's music.

Ulyana Lopatkina (1973-)

A principal dancer with Mariinsky Ballet from 1995 to 2017, Ulyana Lopatkina played Nikiya in *La Bayadère* in 2011 at the Royal Opera House in London. Critic Ismene Brown stated: "Lopatkina transfigures it, so that there is no more effort, no more training—there is only the poetry." Dubbed "the soul of Russia," she excelled at Romantic and classical ballet, and performed in *Giselle*, *Le Corsaire*, *The Sleeping Beauty*, and *Swan Lake*, among many others. Her performances as Odette/Odile and The Dying Swan were legendary, but she was equally convincing as a sensual gypsy girl in *Carmen Suite*.

The Royal Ballet, 2009
Having forgotten his vow of celibacy, the High Brahmin (Gary Avis) declares his love for Nikiya (Tamara Rojo), but is rejected by her.

STORY LINE La Bayadère

Handsome warrior Solor falls in love with bayadère (temple dancer) Nikiya, who is also coveted by High Brahmin (the temple's high priest). Solor and Nikiya swear their eternal love but Solor then becomes engaged to Gamzatti, the Rajah's daughter, who murders her rival with a poisonous snake hidden in a basket of flowers. In the aftermath, Solor dreams of his beloved, who appears to him in the Kingdom of the Shades in an opium-induced dream. Having provoked the wrath of the deities, Gamzatti's murderous triumph is short-lived as the gods destroy the temple during her wedding, killing everyone. Solor and Nikiya are reunited in heaven.

EKATERINA VAZEM AS NIKIYA IN THE IMPERIAL BALLET PRODUCTION, 1877

ACT I, SCENE 1

PLOT OVERVIEW

Solor and warriors return to the temple from a tiger hunt in the sacred forest. Solor asks head fakir (holy man) Magdaveya to arrange a rendezvous for him with Nikiya. There is a celebration of the lighting of the temple's sacred fire.

Nikiya rejects the High Brahmin's declaration of love, and waits in solitude for Solor. Nikiya and Solor meet secretly.

The High Brahmin sees the couple and vows to kill Solor.

THE DANCES

The fakirs whirl in a frenzied dance.

The bayadères emerge from the temple and dance. Their gestures mimic the multi-arm nature of Indian deities.

Nikiya and Solor's pas de deux becomes increasingly passionate as they swear eternal love over the sacred fire.

Nikiya dances a delicate solo that includes low, deep movements, and hands and arms raised to the gods.

SVETLANA ZAKHAROVA AS NIKIYA, 2003

ACT I, SCENE 2

PLOT OVERVIEW

In a room in the palace, warriors honor Solor. The Rajah announces that he may marry his daughter, Gamzatti, as a reward for his valor.

Solor is overcome by Gamzatti's beauty, even though he has sworn eternal love to Nikiya. The couple are betrothed.

Overheard by Gamzatti, the High Brahmin tells the Rajah of Nikiya and Solor's love. Gamzatti tries to bribe Nikiya to leave Solor but she refuses. Nikiya attempts to stab Gamzatti, then flees. Gamzatti determines to kill Nikiya.

THE DANCES

Gamzatti dreams of her wedding day.

The Djampe dance is a balletic version of a local dance for eight women with scarves.

ACT I, SCENE 3

PLOT OVERVIEW

In the palace garden, there are celebrations for Gamzatti and Solor's engagement.

YEKATERINA GELTZER AS NIKIYA IS BITTEN BY THE SNAKE

THE DANCES

The women waltz with fans, attended by male dancers.

Four women tutus dance grand pas d'action.

LIGHTING THE SACRED FIRE, BOLSHOI BALLET, 2013

BETROTHAL CELEBRATIONS IN THE PALACE GARDEN, KREMLIN BALLET THEATER, 2016

Russian versions usually include an athletic adagio for Nikiya with a slave partner, during which she scatters flowers upon Gamzatti.

RUSSIAN NATIONAL BALLET THEATER, KURGAN, RUSSIA, 2008

DAVID MIKLOS KERENYI AS THE BRONZE IDOL, HUNGARIAN NATIONAL BALLET GROUP, 2008

Most productions in Russia divide the acts differently and conclude with the Kingdom of the Shades, omitting the destruction of the temple at Solor and Gamzatti's wedding.

Nikiya is commanded to dance but cannot hide her grief. Her eyes are fixed on Solor. She is given a basket of flowers, which she believes to be from Solor but is actually from Gamzatti. She dances with happiness until a snake crawls out of the flowers and bites her. Nikiya sees Solor leave with Gamzatti, refuses an antidote, and decides to die.

Solor and Gamzatti's grand pas de deux has variations for both.

ACT II

Solor, grief stricken and under the influence of opium, dreams of being reunited with Nikiya. The Kingdom of the Shades takes place.

In the Kingdom of the Shades, a perfect example of ballet blanc, 32 or 48 ballerinas appear, identically dressed in white.

Solor performs a series of large jumps, suggesting the fervor of his quest for the dead Nikiya.

Solor and Nikiya dance an adagio. Nikiya seems almost weightless. The pair slowly come closer.

As the warriors enter Solor's tent to prepare him for his wedding to Gamzatti, the vision of Nikiya continues to haunt and confuse him.

Solor and Nikiya perform the Scarf Dance (Adagio with Gauze).

ACT III

The High Brahmin and the priests prepare for the wedding of Gamzatti and Solor.

The bronze idol performs an athletic male solo with references to Shiva and gestures borrowed from Southeast Asian dance.

The betrothed couple enters.

The bayadères perform a ritual candle dance around them.

There is a swirling solo for Gamzatti, followed by a dramatic quartet in which Gamzatti and Nikiya's ghost are rivals as the tension builds.

Solor remains haunted by the vision of Nikiya and cannot force himself to say his marriage vows to Gamzatti. The infuriated gods destroy the temple and bury everyone under its ruins. The spirits of Nikiya and Solor are reunited in eternal love.

SOLOR SMOKES OPIUM, THE ROYAL BALLET, 2013

THE MARIINSKY BALLET, THE ROYAL OPERA HOUSE, 2011

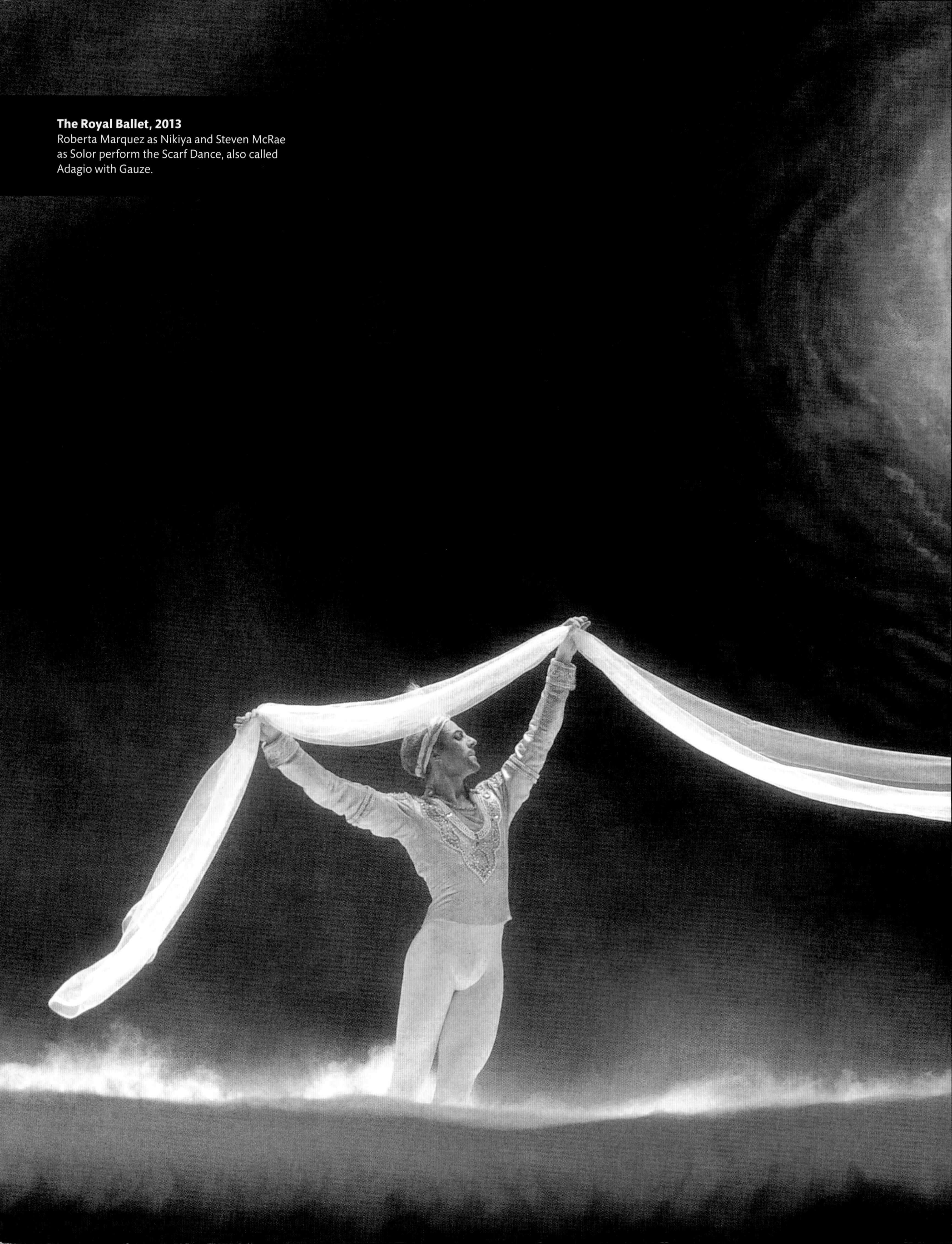

The Royal Ballet, 2013
Roberta Marquez as Nikiya and Steven McRae as Solor perform the Scarf Dance, also called Adagio with Gauze.

Pyotr Ilyich Tchaikovsky

Composer • 1840–1893

One of the first Russian composers to make a lasting international impression, Tchaikovsky's works included symphonies, concertos, operas, chamber music, and choral work. Though few in number, his contributions to the ballet canon will forever mark him as a central figure in the development of the art form. His scores for *Swan Lake*, *The Sleeping Beauty*, and *The Nutcracker* are synonymous with classical ballet, and remain the most popular and well-known works in the classical repertoire.

▲ **Country retreat**
In search of the quiet essential for composition, Tchaikovsky lived in numerous rented houses in Klin, near Moscow. He moved to the one pictured here in 1892 and his piano took center stage.

Tchaikovsky learned the piano at a young age and showed promise in composition. Despite his talents, his family persuaded him to study law, and upon graduating he became a civil servant.

In 1863, Tchaikovsky enrolled to study with Russian composer Anton Rubinstein at the St. Petersburg Conservatory. After graduating he went on to teach at the Conservatory, as well as compose. Tchaikovsky's work, with its Western elements and influence, differed from other Russian composers of this era who created a distinct Russian style using folk tunes and themes as a basis.

The ballet trilogy

In 1875, Tchaikovsky was commissioned by the Imperial Bolshoi Theater, Moscow, to create the score for *Swan Lake*, his first full-length ballet. Fables involving swan princesses were familiar to Tchaikovsky, who had composed a small "ballet," *The Lake of the Swans*, for his nieces and nephews. Yet when it premiered in 1877, *Swan Lake* was not deemed a success, and it had been dropped from the repertoire by 1883. Tchaikovsky would not compose another ballet for more than 10 years.

The director of the Imperial Theater, Ivan Vsevolozhsky, was an avid fan of Tchaikovsky. In 1886, he abolished the position of official ballet composer in order to allow more musical diversity and to be able to commission a range of composers. After some negotiation, Tchaikovsky agreed to create the score for the new ballet *The Sleeping Beauty* in 1888. He wrote to Vsevolozhsky: "I have just seen the scenario of *The Sleeping Beauty* ... the idea appeals to me and I wish nothing better than to write the music for it." The ballet was Tchaikovsky's first collaboration with Imperial choreographer Marius Petipa.

Petipa was extremely exacting and specific when it came to creating a ballet. He would draw up a complete plan of the ballet before choreographing it, and often devised the groupings using small figures. Petipa provided Tchaikovsky with an outline of the dances and mimes, and indications of the type of music needed for each, often including duration, bars, tempo, and rhythm. While this style of working took Tchaikovsky some getting used to, the pair collaborated well, and the ballet premiered early in 1890.

A year later, the Imperial Theater commissioned Tchaikovsky to compose two more works: the one-act opera *Iolanta* and the two-act ballet *The Nutcracker*. Once again Petipa provided a hugely detailed plot and plan for the latter, around which the score needed to be created. While it received a mixed reception at its premiere in 1892, *The Nutcracker* remains one of the most-performed works today.

Legacy and revivals

Tchaikovsky died in 1893, officially from cholera contracted from unboiled water, although speculation remains regarding the exact nature of his death—suicide and even murder are among the theories to have circulated. At a memorial concert for Tchaikovsky in 1894, Petipa and Lev Ivanov staged Act II of *Swan Lake*. It was so successful that it prompted a revival of the whole production, with new choreography and additional orchestration. Today, *Swan Lake* remains the most famous of Tchaikovsky's three ballets, though not the version he himself saw performed.

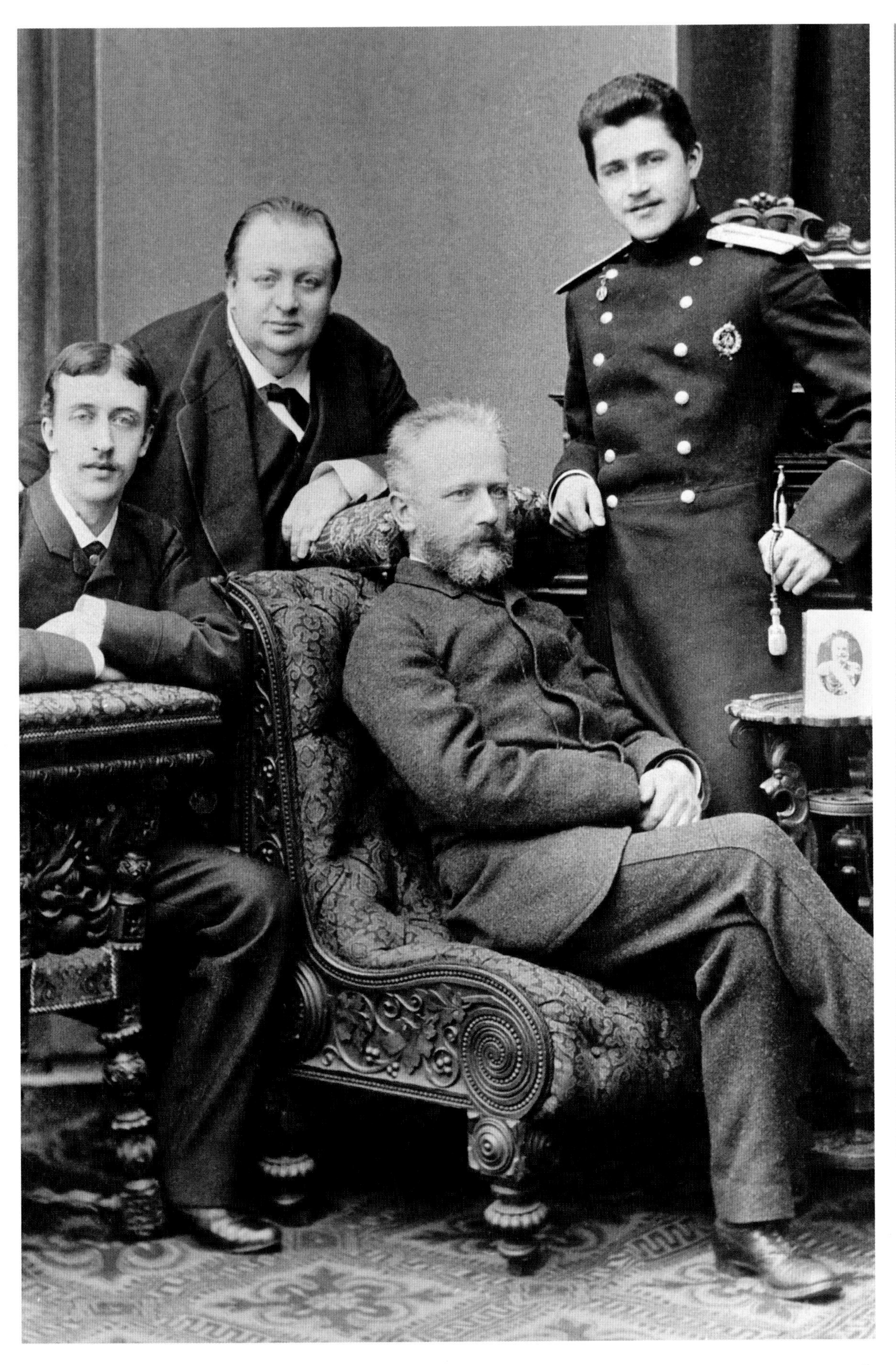

▲ **Keeping company**
Tchaikovsky, pictured in 1888 with nephew Georgy Kartsev (right), Vladimir Zhedrinsky (far left), and lifelong friend and poet Alexei Apukhtin (left), enjoyed conversation to relax after composing.

KEY WORKS

Swan Lake, 1877 • *Eugene Onegin*, 1878 (opera) • *Romeo and Juliet*, 1880 (overture) • *The Sleeping Beauty*, 1889 • *The Queen of Spades*, 1890 (opera) • *Iolanta*, 1891 (opera) • *The Nutcracker*, 1892

TIMELINE

- **May 7, 1840** Born in Votkinsk, Russia, the son of a metal-works manager.
- **1844** Makes his first recorded composition, a song written with his sister Alexandra. A year later he begins piano lessons with a local tutor.
- **1850** Enrolls in the prestigious St. Petersburg boarding institution, the Imperial School of Jurisprudence.
- **1857** Encouraged by Italian singing instructor Luigi Piccioli to develop his musical talent.
- **1861** Travels outside Russia for the first time—to Germany, France, and Britain—and takes up music classes at the new Russian Musical Society on his return.
- **1863** Studies at the St. Petersburg Conservatory, learning harmony and counterpoint under Nikolay Zaremba and composition and instrumentation under Anton Rubinstein.
- **1868** His first opera, *The Voyevoda*, is well received by principal Russian composers.
- **1876** Opens correspondence with Nadezhda von Meck, a wealthy widow who funds his activities for more than a decade, allowing him to give up teaching.
- **1877** Composes the score for *Swan Lake*.
- **1878** Completes his best-known opera, *Eugene Onegin*, which in the 20th century is adapted by choreographer John Cranko.
- **1888** Returns to composing for ballet, creating the score for *The Sleeping Beauty*, followed by *The Nutcracker* in 1892.
- **November 6, 1893** Dies of cholera in St. Petersburg, Russia.

TCHAIKOVSKY'S *ROMEO AND JULIET* OVERTURE, FIRST VERSION, 1869

Swan Lake

First performed: March 4, 1877 ▪ Venue: Imperial Bolshoi Theater, Moscow ▪ Choreography: Julius Reisinger ▪ Music: Tchaikovsky ▪ Story: Possibly Vladimir Begichev and Vasily Geltser

The combination of sublime score, fantasy moonlit setting, yearning love story, clash of good and evil, archetypal classical choreography, and corps de ballet of swans in white tutus has made *Swan Lake* world famous. Based on a variety of European folk tales in which young women are turned into swans, the work features some of the most beautiful dances in the world of ballet.

IN CONTEXT

The drama and romance of *Swan Lake* have prompted many choreographers to create their own version. Perhaps the most famous is Matthew Bourne's production of 1995, but there are several other notable retellings.

John Neumeier created *Illusions—Like Swan Lake* for the Hamburg Ballet in 1976. He based his plotline on Ludwig II of Bavaria, who loved the music of Richard Wagner and built fantasy castles. Contemporary choreographer Graeme Murphy created his neoclassical version for The Australian Ballet in 2002, based on a love triangle between Siegfried, Odette, and Baroness Rothbart. In 2011, Darren Aronofsky's film *Black Swan*, choreographed by Benjamin Millepied, in which Natalie Portman played a ballerina debuting as Odette/Odile, catapulted *Swan Lake* into popular culture.

It was the second staging of *Swan Lake* that took its Russian audience by storm. The first production had not been well received but, in the early 1890s, after the successes of Tchaikovsky's *The Nutcracker* and *The Sleeping Beauty*, discussions began at the Imperial Theater, St. Petersburg, about reviving *Swan Lake* with new choreography by Marius Petipa.

Tchaikovsky died before this plan could be put into action, but, at a memorial concert for the great composer, Petipa and his fellow choreographer Lev Ivanov staged Act II of the ballet. It was so successful that they went on to revive the whole production with additional orchestration by Riccardo Drigo.

For the new production of *Swan Lake*, Petipa choreographed Act I and Act III, and Ivanov created Act II and Act IV. The ballet opened in 1895. Pierina Legnani danced the dual role of Odette/Odile. Petipa included Legnani's specialty, the sequence of 32 fouettés (whipping turns) in Act III, in what is now the famous Black Swan pas de deux.

While many elements from this version survive today, the infamous character of the Black Swan is a relatively recent creation. In Petipa's production, Odile, Rothbart's evil daughter disguised to resemble Odette, wore a colored tutu with no feather pattern. It is believed that Mathilde Kschessinska first wore a black

▼ **Mariinsky Ballet, 2015**
Viktoria Tereshkina (on floor) as Odette/Odile and Andrei Yermakov as the evil Rothbart perform in this production using Konstantin Sergeyev's revised choreography and staging of 1950.

▲ **Nureyev and Fonteyn, 1963**
"At the end of *Swan Lake*, when she left the stage in her great white tutu, I would have followed her to the end of the world," said Nureyev of his partner.

> *Swan Lake* is the most difficult thing to portray for a female ballet dancer; it really requires such specific qualities of articulation, agility, and strength.
>
> BENJAMIN MILLEPIED

tutu for the role at the beginning of the 20th century, and the evolution of this character into a black swan may not have happened until as late as the 1940s.

Swan Lake travels

Elements of *Swan Lake* arrived in Western Europe in waves. Anna Pavlova performed an abridged version on her early tours, in 1907 and 1908, while the Ballets Russes staged a shortened version for their 1911 season. The same year, Mikhail Mordkin and his All Star Imperial Russian Ballet traveled to the US, where it is thought they incorporated Fokine's *Dying Swan* solo into *Swan Lake.*

In 1951, George Balanchine created a version of *Swan Lake* for New York City Ballet with Maria Tallchief and André Eglevsky in the lead roles. Balanchine's version was based on Act II without the mime, and with a larger corps de ballet.

Such was the popularity of *Swan Lake* that Nicholas Sergeyev (former régisseur of the St. Petersburg Imperial Ballet) staged the work for the Vic-Wells Ballet in 1934. This was the first full-length British production, with Alicia Markova as Odette/Odile and Robert Helpmann as Prince Siegfried. In 1987, Anthony Dowell put on a production based on the Petipa/Ivanov version. The Royal Ballet continued to perform it until 2015. Since then, Liam Scarlett has produced a new version with additional choreography.

Even traditional productions of *Swan Lake* vary hugely from company to company, with each having their own interpretation. Some have happy endings (particularly in Russia), while others finish on a dark and tragic note.

Maya Plisetskaya (1925–2015)

Russian ballerina Maya Plisetskaya is most famous for her dual role as Odette/Odile in *Swan Lake*, a part she played more than 800 times from 1945. She had a striking presence on stage with flaming red hair, a massive jump, and extremely flexible back and arms. When Galina Ulanova retired, Plisetskaya became the Bolshoi Ballet's leading ballerina, and she continued performing into her 80s.

▶ **Bolshoi Ballet, 2014**
Russian dancers Artem Ovcharenko (as Prince Siegfried) and Anna Nikulina (as Odette/Odile) perform at the Lincoln Center's David H. Koch Theater, New York.

STORY LINE Swan Lake

Friends come to the palace grounds to celebrate Prince Siegfried's coming of age. At dusk, Siegfried and his friends go swan-hunting in the woods. Siegfried becomes separated from his friends. He sees one of the swans transform into a maiden—the swan queen Odette. At dawn, the evil Rothbart appears, and Odette and her friends become swans. The action switches to a ball at the palace. Rothbart arrives with his daughter Odile, disguised as Odette. Siegfried mistakenly swears his love to Odile, and Rothbart reveals the deception. He insists that Siegfried fulfill his vow to Odile. Odette must become a swan forever.

OLGA PREOBRAJENSKAYA AS ODETTE, IMPERIAL BALLET, 1895

ACT I

PLOT OVERVIEW

Guests have gathered to celebrate Prince Siegfried's coming of age. His friends, including Benno, his tutor, and the court jester are present. The court ladies arrive.

SIEGFRIED ABOUT TO HUNT SWANS

The queen and royal party arrive. The queen mimes that Siegfried must marry, and should choose a bride from the princesses who will attend a ball the following night.

Siegfried sees a flock of swans fly over. Taking his crossbow, he follows them.

THE DANCES

The jester dances a short solo of virtuosic jumps.

The couples dance together; Prince Siegfried joins them.

A lively pas de trois is performed with one male and two female dancers.

ACT II

PLOT OVERVIEW

The evil Rothbart lurks beside the lake. Siegfried arrives and sees the swans. Odette, who transforms back into a woman at night, enters. Siegfried startles her, then tries to catch her.

The corps de ballet of swans makes a dramatic entrance and crosses the stage. There are normally at least 24 swans.

Odette mimes that the evil Rothbart has cast a spell, forcing them to be swans by day and human at night. The spell can only be broken if a man swears true love to Odette.

Siegfried decl... his love for Od... As dawn breaks the maidens tur... back into swans and Odette leav...

THE DANCES

Odette and Siegfried dance together (in some productions Rothbart is behind them).

The swans dance around Siegfried. They are followed by eight more swans, and finally Odette.

Siegfried and Odette dance the famous White Swan pas de deux.

Four of the swans perform the Danc... the Cygnets; anot... four the Dance of Big Swans.

Odette perform... solo that expres... her love.

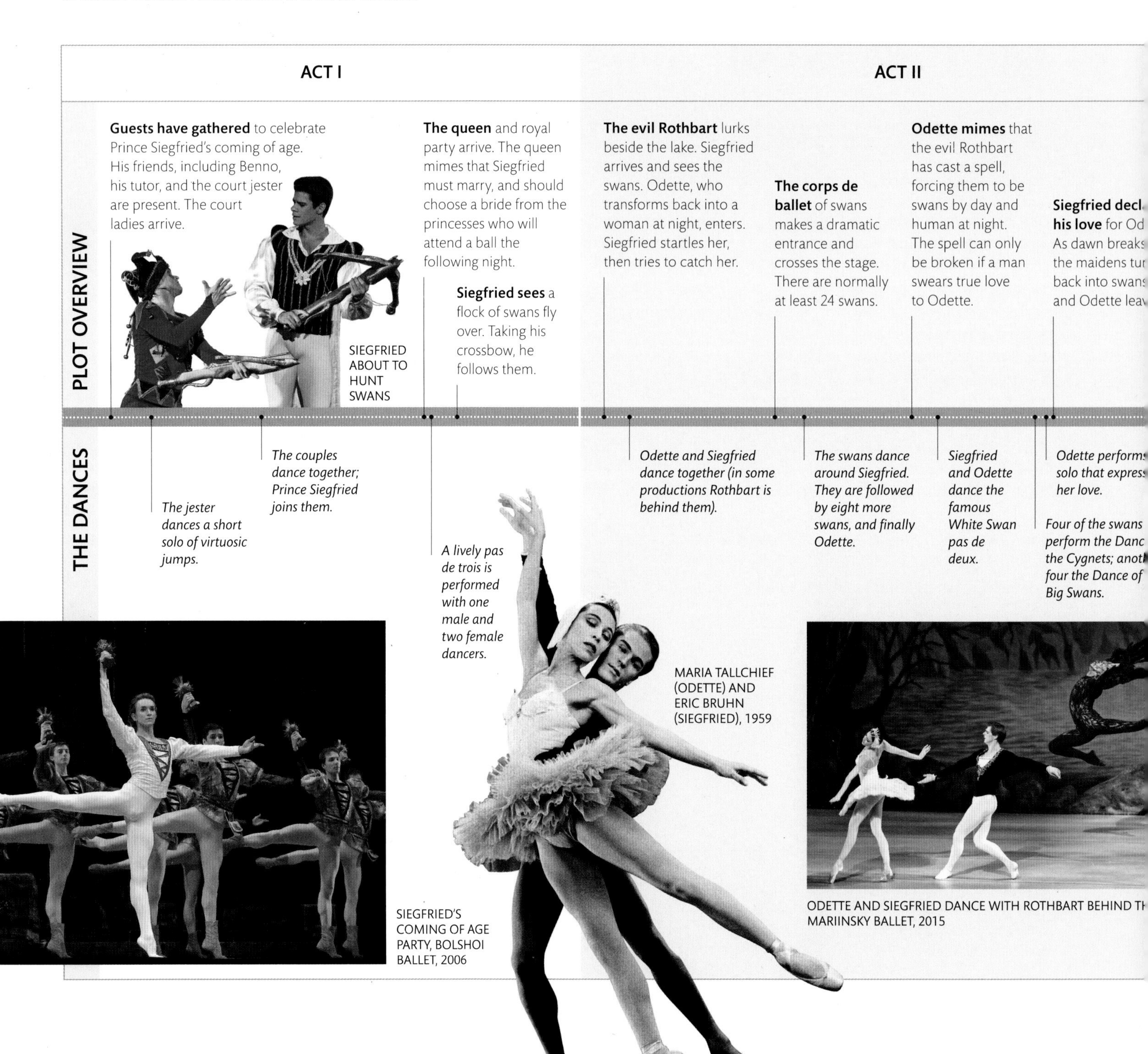
SIEGFRIED'S COMING OF AGE PARTY, BOLSHOI BALLET, 2006

MARIA TALLCHIEF (ODETTE) AND ERIC BRUHN (SIEGFRIED), 1959

ODETTE AND SIEGFRIED DANCE WITH ROTHBART BEHIND TH... MARIINSKY BALLET, 2015

MAYA PLISETSKAYA AS ODILE AND NIKOLAI FADEYECHEV AS SIEGFRIED, BOLSHOI BALLET, 1957

MARIANELA NUNEZ AS ODETTE AND THIAGO SOARES AS PRINCE SIEGFRIED, THE ROYAL BALLET, 2008

ACT III

A ball takes place at the palace. A crowd is gathered, and Siegfried and the queen enter.

Six princesses arrive.

The jester dances.

Siegfried dances with the six princesses.

Rothbart enters with his daughter Odile disguised as Odette. There is a series of national dances.

Spanish, Neapolitan, Hungarian, and Russian dances are performed.

Odile and Siegfried perform the famed Black Swan pas de deux. Odile executes the famous series of 32 fouettés (whipping turns).

Siegfried declares his love and chooses Odile as his bride. Rothbart's deception is revealed; he and Odile vanish.

ACT IV

The swans are on stage. Odette enters, distraught at Siegfried's betrayal, and the swans try to console her.

The swans dance for Odette.

Rothbart appears, followed soon by Siegfried. A battle between Rothbart, Siegfried, and Odette ensues, the outcome of which varies from company to company.

Siegfried and Odette decide to die together and throw themselves into the lake, breaking Rothbart's spell.

Alternatively, Siegfried fights Rothbart. The power of Siegfried and Odette's love breaks the spell, and they are united.

There are two alternative endings to Swan Lake. One version ends happily; the other tragically.

ODILE AND ROTHBART, MARIINSKY BALLET, 2015

SIEGFRIED FIGHTS ROTHBART, ENGLISH NATIONAL BALLET, 2015

Birmingham Royal Ballet, 2015
The corps de ballet of swans provides much of the classic beauty of *Swan Lake*, enhancing the starring role of their queen, Odette.

Pierina Legnani

Dancer ▪ 1868–1930

Italian dancer Pierina Legnani is considered by many to be the greatest ballerina produced by La Scala, Milan, in the latter part of the 19th century. She started her career touring Europe before becoming a famed ballerina in Russia—her career reflecting Russia's dominance in classical ballet. Legnani's skill and technique paved the way for a new generation of female dancers, and she established many of the roles that we know and associate with ballerinas today.

▲ **Dancing *Le Jardin animé***
Pierina Legnani (left) dances with Olga Preobrajenska in the fantasy garden scene in Act III of *Le Corsaire* in 1899. Together with Mathilde Kschessinska, the three were the greatest ballerinas in Russia in the late 19th century.

KEY WORKS

Princess, *Aladdin*, 1893 • Title role, *Cinderella*, 1893 • Odette/Odile, *Swan Lake*, 1895 • White Pearl, *La Perle*, 1896 • Ysaure de Renoualle, *Bluebeard*, 1896 • Title role, *Raymonda*, 1898 Title role, *Camargo*, 1901

Pierina Legnani began dancing at the age of seven, and after a year was accepted to study at La Scala Theater Ballet School, Milan. She trained there for the next 10 years.

After her graduation, Legnani danced with great success throughout Italy and Europe for several years. In 1892, she was appointed prima ballerina at La Scala. She appeared as the Princess in the ballet *Aladdin* at the Alhambra Theatre in London a year later. It was in this ballet that Legnani first performed a series of 32 consecutive fouettés, the first ballerina to do so. After being asked about her ability to perform this move, Legnani credited her ballet shoes from Italy, which reportedly had "a rather Indian canoe shape in front."

While in London, Legnani gave an interview to a journalist from the illustrated newspaper *The Sketch*, published in April 1893. In this she described her day-to-day routine, and the rather surprising amount of food she ate, including, at 2pm, "a good dinner, five or six dishes, and some Chianti."

Sensation in Russia

In 1893, Legnani was invited to join the Imperial Theater, St. Petersburg, where she remained until 1901. She made her debut there in December 1893, in *Cinderella*, supervised by Marius Petipa. In the final act, she performed the famed series of 32 fouettés again, the first time this had been seen in Russia. Legnani's performance caused a sensation in the audience and among the critics, who urged her to repeat the sequence.

Legnani became a muse to Marius Petipa. He created several roles for her, including Odette/Odile in *Swan Lake* in 1895, the title role in *Raymonda* in 1895, and in *Camargo* in 1901. He also revived many works, adapting and creating variations to show off Legnani's talents. These included *Coppélia*, *The Talisman*, *The Little Humpbacked Horse*, and *Le Corsaire*.

Legnani was given the title prima ballerina assoluta, an honor that had only been bestowed on one other dancer (Mathilde Kschessinska, below) with whom Legnani had a great rivalry. After she left Russia in 1901, she continued to dance as a guest artist in Europe, especially in Italy, the UK, and France, until 1910. After this, Legnani retired to her villa at Lake Como in northern Italy. She served on the examining board of La Scala Theater Ballet School until a few months before her death in 1930.

Mathilde Kschessinska (1872–1971)

Legnani's Russian rival, Kschessinska was an Imperial ballerina and mistress to the future Czar Nicholas II before his marriage. She allegedly wore gifts of jewelry on stage and ushered live chickens on for the solo of rival Preobrajenska in *La Fille mal gardée*.

I have breakfast, quite a heavy breakfast—café au lait, with yolks of egg in it, and fillet of beef …

PIERINA LEGNANI IN AN INTERVIEW FOR LONDON'S *THE SKETCH*, 1893

TIMELINE

- **September 30/October 1, 1868** Born in Milan, Italy.
- **1876** Enters Milan's La Scala Theater Ballet School, where she studies with the school's future director, Caterina Beretta.
- **1886** To close a decade at La Scala, understudies prima ballerina Maria Giuri.
- **1889** Performs as prima ballerina in Paris during the Exposition Universelle.
- **1890** Makes her first appearance as prima ballerina at the Alhambra Theatre in London, in *Salandra* by Eugenio Casati.

THE ALHAMBRA THEATRE, LONDON, 1858

- **1892** Dances the Princess in *Aladdin* at the Alhambra Theatre in London.
- **1892** Returns to Milan's La Scala as prima ballerina.
- **December 17, 1893** Debuts with the Imperial Ballet in St. Petersburg, dancing the title role in *Cinderella*. She is made the company's second prima ballerina assoluta.
- **1901** After dancing her final role for the Imperial Ballet in *La Camargo*, leaves Russia for a series of guest performances in France, Italy, and Britain.
- **1910** Retires from the stage, moving to a villa on Lake Como, Italy.
- **November 15, 1930** Dies at her home in Pognara Lario, Lake Como, Italy.

◀ **Muse of choreographer Marius Petipa** Legnani dances in the original production of *La Perle* at the Imperial Mariinsky Theater, St. Petersburg, Russia, in 1896. Marius Petipa created the lead role of White Pearl for her.

CHARACTER DANCES

The phrase "character dance" can have two meanings in ballet. It can refer to the traditional folk dances that appear in many of the best-known ballets, or taking a role that involves acting, maybe as a grotesque or comic person or even an animal. Character dances appear in many 19th-century ballets, including *Coppélia*, *Swan Lake*, *The Sleeping Beauty*, and *Raymonda*, as well as in modern and contemporary works, such as David Bintley's *"Still Life" at the Penguin Cafe*.

The traditional character dances include czardas, mazurka, and polonaise. These would have been known to many of the audiences at the time as they were popular ballroom dances, and court scenes often began with a processional polonaise, used as an entrance for the courtiers. Many popular works, such as *The Nutcracker*, use balletic versions of national dance to add a contrast to the classical steps and some diversity to the entertainment. Spanish, Arabic, Chinese, or Italian dances may appear, for instance, sometimes inserted to impress foreign diplomatic visitors. Professional ballet schools still teach classes in character dance, which include barre and center work as well as the set dances from ballets.

Character roles differ as they create an individual personality such as the cruel Rothbart in *Swan Lake* or, more recently, the comical Widow Simone enjoying her clog dance in Ashton's *La fille mal gardée*. The dancers in these roles tend not to wear traditional ballet costumes or footwear. The parts are usually taken by older dancers who have the stage experience to play a larger-than-life character as well as the movement quality required.

> He does not seek to depict the actions and gestures of an isolated type of the character he assumes; rather does he portray the spirit or essence of all types of that character.
>
> CYRIL BEAUMONT, BALLET HISTORIAN, DESCRIBING NIJINSKY

◀ ***"Still Life" at the Penguin Café*, The Royal Ballet, 2011**
The Southern Cape Zebra (here, Eric Underwood) in the White Mischief semaphore dance is a highlight of David Bintley's set pieces of 1988. The witty and eclectic character dances underpin a serious message, as each animal represents an endangered species.

The Sleeping Beauty

First performed: January 15, 1890 ▪ Venue: Mariinsky Theater, St. Petersburg ▪ Choreography: Marius Petipa ▪ Music: Tchaikovsky ▪ Story: Ivan Vsevolozhsky

In 1888, the director of the Imperial Theaters, Ivan Vsevolozhsky, proposed the idea for a new ballet based on Charles Perrault's fairytale *The Sleeping Beauty*. Petipa and Tchaikovsky collaborated closely: Petipa planned out scenes using papier-mâché figures, and then gave Tchaikovsky a request for the number of bars and tempo for each scenario. The tightly knit result is the classic entertainment enjoyed by audiences around the world today.

IN CONTEXT

The names of the fairies that attend Aurora's christening vary from company to company. In the 1890 production, the fairies were Candide (Candor), Coulante or Fleur-de-Farine (Fine Wheat Flour), Miettes-qui-Tombent (Falling Breadcrumbs), Canari-qui-Chante (Songbird), and Violente (Temperament). The Lilac Fairy is thought to owe her name to the Russian tradition of placing a baby under a lilac tree to bring the child fortune and wisdom. There are many theories surrounding the names of the other fairies. Miettes-qui-Tombent probably recalls the tradition of spreading breadcrumbs on a girl's cradle as a blessing. Violente, who dances with pointed fingers, perhaps resembles electricity, which had recently been installed at the Mariinsky Theater.

The ballet contains characters from other Perrault stories besides Princess Aurora from The Sleeping Beauty, such as Puss-in-Boots, Little Red Riding Hood, Cinderella, Bluebeard, and Hop-o'-My-Thumb, and additional fairytale characters including Belle from Beauty and the Beast, Goldilocks, the White Cat, Princess Florine, and the Bluebird. *The Sleeping Beauty* premiered with Carlotta Brianza as Princess Aurora, the 45-year old Pavel Gerdt as Prince Désiré (in later productions sometimes called Prince Florimund), Marie Petipa (Petipa's daughter) as the Lilac Fairy, and Enrico Cecchetti (later the famous ballet pedagogue) as both Carabosse and the Bluebird. The ballet received mixed reviews, but overall was popular.

▲ **The original cast, 1890**
Key members of the huge cast of this sumptuous Russian production included Carlotta Brianza as Princess Aurora (center).

It inspired artists Alexandre Benois and Léon Bakst, as well as Diaghilev—and also an eight-year-old Anna Pavlova.

In the summer of 1916, Pavlova and her company agreed to appear in Charles Dillingham's *The Big Show* at the New York Hippodrome, where they performed a condensed version of *The Sleeping Beauty*. Léon Bakst designed the production, but the Hippodrome management demanded "more spangles" (sequins) on the costumes. Sharing the bill with Pavlova were the Mammoth Minstrels, Powers' Performing Elephants, and an ice ballet.

Alexei Ratmansky (1968–)

Russian-American choreographer Alexei Ratmansky went back to first principles for his staging of *The Sleeping Beauty* for American Ballet Theatre in 2015, poring over old notation to recover the authentic choreography of Marius Petipa from 1890. His restoration received positive reviews, with critics describing it as a refreshing triumph that brought out the romance of the story and featured meshed moves to music with soft curves and bends rather than sharp extensions and vertical lines.

The Ballets Russes production

In 1921, the Ballets Russes staged its most ambitious project to date—a full-length production of *The Sleeping Beauty*, renamed *The Sleeping Princess.* Diaghilev employed Nicholas Sergeyev, the former régisseur of the Mariinsky, to produce Petipa's choreography. Diaghilev himself altered the score with additions from *The Nutcracker* and other ballets, and employed Bronislava Nijinska to create extra choreography. He commissioned Bakst to design the opulent costumes and sets.

The Sleeping Princess opened on November 2, 1921, at the Alhambra Theatre, London. A full-length ballet was a new experience for British audiences (the Ballets Russes primarily performed one-act ballets), and initially was a great success. After the buzz of the Christmas run-up, sales flagged in the New Year, but it nevertheless remains one of the longest-running ballets in London's West End at 105 performances.

▲ **Design for the Queen**
Léon Bakst designed this costume, annotating it in French with details of materials, trims, patterns, and color, in 1921.

The Royal Ballet

The Sleeping Beauty is a favorite of The Royal Ballet. Nicholas Sergeyev staged it for the Vic-Wells Ballet (forerunner of The Royal Ballet) in 1939. When the Sadler's Wells Ballet (before their Royal warrant) moved into their new home at the Royal Opera House in 1946, *The Sleeping Beauty* was the ballet chosen to open the season. The production, staged by Ninette de Valois and designed by Oliver Messel, featured Margot Fonteyn and Robert Helpmann in the lead roles. The fairies had different names from the original: Fairy of the Crystal Fountain, Fairy of the Enchanted Garden, Fairy of the Woodland Glade, Fairy of the Song Bird, and Fairy of the Golden Vine.

The Royal Ballet has since staged many versions of *The Sleeping Beauty.* In 2006, however, the 1946 version of the ballet was revived, and it continues to be performed today.

▶ **The Royal Ballet, 2006**
Alina Cojocaru as Aurora collapses after pricking her finger, and is comforted by the Queen (Elizabeth McGorian) and the King (Christopher Saunders) in this revival of the 1946 version.

STORY LINE Sleeping Beauty

The ballet begins with the christening of baby Princess Aurora. Six Good Fairies arrive to bestow gifts on the infant before the wicked Fairy Carabosse arrives. She puts a curse on Aurora, stating she will prick her finger on a spindle and die on her 16th birthday. The good Lilac Fairy amends the curse so that Aurora will fall asleep for 100 years—but may only be awoken by a Prince's kiss. On Aurora's 16th birthday, an old woman (Carabosse disguised) appears and gives Aurora a spindle. Aurora pricks her finger and collapses. The Lilac Fairy puts the court into an enchanted sleep. After 100 years, a Prince finds the sleeping Princess and wakes her with a kiss. They marry.

THE WOLF AND LITTLE RED RIDING HOOD'S CHARACTER DANCE IN ACT III, SADLER'S WELLS BALLET, 1946

PROLOGUE

PLOT OVERVIEW

The Master of Ceremonies welcomes members of the royal court, followed by the King and Queen, to the christening of the baby Princess Aurora.

The five Good Fairies arrive, each accompanied by her cavalier. The Lilac Fairy, her cavalier, and attendants (a corps de ballet of female dancers) appear on stage.

The wicked Fairy Carabosse storms into the celebration, angry at not having been invited. She is often accompanied by rats and monstrous attendants. Carabosse puts a curse on the baby Princess. The Lilac Fairy amends the curse so that Aurora will fall asleep.

THE DANCES

The fairies and attendants all dance together.

Each fairy performs her own solo and presents a gift to baby Aurora. Another group dance follows.

ACT I

PLOT OVERVIEW

It is Aurora's 16th birthday. Some productions begin this act by showing a group of women knitting, a crime punishable by death, as the King has banished the use of all needles and spindles. The group is arrested but pardoned, as it is the Princess's birthday.

Four princes arrive from faraway lands.

An old woman arrives and gives Aurora a spindle. She accepts it and dances before pricking her finger. The old woman reveals herself as Carabosse, and Aurora collapses. The Lilac Fairy appears and casts a spell of sleep on the entire court. Lilac trees and thorn bushes grow to cover the court.

THE DANCES

The Garland Dance begins. Peasant boys and girls dance with flower garlands in the palace garden.

Aurora enters and dances a happy, lively solo.

In the Rose Adagio, Aurora dances with each Prince. This is a difficult dance requiring multiple balances.

Aurora's friends dance, and Aurora joins them.

THE CHRISTENING, WITH CLAIRE CALVERT ALOFT AS THE LILAC FAIRY, THE ROYAL BALLET, 2011

AURORA SWOONS UNDER THE SPELL, ENGLISH NATIONAL BALLET, 2012

CARABOSSE AND THE QUEEN, DEUTSCHE OPER, BERLIN

> [The Sleeping Beauty] is the last relic of the great days of St. Petersburg.
>
> SERGEI DIAGHILEV

GRAND PAS DE DEUX, IRINA SURNEVA (AURORA) AND ANDREI UVAROV (THE PRINCE), MOSCOW INTERNATIONAL BALLET FESTIVAL, 2002

MARIANELA NUNEZ AS THE LILAC FAIRY

ACT II

One hundred years have passed, and the Prince is hunting with friends, including a beautiful Countess. Eventually the party disperses, leaving the Prince alone. The Lilac Fairy appears and shows him a vision of the Princess Aurora.

The Prince dances with Aurora and a corps de ballet of "visions."

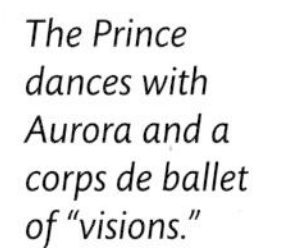

The "visions" disappear, and the Lilac Fairy leads the Prince to the castle, sometimes via her magical boat or gondola.

The Prince arrives at the castle, which is covered in thorns and cobwebs. He kisses Aurora. The court transforms and awakens, and the cobwebs disappear. The Prince asks for the hand of Aurora.

The Prince awakens Aurora with a kiss.

THE PRINCE BREAKS THE SPELL BY KISSING AURORA

ACT III

The wedding of Princess Aurora and the Prince takes place with a great and colorful celebration. A series of court couples enters, followed by a host of fairytale characters. Their dances vary from company to company.

The jewel fairies (Diamond, Sapphire, Gold, and Silver) perform a pas de quatre.

Puss in Boots and the White Cat dance.

Little Red Riding Hood and the Wolf share a dance.

Fairytale dances may also include Bluebird and Princess Florine.

The Three Ivans perform a comic Russian-inspired acrobatic pas de trois.

Aurora and the Prince dance a Grand Wedding pas de deux.

The court couples dance a mazurka. The fairytale characters join them and all dance together. The Lilac Fairy blesses Aurora and the Prince. The entire cast joins in for a final dance, the Apotheosis.

THE WHITE CAT AND PUSS IN BOOTS, ENGLISH NATIONAL BALLET, 2012

Moscow Ballet of Classical Choreography, 2017
Director Elik Melikov started "La Classique," as the company is known for short, in 1990, using top Russian dancers to tour the world with classical ballets such as *The Sleeping Beauty*.

Anna Pavlova

Dancer ▪ 1881–1931

A household name for more than a century, Anna Pavlova is most famous for her *Dying Swan* solo. Her charismatic dancing drew audiences like a magnet, and schools and companies sprang up wherever she had performed. She was born in St. Petersburg, Russia, in 1881 and raised by her mother; the identity of her father is uncertain. In 1890, she was taken to see the newly created ballet, *The Sleeping Beauty*, at the Mariinsky Theater and decided her destiny was to become a ballerina.

▲ **Training with a maestro**
In her mid-20s, Pavlova trained with renowned Italian ballet teacher Enrico Cecchetti. Under the "Cecchetti method," dancers perform strict daily exercises and routines. It is still taught today.

In 1891, at the age of 10, Pavlova was accepted into the prestigious Imperial Ballet School and graduated in 1899 into the Imperial Ballet Company. Seven years later, she was promoted to prima ballerina.

Short tours in Europe in 1908–1909 with fellow-dancer Adolph Bolm included visits to Copenhagen, Prague, Stockholm, Berlin, Leipzig, and Vienna. In the spring of 1909, she joined Sergei Diaghilev's Ballets Russes' first season in Paris. Here, Pavlova performed with Vaslav Nijinsky in the ballets *Les Sylphides*, *Cléopâtre*, and *Le Pavillon d'Armide*, created by Michel Fokine. Pavlova and Nijinsky, along with Tamara Karsavina, became overnight sensations.

After the success of this Paris season, Pavlova, with fellow Russian dancer Mikhail Mordkin, paid their first visit to London. Dubbed the "Modern Taglioni," Pavlova first danced at a soirée attended by King Edward and Queen Alexandra.

Pavlova made her US debut in New York in 1910, followed by an engagement at the Palace Theatre, London. Theater impresario Sir Alfred Butt engaged her for $778 a week, but was soon paying her a princely $5,840 weekly. After this success, Pavlova formed her own company, the Pavlova Company, managed by Victor Dandré, a Russian businessman who also claimed to be her husband. In 1914, Pavlova bought Ivy House in London, which became her home and the artistic hub of her company.

Curtain call on Russia

Pavlova was traveling through Germany when war was declared with Russia in 1914; as a Russian national, she was immediately arrested and faced possible internment. Upon her release, she made her way to London and eventually North America with her company. This year also marked the official end of her association with the Imperial Ballet. For the next two years Pavlova and her company performed a flurry of one-night shows in Canada and the US.

Pavlova's time in the US proved eventful. In 1916, her first (and only) appearance in a Hollywood film was released. *The Dumb Girl of Portici* featured three dance interludes to ensure that the audience still saw Pavlova the dancer. The following year, faced with creditors, she agreed for her company to appear in Charles Dillingham's *The Big Show* at the New York Hippodrome. They performed a shortened version of *The Sleeping Beauty*.

In 1917–1918, the company toured Latin America, and it was here that Pavlova developed an interest in traditional dances. For the next decade, she would seek out and learn the national dance of every country she visited, inspiring her to choreograph works including *Mexican Dances*, *Oriental Impressions*, and *Ajanta's Frescoes*.

Going global

During the 1920s, the Pavlova Company toured extensively, traveling an estimated 500,000 miles and giving thousands of performances to millions of people. A famed dancer and businesswoman, Pavlova was also a modern celebrity, endorsing countless products and creating a popular public image. Her close friends included film star Charlie Chaplin, opera singer Feodor Chaliapin, and business magnate Gordon Selfridge.

Despite her global success, the Pavlova Company stayed true to Anna's roots, and

paid homage to the repertoire of the Imperial Theater and prerevolutionary Russia rather than pushing the bounds of classical technique, as Diaghilev's Ballets Russes did. Works performed included *The Fairy Doll*, *Don Quixote*, and *Raymonda*, as well as divertissements arranged by Pavlova herself.

Throughout her career, Pavlova's most famous work was the short solo *The Swan* or *The Dying Swan*. Created for her in around 1907 by Michel Fokine, she performed this evocative solo throughout her career, and it remains a rite of passage for ballerinas today.

▲ **Creature comforts**
In this image from 1920, Pavlova is seen relaxing at her London home with a pet—aptly a swan. *The Swan* or *The Dying Swan* was Pavlova's signature solo dance.

KEY WORKS

Title role, *Paquita*, c. 1901/1902 • Title role, *Giselle*, 1903 • *The Swan* (*Dying Swan*), c. 1907 *Autumn Bacchanal*, 1910 • *The Dragonfly*, c. 1914/1915 • *Autumn Leaves*, 1920 • *Oriental Impressions*, c. 1923 • *The Immortal Swan*, 1935 (a posthumous film collection of her dances)

TIMELINE

- **January 31, 1881** Born in the suburb of Ligovo, St. Petersburg, Russia, to her unmarried mother, Lyubov Feodorovna.
- **1891** Accepted into the Imperial Ballet School, St. Petersburg, on her second try.
- **1892** Makes her first recorded appearance, dancing in the school's production of *The Magic Fairy Tale*.
- **1899** Graduates into the Imperial Ballet Company, taking the role of Zulme in *Giselle*.
- **1900** Eager to further her art, travels to Milan to study under Catarina Beretta.
- **1906** Becomes prima ballerina at the Imperial Ballet Company, and appoints Enrico Cecchetti as her private teacher.
- **1908** Her first foreign tour, visiting Latvia and Scandinavia, receives great acclaim.
- **1909–1910** Tours central Europe with the Ballets Russes, continuing to Paris and London, then on to New York, Boston, and Baltimore.
- **1910** Engaged at the Palace Theatre, London, a city she makes her base two years later.
- **1913** Dances in St. Petersburg for the last time, World War I and the Russian Revolution preventing her return to Russia.
- **1916** Features in the film *The Dumb Girl of Portici* to finance her tour of the US.
- **1917–1929** Tours relentlessly around the world with her company.
- **January 23, 1931** Following a bout of pneumonia, dies of pleurisy at the Hôtel des Indes in The Hague, Netherlands.

BALLET SHOES WORN BY PAVLOVA DURING HER PERFORMANCE OF *BALLET IN THREE MINIATURES* IN 1923

ROYAL OPERA HOUSE

Old meets new in London's Royal Opera House (ROH), which dates back to the 18th century but is now at the technical forefront of ballet and opera. The building has twice been destroyed by fire, in 1808 and 1856, and today only the portico, foyer, and auditorium date from its third incarnation. This third building, and the Paul Hamlyn Hall next door, were designed by E.M. Barry and opened in 1858. Today, the ROH houses The Royal Ballet, The Royal Opera, and their orchestra.

The original theater was dreamed up by actor-manager John Rich in 1732, and funded by his profits from commissioning *The Beggar's Opera*. He had the Theatre Royal, as it was called, built on the site of an old convent garden—a space that also accommodated Covent Garden's fruit and vegetable market until 1974 and is now home to a piazza buzzing with shops and performance artists. The first ballet to be performed at the Theatre Royal was *Pygmalion*, in 1734.

War interrupted entertainment in the 20th century. In World War I, the building (renamed the Royal Opera House in 1892) was put to practical purpose as a furniture repository. During World War II, the ROH was used as a dance hall, raising morale in dismal times and, in 1946, it reopened with a lavish ballet production of *The Sleeping Beauty*. Lottery funding in the 1990s to update the ROH for the 21st century allowed a huge refurbishment to take place. Backstage, studios were built and new stage and technical equipment installed, and freight trucks were given access to drive straight into the theater to drop off and collect scenery. Another refurbishment program is underway, including a redesign of The Linbury Studio Theatre and public areas, to enhance the experience of visiting the building.

> The Royal Opera House has the most beautiful auditorium in Great Britain.
>
> F.H.W SHEPPARD, HISTORIAN, 1970

◄ **Bow Street facade**
The imposing main entrance dates back to 1856. It has a classical-style portico of Corinthian columns, raised on a rusticated (deeply-grooved) base and with a stunning glazed conservatory behind.

The Nutcracker

First performed: December 7, 1892 ▪ Venue: Mariinsky Theater, St. Petersburg ▪ Choreography: Lev Ivanov ▪ Music: Tchaikovsky ▪ Story: Marius Petipa

Part of the festive season along with Christmas trees and carols, *The Nutcracker* is the ballet that companies worldwide return to year after year, and that audiences flock to see. For many, it provides their first experience of ballet. Key to its popularity is its music. However, composer Tchaikovsky never knew what a huge success the ballet became, as he died less than a year after the first performance.

IN CONTEXT

The story, based on E.T.A. Hoffmann's tale *The Nutcracker and the Mouse King*, varies from production to production. Clara may be portrayed as a child, or as a teenager and danced by an adult. In the US, she is usually known as Marie, and in Russia as Masha. Clara and the Sugar Plum Fairy may be portrayed as different characters, or Clara can imagine herself as the Sugar Plum Fairy. Underlying many versions is Clara awakening to the wider world and romantic love.

For his Royal Ballet production, Peter Wright provides a prologue: the Nutcracker is actually Drosselmeyer's nephew, Hans Peter, who was transformed into the doll by the Mouse Queen after his uncle killed half the mice in the palace. He can only be released from the spell by killing the Mouse King and falling in love with a girl.

The Russian Imperial Theaters in St. Petersburg commissioned the ballet from Tchaikovsky as a follow-up to the hugely successful *The Sleeping Beauty* (1890). The more popular pieces of the score, forming the *Nutcracker Suite*, were premiered about six months ahead of the ballet and became instantly popular.

The full ballet, which turned out to be Tchaikovsky's last, did not fare so well. Critics liked the first act with its children, Christmas tree, and battle, but found that Act II lacked drama and was unconvincing—and the fact that it formed part of a double bill, so the audience had to wait until midnight before they saw the grand pas de deux, may not have helped. After rare stagings, the first complete performance outside Russia was held in 1934 in London, by Nicholas Sergeyev for the Vic-Wells Ballet. In the US, audiences saw *The Nutcracker* in full when William Christensen staged it for San Francisco Ballet in 1944. Then Sadler's Wells Theatre Ballet had an American tour with a version by Frederick Ashton in 1951.

However, the fact that *The Nutcracker* became an American institution is down to George Balanchine. Stripped of any dark elements, his 1954 production for New York City Ballet became the template for versions across the US. It became even more popular after being televised in 1957 and 1958.

▲ **The Royal Ballet, 2009**
Iohna Loots (Clara) and Ricardo Cervera (the Nutcracker, transformed into the handsome Prince) travel through the Land of Snow.

▲ **Matthew Bourne's *The Nutcracker*, 2011**
Bourne's Kingdom of Sweets characters in Act II make a big visual impact, in contrast with the drab Victorian orphanage setting of Act I.

The Nutcracker is a fantasy ballet for children, like a toy that a grown-up makes with thoughtful care.

CRITIC EDWIN DENBY ON GEORGE BALANCHINE'S *THE NUTCRACKER*, 1954

Peter Wright popularity

All that survives of the original choreography in most productions is the grand pas de deux between the Sugar Plum Fairy and her cavalier. In the UK, Peter Wright's richly traditional productions for The Royal Ballet (1984, revised 1999) and Birmingham Royal Ballet (1990) are the main source of the work's popularity. After much research, Wright went back to the original patterns, if not the actual steps, from the notation for the snowflake dance.

Both his productions are strong on narrative, and having Clara join in the divertissements in Act II keeps the story going. His Birmingham production has more of Hoffmann's original tale in it than most, and is particularly noted for its dramatic transformation scene, in which the Christmas tree swamps the whole stage.

Lev Ivanov (1834–1901)

Russian Lev Ivanov was second ballet master of the Imperial Theaters, where Petipa was chief ballet master. Petipa originally intended to choreograph *The Nutcracker*, but he fell ill and Ivanov took over. He was restricted by Petipa's detailed notes on the plot, but had the freedom to express his genius in the snowflake sequence and the grand pas de deux. Ivanov is best known for this and two other works he created in the 1890s—*The Magic Flute*, a one-act ballet, and *Swan Lake*.

Probably the most performed ballet in the world, *The Nutcracker* is, however, far from uniform. Productions often take local inspiration. Christopher Wheeldon's for the Joffrey Ballet is set in Chicago just before the 1893 World's Fair and relates the story to immigrants. In South Africa, Joburg Ballet's *The Nutcracker, Re-Imagined* has Drosselmeyer as a traditional African healer, who shows Clara the beauty of the continent, and includes gumboot dancing alongside classical ballet in the Russian dance.

The National Ballet of China's version is Chinese New Year–themed and features Tuantuan (Fritz) bullying Yuanyuan (Clara) with nunchucks while wearing a green dragon mask, and her being helped by sword-wielding tigers. Meanwhile, Rudolf Nureyev's *The Nutcracker*, in the Paris Opéra Ballet repertoire, has no Sugar Plum Fairy or Kingdom of Sweets, and Drosselmeyer and the Prince as the same person.

◀ **Peter Wright's version**
Yuhui Choe (as the Sugar Plum Fairy) and Sergei Polunin (as the Prince) perform in this Christmas favorite with The Royal Ballet in 2008.

STORY LINE The Nutcracker

At a family Christmas party, young Clara Stahlbaum is given a beautiful wooden nutcracker doll by the mysterious Herr Drosselmeyer. In the night, Clara creeps downstairs to check on her new toy, but Drosselmeyer is waiting to sweep her off on a magical adventure. By helping the Nutcracker defeat the Mouse King in battle, Clara breaks a spell. The Nutcracker is transformed into the handsome Prince. Clara and the Prince travel through the Land of Snow to the Kingdom of Sweets where they meet the Sugar Plum Fairy, who introduces her friends. Everyone dances in celebration, but it is getting late and soon Clara finds herself back at home.

THE CHINESE DANCE, THE ROYAL BALLET, 2015

ACT I

PLOT OVERVIEW

At the Stahlbaum's house, everyone is busy preparing for the Christmas party. The guests arrive, bringing gifts for Clara and her younger brother, Fritz. Drosselmeyer makes a dramatic entrance. Amid much excitement, the tree is lit, and Clara is enchanted.

MEAGHAN GRACE HINKIS AS CLARA, 2012

Drosselmeyer entertains the guests with mechanical toys, and presents Clara with a nutcracker doll. Fritz snatches the doll and breaks it, but Drosselmeyer then repairs it. The guests leave and everyone goes to bed. Clara creeps back downstairs to find her Nutcracker.

Clara is surprised by Drosselmeyer, then frightened by the life-size mice that appear. Drosselmeyer works his magic and the room and Christmas tree grow. The mice reappear, and the Nutcracker leads his soldiers into battle against them and the Mouse King. Clara saves the day by hitting the Mouse King on the head with a ballet slipper.

The scene mysteriously changes as Clara and the Nutcracker, now the Prince, glide to the Land of Snow.

THE DANCES

There are dances for Clara, her family, and guests, including a polite, formal quadrille for the children.

Clara's mother performs an elegant solo, and the others join in.

The mechanical dolls dance, and Clara happily dances with the Nutcracker. Dr. Stahlbaum and his wife lead the guests in a final dance.

Clara dances a joyous and romantic pas de deux with the Nutcracker-Prince (Drosselmeyer's nephew Hans Peter in The Royal Ballet productions).

In a snowy forest, the snowflakes dance. Clara and the Prin join in.

ERNST MEISNER AS THE MOUSE KING, 2008

CHRISTMAS PARTY, ORIGINAL PRODUCTION, ST. PETERSBURG, 1892

ALEXANDRA ANSANELLI, AS THE SUGAR PLUM FAIRY, AND VALERI HRISTOV, AS THE PRINCE, 2007

STAGE DESIGN FOR THE ORIGINAL PRODUCTION, 1892

ACT II

Set in the Kingdom of Sweets, Clara and the Nutcracker-Prince arrive. The Sugar Plum Fairy and her cavalier greet them. The Prince tells the Sugar Plum Fairy what happened and how Clara saved him.

In Peter Wright's Birmingham production, Drosselmeyer greets Clara. The Mouse King, who was only wounded, arrives. There is a short fight, and he is captured and taken away.

In the Birmingham production, Clara transforms into the Sugar Plum Fairy at the end of the Waltz of the Flowers, then returns to her real self as the scene melts away.

Clara and the Nutcracker-Prince return home in the sleigh. Back at the Stahlbaum house, Clara wakes up on Christmas morning to find that all is normal, and wonders if it was all a dream. Wright's Royal Ballet production ends, as it began, in Drosselmeyer's workshop.

Surrounded by angels, the Sugar Plum Fairy dances a variation to the celeste (a keyboard instrument). At The Royal Ballet, this is a short pas de deux with the Prince.

There are four character dances: a lively Spanish dance (sometimes known as Chocolate), a sultry Arabian dance (Coffee), an amusing Chinese dance (Tea), and an upbeat Russian trepak (Candy Canes).

The perky Dance of the Mirlitons is usually for four ballerinas and a lead dancer.

In the US, Mother Ginger's children, the Polichinelles, emerge from under her enormous hoop skirt to dance.

The Waltz of the Flowers is a large ensemble dance.

The Sugar Plum Fairy and the Prince or her cavalier perform a grand pas de deux.

Clara and the Nutcracker-Prince join in as everyone returns for a finale to bid them farewell.

ARABIAN DANCE, BIRMINGHAM ROYAL BALLET, 2011

In Peter Wright productions, Clara joins in with all the character dances, instead of just watching them, so Act II is well integrated with Act I.

CHINESE DANCE, BIRMINGHAM ROYAL BALLET, 2009

English National Ballet, 2015
The corps de ballet dance the Waltz of the Snowflakes in Wayne Eagling's production of *The Nutcracker* at the London Coliseum.

Raymonda

First performed: January 19, 1898 ▪ Venue: Mariinsky Theater, St. Petersburg ▪ Choreography: Petipa ▪ Music: Alexander Glazunov ▪ Story: Lydia Pashkova

Choreographed by Marius Petipa in his 80th year, *Raymonda* is set in medieval Europe and draws many parallels with his earlier work, *The Sleeping Beauty*. The ballet was one of Petipa's last and most successful, and is renowned for its sumptuous dances, particularly the female solos. It has been revived many times, notably by Anna Pavlova, who condensed it into two acts, and Rudolf Nureyev, who recreated it mostly from memory after defecting to the West.

STORY LINE

Act I Scene 1 Raymonda is celebrating her birthday. She is engaged to Jean de Brienne, who is due to return from the Crusades the following day. At the party, a Saracen Lord, Abdérâme, tries to woo Raymonda but she rejects him.

Act I Scene 2 Raymonda falls asleep. In her dream, the White Lady, who protects family tradition, leads her to Jean and she dances with him. Jean vanishes and Abdérâme appears declaring his love for her.

Act II Abdérâme and his accomplices try to abduct Raymonda but Jean returns to save her. Abdérâme is killed in a duel with Jean.

Act III Everyone gathers to celebrate the marriage of Raymonda and Jean.

◀ **Anna Pavlova**
The Russian prima ballerina dances in the eponymous role. The Pavlova Company's revival of the ballet premiered in New York in 1915.

Following the death of Tchaikovsky in 1893, the director of the Imperial Theaters searched for a new composer to collaborate with choreographer Marius Petipa. Alexander Glazunov, a student of Nikolay Rimsky-Korsakov, was chosen and *Raymonda* was his first ballet. Petipa specifically choreographed the role of Raymonda for Italian prima ballerina Pierina Legnani, who had originated the role of Odette/Odile in *Swan Lake*.

Although *Raymonda* has a very simple plot, it can be hard to follow and runs at over two hours long. Rather than a strong story line, it presents a series of divertissements in which the dancers, especially the soloists, are allowed to shine, most spectacularly during the wedding scene in Act III.

Modern revivals

In 1915, Anna Pavlova and her company produced a two-act version of *Raymonda*, including the birthday scene and dream sequence, with choreography by Ivan Clustine. This new abridged version opened on the first night of Pavlova's season at the Century Opera House, New York, in February 1915.

Rudolf Nureyev was familiar with *Raymonda*, having performed in Konstantin Sergeyev's 1948 version with the Kirov Ballet. It was also the first ballet he staged after defecting to the West. His premiere production was for The Royal Ballet, London, and was performed again in 1964 at the Spoleto Festival in Italy.

Nureyev put on further productions for The Australian Ballet in 1965, The Zurich Opera Ballet in 1972, and American Ballet Theatre in 1975. In 1983, as artistic director of the Paris Opéra, he staged a final version for his inaugural season. This production followed Petipa's arrangements but enhanced the male dancing roles.

Stephen Baynes choreographed a new version for The Australian Ballet in 2005. Set in Hollywood's Golden Age, it was loosely based on the life of Grace Kelly, with Raymonda danced by Kirsty Martin.

▼ **Hollywood glamour**
In The Australian Ballet's 2005 version of *Raymonda*, medieval Europe becomes 1950s Hollywood, with Raymonda herself now a film star who marries a European prince.

▶ **Nureyev variations**
Nureyev produced a number of variations of *Raymonda* between 1964–1983. He is shown here dancing with Margot Fonteyn in 1965 for The Australian Ballet.

PAS DE DEUX

A defining feature of classical ballet, a pas de deux is a duet usually danced by a ballerina and a male partner, but may also be performed by two men or two women. The first recorded pas de deux was in the early 18th century when ballets were mostly allegorical, and the figures often displayed characteristics to help tell the story; the male dancer would be strong, gallant, and noble, while the female would be submissive and wistful, or even flirtatious and bold. As such, the male partner acted as a support for the ballerina, who could appear to defy gravity in a jump or remain suspended at the end of a turning movement with his help.

With the rise of Romantic ballet in the late 18th and early 19th centuries, more ballerinas began to dance en pointe, and so the male dancer became even more important in a pas de deux. The need for strength, physical contact, and skill increased as the ballerinas literally put themselves in the capable hands of their partners. As ballet technique continued to evolve, the pointe shoes worn by dancers became more functional, and changes in dance clothing (such as the use of stretch fabrics) allowed for much greater athleticism and daring moves—particularly more demanding jumps.

The grand pas de deux, which often appears as the climax of a scene or performance, was introduced in the late 19th century. It usually consists of a supported adage, followed by virtuoso solos—the male and then the female dancer—and a finale. Iconic examples include the dance of the Sugar Plum Fairy and her Prince in *The Nutcracker*, and Odile and Prince Siegfried in *Swan Lake*. Since the 20th century, the grand pas de deux has become more integrated with the story of the ballet, and showcases the dancers' skills.

> A pas de deux is a dialogue of love. How can there be conversation if one partner is dumb?
>
> RUDOLF NUREYEV

Margot Fonteyn and Rudolf Nureyev, 1966 ▶
Some of the most iconic love pas de deux appear near the end of each act in Kenneth MacMillan's *Romeo and Juliet*, charting the development of romance to tragedy.

The Dying Swan

First performed: 1905 or 1907 ▪ Choreography and story: Michel Fokine ▪ Music: Camille Saint-Saëns from *The Carnival of the Animals*

Originally called *The Swan*, *The Dying Swan* is one of the most famous dance pieces of all time. The four-minute solo was created by Russian choreographer Michel Fokine for ballerina Anna Pavlova, who performed it around the world for more than 20 years. When Pavlova approached him to create a solo for her, Fokine composed the dance in just a few minutes, to music he had recently heard—Saint-Saëns's *The Swan*.

The piece was created for Pavlova to perform at a charity event. While there is debate over whether it was created in 1905 or 1907, certainly she danced *The Dying Swan* on December 22, 1907, at The Mariinsky Theater, St. Petersburg, Russia. This performance was in aid of a charity for newborn children and impoverished mothers.

Michel Fokine had known Pavlova from childhood (the two having trained at the Imperial Ballet School together). He later wrote, "The dance was composed in a few minutes. It was almost an improvisation. I demonstrated for her, she standing behind me. Then she danced and I walked alongside her, curving her arms and directing details of the poses." *The Dying Swan* relies on a series of pas de bourrées (a rapid movement of the feet en pointe) and an expressive use of arms to depict a swan's last moments. Fokine believed this solo was one of the first illustrations of a new form of Russian ballet.

Pavlova's white tutu, designed by Léon Bakst, represented the swan's wings, and was decorated with real goose feathers. Pavlova's costume-maker, Madame Manya, stated that Pavlova "never wore her Swan costume more than twice without the skirts of the tutu being renewed." This was most likely because tarlatan and tulle were much softer than today and required constant stiffening.

▲ **Pavlova's triumph**
After achieving the title of prima ballerina in 1906, Pavlova went on to perform this solo thousands of times.

In the 1930s and '40s dancers tended to have a red jewel set into the center of their costume, symbolizing the wound where the swan had been shot. However, this was not the original intention of the story, and Pavlova's costumes had blue or green gems, to represent the creature's soul.

STORY LINE

Inspired by Alfred, Lord Tennyson's poem, also titled "The Dying Swan," and swans that Pavlova had observed in parks, this ballet depicts the final minutes of a swan's life. The work requires great control to portray the longing to remain alive, but the struggle to do so. Renowned Russian dance critic André Levinson wrote of Pavlova's portrayal of the dying swan, "Arms folded, on tiptoe, she dreamily and slowly circles the stage ... she seems to strive toward the horizon, as though a moment more and she will fly ... faltering with irregular steps toward the edge of the stage—leg bones quiver like the strings of a harp ... she sinks on the left knee—the aerial creature struggling against earthly bonds; and there, transfixed by pain, she dies."

In 1913, a young Ninette de Valois (who later founded The Royal Ballet) notated the solo while in the audience at the Palace Theatre. Today, *The Dying Swan* has been reinterpreted and copied by dancers all over the globe, and famously parodied by Les Ballets Trockadero de Monte Carlo.

◀ **Expressive solo**
The dance requires the use of the whole body, not just the legs, to convey a swan's movements and to symbolize the "longing for life by all mortals."

▶ **Signature dance**
Performed under a single moving spotlight, *The Dying Swan* would remain Pavlova's most famous work. On her deathbed in 1931 she is said to have asked for her swan costume to be prepared.

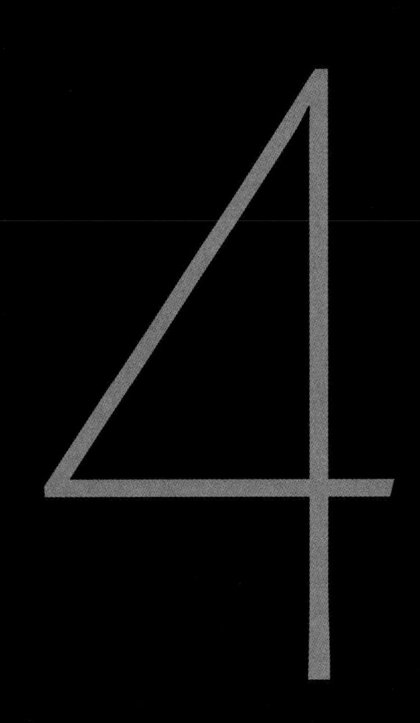

4 MODERN BALLET

(1905–1945)

Modern ballet 1905–1945

The early 20th century saw considerable changes in ballet, including how it was danced, where, and even why. In Western Europe, the art had gradually declined in popularity among mainstream audiences, and had been relegated to a music-hall novelty. Meanwhile in Russia, ballet had continued to thrive, although a new generation of dancers and choreographers was emerging, eager to break free from the strict regime of the Imperial Theaters. For many, their opportunity came with Sergei Diaghilev's hugely influential company, Ballets Russes.

After the success of several early forays in Paris showcasing Russian art, music, and opera, Diaghilev was invited to present a program at the Paris Opéra in 1909, in which he included the groundbreaking ballets *Les Sylphides* and *Cléopâtre*. The program was an overnight sensation, and made household names of dancers such as Vaslav Nijinsky, Anna Pavlova, and Tamara Karsavina.

The company quickly became the driving force of ballet in Western Europe, where it revived a passion for the art, with the premiere of *The Rite of Spring* (*Le Sacre du Printemps*, 1913) even resulting in a riot. Touring Europe and North and South America, the Ballets Russes was also the leading platform for some of the art world's greatest talents, including composers Igor Stravinsky, Claude Debussy, Erik Satie, and Maurice Ravel; choreographers Léonide Massine, Bronislava Nijinska, and George Balanchine; and designers and artists Alexandre Benois, Léon Bakst, Pablo Picasso, Henri Matisse, and even Coco Chanel.

Reinvigorated, ballet prospered outside Russia once more as brave new works were staged, such as *Parade* (1917), with its Cubist set, and *Apollo* (1929), the first neoclassical ballet. In the US, Martha Graham founded her own dance company in 1926, The Martha Graham Dance Company, while Russian George Balanchine established the School of American Ballet in New York in 1934. Meanwhile, in the UK, Polish-born Marie Rambert founded Ballet Club in London in 1928, the country's first dance company, followed by Ninette de Valois's Vic-Wells Ballet and ballet school in 1931, the precursor to London's The Royal Ballet.

Following World War I and the Russian Revolution, ballet in Russia itself faced incredible challenges. Initially considered decadent and nearly banned, ballet became a mouthpiece of the new Soviet system, used to uphold Socialist ideals, as seen in works such as *Les Noces* (1923). However, theaters were frequently purged and artists feared state-sponsored public ridicule, or worse. Many of Russian ballet's greatest talents fled to the West or never returned home from it, including Diaghilev, who died in a hotel room in Italy in 1929.

Sergei Diaghilev

Impresario and founder, the Ballets Russes ▪ 1872–1929

Larger-than-life Russian Sergei Diaghilev is known for the sheer force of his character. He brought together the Ballets Russes and pulled off the company's triumphant 1909 season in Paris. He and his colleagues were hugely influenced by the Wagnerian concept of *Gesamtkunstwerk* ("total work of art"), in which each art form comes together to create a whole. This concept became their central philosophy. With Diaghilev at the helm, the Ballets Russes electrified the world of ballet.

▲ Diaghilev (right) with Jean Cocteau
Sergei Diaghilev famously challenged the French poet, playwright, and film director Jean Cocteau to "Astonish me!" in his search for new and thought-provoking artistic expression that would surprise society.

Sergei Diaghilev's mother died shortly after his birth and his officer father remarried when his son was two. It was Diaghilev's stepmother, Yelena, who encouraged him to take an interest in the arts. The family moved to Perm on the Siberian border when he was 10, where Diaghilev and his half-brothers saw amateur performances of opera, concerts, plays, and poetry. In 1890, Diaghilev left for St. Petersburg to study law, while also attending music and singing classes at the Conservatory of Music.

Artistic ambitions

In St. Petersburg, Diaghilev joined a literary circle through his cousin, Dmitry Filosofov, which included the artists Alexandre Benois and Léon Bakst and writer Walter Nouvel. Diaghilev was eager to learn all he could at these intellectual gatherings. After graduating in the mid-1890s, he sought a career in music, and he showed some of his compositions to Nikolay Rimsky-Korsakov. The great composer was not encouraging.

In 1898, Diaghilev and his group launched the magazine *Mir Iskusstva* ("World of Art"), which aimed to educate artistic tastes and liberate art. This helped to establish Diaghilev's reputation. *Mir Iskusstva* appeared fortnightly until 1900 and then monthly until 1904.

In 1899, Diaghilev became a special assistant to Prince Volkonsky, director of the Imperial Theaters. His role included compiling the yearbook, and he vastly overspent on a lavish volume. He was dismissed from this position, but had become well acquainted with the world of the Imperial Ballet.

The next venture for Diaghilev was a well-received portrait exhibition of Russian art treasures in St. Petersburg in 1905. Fueled by this success, he mounted an exhibition of Russian art in Paris. He followed with a series of Russian music concerts in 1907, and in 1908 a production of the opera *Boris Godunov* starring Feodor Chaliapin. In 1909, Diaghilev planned a second season of Russian opera in Paris but, to save money, he opted to stage a program of ballets and opera excerpts instead.

Diaghilev chose dancer and up-and-coming choreographer Michel Fokine to choreograph the pieces. He supplemented the best of the new generation of dancers from St. Petersburg and Moscow with some of the finest singers from the Imperial Theaters. Members of the *Mir Iskusstva* circle, including Bakst and Benois, designed sets. The 1909 season hooked Paris and assured the success of what was now the Ballets Russes.

Charisma, control, and compassion

The Ballets Russes régisseur Serge Grigoriev described Diaghilev as a tall, solid man, with a large head and interesting face. Diaghilev was phobic about illness and water—a gypsy once told him he would die on the water. He was a dogmatic leader who micromanaged every aspect of the Ballets Russes from checking sets and costumes to choreography, music, and lighting. Diaghilev supported all of the artists, musicians, and writers in his company, and influenced their search for the new and inventive. A short-tempered man, he could also show pity. During the struggling tour of Spain in 1918, he gave his last handful of coins to dancer Lydia Sokolova to buy medicine.

The impresario promoted the careers of male Ballets Russes dancers, whom he

> First of all, I am a great charlatan … second, I'm a great charmer; third, I've great nerve; fourth, I'm a man with a great deal of logic and few principles; and fifth, I think I lack talent; but … I think I've found my real calling—patronage of the arts …

SERGEI DIAGHILEV, 1895

▲ **The Ballets Russes in Seville, Spain, 1916**
Diaghilev (center, with a white streak in his dark hair) surrounded himself with artists, writers, and musicians as well as ballet dancers. He fostered their talents and encouraged them to innovate. The company toured extensively from 1909 to 1929, often relying on wealthy benefactors to keep it afloat.

often took as lovers. These included Vaslav Nijinsky, Léonide Massine, and Serge Lifar. He fired both Nijinsky and Massine after they became involved with women, a scenario retold in the ballet film *The Red Shoes* (1948).

Diaghilev never returned to Russia after World War I and the Russian Revolution. Upon his death in 1929, Russian composer and writer Nicolas Nabokov wrote that Diaghilev died as he lived, "in a hotel room, a homeless adventurer, an exile, and a prince of the arts." His grave in Venice is covered in ballet shoes and other tokens.

KEY WORKS

The Firebird, 1910 • *Petrushka*, 1911 • *The Rite of Spring*, 1913 • *Jeux*, 1913 • *Pulcinella*, 1920
The Sleeping Beauty, 1921 • *Les Noces*, 1923

TIMELINE

- **March 19, 1872** Born in Novgorod, Russia, into a wealthy family. Takes piano lessons and composes.
- **1893** Promotes his love of art and literature by joining a social circle of St. Petersburg intellectuals, and traveling to Europe, visiting Germany, France, and Italy.
- **1896** His studies in St. Petersburg concluded, resolves to establish himself as a patron of the Russian arts.
- **1898** Sets up artistic review *Mir Iskusstva* ("World of Art") as editor-in-chief.
- **1899** Becomes special assistant to Prince Volkonsky, director of Imperial Theaters.
- **1900** Charged by Volkonsky with staging Léo Delibes' ballet *Sylvia*, a controversial production that contributes to ending his association with Imperial Theaters.
- **1906** Moves to Paris, staging exhibitions and concerts that showcase Russian talent.
- **1909** Founds the Ballets Russes in Paris, a company that includes dancers Anna Pavlova, Vaslav Nijinsky, and Michel Fokine.
- **1910** Tours the Ballets Russes widely, taking in Europe, the US, and South America.
- **1916** Takes his company to the Metropolitan Opera in New York.
- **1920** Works with famous artists including Léon Bakst, Joan Miró, Alexandre Benois, and Henri Matisse. Pablo Picasso designs costumes and set for *Pulcinella*.
- **August 19, 1929** Dies at the Hotel des Bains in Venice, Italy, following the end of a rapturously received season at the Covent Garden Theatre, London.

THE RED SHOES (1948) BORROWS ELEMENTS FROM DIAGHILEV'S COLORFUL LIFE

Les Sylphides

First performed: June 2, 1909 ▪ Venue: Théâtre du Châtelet, Paris ▪ Choreography: Michel Fokine ▪ Music: Frédéric Chopin

Les Sylphides is a one-act romantic reverie. It is a plotless work in which a poet dances by moonlight with ethereal winged sylphs in a forest. Fokine set out to recreate the mood of Romanticism, at its height 70 years earlier with Marie Taglioni, and he reworked the piece twice, creating what is regarded as the first abstract ballet. In its first two incarnations, *Les Sylphides* was called *Chopiniana*, and it still goes by this title in Russia.

STORY LINE

Les Sylphides evokes a mood rather than telling a story. The setting is a moonlit woodland glade and the female dancers wear long tulle skirts.

The overture This is Chopin's Prelude op.28, no. 7, and in Russia usually the Polonaise op.40, no. 1. The curtain rises on a symmetrical tableau. The dancers—one ballerina, two female soloists, and a female ensemble—are arranged around the Poet.

Variations There are a series of solos by the first soloist, the ballerina, the Poet, and the second soloist. The Poet and the ballerina dance a pas de deux. The ensemble dances together, returning to the original tableau at the end of the ballet.

It took a while for Fokine to reach the work of 1909 that is still performed today. In 1907, he created a ballet entitled *Chopiniana*, which consisted of a series of divertissements set to the music of Chopin. It was very different from *Les Sylphides* of today, consisting of five short tableaux, each independent of the next. Fokine rechoreographed the ballet the following year, retaining only the waltz pas de deux. This new ballet took Fokine just three days to create, and was designed, not to portray dramatic or acrobatic feats, but to embody true poetry. Fokine was greatly inspired by the ballerinas of the Romantic period, and dressed the female dancers in long Romantic tutus, giving them an ethereal appearance. As he later recalled, "I was surrounded by 23 Taglionis." With no story line or named characters, the ballet veers between reality and dream.

The second *Chopiniana*

The new ballet required a corps de ballet of female dancers, three female soloists, and one male soloist. The male role, danced by Vaslav Nijinsky, was according to Fokine, not a character but "the personification of a poetic vision."

The ballet itself consisted of four variations (performed by each of the soloists), a pas de deux, and two ensemble pieces. It opened at the Mariinsky Theater on March 20, 1908.

Renaming the work

The following year, preparations began in St. Petersburg for the premiere of Sergei Diaghilev's Ballets Russes in Paris. Fokine was employed as choreographer, and proposed including *Chopiniana* in the repertoire. Diaghilev agreed, but renamed the work *Les Sylphides*. It opened as part of the Ballets Russes' first season, in Paris. The four soloist roles were danced by Tamara Karsavina, Anna Pavlova, Alexandra Baldina, and Vaslav Nijinsky. *Les Sylphides* became one of the most popular works in the Ballets Russes repertoire, and was performed regularly by the company. It continues to be performed today by companies around the globe.

Inspired by Pavlova

Anna Pavlova's performance of the waltz pas de deux in Fokine's original version of *Chopiniana* may have been the inspiration for his rework of the ballet. She also danced it in the 1908 version, and again in *Les Sylphides* in 1909.

In 1913, Ivan Clustine, the Pavlova Company's choreographer, created a new version of Fokine's second *Chopiniana* for Pavlova, retaining only the waltz pas de deux. Clustine's *Chopiniana* was successful, and was performed until the company closed in 1931, following Pavlova's death.

▶ **The Ballet Russe de Monte Carlo**
Alexandra Danilova as one of the winged sylphs strikes the note of Romanticism without sentimentality that Fokine strove after.

▼ **Bolshoi Ballet, 1974**
The strong lines and eloquent stillness of the Poet center stage contrast with the billowing gauze of the female ensemble.

THE EXOTIC ORIENT

The Orient, in the late 19th century, referred to present-day Turkey, Greece, the Middle East, and North Africa. The way in which Western cultures imagined these countries and their art and culture became known as Orientalism.

In 1910, Sergei Diaghilev's Ballets Russes premiered the Eastern-inspired ballet *Schéhérazade*. With its exotic theme taken from *One Thousand and One Nights (The Arabian Nights)*, score by Nikolay Rimsky-Korsakov, and choreography by Michel Fokine, the production enraptured the Parisian audience. The most dramatic elements, however, were the exotic set and costumes designed by Léon Bakst. This ballet sparked "*Schéhérazade* fever," and came to personify the Ballets Russes and Orientalism. Turbans and harem pants found their way into the world of fashion and in 1911 French fashion designer Paul Poiret hosted a *Thousand and Second Night* costume party, inspired by *Schéhérazade*.

Before World War I, the Ballets Russes' exotic and Orient-inspired ballets—which included *Cleopatra*, *Thamar*, *Le Dieu Bleu*, and the *Polovtsian Dances from Prince Igor*—were the most popular in their repertoire, and they defined the company for years to come. Fokine choreographed all of these ballets—he did not base his choreography on genuine Oriental dance steps but on the idea of these.

Fokine was not the only choreographer to be inspired by Orientalism. Anna Pavlova had a range of Eastern-themed ballets in her company's repertoire, and American modern dance pioneer Ruth St. Denis made her name by performing a range of Orient-inspired works.

> Perceptions of the East, however artificial and synthetic, produced a genuine revolution.
>
> JOHN M. MACKENZIE, HISTORIAN, 1995

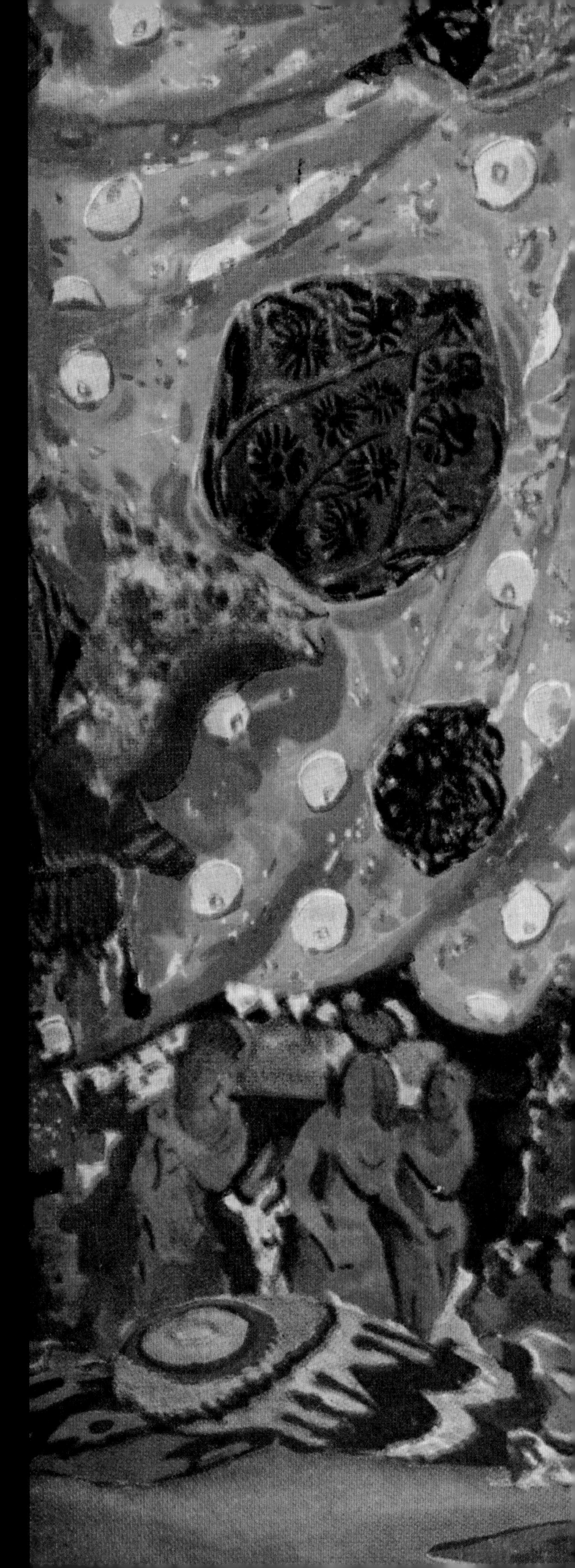

Set design for *Schéhérazade*, 1910 ▶
Russian artist Léon Bakst's bold use of red and emerald green in his design for the set of *Schéhérazade* created a striking backdrop for the Ballets Russes production.

Isadora Duncan

Dancer ▪ 1877–1927

Today, Isadora Duncan is known as much for her turbulent private life and dramatic death as she is for her dancing. However, it was her radical rejection of the formality of theater ballet, naturalistic approach to movement, use of music, and insistence on dance as art rather than mere entertainment that sowed the seeds for many future developments. Although often called the "mother of American modern dance," an epithet also given to Martha Graham, it was in Europe that she found fame.

◀ **The Isadorables**
Isadora Duncan (reclining) poses with pupils from the school she opened in 1904 in Germany. She adopted six of them, dubbed the "Isadorables" in the media.

Dance was in Duncan's genes—by the age of six she was teaching movement to other children in her neighborhood in Oakland, CA, and left school at 10 to earn income from giving classes. Later, as her family moved east, she worked with dance companies in Chicago and New York but disliked theater hierarchy.

To Europe and success

Despite earning extra money by dancing at parties, Duncan sought success and recognition, and so moved to London with her family in 1899. Having long been drawn to the myths and traditions of ancient Greece and its philosophy of freedom, she immersed herself in the collections of the British Museum. These, and the teachings of François Delsarte, who proposed that every outward gesture or posture corresponds to, or expresses, inner emotion, were to provide much inspiration for her dance.

Her London debut was in 1900 as a fairy in Frank Benson's production of *A Midsummer Night's Dream* (coincidentally, her New York debut was in the same role), but it was after solo performances later that year that her career took off. Upon moving to Paris, she initially toured with Loie Fuller's company, Loie Fuller and Her Muses, but went on to dance solo in the cities of Europe. She was a sensation wherever she performed, and her famous encore of *The Blue Danube* during her solo tour in Hungary in 1902 was an audience favorite. Duncan refused to be filmed, saying she preferred to be remembered as a legend. She was not interested in telling stories. Rather, her dance, often partly improvised, was a personal response to the music, which frequently came from composers such as Beethoven (reflected in her performance of *Beethoven's Seventh Symphony* in c. 1905) and Wagner—to the horror of some music critics, who considered them to be above dance accompaniment.

Duncan made the most of her female form, performing without a corset in flowing, revealing, and delicate Grecian-style costumes, usually against voile curtains and under soft lights.

Kindred spirits

While Duncan may have disliked ballet's affected grace and rules, she had a significant impact on classical dance. After seeing her in St. Petersburg, Michel Fokine, seeking a new, expressive style for the Ballets Russes, recalled how, "Duncan reminded us of the beauty of simple movements." Sergei Diaghilev called her a "kindred spirit" and proclaimed that, "We carry the torch that she lit."

Frederick Ashton saw Duncan dance in London in 1921. Although she was well past her prime, her freedom, pliancy, and fusion of music and dance were all to influence his own style. Over 50 years

▶ **Free spirit**
Isadora Duncan danced barefoot, in Grecian-style robes, with her hair down. While acknowledging gravity and the body's weight in her dancing, she was often light and playful, skipping and jumping as if carried by the music.

later, he made *Five Brahms Waltzes in the Manner of Isadora Duncan* (1976)—not a re-creation but a dialogue with her spirit. However, it was Duncan's private life that Kenneth MacMillan chose to focus on five years later in his *Isadora* (1981).

Tale of love and tragedy

A firm feminist, Duncan's liberated sexuality made as many headlines as her dancing. Her lovers included stage designer Gordon Craig (son of the actress Ellen Terry), and sewing-machine millionaire Paris Singer. She had a child by each, but both children were drowned in 1913 when the car they were in rolled into the Seine. Duncan never got over the tragedy.

In MacMillan's ballet *Isadora*, the main character is portrayed by two performers—a dancer, and an actress who speaks the words of Duncan taken from her memoirs (Merle Park and Mary Miller in the original cast). The tragedy of Duncan's children drowning is evoked in a dramatic and moving pas de deux with Paris Singer, first played by Derek Wrencher.

Duncan made headlines to the end. In 1927, sitting in a sports car driven by the man she had eyes on as her next lover, the fringes of her scarf caught in the rear wheel, breaking her neck.

KEY WORKS

The Blue Danube, 1902 • *Parsifal*, c. 1905 *Tristan und Isolde*, c. 1905 • *Beethoven's Seventh Symphony*, c. 1905 • *Dance of the Furies*, 1905 • *Iphigenia in Aulis*, 1917

TIMELINE

- **May 27, 1877** Born in San Francisco, the youngest of four children.
- **1896** Joins Augustin Daly's theater company, performing in Chicago, New York, and London.
- **1899** Sets sail with her family aboard a cattle boat bound for the UK, with an eye to expressing her art in the more receptive climate of Europe.
- **1900** Moves to Paris, studying the Greek vase collection at the Louvre and touring with Loie Fuller before going solo.
- **1902** Performs her own dances to sold-out crowds in Budapest, Hungary.
- **1903** Visits Greece, the homeland of her classical inspiration, purchasing land, and dancing before King George and the Greek royal family.
- **1904** Opens a dance school in Berlin-Grunewald, Germany, tutoring 20 girls.

ISADORA DUNCAN ON THE COVER OF *JUGEND* MAGAZINE, 1904

- **1905** Visits Russia for the first time, dancing before choreographer Michel Fokine and impresario Sergei Diaghilev.
- **1914** Moves back to the US, opening a dance school in New York.
- **July 8, 1927** Performs in public for the last time, at the Mogador Theatre in Paris.
- **September 14, 1927** Dies in a car accident in Nice, France.
- **December 1927** Her autobiography, *My Life*, is published posthumously.

The Firebird

First performed: June 25, 1910 ▪ Venue: Grand Opéra, Paris ▪ Choreography and story: Michel Fokine ▪ Music: Igor Stravinsky

The first Ballets Russes production to feature an original score, *The Firebird* was a turning point for both Diaghilev's fledgling company and its composer, Igor Stravinsky. Based on a traditional Russian folk tale, the choreography, staging, and costumes introduced more realist, less classical, folk-inspired themes to ballet. Since its premiere, the work has been reinvigorated by numerous companies around the world.

STORY LINE

Prince Ivan (Ivan Tsarevich) steals into an enchanted garden where he tries to catch the magical Firebird. The Firebird pleads for her freedom and gives Ivan a feather, promising to protect him if he is ever in need. A group of princesses, bewitched by the Immortal Kostcheï, begins to dance. Ivan falls in love with one of them, Tsarevna, who warns him that every previous rescuer has been turned to stone. A slew of monsters and enchanted characters appear, followed by Kostcheï himself. Ivan brandishes the magical feather and the Firebird appears, forcing the creatures to dance until they fall asleep. Ivan finds an egg that contains Kostcheï's soul and destroys it, breaking the spell and freeing the princesses. The story ends with a wedding procession for Ivan and Tsarevna.

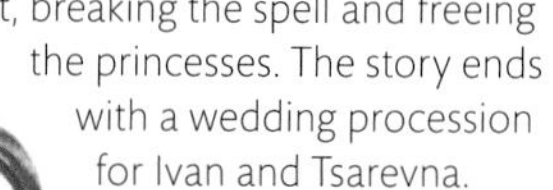

Choreographer Michel Fokine had long wanted to a create a ballet based on the Russian fairytale of the Firebird. He proposed the idea to Sergei Diaghilev, impresario of the Ballets Russes, and the project was agreed. The score for the one-act ballet was composed by the 28-year-old then-unknown Igor Stravinsky, who worked closely with Fokine, the latter miming an intended role while the former played.

The Firebird premiered in 1910 as part of the Ballets Russes' debut season in Paris, with Tamara Karsavina as the Firebird. The ballet continued to be performed throughout the company's existence. It was redesigned by Natalia Goncharova in 1926, and revived by Les Ballets Russes de Monte Carlo in 1934.

▲ **Striking plumage**
The part of the Firebird was created for prima ballerina Tamara Karsavina, who in 1910 wore this bold costume designed by Léon Bakst.

Modern stagings

Artist Marc Chagall designed sets and costumes for a 1945 staging American Ballet Theatre (then Ballet Theatre). With Chagall's modernist designs, the ballet was taken to New York City Ballet in 1949 by George Balanchine, who in 1970 renewed the choreography with Jerome Robbins.

The Royal Ballet (then Sadler's Wells Ballet) based its 1954 production on the 1926 version. The former Ballets Russes ballet master Sergei Grigoriev and his wife Lubov Tchernicheva created the choreography, while Karsavina coached Margot Fonteyn as the Firebird.

Australian Ballet premiered *The Firebird and Other Legends* in 2009, inspired by Les Ballets Russes de Monte Carlo's 1936 tour of Australia. This re-imagining by contemporary choreographer Graeme Murphy featured a lizardlike Kostcheï on a stage littered with large egg shells.

◀ **Incendiary embrace**
Maria Tallchief and Francisco Moncion in a 1964 restaging of Chagall's production of *The Firebird*, choreographed by Balanchine.

▶ **Birdlike poise**
The Firebird, played here by Maria Tallchief, was originally the only part en pointe, but many productions now put the princesses en pointe, too.

> Stravinsky wrote many ballets, but none of them so great as *The Firebird*. In *The Firebird* there is poetry and beauty.
>
> MICHEL FOKINE

Igor Stravinsky

Composer ▪ 1882–1971

One of the most important and influential composers of the 20th century, Russia's Igor Fyodorovich Stravinsky is best known for the many works he created for the ballet. His break came in 1909, when his orchestral piece *Fireworks* was performed at the Academy of Music, St. Petersburg. In the audience was the impresario Sergei Diaghilev, and there followed a meeting that would change Stravinsky's life forever. He collaborated with the Ballets Russes for the next two decades.

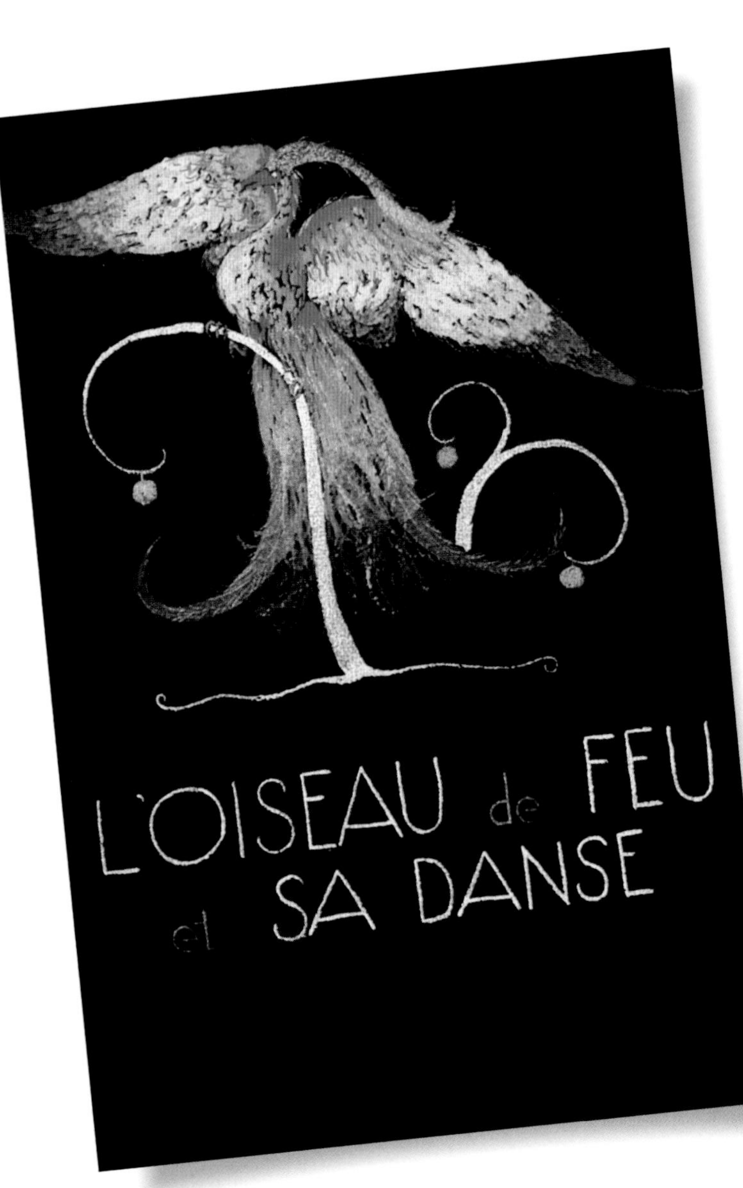

▲ ***The Firebird* program cover, 1926**
Illustrator Edmund Dulac painted this watercolor of the magical glowing bird (*l'oiseau de feu* in French) at the heart of the Russian fairytale that inspired Igor Stravinsky's composition of 1910. The music and ballet, with its fluttering bird dance and striking wedding march at the end, brought Stravinsky immediate recognition.

The son of a famous singer, Stravinsky showed early signs of musical talent and, while at university, took lessons in composition and orchestration with Nikolay Rimsky-Korsakov. The lessons went on until the composer died in 1908.

Stravinsky married his cousin Katherine (Katya) Gavrylivna Nosenko in 1906. The couple had four children: Fyodor, 1907; Ludmila, 1908; Sviatoslav Soulima, 1910; and Marie Milène, 1914.

Working with the Ballets Russes

In 1909, Diaghilev and the Ballets Russes were planning a new ballet based on the Russian fairytale of the Firebird, with choreography by Michel Fokine. Diaghilev had asked Anatoly Liadov to create the score, but the composer had made little progress. Frustrated, Diaghilev decided to commission the unknown 27-year-old Stravinsky, whose piece *Fireworks* had impressed him. *The Firebird*, which premiered in Paris in 1910, was a huge success. The following year, Diaghilev commissioned Stravinsky to compose *Petrushka*, also choreographed by Fokine, and based on the theme of the Russian Shrovetide Fair. In 1913, the Ballets Russes premiered *The Rite of Spring* (*Le Sacre du Printemps*), their most controversial work to date, with Vaslav Nijinsky's avant-garde choreography and Stravinsky's striking contemporary score. It became Stravinsky's most famous work.

The outbreak of World War I, closely followed by the Russian Revolution, made it impossible for Stravinsky to leave France (where he and his family stayed after *The Firebird* premiere) and return to Russia—a country he would not visit again until 1962. Instead, the family moved to Switzerland. Stravinsky continued to work with the Ballets Russes. In 1920, *Pulcinella* and *Le Chant du Rossignol* debuted, choreographed by Leonide Massine. In the same year, *The Rite of Spring* was revived, with financial backing from fashion designer Coco Chanel and new choreography by Massine.

Stravinsky worked with each new Ballets Russes choreographer in turn, and Bronislava Nijinska choreographed both *Renard*, 1922 and *Les Noces*, 1923. In 1925, the young dancer George Balanchine revived *Le Chant du Rossignol* with new choreography. So began one of the most significant choreographer-composer partnerships in modern ballet history.

Forging links with the US

During the 1920s and '30s, Stravinsky and his family returned to France and became French citizens in 1934. By now, Balanchine had moved to the US and, in 1937, Stravinsky composed *Card Game* and reworked *The Fairy's Kiss* of 1928 for Balanchine's company American Ballet.

Stravinsky's eldest daughter and wife tragically died just three months apart from tuberculosis in 1938–1939, followed by his mother shortly after. Stravinsky left for the US at the end of 1939, and there married Vera de Bosset. The couple had met through the Ballets Russes in 1921.

Once in the US, Stravinsky again collaborated with Balanchine. In 1942, they created *Circus Polka* for Ringling Brothers and Barnum & Bailey Circus. The work included 50 elephants and 50 ballerinas. In 1947, the two created *Orpheus* for Ballet Society and, 10 years later, *Agon* for New York City Ballet. After Stravinsky's death in 1971, Balanchine continued to use the composer's music for his creations.

▲ **Great minds: composer and impresario** Igor Stravinsky (left) and Sergei Diaghilev meet at Croydon Airport, UK, in 1926. The last ballet Stravinsky composed for Diaghilev and the Ballets Russes was *Apollo (Apollon Musagète)*, choreographed in 1928 by George Balanchine.

KEY WORKS

The Firebird, 1910 • *Petrushka*, 1911 • *The Rite of Spring*, 1913
Le Chant du Rossignol, 1914 • *The Wedding*, 1923 • *Apollo (Apollon Musagète)*, 1928 • *Agon*, 1957

TIMELINE

- **June 5, 1882** Born in a suburb of St. Petersburg, the son of celebrated operatic bass singer Fyodor.
- **1901** Despite his clear musical promise, enrolls at St. Petersburg University, studying law and philosophy.
- **1902** Becomes a pupil of composer Nikolay Rimsky-Korsakov, the father of a fellow law student.
- **1908** St. Petersburg Court Orchestra plays his *Symphony in E-flat Major* and *The Faun and the Shepherdess*, the first time his work is heard in public.
- **February 1909** Brought to the attention of impresario Sergei Diaghilev, heralding a long association with the Ballets Russes.
- **June 25, 1910** *The Firebird*, a full-length ballet commissioned by Diaghilev, debuts in Paris, announcing Stravinsky's arrival as a prodigiously talented young composer.

REHEARSING *THE FIREBIRD*: STRAVINSKY SEATED, FOKINE LEANING AGAINST PIANO, 1910

- **May 29, 1913** *The Rite of Spring* premieres at Théâtre des Champs Élysées, Paris, sparking rioting in the audience.
- **1914** Settles with his family in Switzerland due to the outbreak of war.
- **1920** Takes up residence in France, having lost all of his property in his native land following the Russian Revolution.
- **1928** Finishes *The Fairy's Kiss* for the Ballets Russes, based on the music of Tchaikovsky.
- **1939** Moves to the US after the deaths of his daughter, wife, and mother.
- **1940** Marries his long-term mistress, Vera de Bosset, who had been a character dancer with the Ballets Russes.
- **April 6, 1971** Dies of heart failure in New York.

Le Spectre de la rose

First performed: April 19, 1911 ▪ Venue: Théâtre de Monte Carlo ▪ Choreography: Michel Fokine ▪ Music: Carl Maria von Weber ▪ Story: Jean-Louis Vaudoyer

With its use of truly expressive dances, rather than combinations of established steps, Michel Fokine saw his work as part of the canon of new ballet. Vaslav Nijinsky's dramatic leap through a window as the character of the Rose made the ballet world-famous as well as making the role a defining one in Nijinsky's career. The ballet was also remarkable for Rudolph Nureyev, being the first he danced after defecting to the West, and one of his last with Margot Fonteyn.

STORY LINE

A young girl returns home with a rose after attending her first ball. She sinks into a chair and falls asleep. The Spirit of the Rose appears at the window. He dances around the sleeping Young Girl before dancing with her. The girl, still asleep, dances with her eyes closed. As suddenly as he arrived, the Rose leaps through an open window and vanishes. The Young Girl awakes and picks up her dropped rose from the floor.

At just 11 minutes long, *Le Spectre de la Rose* was one of the shortest ballets in the Ballets Russes repertoire, and one of its most popular. The idea for the piece came from French writer Jean-Louis Vaudoyer, who wrote to the company suggesting a ballet based on a poem by Théophile Gautier, set to Weber's *Invitation à la valse.* Diaghilev commissioned Fokine to create the choreography and Léon Bakst the design.

The ballet, a pas de deux, opened in Monte Carlo, with Vaslav Nijinsky as the Rose, and Tamara Karsavina as the Young Girl. It became one of Nijinsky's most famous roles due to his magnificent exit leap through a window—allegedly caught on the other side by stagehands.

For his role Nijinsky wore a silk jersey bodysuit, sewn with silk rose petals that often fell off. His servant, Vasili, is said to have collected the petals to sell to fans, and built his house, Le Château du Spectre de la Rose, from the proceeds.

The ballet was first revived in 1935 by Les Ballets Russes de Monte Carlo, with Irina Baronova and Paul Petrov. Other notable performances include Fokine's 1941 production with the Ballet Theatre company, New York—the last before his death—which opened at the Palacio de Bellas Artes in Mexico City, and went to New York the same year. In 1997, an extract of the ballet was adapted for an American Ballet Theatre gala, performed by Ukrainian Vladimir Malakhov, and 75-year-old Cuban ballerina, Alicia Alonso.

▲ **Ballets Russes poster, 1911**
Depicting Tamara Karasavina as the Young Girl, this poster advertises *Le Spectre de la rose* at Théâtre du Châtelet in Paris.

◀ **Nijinsky and Karsavina**
Few dancers ever achieved the magnificence of Nijinsky's performance as the Rose, because the role was created and the dances choreographed with his unique talents in mind.

▶ **Russian revival**
Performing at the London Coliseum, Russian Yuliya Makhalina and British Xander Parish dance as the Young Girl and the Rose for the Kremlin Ballet in 2013.

> I choreographed it very rapidly, for it was almost an improvisation—and yet, like the rest of my best works, I never altered it.
>
> MICHEL FOKINE

Petrushka

First performed: June 13, 1911 ▪ Venue: Théâtre du Châtelet, Paris ▪ Choreography: Michel Fokine ▪ Music: Stravinsky ▪ Story: Stravinsky and Alexandre Benois

In 1911, Sergei Diaghilev's Ballets Russes premiered their most Russian work to date. A one-act ballet in four scenes, *Petrushka* is based on the iconic Russian fairground puppet that Stravinsky dubbed "the immortal and unhappy hero of every fair in all countries." Set in St. Petersburg during the Butter Week Fair of the 1830s, a week of celebrations prior to the beginning of the Christian tradition of Lent, *Petrushka* is packed full of nostalgia.

STORY LINE

Scene 1 In St. Petersburg the fair is underway. The Charlatan brings three puppets to life: a Ballerina, Petrushka, and a Moor.

Scene 2 Locked in his cell, Petrushka is in despair over his fear of the Charlatan and his unrequited love for the Ballerina. She enters, but Petrushka scares her and she leaves.

Scene 3 The Ballerina goes to the cell of her lover, the Moor. Petrushka interrupts them and is chased away by the Moor.

Scene 4 At the fair, the Moor catches and kills Petrushka.

A masterpiece of design, composition, and choreography, the tragic tale of *Petrushka* features a dramatic, discordant score by Stravinsky, and set and costumes filled with Russian references by Alexandre Benois, who, together with Stravinsky, wrote the libretto. In his design, Benois tried to recreate a fairground atmosphere, with large crowds of supers (costumed extras) and props, such as merry-go-rounds, swings, and booths. Benois later recalled, "Petrushka, the Russian Guignol, or Punch, no less than Harlequin, has been my friend since my earliest childhood … I immediately had the feeling that it was a duty I owed to my old friend to immortalize him on the real stage."

Playing the puppet

Fokine created the role of the Ballerina for Tamara Karsavina, the Moor for Alexander Orlov, and Petrushka for Vaslav Nijinsky. The puppet master or Charlatan was danced by Enrico Cecchetti. Petrushka became an iconic role for Nijinsky, showcasing his skills as both a dancer and actor, and drawing many other male dancers to the ballet, including Rudolf Nureyev, who went on to perform many of Nijinsky's ballets. Nureyev first danced the role of Petrushka in 1963 with The Royal Ballet in London, and continued to perform it throughout his career to great acclaim and all over the world.

▲ **Clash of chords**
This page is from the second draft of Igor Stravinsky's score for the ballet *Petrushka*. Allegedly, when the orchestra first saw the score, they laughed, thinking it was a joke.

▲ **Made for the part**
Renowned beauty Tamara Karsavina, a principal artist of the Ballets Russes, danced the role of the Ballerina in the 1911 premiere.

▶ **Off to the fair**
This costume sketch for *Petrushka* shows the Court Coachman. Benois' designs were inspired by the fairs he had been to as a child.

L'Après-midi d'un faune

First performed: May 29, 1912 ▪ Venue: Théâtre du Châtelet, Paris ▪ Choreography: Nijinsky ▪ Music: Debussy ▪ Story: Jean Cocteau and Stéphane Mallarmé

The first ballet that Russian dancer Vaslav Nijinsky choreographed, *L'Après-midi d'un faune's* groundbreaking style of choreography led to mixed reactions from audiences when it premiered as part of the Ballets Russes 1912 season. However, the approximately ten-minute work is now considered to be a turning point in choreographic history, and it has continued to be revived and performed by ballet companies around the globe.

STORY LINE

L'Après-midi d'un faune is a choreographic tableau in one act. The ballet opens with the faun seated on a rock. Six nymphs enter, followed by the senior nymph. They have come to bathe in the stream. The senior nymph takes off some layers of her costume, assisted by the nymphs. The faun, intrigued and entranced, comes down from his rock. He scares the other nymphs away and tries to interact with the senior nymph, but eventually she, too, flees from the amorous faun, dropping her scarf as she runs. The faun takes the scarf back to his lair where he lovingly caresses it before the ballet ends in an erotic final tableau.

The ballet was set to the symphonic poem, *Prélude à l'après-midi d'un faune*, by Claude Debussy. Written in 1894, Debussy's work was based on a poem by Stéphane Mallarmé, which portrays a faun's encounter with a group of nymphs.

Nijinsky's challenging choreography for *L'Après-midi d'un faune* evoked ancient Greek vase paintings, and was performed as if the dancers were flattened and moving in slots across the stage. Set and costume designer Léon Bakst echoed this two-dimensional style in the design of the costumes, particularly in the geometric patterning and shape of the nymphs' silk dresses.

Controversial but inspiring

Audience reactions were mixed due to the radical choreography and sexual undertones, but this did not stop the ballet being a success. Serge Grigoriev recalled, "Our other first nights had been rather dull; but on this occasion the audience were electrified from the start. The ballet was watched with intense interest, and at the end one half of the spectators broke into frantic applause, and the other into equally frantic protests."

In 1953, dancer and choreographer Jerome Robbins created a new version of the ballet, set to Debussy's score and entitled *Afternoon of the Faun*. The resulting pas de deux, set in a dance studio, was premiered by New York City Ballet.

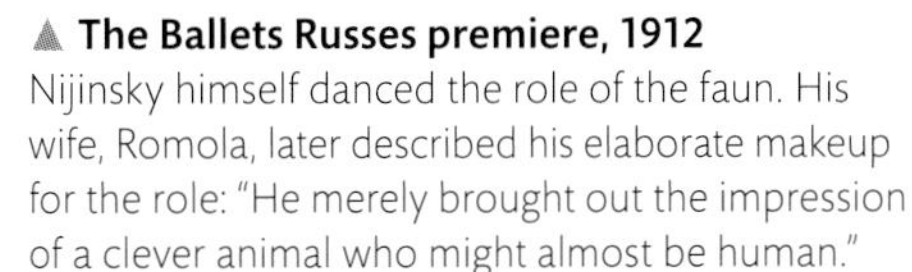

▲ **The Ballets Russes premiere, 1912**
Nijinsky himself danced the role of the faun. His wife, Romola, later described his elaborate makeup for the role: "He merely brought out the impression of a clever animal who might almost be human."

◄ **Setting the scene**
L'Après-midi d'un faune was designed by Léon Bakst—his second ballet based on a Greek theme. The nymphs wore long wigs of twisted golden rope and Grecian-style sandals, not ballet shoes.

Vaslav Nijinsky

Dancer and choreographer ▪ 1889–1950

One of the most celebrated male ballet dancers of all time, Nijinsky's talent was obvious from an early age. With his strength and lightness, his incredible leaps, and his ability to appear to float on air, he was soon trumpeted as the "eighth wonder of the world." All was not well, however. What at first appeared to be fidgety nervous tension gradually revealed itself to be a serious mental health condition that robbed Nijinsky of his career, and ballet lovers of a remarkable dancer.

▲ **Design for faun costume**
This illustration by Léon Bakst depicts Nijinsky's costume for his role as The Faun in Ballet Russes's 1912 production of *L'Après-midi d'un faune*. It was published in *L'Art Decoraif de Léon Bakst*, 1913.

The son of celebrated dancers Thomas Nijinsky and Eleonora Bereda, dance was in Nijinsky's blood. At the age of nine, he was accepted into the Imperial Ballet School in St. Petersburg, and after graduating, he joined the Imperial Ballet Company. By this time his balletic talents, including his phenomenal leaps, had already been noticed and praised.

The Ballets Russes

In 1909, Nijinsky joined Sergei Diaghilev's premiere season of the Ballets Russes in Paris, making him a household name. He was made principal dancer of the Ballets Russes and left the Imperial Ballet. He worked closely with the company's choreographer Michel Fokine, creating roles in ballets such as *Le Carnaval*, *Les Sylphides*, and *Petrushka*. But even in these early years he showed signs of the mental illness that would consume him, such as delusions and disorganized behavior.

Nijinsky the choreographer

Diaghilev had encouraged Nijinsky to experiment in choreography, and in 1912 he starred in his first work, *L'Après-midi d'un faune*. The ballet took the form of an animated Greek frieze, with movements conducted in profile to the dreamlike music of Debussy. Although only around ten minutes long, it represented the birth of a new style of experimental productions in the Ballets Russes repertoire.

However, this shift of focus and Nijinsky's growing interest in choreography caused friction with Diaghilev's resident choreographer, Fokine. During the company's London season, Fokine resigned, and Nijinsky became both principal dancer and choreographer. In 1913, the company premiered Nijinsky's works, *Jeux* and *Le Sacre du Printemps*. Nijinsky's unconventional, even shocking, choreography had by now become the foundations of modern ballet.

Marriage and the Great War

Later the same year, the Ballets Russes left Europe to tour South America, taking with them a young Hungarian socialite, Romola de Pulszky, who had been having classes with the company. During the trip an unlikely friendship emerged between her and Nijinsky. Their engagement was announced two weeks later and they married in Buenos Aires. Upon hearing this, Diaghilev dismissed Nijinsky from the company. The following year Romola gave birth to a daughter, Kyra, and in 1920 their second daughter Tamara was born.

At the outbreak of World War I, Nijinsky was interned in Hungary and placed under house arrest. In 1916, Diaghilev, with the assistance of the king of Spain, secured his release on the premise that he would join the company's tour of North America. Once in New York, members of the company noticed a change in Nijinsky, who was now hostile and suspicious of everybody. It was on this tour that Nijinsky choreographed his last ballet, *Till Eulenspiegel*. The work was not a success, and was the only piece produced for the Ballets Russes that Diaghilev never saw, as he had stayed in Europe.

In 1917, he danced with the Ballets Russes for the last time in his most famous roles, *Le Spectre de la rose* and *Petrushka*. His behavior was increasingly erratic, and upon retiring to Switzerland, he was diagnosed with schizophrenia. He spent the rest of his life in psychiatric hospitals in Switzerland, France, and the UK.

Nijinsky's triumph
Here, Nijinsky is dressed as the Rose from the 1911 ballet, *Le Spectre de la rose*. It was one of his most famous roles, in which he performed a magnificent leap at the end of the ballet, and one of the last roles he ever danced.

His feats in dancing border on the miraculous, he hardly seems to touch the stage … supported by invisible wings.

DAILY NEWS CRITIC, JUNE 22, 1911

KEY WORKS

Dancer: The Poet, *Les Sylphides*, 1909 • The Golden Slave, *Schéhérazade*, 1910 • The Rose, *Le Spectre de la rose*, 1911 • Title role, *Petrushka*, 1911 • The Faun, *L' Après-midi d'un faune*, 1912 Choreographer: *Jeux*, 1913 • *Le Sacre du Printemps*, 1913 • *Till Eulenspiegel*, 1916

TIMELINE

- **March 12, 1889** Born in Kiev, Russia, to Polish dancers Thomas Nijinsky and Eleonora Bereda.
- **1907** Joins the Imperial Ballet Company at 18. He is immediately chosen by the company's foremost ballerina as her partner.
- **1908** Introduced to Sergei Diaghilev, who invites him to join the Ballet Russes for its first Paris season a year later.
- **1909** Acclaimed as "a god of dance" by Parisian audiences at the spectacular premiere season of the Ballet Russes.

NIJINSKY PERFORMING IN *THE RITE OF SPRING* FOR THE BALLETS RUSSES, 1913

- **1912** Choreographs his first ballet, *L' Après-midi d'un faune*, becoming the Ballets Russes' principal choreographer a year later.
- **September 10, 1913** Marries Romola de Pulszky while on tour with the Ballet Russes.
- **March 1914** After being dismissed by Diaghilev, attempts to form his own ballet company for a billing at the Palace Theatre in London, but the show is cancelled after only two weeks.
- **1916** Rejoins the Ballets Russes to dance a season at the Metropolitan Opera in New York, and then directs a subsequent US tour that proves a financial disaster.
- **1917** Dances for the last time with the Ballet Russes on a South American tour. Then moves to Switzerland with his family.
- **1919** Diagnosed with schizophrenia in Zurich by Swiss psychiatrist Eugen Bleuler.
- **April 8, 1950** Dies in London, after almost 30 years in various psychiatric hospitals.

RETURN OF THE DANSEUR

The French term "danseur" goes back to the early days of ballet when all professional dancers were male. The term is not used today in English, except to describe a particular type of dancer such as a danseur noble (principal dancer) or danseur caractère. The Baroque male danseurs were the stars of the stage, but with the arrival of Romantic ballet in the mid-19th century, they became secondary to the ballerina: when women rose en pointe, men shuffled off the stage. It eventually became difficult to recruit men to become simply the supporters and porters of women, roles that stagehands instead fulfilled.

It was Vaslav Nijinsky's breathtaking jumps, which audiences were introduced to when Diaghilev brought the Ballets Russes to Europe in the early 20th century, that helped propel the male dancer back to center stage. When Rudolf Nureyev started dancing with The Royal Ballet in 1962, he completely changed the role of the male dancer. Nureyev's presence on stage was electrifying and his ambitious technique added excitement to every performance. The male dancer was no longer limited to supporting the female dancer, and became a star once again.

Other great male dancers followed, including Mikhail Baryshnikov, Anthony Dowell, and Vladimir Vasiliev, who raised the standard for all male dancers and helped to change the stigma attached to men building dance careers. At the start of the 21st century, the film *Billy Elliot* (2000)– about a poor boy who wanted to dance against all the prejudice he encountered–led to what is known as the "Billy Elliot effect" when, in 2002, The Royal Ballet Junior School admitted more boys than girls for the first time in its history. This "effect" continues today.

> From the depths of the stage with a single leap, assemblé, entrechat-dix, he flies toward the first wing.
>
> BRONISLAVA NIJINSKA DESCRIBING HER BROTHER NIJINKSY

The rise of the male star ▶

The Rite of Spring

First performed: May 29, 1913 ▪ Venue: Théâtre des Champs-Elysées, Paris ▪ Choreography: Nijinsky ▪ Music: Stravinsky ▪ Story: Stravinsky and Roerich

The third ballet composed by Stravinsky and the third choreographed by Nijinsky, *The Rite of Spring* serves to illustrate that the third time is not always lucky. While it was designed to be experimental, such was the audience's adverse reaction to the discordant score and startling choreography that a riot broke out during its premiere in Paris. Now more widely appreciated and understood, the ballet has been revised more times than any other.

IN CONTEXT

The "riot at the Rite" has become known as the most scandalous event in the history of the arts, creating a mythology bigger than the ballet itself.

Although the ballet was shocking to the audience, especially Stravinsky's challenging score, the trigger for the riot may lie in the politics of Paris at the time. Even before the ballet started, there was animosity between Bohemian members of the audience in the stalls and the wealthy theater-goers in their boxes. There was also an anti-Russian sentiment circulating the city at the time, which may have made this apparent celebration of ancient Russian culture an obvious target to disrupt.

Commissioned by Sergei Diaghilev for the Ballets Russes, the idea behind *The Rite of Spring* came from Stravinsky, who wanted to produce a ballet based on pagan rituals. Nijinsky, then aged 21, was engaged to produce the choreography, and readily took the opportunity to experiment with different styles and movements. To help Nijinsky interpret the complex rhythms of Stravinsky's score, Diaghilev hired Marie Rambert, who was trained in the use of Dalcroze eurhythmics—a concept of rhythm, structure, and musical expression through movement.

Nijinsky also collaborated closely with Nicholas Roerich, the leading expert on prehistoric Russia, who designed the set and costumes to be as historically accurate as possible. These in turn inspired Nijinsky's choreography, with its hunched, almost pre-human movements.

▲ **Authentic revival**
Maia Wilkins dances as The Chosen One in the Joffrey Ballet's 2003 production, featuring Hodson and Archer's reconstructed Nijinsky choreography.

The infamous night

When the ballet premiered in Paris, Stravinsky's score, coupled with Roerich's primitive designs and Nijinsky's avant-garde choreography (in which the dancers adopted a pigeon-toed foot position), seem to have been an overwhelming combination for the audience.

▲ **The Chosen One**
Terese Capucilli took the principal role in Martha Graham's 1984 production—a part which was choreographed especially for Graham's protégé.

Régisseur of the Ballets Russes Serge Grigoriev recalled the opening night vividly in his memoirs: "The audience began shouting its indignation; on which the rest retaliated with loud appeals for order … the hubbub soon became deafening; but the dancers went on, and so did the orchestra, though scarcely a note of the music could be heard … [then] actual fighting broke out among some of the spectators."

Lasting legacy

The ballet was performed just eight times before being dropped. However, while little is known about the original choreography, such is the reputation of *The Rite of Spring* that it has come to be seen as a rite of passage by many choreographers. It is now one of the most reenacted works of the 20th century—the score was even used in Walt Disney's *Fantasia* (1940).

The Rite of Spring was first revised in 1920, when Léonide Massine was commissioned to rechoreograph it for the Ballets Russes. It opened in the US with Martha Graham as The Chosen One. In 1962, British choreographer Kenneth MacMillan created his version for The Royal Ballet. In his research, he drew from the traditional dance forms of the Philippines, Haiti, Guinea, and Senegal to find a "primitive" theme that would resonate with modern audiences. The theme was also reflected in the costumes and set, for which Australian artist, Sydney Nolan, set the work in "a nightmarish vision of Aboriginal Australia."

German contemporary choreographer, Pina Bausch, tackled *The Rite of Spring* in her production in 1975. Though not using the original libretto, the work retained the order of scenes and the concept of a "chosen one," and was performed on a stage covered with earth.

In 1984, at the age of 90, modern dance pioneer Martha Graham produced her re-imagining for the Martha Graham Dance Company. Then, three years later, historians Millicent Hodson and Kenneth Archer created a version using Nijinsky's "original" 1913 choreography.

Their reconstruction was the result of extensive archival research based on a wide range of sources, including annotated scores by Stravinsky and Rambert, and 70 sketches made by artist Valentine Gross during the first performances. Since 1987, the work has toured around the world, and has been restaged by at least nine international ballet companies.

> Exactly what I wanted.
>
> SERGEI DIAGHILEV'S RESPONSE AFTER THE APPARENT FIASCO OF THE OPENING NIGHT

Léonide Massine (1896–1979)

Seven years after the controversial opening of *The Rite of Spring*, Diaghilev wanted to revive the ballet. As there was no record of Nijinsky's original choreography, his young protégé, Léonide Massine, and Stravinsky began afresh. This 1920 version was well received, partly because it was accompanied by two similar works, *Petrushka* and *Le Tricorne*, which better suited Stravinsky's score.

▶ **Prehistoric design**
Roerich's richly colored costumes, which he designed based on his own historical research, were recreated for this production by the Kirov Ballet at the Royal Opera House, London, in 2013.

STORY LINE The Rite of Spring

There is no actual story line to *The Rite of Spring*—instead it depicts a prehistoric pagan ritual whereby a young virgin is selected and sacrificed by her village to thank the sun god, Yarilo. The ballet is divided into two parts. In the first, The Adoration of the Earth, two rival tribes perform a series of ritualistic dances before The Sage, or The Wise Elder, enters and kisses the earth, indicating that spring has broken. In the second part, The Sacrifice, the tribe prepares to sacrifice a virgin. A girl is selected by fate to become The Chosen One. The tribe encircles her and she dances in an increasingly frantic and vicious scene, until she falls exhausted and dies. The sacrificial rite is complete.

ROERICH'S ORIGINAL 1913 COSTUMES FOR THE BALLET INCLUDED HEAVY WOOLEN LEGGINGS AND RICHLY PAINTED SMOCKS

ACT I

PLOT OVERVIEW

VALENTINA FORMANTI ENTERS AS THE HAG, ENGLISH NATIONAL BALLET, 2009

The Hag enters the stage, usually carrying sticks.

The Sage teaches the secrets of the earth to villagers, who dance in celebration of spring.

Girls enter in single file. The villagers enact a mock abduction to honor Yarilo.

The villagers prepare to welcome The Sage.

The Sage processes onto the stage.

The Sage kneels and blesses the earth by kissing the ground. Spring has broken.

THE SAGE ENTERS, PERFORMED BY FABULOUS BEAST DANCE THEATRE, THE COLISEUM, LONDON, 2009

THE DANCES

The Augurs of Spring: The tribes dance in circles, while The Hag appears to teach them.

Ritual of Abduction: The girls dance as a group and are chased by the villagers.

Spring Rounds: The tribes and the girls form into groups and dance in circles.

Ritual of the Rival Tribes: The tribes dance as groups, forming parallel lines facing each other.

Procession of The Sage: The villagers stop dancing and escort The Sage to their midst.

Dance of the Earth: The villagers dance wildly around The Sage in celebration.

TEATRO DELL'OPERA DI ROMA PERFORMS THE AUGURS OF SPRING IN MOSCOW IN 2003

DANCERS OF THE ENGLISH NATIONAL BALLET PERFORM RITUAL OF THE RIVAL TRIBES IN MACMILLAN'S 2012 PRODUCTION

PINA BAUSCH'S PRODUCTION ON A SOIL-COVERED STAGE IN 2008

MARIA MARTA COLUSI REHEARSES THE SACRIFICIAL DANCE WITH BERLIN-BASED DANCE TROUPE, SASHA WALTZ AND GUESTS, 2015

ACT II

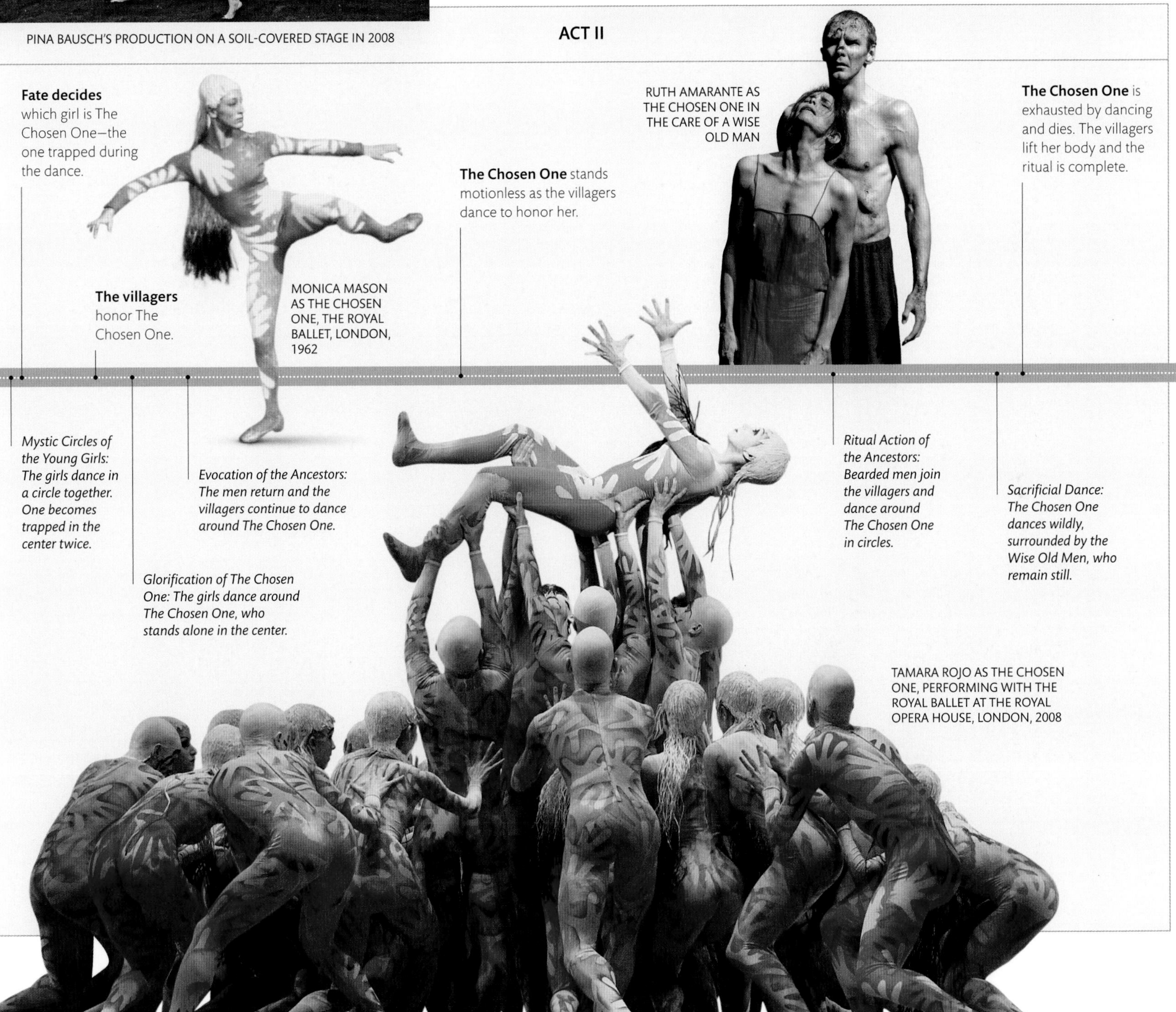

Fate decides which girl is The Chosen One—the one trapped during the dance.

The villagers honor The Chosen One.

MONICA MASON AS THE CHOSEN ONE, THE ROYAL BALLET, LONDON, 1962

The Chosen One stands motionless as the villagers dance to honor her.

RUTH AMARANTE AS THE CHOSEN ONE IN THE CARE OF A WISE OLD MAN

The Chosen One is exhausted by dancing and dies. The villagers lift her body and the ritual is complete.

Mystic Circles of the Young Girls: The girls dance in a circle together. One becomes trapped in the center twice.

Glorification of The Chosen One: The girls dance around The Chosen One, who stands alone in the center.

Evocation of the Ancestors: The men return and the villagers continue to dance around The Chosen One.

Ritual Action of the Ancestors: Bearded men join the villagers and dance around The Chosen One in circles.

Sacrificial Dance: The Chosen One dances wildly, surrounded by the Wise Old Men, who remain still.

TAMARA ROJO AS THE CHOSEN ONE, PERFORMING WITH THE ROYAL BALLET AT THE ROYAL OPERA HOUSE, LONDON, 2008

The Royal Ballet, 2008
Australian dancer Steven McRae performs as The Chosen One—a role usually danced by a female—in Kenneth MacMillan's unsettling and other-worldly production of *The Rite of Spring* at the Royal Opera House, London.

Marie Rambert

Producer and teacher ▪ 1888–1982

Originally from Poland, Marie Rambert moved to London in 1914, where she became a pioneering figure of British ballet in the 1930s. She is credited with discovering choreographers Frederick Ashton and Antony Tudor, and founded today's Rambert Dance Company, the oldest British dance company still performing. She was also known for her unstoppable energy, which saw her performing cartwheels in public until the age of 70, when her concerned husband finally persuaded her to stop.

▲ **Dance rehearsals, 1950**
Marie Rambert is seen here leading rehearsals in Paris alongside dancers of Ballet Rambert Sally Gilmour and Margaret Hill. Gilmour was the company's leading dancer during the 1940s, and was often compared to Margot Fonteyn.

The daughter of a bookseller, Marie Rambert was born Cyvia Rambam into a middle-class family in Warsaw in 1888. As a child, she was extremely active and energetic, which led her nurse to give her the nickname "quicksilver."

Already the star pupil in school dance classes, it was a performance by Isadora Duncan in Warsaw in 1904 that inspired her to pursue a career in dance. However, her increasingly rebellious attitude toward politics led her parents to send her to study medicine in Paris. There, she began to earn money dancing in salons, adopting the name Myriam.

Studying eurhythmics

In 1909, Rambert met the Swiss composer Émile Jaques-Dalcroze, who had developed eurhythmics—a form of musical education that focuses on understanding rhythm through body movements. Having joined his school in 1910, she was then invited by Sergei Diaghilev to teach eurhythmics at the Ballets Russes two years later.

Rambert stayed with the company for less than a year, but it influenced her greatly. There, she worked with Vaslav Nijinsky, advising him in the interpretation of Stravinsky's *The Rite of Spring*. She also studied under Enrico Cecchetti, and danced in the corps de ballet.

With the outbreak of World War I, Rambert moved to London in 1914 and changed her name to Marie Rambert—"Mim" to her closest friends—where she taught ballet and eurhythmics privately. In 1918, she married British playwright Ashley Dukes and opened her dance school two years later.

Pioneering British ballet

As a dance teacher, Rambert's classes were often unruly, mainly due to her histrionics—prone to hysterical tantrums, she would scream insults. However, she was also known to be a warm person, who connected emotionally with her pupils. Most understood that her approach only reflected her passion for theatrical performances. More importantly, Rambert had an extraordinary gift for spotting new talent, and saw a successful choreographer in one of her pupils, Frederick Ashton. In 1926, Rambert produced Ashton's first choreographical work, *A Tragedy of Fashion*.

In 1928, Dukes bought a church hall in Notting Hill, London, and converted it into an 150-seat theater, where Rambert established the Ballet Club, the UK's first dance company. Named the Mercury Theatre (a nod to Rambert's childhood nickname), it soon became a center for experimental new works, including the first performance of Antony Tudor's psychological ballet *Jardin aux lilas* (1936).

In addition to Ashton, other members included choreographers Frank Staff and Andrée Howard, dancers Alicia Markova and Pearl Argyle, and designers William Chappell and Sophie Fedorovitch. The company was renamed Ballet Rambert in 1935 and became a full-time touring company during World War II.

In 1966, Rambert and her associate director, Norman Morris, decided to focus purely on contemporary dance. Today, it is one of the most acclaimed modern dance companies in the world.

Although people complained about her … what she wanted to do was to present the dancer to the public in the best light.

JOHN WEBLEY, BALLET RAMBERT ADMINISTRATOR, 2016

▲ **A class of her own**
While Rambert herself was trained under the highly disciplined Cecchetti method, as a teacher, the classes she held were less structured. Nonetheless, she achieved results, and many of her pupils became long-standing friends.

KEY WORKS

The Rite of Spring, 1913 • *A Tragedy of Fashion*, 1926 • *Jardin aux Lilas*, 1936 • *Dark Elegies*, 1937 • *Judgment of Paris*, 1938 *Lady into Fox*, 1939 • *Two Brothers*, 1958

TIMELINE

- **February 20, 1888** Born Cyvia Rambam in Warsaw, Poland, one of six children of Yokav Ramberg and Yevgeniya Alapina.
- **1904** After seeing Isadora Duncan dance in Warsaw, resolves to become a dancer.
- **1905** Sent to Paris to study medicine by her parents after participating in the Polish uprising against the Czar.
- **1906** Too young to enroll in medical college, instead studies for a *Certificat d'études Français* at the Sorbonne.
- **1910** Learns eurhythmics from Émile Jaques-Dalcroze at a school in Geneva.
- **1912** Begins working for Sergei Diaghilev at the Ballets Russes.

RAMBERT POSES IN COSTUME FOR A RECITAL IN PARIS, c.1909

- **1914** Moves to London after the outbreak of World War I.
- **1918** Marries playwright Ashley Dukes and becomes a British citizen.
- **1920** Opens a ballet school in Kensington, London.
- **1926** Produces *A Tragedy of Fashion*, choreographed by Frederick Ashton.
- **1930** Establishes the Ballet Club (renamed Ballet Rambert in 1935), based at her husband's Mercury Theatre.
- **1962** Awarded Dame of the Order of the British Empire.
- **1966** Transforms Ballet Rambert into a contemporary dance company.
- **June 12, 1982** Dies at home in London.

Parade

First performed: May 18, 1917 ▪ Venue: Théâtre du Châtelet, Paris ▪ Choreography: Léonide Massine ▪ Music: Eric Satie ▪ Story: Jean Cocteau

Acclaimed and derided in equal measure following its Paris premiere, *Parade* courted controversy. With its use of everyday sounds, movements, and settings, it snubbed familiar elitist ballet expectations, instead referencing more popular art forms, including silent films. It is particularly noted for the set and costume designs by Pablo Picasso, and was an exciting collaboration between some of the leading minds of the early 20th century.

STORY LINE

A ballet in one act

Parade depicts a group of musical hall managers and the artists they represent, trying to attract attention for their show by performing on the street outside the theater. The French Manager introduces the Chinese Conjurer, the American Manager introduces the Little American Girl, and finally a horse—originally intended to have a papier-mâché British Manager on its back—introduces the two acrobats.

Inspired by a mix of vaudeville, circus, and music hall, *Parade* was momentous for several reasons. Firstly, the score by Satie included the sounds of a typewriter, pistol shots, sirens, and a fog horn among other commonplace noises. Secondly, Massine's choreography took in everyday moves and steps from popular dance culture and acrobatics alongside classical ballet. Lastly, the Cubist set and costume designs by Pablo Picasso included Managers' costumes 10 ft (3 m) tall. These were constructed from cardboard and contained elements of skyscrapers, staircases, and balconies, with only the semblance of a human outline.

Parade was also the first Ballets Russes production to include a stage curtain—a specially designed drop cloth hung before the performance. Designed and finished by Picasso, it depicted a group of circus performers and a winged horse. This was Picasso's first of many collaborations with ballet productions.

Public reaction

The ballet opened in Paris in May 1917 and divided the critics. Poet Guillaume Apollinaire described *Parade* as "a kind of surrealism" in his program note, coining the word before Surrealism emerged as an art movement. *Parade* was presented to King Alfonso of Spain at his request that same year.

In 1973, City Center Joffrey Ballet, New York, restaged *Parade*—founder Robert Joffrey was passionate about recreating works by choreographic masters, and he considered *Parade* to be "the first multimedia ballet, because not only the dancing was important, the art was, and especially those wonderful cubistic costumes." The company was committed to staging the ballet as authentically as possible, with detailed re-creation of the costumes and set, as well as the original choreography overseen by Massine himself. The company's principal dancer, Gary Chryst, later described Massine's complex directions for the role of the Chinese Conjurer (which Massine had originally danced himself), "I have to say, we thought he was out of his mind because he was asking us to do strange things with our face. 'Flex your cheekbones' … What? What does that mean?"

Before Joffrey's revival, *Parade* had only been seen nine times, and had never been performed in the US. The ballet has since been recreated by several companies, including Crystal Pite's 2013 production for Nederlands Dans Theater, which recaptured the eclectic genius of the original.

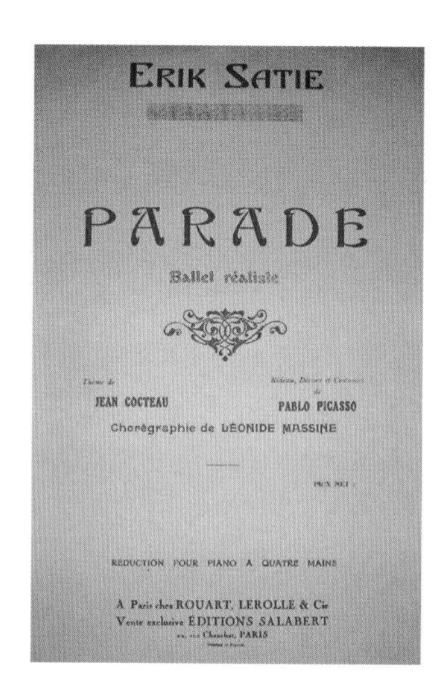

▲ **First *Parade* score**
This title page is from the score for four-handed piano, which Satie wrote at the beginning of 1917. His version for full orchestration was not completed until May that year, just 10 days before the ballet's premiere.

▲ **Preljocal's reinterpretation**
In 1993, Angelin Preljocal choreographed his own version of *Parade*, which was performed at the Palais Garnier in a tribute to the Ballets Russes.

▶ **Picasso stage curtain**
Picasso's depiction of a traditional circus scene, which greeted the audience before the ballet started, was in sharp relief to the startling Cubist costumes and set that were revealed when the curtain was raised.

COSTUME DESIGN

Costumes for ballet are unique in the theater world—not only do they need to portray a character, but they also have to allow movement. Ballet costumes are constructed to have a life of up to 30 years, and to be altered to fit multiple dancers. They also need to have a visual impact ranging from close up to the very back of the balcony in a theater. The designer must take all of these factors into consideration.

During the 19th century, ballerinas wore a tutu and pointe shoes whether they were portraying a princess or a gypsy. At the beginning of the 20th century, however, Sergei Diaghilev's Ballets Russes revolutionized the fields of choreography, composition, and design. Diaghilev employed artists to design the sets and costumes for his ballets, with astonishing results. These artists moved away from ballerinas in tutus, and instead experimented with shape, style, and color. Coupled with avant-garde choreography and composition, these designs pushed Ballets Russes to the forefront of art and culture.

The artists commissioned by Diaghilev included Léon Bakst, Alexandre Benois, Nicholas Roerich, Mikhail Larionov, Natalia Goncharova, Pablo Picasso, Henri Matisse, Coco Chanel, Giorgio de Chirico, Joan Miró, Georges Braque, André Derain, Robert and Sonia Delaunay, and Pavel Tchelitchev.

Russian artist Léon Bakst was the most influential designer of all. He designed most of Ballets Russes' pre-World War I repertoire, then helped by painter Marc Chagall. Bakst's use of contrasting colors and patterns led the worlds of fashion and interior design of the time, and today his work remains synonymous with the Ballets Russes.

> Chagall is my favorite pupil, and what I like about him is that after listening attentively to my lessons he takes his paints and brushes and does something absolutely different from what I have told him.
>
> LEON BAKST

Léon Bakst's costume design for *The Sleeping Beauty* ▶
For his last collaboration with Diaghilev, Bakst reported that he created "more than 200 maquettes (sketches), costumes, and sets" in the space of two months.

vifs

ror

Plumes d'autruches
verts et rouges

Da...

Av...
porta...
(Av...

...isante tres rouge
...lotte en velours
...e

varier la nuance des
cheveux

le haut du corsage
avec gradations mou-
rantes de soie et
dentelles et linons.

...soie

Fourr...
ave...

et...

Traine et manches
en beau velours rouge
de cette nuance vive avec
...ndes appliques de broderie
Louis XIV en argent

Lore...
talon et...

Les Noces

First performed: June 13, 1923 ▪ Venue: Théâtre de la Gaîté, Paris ▪ Choreography: Bronislava Nijinska ▪ Music and story: Stravinsky

The title means "The Wedding," but *Les Noces* is far from celebratory—it is an austere portrayal of Russian peasant life in which individuality is suppressed for the good of the many. Despite André Levinson's remarks that the dancers "look like machinery: Marxist, mechanical, utilitarian, industrial, an entire Red army division," more ballet-lovers agree with fellow-critic Edwin Denby that *Les Noces* "is noble, it is fierce, it is simple, it is fresh, it is thrilling."

STORY LINE

Scene 1 The Blessing of the Bride begins with a lament at the parents' loss of their daughter, Natasia. Her friends plait her hair.

Scene 2 In the Blessing of the Bridegroom, Fetis's friends dress his hair.

Scene 3 At the Bride's Departure from her Parents' House, the two mothers wail because by tradition they may not attend the wedding.

Scene 4 The Wedding Feast takes place after the ceremony, which, like the mothers, the audience does not see. Instead, they watch the young guests perform vigorous dances.

◀ ***Vanity Fair*** **magazine, 1929**
Valentina Koshuba as the bride, Natasia, wears an elaborate costume with extremely long braids. The bride's friends manipulate her long hair into plaits in Scene 1, a symbolic gesture mirrored by the bridegroom's hair-based ritual in the next scene.

This one-act ballet of four scenes is 28 minutes long, and was originally part of a triple bill performed by the Ballets Russes. As always, Sergei Diaghilev harnessed the greatest talents of the day. For the score, Igor Stravinsky set traditional Russian wedding songs to his own compositions, with a concert-style chorus. The music was performed on four pianos with percussion. Diaghilev had the pianos placed on the stage.

Leading Moscow artist Natalia Goncharova designed the sets and costumes. The first designs, based on folkloric costumes, featured bright colors, but choreographer Nijinska wanted more earthy hues so a palette of gray-blue (associated with the proletariat at this time), brown, and cream was used.

The women wore brown woolen pinafore dresses over cream muslin blouses and pointe shoes dyed brown. The men wore similar cream shirts with brown woolen trousers and cream stockings. Their soft shoes had straps laced up to their knees. The stage set had a raised platform at the back of the stage showing the basic interior of a peasant home with a bench, door, and window.

Nijinska's choreography

The female dancers performed en pointe, to help recreate the elongated images suggested by mosaic Byzantine saints. Steps matched the percussive beats of the music. The balletic pas de bourrée step was performed without any turnout, imitating the striking of a clapper in a chiming bell as the dancers' legs swung out from side to side. The energetic jumps of both male and female dancers were often similar. One leap, in which the dancer leaned forward, throwing back their arms while lifting their legs high in a bent position, was later used by Martha Graham and referred to as a "bison jump." Instead of the soft hand movements used in classical ballet, the dancers clenched their fists and held mitten-like positions.

▲ **Strong, sculptural shapes**
In Scene 1, Natasia is attended by her friends. They form a frieze, making a pyramid with their heads. Kristen McNally as Natasia, in the 2012 Royal Ballet production, is at the top. The ballet ends with another pyramid, this time topped by the best man.

Nijinska's work was revived in at least four later productions. There are also several versions with new choreography: Maurice Béjart (1962), Jerome Robbins (1965), and Jiří Kylián (1982) under the Russian title of *Svadebka*.

Les Biches

First performed: January 6, 1924 ▪ Venue: Théâtre de Monte Carlo ▪ Choreography: Bronislava Nijinska ▪ Music: Francis Poulenc

Less than a year after Nijinska choreographed the solemn *Les Noces*, she created, for the Ballets Russes, a work in complete contrast—chic, bright young things of the Jazz Age dance, giggle, flirt, and strike a pose at a party in the South of France. The title *Les Biches* means "the does," colloquially used at the time to refer to coquettish young women. When performed in the UK, the ballet was often entitled *The House Party*.

While no individual personalities were shown by the cast of *Les Noces,* here each dancer is allowed to reveal their own character in a light-hearted, yet sophisticated way. The music is relaxing compared to the dirge-like singing in *Les Noces*. Even the costumes, suggesting wealth, confidence, and glamour with their fashionable designs and delicate colors, contrast with the brown and cream work clothes of the previous year.

Music, set, and costumes

Diaghilev commissioned the then little-known Francis Poulenc to write the music, based on a piece written 17 years earlier. Instead, Poulenc took inspiration from the paintings of French Rococo artist Antoine Watteau, depicting Louis XV passing the time with various women in his Parc aux Biches (Deer Park). Poulenc composed eight pieces of jazz-based music, and the dances of *Les Biches* were originally named after the musical titles: Rondeau, Chanson Dansée, Adagietto, Jeu, Rag Mazurka, Andantino, Chanson Dansée, and Finale.

Marie Laurencin, known for her stylized, delicate paintings of chic Parisian women, designed the set of an elegant room with white walls, a window, a curtained balcony, and lilac sofa, all suggesting a fashionable home. Her costume colors were sophisticated, with pale pink dresses for the young women, an additional long string of pearls and cigarette holder for the Hostess, and a short blue velvet coat with white tights and gloves for La Garçonne (the Bachelor Girl). Three of the men appeared to have come straight from the beach in their swimsuits.

Roles and revivals

The Hostess, a sophisticated woman who likes to cling to her youth by surrounding herself with young people, does not appear until over halfway through the ballet. Nijinska herself took the role of the Hostess in the opening performances. Ninette de Valois appeared as one of the young women.

STORY LINE

There is no story to *Les Biches*, just guests at a house party in the South of France during the 1920s. This is precisely where and when Nijinska was based with the Ballets Russes.

The ballet opens with young women dancing. Three young men appear and, after their pas de trois, they dance and flirt with the women. One remains on stage, and a boyish woman, La Garçonne, appears. She moves across the stage en pointe. She dances with the man and leaves as two young women dance together. Sexual identity is deliberately ambiguous.

▼ **The Royal Ballet, 2000**
Dancing with Jonathan Cope, Mara Galeazzi plays La Garçonne (the Bachelor Girl). En pointe, and in a short tunic, her identity is something of a mystery.

Martha Graham

Dancer and choreographer ▪ 1894–1991

American Martha Graham reshaped modern dance to offer the first significant alternative to classical ballet. Never afraid of controversy, she tackled social, political, and sexual themes through innovative choreography that often explored the complexities of human emotion. She created over 180 works dedicated to expressing the inner human through physical movement, a concept she introduced to the world of dance in the 1920s, and continued to nurture right up until her death.

▲ ***Night Journey*, 1947**
Martha Graham played the remorseful Queen Jocasta in this ballet. She choreographed the work, with music by William Schuman and set by American-Japanese sculptor Isamu Noguchi. This was the third ballet that Graham based on Greek mythology.

Graham saw her first modern dance performance at the age of 17 in California—a production by Ruth St. Denis, who was famous for incorporating Eastern influences such as Japanese and Egyptian dance into her choreography. Graham was captivated. She auditioned to enter Los Angeles's Denishawn School, founded by St. Denis and her husband Ted Shawn. The school taught various international dances, from folk techniques to yoga and ballet.

Graham trained under Shawn and progressed quickly. She made her professional debut in 1920 in Shawn's *Xochitl*, dancing the lead role of a Toltec Princess. Graham left Denishawn in 1923 to take a well-paid dance position, and then, in 1926, started the Martha Graham Dance Company.

Louis Horst, whom Graham met at Denishawn, became her musical director, and remained a strong influence up until his death in 1964. He pushed her to move on from Denishawn styles, and introduced her to abstract art as well as new, modern music. He became her mentor and her lover, though he remained married.

Reshaping modern dance

By the 1930s, Graham was experimenting with choreography that was independent of any other dance form. She developed her technique of "contraction and release," which involved contraction of the torso and deep pelvic muscles followed by relaxation. Spiraling, a movement originating from the pelvis, and falls, which acknowledged the power of gravity, were also part of her technique.

Graham believed that the floor and the space of the stage were as important as the dance. In her company's early years, Graham and her dancers performed on a bare stage but, in 1935, she collaborated with sculptor Isamu Noguchi to create the set for *Frontier*. The two shared a love for stark, stripped-back designs at a time when painted backdrops dominated.

Controversial themes

Graham's themes, whether grief, lust, greed, society, or politics, were as controversial as her choreography. In *Lamentation* (1930), she depicted sorrow in a four-minute solo, her angular movements stretching her purple, tube costume that symbolized human skin.

Graham made sure that her voice was heard offstage as well as on. In 1936, she rejected Hitler's invitation to dance at the International Arts Festival in Berlin. Two years later, she created *American Document* in response to European Fascism. One of her many US-themed works, it explored what it means to be American, with recitations of the Declaration of Independence and Emancipation Proclamation. The same year, 1938, Graham became the first dancer to perform at the White House, invited by the Roosevelts. In another first, *American Document* was her first work to feature a male dancer, Erick Hawkins, whom Graham married in 1948.

Graham also drew from Greek mythology in such works as *Cave of the Heart* (1946) and *Errands into the Maze* (1947). In 1958, she presented her only full-length work, *Clytemnestra*, a tale of lust, betrayal, and revenge based on the ancient Greek legend of the same name.

In 1969, Graham retired from dancing, aged 75, but struggled with the transition and became depressed. Nonetheless, she continued to choreograph until her death in 1991.

▲ ***Salem Shore*, 1943**
Martha Graham danced in this "ballad of a woman's longing for her beloved's return from the sea," for which she also did the choreography. As always, each movement was executed with strength, often resulting in angular and forceful dances. Props were also made part of the dance.

KEY WORKS

Revolt, 1927 • *Frontier*, 1935 • *Appalachian Spring*, 1944
Cave of the Heart, 1946 • *Clytemnestra*, 1958 • *Acrobats of God*, 1960 • *Cortege of Eagles*, 1967

TIMELINE

- **May 11, 1894** Born in Allegheny, PA, one of three daughters of Dr. George Graham, a physician who utilizes physical movement to remedy nervous disorders.

- **1916** Enters the Denishawn School in Los Angeles, learning the founders' non-Western styles and techniques of dance.

- **1920** Takes the lead role in Ted Shawn's Aztec-themed ballet, *Xochitl*, and becomes Denishawn's star dancer.

- **1923** Leaves Denishawn, moving to New York to join the Greenwich Village Follies, a musical revue at which she performs over the next two years.

- **1924** Takes a teaching role at the Eastman School of Music in Rochester, New York.

- **1926** Establishes the Martha Graham Dance Company in New York.

- **1927** Presents what becomes her characteristically expressive form of dance for the first time in *Revolt*, a work received with dismay by New York audiences and critics alike.

- **1929** Founds her own dance troupe in New York.

- **1948** Marries dancer Erick Hawkins, but the couple divorce in 1954.

MARTHA GRAHAM PROGRAM COVER, c. 1954

- **1969** Announces her retirement as a dancer, at the age of 75.

- **1975** Choreographs *Lucifer* for Margot Fonteyn and Rudolf Nureyev.

- **1990** Creates what turns out to be her final complete ballet, *Maple Leaf Rag*.

- **April 1, 1991** Months after completing her autobiography, *Blood Memory*, dies from pneumonia at the age of 96, in New York.

Apollo

First performed: June 12, 1928 ▪ Venue: Théâtre Sarah Bernhardt, Paris ▪ Choreography and story: George Balanchine ▪ Music: Igor Stravinsky

One of the most transformational works of the 20th century, George Balanchine's *Apollo*, known as *Apollon Musagète* until 1957, was the first example of neoclassical ballet. The ballet, which depicts the coming of age of Apollo, the Greek god of music, was created by Balanchine during his early years as a choreographer for Sergei Diaghilev's Ballets Russes. From the moment the ballet premiered, it was a huge success.

One of the few works Balanchine created to highlight the male dancer, *Apollo* represented a new vision of classicism that embraced both tradition and modernity through its decisive pairing of music and movement. Writing in 1928, critic Edwin Denby christened the ballet, "The first work in the contemporary style." With *Apollo*, the 24-year-old Balanchine had embarked on the neoclassical line of development that would become central to his later work.

▲ **New York City Ballet, 2015**
Most versions of *Apollo* feature just four dancers. This production starred Tiler Peck, Ashly Isaacs, Lauren Lovette, and Adrian Danchig-Waring.

STORY LINE

Apollo In his first dance, Apollo, god of music, is young and inexperienced, and just beginning to discover his own weight and mobility. With the help of the three muses, he grows up, discovers his creative powers, and ascends Mount Parnassus. Apollo's second solo begins with him extending his arms above his head—now mature, he is refined and in control of his power.

The Three Muses Each with their own gift, the muses teach Apollo their arts. The muse of poetry, Calliope, idly scribbles on her tablet, yet her body contorts to expel her deeper truths. Polyhymnia, the muse of mime, discards her mask but keeps her code of silence by covering her mouth during her solo. Strumming her lyre, Terpsichore, the muse of dance, invites him to dance a duet.

Dream team

Apollo marked Balanchine's first collaboration with Stravinsky—an occasion that the choreographer considered to be the turning point of his life. Stravinsky envisioned *Apollo* to be a grand ballet presented in a simple manner and suggested focusing the score on just one family of instruments, the strings. Balanchine found the restrained and disciplined qualities of Stravinsky's composition to be a "revelation" that encouraged him to clarify his movements and distill his ideas. "It seemed to tell me that I could dare not to use everything," he said. Backstage, Balanchine watched the premiere while Stravinsky conducted from the orchestra pit—it was the start of a lifelong artistic alliance and friendship.

It was not just *Apollo*'s name that was later simplified. The original version, still performed by some companies, included Apollo's mother, two nymphs, a prologue, and birth scene, all of which Balanchine eliminated for his 1951 New York City Ballet production. The sets and costumes were gradually reduced, too. Coco Chanel reworked the costumes in 1929, outfitting Apollo in a diagonal-cut toga, and the muses in white tutus. Today, *Apollo* is danced on a bare stage in white tights for the man and white leotards with skirts for the women.

The choreography requires pristine technique, but the angular distortions of the movements and intimate modern gestures, with dancers shuffling on their heels, their wrists fixed and legs inverted like Greek statues, are what make *Apollo* a neoclassical ballet.

◀ **The Ballets Russes, 1928**
The first version of *Apollo* starred Alice Nikitina, Lubov Tchernicheva, Felia Doubrovska, and Serge Lifar, and featured Baroque sets and costumes designed by French artist André Bauchant.

▶ **The Royal Ballet, 2013**
Here, Rupert Pennefather plays Apollo, with muses Olivia Cowley, Sarah Lamb, and Itziar Mendizabal posing behind one another as beautiful goddesses with their legs at varying heights of arabesque.

THE ROYAL BALLET

In the 18th century, many European courts followed France and supported their own ballet companies. However, it was not until the 20th century that the UK acquired a national ballet company, thanks to the vision of Ninette de Valois. After dancing with the Ballets Russes for two years, she opened The Academy of Choregraphic Art (she opted for the 18th-century spelling of "choreographic") in London in 1926. Her students danced in occasional opera performances at The Old Vic theater and, when Lilian Baylis reopened Sadler's Wells Theatre in 1931, de Valois moved her school there. The dancers then performed at both venues and so were called the Vic-Wells Ballet and Vic-Wells School. In 1940–1941, they became known as the Sadler's Wells Ballet and School.

Ninette de Valois and Frederick Ashton created works especially for the company, developing an English style that was noted for its neat footwork and lyrical movement. The Sadler's Wells Ballet became resident at the Royal Opera House after World War II and reopened Covent Garden as a lyric theater in 1946 with *The Sleeping Beauty*, featuring Margot Fonteyn as Princess Aurora.

Sadler's Wells became the home of a second ballet company, Sadler's Wells Theatre Ballet, in 1946, and the following year the school moved to west London. A royal charter was granted in 1956, and the companies became The Royal Ballet and Sadler's Wells Royal Ballet (later to be called Birmingham Royal Ballet when it moved to the Midlands in 1990). The school was also given royal status. In 2003, the upper forms of The Royal Ballet School moved to Covent Garden, linked to their adult counterparts at The Royal Ballet by a bridge, and realizing de Valois' dream of having the school and company on one site.

> One of the few things in dance to match The Royal Ballet's curtain calls is The Royal Ballet's dancing.
>
> CLIVE BARNES, DANCE CRITIC, 1966

In rehearsal—the work behind the dream ▶
After a morning warm-up class, rehearsals at The Royal Ballet usually last from noon until 5:30 pm. Then there is time for dinner before warming up again and getting into costume for the evening performance.

Ninette de Valois

Dancer, choreographer, director, and founder of British ballet ▪ 1898–2001

De Valois is credited with changing the face of British ballet and launching the careers of some of the 20th-century's iconic dancers. Despite suffering from spinal pain caused by undiagnosed childhood polio, she carried on dancing until 1937, reprising Swanhilda in *Coppélia* just a few weeks before her 39th birthday. Her drive and determination saw her become an acclaimed choreographer, and establish ballet schools and companies in the UK, Ireland, and Turkey—most notably The Royal Ballet in London.

▲ ***Douanes*, 1935 revival**
Ninette de Valois choreographed *Douanes* (1932) and took the leading role of the Tightrope Walker. In this studio photograph, the shadow of Robert Helpmann looms large as the Cook's Man.

It began with an Irish jig learned from the cook in the large country house in County Wicklow, Ireland, where Edris Stannus lived with her British army officer father, mother, and three siblings. Later, when Edris insisted on performing the dance at a party, first checking that the pianist would accompany her correctly, it was obvious that this seven-year-old had a rare determination.

After moving to the UK, Edris began dance lessons, and then joined the Lila Field Academy at the age of 13, becoming part of a touring group called the "Wonder Children." While touring, she was most celebrated for her exact replication of Anna Pavlova's *Dying Swan*. It was at this time that she adopted the stage name, Ninette de Valois, based on her Huguenot ancestry.

First steps

By the age of 21, de Valois was a principal dancer in pantomimes and opera ballets at Covent Garden, but decided to take classical training with world-class teachers, such as Edouard Espinosa and Enrico Cecchetti, to further her career.

Her next move was to join Sergei Diaghilev's Ballets Russes in France, where his particular achievement was to commission groundbreaking choreographers, composers, and designers, working in close collaboration to create exciting new ballets.

At 24, de Valois was promoted to soloist, but the pain she suffered when dancing was extraordinary. When she was diagnosed with spinal problems, she knew her career as a dancer was compromised. However, two years with the Ballets Russes furnished her with the skills she needed to launch her own dance academy on her return to London, The Academy of Choregraphic Art. Then, a meeting with Lilian Baylis, manager of the Old Vic theater, became the catalyst for her plans for a future national ballet in the UK. In exchange for coaching and staging short dances, de Valois was promised space for a dance company and school when the derelict Sadler's Wells theater was rebuilt.

A new direction

With the opening of Sadler's Wells in 1931, de Valois founded the Vic-Wells Ballet company (later renamed Sadler's Wells Ballet), and assembled a superlative company of choreographers, dancers, composers, and music directors. Constant Lambert was musical director and Nicholas Sergeyev was hired to produce classics, such as *Giselle* and *Swan Lake*. De Valois supplemented these works with her own avant-garde short ballets. *Job*, based on the Hebrew Bible and William Blake's engravings, with music by Vaughan Williams, featured guest artist Anton Dolin in the role of Satan. *The Rake's Progress*, inspired by Hogarth's paintings, moved from drawing room to brothels and Bedlam. *Checkmate* was a symbolic ballet about a game of chess with June Brae as the Black Queen. Sadler's Wells dancers also included an adolescent Margot Fonteyn, Moira Shearer, and Beryl Grey.

The Royal Ballet is born

After World War II, Sadler's Wells Ballet was chosen to reopen London's Royal Opera House, and in 1956 it was granted a charter as The Royal Ballet. De Valois recruited a generation of dancers that included Lynn Seymour, Antoinette Sibley, and Anthony Dowell, and drew choreographers Frederick Ashton, John Cranko, and Kenneth MacMillan to work

KEY WORKS

Choreographer: *Job*, 1931 • *Douanes*, 1932 • *Bar aux Folies Bergère*, 1934 • *The Rake's Progress*, 1935 • *Checkmate*, 1937 *The Prospect Before Us*, 1940 • *The Sleeping Beauty*, 1946 *Don Quixote*, 1950

with her. She was also the first in the UK to give Russian émigré Rudolf Nureyev work in 1962, and to partner him with Margot Fonteyn—reviving her career.

De Valois retired as director of The Royal Ballet in 1963, and from its school in 1970. In honor of her contribution to British ballet, she was made a dame in 1947, awarded the Companion of Honour in 1983, and the Order of Merit in 1992. She died in 2001.

Rehearsing, 1931
Ninette de Valois practises a Spanish dance at Sadler's Wells Theatre in London in 1931, the same year she opened her ballet school and company there.

TIMELINE

- **June 7, 1898** Born Edris Stannus in County Wicklow, Ireland, the second of four children in a military, aristocratic family.
- **1905** Moves with her family to Kent, where she receives weekly dance lessons with her sister and governess.
- **1911** Learns classical ballet at the Lila Field Academy for Children in London.
- **1914** Becomes principal dancer in the annual pantomime at the Lyceum Theatre in London.
- **1915** Studies under Edouard Espinosa.
- **1919** Trains with Enrico Cecchetti to refine her technique, becoming principal dancer at the Covent Garden Opera House in London.
- **1923** Becomes a soloist at the Ballets Russes in Paris.
- **1926** Sets up her own ballet school, The Academy of Choregraphic Art, in London.
- **1931** Founds the Vic-Wells School and Company at Sadler's Wells Theatre, London (later known as the Sadler's Wells Ballet).
- **1946** The Sadler's Wells Ballet becomes the resident company of the Royal Opera House, Covent Garden, London.
- **1947** Travels to Turkey to help establish the country's first national ballet.
- **1949** Debuts the Sadler's Wells Ballet in New York.
- **1956** Her Sadler's Wells company is granted a royal charter, changing its name to The Royal Ballet.
- **1961** Takes The Royal Ballet to the Soviet Union, staging productions in St. Petersburg and Moscow.
- **1963** Retires as director of The Royal Ballet, but stays on as head of the Sadler's Wells School for seven years.
- **March 8, 2001** Dies at home in Barnes, London, at the age of 102.

SET DESIGN BY EDWARD MCKNIGHT KAUFFER FOR THE BALLET *CHECKMATE*

The Prodigal Son

First performed: May 21, 1929 ▪ Venue: Théâtre Sarah Bernhardt, Paris ▪ Choreography: George Balanchine ▪ Music: Sergei Prokofiev ▪ Story: Boris Kochno

Dramatic, experimental, and filled with acrobatic choreography, *The Prodigal Son* was an immediate hit with critics and audiences when it premiered in 1929. The last ballet created by George Balanchine for the Ballets Russes, which disbanded three months later upon the sudden death of its founder Sergei Diaghilev, it represented Diaghilev's great skill in bringing together the best of contemporary dance, art, music, and writing to make inspiring works.

STORY LINE

A retelling of the Biblical fable in one act and three scenes.

Scene 1 The ballet begins with the Prodigal Son's rebellious departure from his home and father in the company of two friends.

Scene 2 The Prodigal Son arrives in a strange and exotic city. He meets revelers and joins a feast. The Siren enters and dances with the Prodigal Son. She and the revelers encourage the Prodigal Son to drink, then strip him of all his possessions.

Scene 3 The repentant Prodigal Son, clad in rags and weak with exhaustion, returns home where he is welcomed and forgiven by his father.

Taking its theme from St. Luke's Gospel, *The Prodigal Son* was created by Boris Kochno (Sergei Diaghilev's librettist since 1920) and choreographer George Balanchine. The music was composed by Sergei Prokofiev, who was allegedly unhappy with the Ballets Russes production, especially the portrayal of the Siren whom he had envisaged as demure, in contrast to Balanchine's strong and more sinister depiction. Georges Rouault, a French religious artist, was approached to design the sets and costumes.

Balanchine used movements taken from gymnastics and circus acrobatics to create a new and experimental language of movement for the ballet. The pas de deux between the Siren and Prodigal Son was especially challenging, with many complex moves and lifts.

The dramatic choreography was complemented by striking costumes. To portray the Siren, Russian ballerina Felia Doubrovska, already a tall dancer, wore a high headdress and danced en pointe to intimidating effect. The multipurpose use of simple stage props was also novel. A single prop was used as a fence, a boat, a banquet table, a pillar, and finally a gate.

Reworkings and revivals

In the 1930s, Balanchine refused to allow Colonel W. de Basil's Covent Garden Russian Ballet (as it was then called) to revive *The Prodigal Son*. Determined to stage the ballet, de Basil engaged dancer David Lichine to create new choreography. The work premiered in Australia in 1938 and was performed until 1948. In 1977, it was revived for the Dallas Ballet, and in 1985 for the Tulsa Ballet.

Balanchine restaged *The Prodigal Son* for New York City Ballet in 1950 with his wife, Maria Tallchief, as the Siren. Still performed by companies around the world, the ballet remains one of the most popular of Balanchine's early works.

▲ **Original production**
Ukrainian dancer Serge Lifar (the Son) and Russian ballerina Felia Doubrovska (the Siren) star in the first production of *The Prodigal Son* in May 1929.

▶ **Carlos Acosta**
In 2004, The Royal Ballet performance of *The Prodigal Son* at the Royal Opera House, London, featured Carlos Acosta and Sylvie Guillem in the lead roles.

The Russian Ballet does not try to be what it used to be. It seizes and assimilates the latest developments in painting and music.

A LONDON REVIEWER, 1929

The Bolt

First performed: April 8, 1931 ▪ Venue: State Academic Theater of Opera and Ballet, Leningrad ▪ Choreography: Fedor Lopukhov ▪ Music: Dmitri Shostakovich
Story: Viktor Smirnov

Fiercely criticized for being un-Soviet, especially for putting negative characters at its center, *The Bolt* was banned after its dress rehearsal in 1931. Satirical in tone, and a thinly disguised caricature of the stories of the Workers' Youth Theater, the ballet was judged too playful and avant-garde in its treatment of serious issues relating to work at a time when Stalin was promoting industrialization and hardening his state policy on culture.

▲ **Costume for Kozelkov, the factory clerk**
Tatiana Bruni's graphic costume designs for *The Bolt* show the influences of contemporary Soviet propaganda posters and constructivism.

▼ **Bolshoi Ballet performance**
After a gap of 74 years, *The Bolt* received its world premiere in Russia in a production by the Bolshoi Ballet, directed by Alexei Ratmansky in 2005.

Not many ballets get just one performance, but that is precisely what happened with *The Bolt*. Wreckers were commonly blamed for the failure of Soviet industrial projects at the time, and while *The Bolt* was based on just such a tale of industrial sabotage by Viktor Smirnov, its use of comedy and satire proved too much for the Soviet authorities, who banned the work.

Shostakovich's score blended serious music with take-offs of popular and circus tunes, waltzes, Red Army marches, and tangos. Lopukhov's choreography was similarly modern in approach, combining classical ballet with circus acrobatics, sports, vaudeville, and jazz dance. Characters and costumes were comically stereotyped—the pompous Bureaucrat appeared in paper trousers, while the Terrorist wore an elaborate funereal black dress. A victim of the changing mood in Russia, this level of parody and mixture of mass entertainment with ballet were considered too dubious to be allowed.

STORY LINE

In revenge for being fired from his factory job, indolent worker Lenka Gulba (Russian for "Lazy Idler") convinces a young boy, Goshka, to throw a huge bolt into one of the workshop lathes. The plan works. Lenka blames a member of the team, Boris, before Goshka admits his guilt and reveals who was behind the sabotage. Lenka is captured, the lathe is repaired, and, victory over counter-revolutionary subversion achieved, the laborers go back to their work.

Russian revival

Shostakovich later created a suite from the score, and put selections in other compositions, but he refused to let *The Bolt* be heard in full separately from the dance. It was finally recorded in 1995, but not heard in a theater again until 2005. In this production for the Bolshoi Ballet, Alexei Ratmansky reimagined the work—keeping the ballet's plot, but adapting some of the action and music.

SOVIET BALLET

Impresario Sergei Diaghilev left Russia with the dancers who comprised the Ballets Russes shortly before the Russian Revolution of 1917. While their talent and passion reignited ballet in Europe, many of them never danced in Russia again, as movement between Russia and the West became severely restricted. After the Revolution, Lenin questioned the need for ballet, but it survived to become an important socialistic art form during the 1920s and '30s, and heralded works such as *The Red Poppy* (1927) and *The Golden Age* (1930). St. Petersburg became Leningrad, the Imperial School of Ballet was renamed the State Choreographic Institute, and the ballet company became the Kirov. Dance was increasingly politicized and heavily censored: ballets were there to promote sound political ideas, and any suspect works such as *The Bolt* were hastily removed. A few choreographers, such as Leonid Yakobson and Fyodor Lopukhov, risked creating ballets with hidden messages of individuality and social reform, much as composer Dmitri Shostakovitch did with music.

Soviet dancers, with their long training regime and dedication to their art, became models of strength and superiority to the West. Although the Kirov and Bolshoi (Moscow) Ballets seldom toured, when they did they stunned audiences with their breathtaking technique and fearless athleticism. In 1921, Agrippina Vaganova, who had trained during the dying days of the Imperial School, began to teach at the Choreographic Institute, and in 1934 she published her famous book *Fundamentals of Classical Dance.*

Later in the 20th century, defecting Russian artists such as Rudolf Nureyev, Mikhail Baryshnikov, and Natalia Makarova entranced ballet audiences everywhere. Since the demise of the USSR in 1991, exchange of dancers between Russia and the West has increased, to the delight and excitement of ballet-goers around the world.

> I was not extremely patriotic about Mother Russia. I played their game, pretending.
>
> MIKHAIL BARYSHNIKOV

◄ ***The Bolt*, Bolshoi Ballet**
The original press showing of *The Bolt* in 1931, choreographed by Fyodor Lopukhov to Shostakovich's score in the age of socialist realism, insulted everyone with its satire of factory life. Both the workers it depicted and the Soviet establishment were infuriated, and the ballet was instantly shelved.

Serenade

First performed: June 10, 1934 ▪ Venue: Estate of Felix M. Warburg, White Plains, New York ▪ Choreography: George Balanchine ▪ Music: Tchaikovsky

The first work he created in the US, George Balanchine's *Serenade* to Tchaikovsky's *Serenade for Strings* is a milestone in ballet history. It is the signature work of New York City Ballet and one of Balanchine's most widely performed works. Narrative-free, Balanchine's choreography took its lead from Tchaikovsky's score. Each of the four movements—Sonatina, Waltz, Tema Russo, and Elegy—touch on different human emotions, such as love, loss, and yearning.

STORY LINE

Serenade does not have a plot, instead Balanchine saw it as "dancers in motion to a beautiful piece of music." Its choreography reflects it origins—it was created to give students at the School of American Ballet classes in stage technique. The first class contained 17 girls, and to make them look interesting, Balanchine placed them on diagonal lines. Only nine girls attended the second class, and six the third. Balanchine worked with whomever was there and incorporated class events—such as one girl being late and another falling—into his work.

The *Serenade* of today is the product of Balanchine's continual revising. He did not include Tchaikovsky's Tema Russo movement, for example, until 1941. Balanchine also consolidated parts into one principal female role before breaking them up again into today's Waltz Girl, Russian Girl, and Dark Angel; and the noted moment when the Tema Russo soloist lets down her hair for the Elegy did not appear until as late as 1981.

The opening tableau is iconic. A group of women stand motionless in the soft moonlight, their right arms out, palms lifted as if catching its beams before touching their wrists to their foreheads as if in despair. Modern touches are immediately apparent. The arms are not classical, wrists are flexed, and feet parallel. Yet once the dancers move, they turn out their feet and begin to move in a way seen in any ballet class. The meeting of the Romantic, classical, and modern continues throughout, Balanchine acknowledging but disrupting his Russian traditions. Modern details include the lack of obvious hierarchy. Dressed identically to the corps, the three soloists are not afforded their own entrances and exits but emerge from the group before retreating. The partnering of the women is often off-center—when they waltz, the man has his arms around the woman's waist; and in the Elegy, he assists her promenade in arabesque by holding her thigh rather than her hand.

Despite moments such as the haunting end when the heroine seems to die as she is carried aloft, Balanchine was adamant *Serenade* had no plot. "The only story is the music's story, a serenade, a dance, if you like, in the light of the moon."

▼ **Romantic elements**
The New York City Ballet dancers wear long skirts, influenced by Karinska's famous 1952 ocean-blue skirts, reminiscent of traditional Romantic tutus. These contrast with the chic, knee-length dresses in gray and red worn in earlier productions.

Jardin aux lilas (Lilac Garden)

First performed: January 26, 1936 ▪ Venue: Mercury Theatre, London ▪ Choreography and story: Antony Tudor ▪ Music: Ernest Chausson

Considered by many to be the first in a new genre of psychological ballets, *Jardin aux lilas* (known in North America as *Lilac Garden*) is one of English dancer and choreographer Antony Tudor's most significant works. Set in the Edwardian era, the main character, Caroline, forsakes the man she loves for an advantageous match, stifled by, yet ultimately conforming to, society's protocols.

▲ **Original production, 1936**
Maude Lloyd as Caroline and her Lover, played by Hugh Laing, portray their anguish, all the more palpable at the tiny Mercury Theatre in London.

Many view this ballet as a commentary on the social conventions and suppression of emotions among the British upper classes at the turn of the 20th century. *The New York Times* critic Alastair Macaulay later expressed in a review of the work that the ballet's "steps, gestures, and phrases showed flickering aspects of repression, denial, private longing, heartbreak, personal conflict, and hypocrisy."

Tudor created the ballet for the Ballet Club, soon to be known as Ballet Rambert. He chose to choreograph the ballet to Ernest Chausson's *Poème (Op. 25)* for violin and orchestra, because he liked to use unusual music that was not intended for dance. *Jardin aux lilas* made its première at the home of the Ballet Club, the Mercury Theatre, in London's Notting Hill, in January 1936. In this small and intimate theater, which seated only about 150, the contrast of the romantic setting of a lilac garden at dusk with characters in formal Edwardian dinner dress doing the unthinkable—expressing strong emotions—was all the more shocking.

The principal casting at the premiere comprised Maude Lloyd (Caroline), Hugh Laing (her Lover), Antony Tudor (the Man she must Marry), and Peggy van Praagh (the Woman from his Past). As *Lilac Garden*, the ballet premiered in the US in 1940. Since then the ballet has gone on to be performed around the globe, and continues to be popular today.

STORY LINE

This one-act ballet is set in the Edwardian period and occurs in the lilac garden of bride-to-be Caroline's house.

The action takes place at a reception the night before Caroline (the only character to have a name) is due to marry a man she does not love. Caroline tries to find a moment to bid a last farewell to her lover, but in the end she leaves on the arm of the man she must marry.

▼ **American Ballet Theatre, 1961**
Dianne Richards and Royes Fernandez give a heartrending performance in *Lilac Garden*.

> The interplay of feelings between these characters was revealed in beautiful dance movements and groupings, with subtle changes of expression … without any recourse to mime or gesture.
>
> MARIE RAMBERT

Checkmate

First performed: June 15, 1937 ▪ Venue: Théâtre des Champs-Élysées, Paris ▪ Choreography: Ninette de Valois ▪ Music and story: Arthur Bliss

One of Ninette de Valois' most significant works, *Checkmate* tells the tragic story of the Red Knight's unfulfilled love for the Black Queen against the backdrop of a game of chess. First performed by the Vic-Wells Ballet, with June Brae as the Black Queen and Harold Turner as the Red Knight, the battle between love and death has proved an enduring theme, and the ballet has since been staged by The Royal Ballet and Birmingham Royal Ballet, among other companies.

STORY LINE

Prologue Two people are playing chess—one represents death; the other, love.

Act I The chess pieces all arrive on stage, taking up their various positions on the board. The first Red Knight is transfixed by the Black Queen. The frail Red King enters and totters feebly to his throne. The Black Queen and her pieces attack the Red King and the loyal Red Knight tries to defend his master. He duels with the Black Queen, but cannot bring himself to kill the woman that he loves. She fatally stabs him in the back, and checkmate soon follows.

▲ **Sadler's Wells Ballet, 1947**
In one of her iconic roles, Beryl Grey plays the Black Queen, alongside Philip Chatfield and Richard Ellis as the Black Knights.

◀ **The Royal Ballet**
Performing in 2007, Bennet Gartside plays the first Red Knight, with Ryoichi Hirano as the first Black Knight.

British composer Arthur Bliss became interested in ballet after seeing Diaghilev's Ballets Russes perform in London. He approached Ninette de Valois, founder of The Royal Ballet, with the idea of a ballet based on chess and she devised an allegorical dramatic piece, with love, power, and death at its heart. While the game of chess has been used as a theme for ballets since 1607 (when *Ballet des Echecs* was performed for French king Louis XIV), unlike earlier works, with dancers enacting a game as giant chess pieces, de Valois' pieces come to life, filled with emotion.

The first of many ballet commissions for Bliss, *Checkmate* begins with a prologue entitled The Players and culminates in Checkmate. In the opening scene, two men are playing chess: one in red and gray armor representing death; the other in blue and yellow portraying love. The music is ominous, foretelling the disaster that is to come. The choreography uses stabbing movements en pointe for the red pawns' entrance, while the black pawns reflect de Valois' fondness of national dance. Bliss had to teach de Valois and the set and costume designer, Edward McKnight Kauffer, about chess: "… I moved the pieces about on a big chessboard and demonstrated their characteristic moves—the knight's jump, the bishop's diagonals, the queen's mobility, the king's tottering shuffle …." *Checkmate* remains popular with audiences today, and was staged by the American Sarasota Ballet in 2017.

▶ **Love versus death**
Bennet Gartside's Red Knight takes on Zenaida Yanowsky's Black Queen in The Royal Ballet's 2007 production of *Checkmate*.

Romeo and Juliet

First performed: December 30, 1940 ▪ Venue: Mariinsky Theater, St. Petersburg ▪ Choreography: Lavrovsky ▪ Music: Prokofiev ▪ Story: William Shakespeare

While Shakespeare's timeless tale of love and tragedy had formed the basis of previous ballets, it was Prokofiev's eponymous three-act score, originally commissioned in 1934 for a new production for the Bolshoi Theater, that laid the foundations for many future versions. Immediately hailed as the pinnacle of Soviet ballet following its premiere, while the choreography has since been revised for later productions, Prokofiev's masterpiece remains a constant.

The idea of staging a new version of *Romeo and Juliet* at the Bolshoi was first suggested in 1934 by the Leningrad Film Institute's artistic director, Adrian Piotrovsky. Sergei Prokofiev, who was living in the West at the time, was invited to compose the score as an inducement to return to Russia. He completed the work the following year. To produce the scenario, Piotrovsky worked with dramatist, Sergei Radlov, and Ivo Psota developed the choreography. However, as new art forms were strictly regulated in Soviet Russia, the work had to take the form of a "drambalet"—devoid of decadence, it had to have a strong narrative that upheld Communist ideals.

As conservatism intensified in Soviet Russia, the arts were placed under increasing scrutiny, and *Romeo and Juliet* was postponed. When permission was finally granted in 1938, it was staged as a single act piece at a theater in Brno, in Soviet-occupied Czechoslovakia. However, it was enough to interest the Kirov Theater, which decided to present the ballet in 1940, to be choreographed by Leonid Lavrovsky.

By then, Prokofiev's original score, which radically featured a happy ending for the lovers, was deemed too modernist. Ballerina Galina Ulanova, set to dance as Juliet, commented, "For never was a story of more woe than Prokofiev's music for Romeo." Lavrovsky demanded that Prokofiev amend the ending and make the score sound more monumental and traditional overall. Under duress, Prokofiev begrudgingly obliged. With Konstantin Sergeyev as Romeo partnering Ulanova, Lavrovsky's ballet, with its communicative mime, romantic pas de deux, and spectacular crowd scenes opened to huge acclaim.

Romeo revisited

Romeo and Juliet has been restaged many times since the St. Petersburg premiere. John Cranko's highly atmospheric production for Stuttgart Ballet in 1962, set to Prokofiev's score, featured powerful ensemble dances and pas de deux that showed a heavy Russian influence. In 1965, Kenneth MacMillan staged his version for The Royal Ballet in London, also set to Prokofiev's score. With its focus on Juliet, danced by Margot Fonteyn—opposite Rudolf Nureyev as Romeo—it gave greater emphasis to the characters, and proved the perfect vehicle for the obvious bond between its lead dancers.

STORY LINE

Act I Romeo is caught up in a street brawl. Juliet, in contrast, plays childishly with her Nurse before her society introduction at a masked ball. The couple meet and fall in love, Romeo wooing Juliet from her balcony.

Act II Due to their families' enmity, the lovers marry in secret. Romeo kills Juliet's cousin, Tybalt, to avenge the death of his friend Mercutio, and is banished.

Act III To escape her forced marriage, Juliet drinks a potion that makes her seem lifeless. Romeo does not receive her note explaining the plan; thinking her dead, he goes to her tomb and kills himself. Juliet wakes, sees Romeo's corpse, and stabs herself.

▼ **Renaissance grandeur**
MacMillan portrays the young lovers as subject to the will of their wealthy families. The sense of oppression is emphasized by Nicholas Georgiadis's lavish sets and costumes.

◀ **New heights**
Although MacMillan choreographed *Romeo and Juliet* for Christopher Gable and Lynn Seymour, the premiere was danced by Rudolf Nureyev and Margot Fonteyn, reviving the latter's career.

Danses Concertantes

First performed: September 10, 1944 ▪ Venue: City Center of Music and Drama, New York ▪ Choreography and story: Balanchine ▪ Music: Igor Stravinsky

Stravinsky's 20-minute orchestral piece, *Danses Concertantes* has proven a fertile backdrop for a succession of leading choreographers. Composed in 1942, it made its first dance appearance in George Balanchine's 1944 ballet of the same name, and has since been choreographed more than a dozen times. Balanchine said that "the music embodied dancing" and to hear it "was also to visualize a ballet."

STORY LINE

A plotless ballet, it begins with a parade before the front cloth that introduces the dancers, who appear as if a group of strolling players. Then come four trios and a pas de deux, each color-coded, and a swift finale.

In his 1972 re-creation, while the structure remains the same, Balanchine's new, bright, and upbeat choreography is non-stop. The dancers appear to be having fun and gesture as if in animated conversation. At the time, a general feeling was that the ballet promised somewhat more than it delivered, perhaps due in part to the reputation of the original.

▼ **Quirky choreography**
The Sadler's Wells Theatre Ballet's 1955 production featured pointing fingers, hands as spectacles, angled ports de bras, and twisted pirouettes.

Although it was commissioned by Werner Janssen for his Los Angeles–based orchestra, *Danses Concertantes* was structured for ballet. Igor Stravinsky's correspondence with friend and colleague George Balanchine indicates that the work was conceived for performance at the latter's suggestion. In fact, Balanchine's work of the same name was his first as choreographer for the Ballet Russe de Monte Carlo.

While critical opinion was divided, Balanchine's 1944 *Danses Concertantes* proved popular on tour. Reports indicate it was witty and effervescent, with the dances following the score. It began and ended with parades, between which came several rhythmically quirky pas de trois and a demanding pas de deux. The complex score was problematic, however, and it was dropped from the repertory in 1948 and the original choreography lost.

Sadler's Wells premiere

Kenneth MacMillan had created several well-received workshop pieces, and in 1955 produced *Danses Concertantes* for his first Sadler's Wells Theatre Ballet commission. The playful score—rhythmically complex and exact, with rapid changes of pace and mood, and a hint of jazz—appealed to him greatly.

By choreographing an abstract ballet, MacMillan moved away from the dance-drama that formed the core of the company's repertoire. Paralleling the off-beat qualities of the music, his busy, sharp choreography is an eccentric distortion of the classical ballet vocabulary.

▲ **Striking sets**
Nicholas Georgiadis's skeletal set designs for MacMillan's 1955 version, matched the spikiness of the score and the dance.

He even asked lead dancer Maryon Lane to wiggle her hips and break into a kind of tap routine.

The ballet met with universal acclaim and gave MacMillan the courage to retire from the stage and take up choreography full-time. It was later incorporated into the repertory of The Royal Ballet.

Stravinsky celebrated

After making his name with New York City Ballet, the company he cofounded in 1948, George Balanchine returned to *Danses Concertantes* later in his career. He rechoreographed it for the company's Stravinsky Festival in 1972, a celebration to mark the 90th anniversary of the composer's birth. While the structure of the ballet was the same, much of the detail was different. His reasons were partly because—so he claimed—he could not remember what he had done the first time, and partly because he wanted to do something different with new dancers.

▶ **Daring designs**
The vividly colored costumes that Georgiadis designed featured contrasting black accents, which became one of his trademark design features.

5

INTERNATIONAL BALLET

(1945–1975)

International ballet 1945–1975

Following the success of international tours by companies such as Ballets Russes, later under the guise of Les Ballets Russes de Monte Carlo, and the Pavlova Company, ballet reached new heights of popularity in the mid-20th century. Countless articles were written about it, ballet magazines started, and images of tutu-clad dancers became the motif of choice on furnishings and housewares. Ballet was even the subject of films, including Oscar-winning *The Red Shoes* (1948).

While Russia remained the spiritual home of ballet, companies were emerging around the world and developing their own styles. In the US, George Balanchine and Lincoln Kirstein founded New York City Ballet in 1948, while in 1957 Antony Tudor developed the city's Ballet Theatre into the leading American Ballet Theatre. In the UK, Ninette de Valois's Sadler's Wells Ballet debuted in 1949, transforming into The Royal Ballet seven years later, while in Germany, Stuttgart Ballet was reborn in 1961 under John Cranko. Ballet companies also appeared in Canada, Australia, and New Zealand, as well as in Cuba and Iran. While many ballet companies' origins lay in the diaspora of Ballets Russes, Soviet ballet was also an influence. This was most evident in the founding of the Beijing Dance Academy in China in 1954, and the National Ballet of China in 1959, where works such as *The Red Detachment of Women* (1964) were staged as propaganda.

As new ballet companies evolved, modern forms of choreography appeared. In the US, Balanchine created a school of ballet that stripped away the pomp of Imperial ballet and the visual splendor of Ballets Russes in favor of pure balletic movement. In Europe, too, slick productions sought to portray human emotion through movement, such as Maurice Béjart's hypnotic *Bolero* (1960). While traditional story ballets still had a place, Russian and French classics were frequently restaged for new audiences, such as Frederick Ashton's theatrical reworking of *Cinderella* (1945).

Where once ballet had looked to the past and fantasy for inspiration, it now more readily embraced contemporary themes, as seen in Alvin Ailey's highly influential *Revelations*, which depicted the rise of black Americans from slavery at the cusp of the Civil Rights Movement in 1960. In a different vein, following the lunar landings, Ashton speculated how humans might move on the moon in his *Monotones* of 1965. However, in this period of innovative national and international companies, one of the most transforming influences on ballet, and in particular the role of the male dancer, still came from the Soviet Union. As many of its most celebrated stars, such as Rudolf Nureyev and Mikhail Baryshnikov, defected to the West, they brought the perfection of Russian ballet training to the global stage.

Cinderella

First performed: December 23, 1948 ▪ Venue: Royal Opera House, London ▪ Choreography: Frederick Ashton ▪ Music: Prokofiev ▪ Story: Charles Perrault

Frederick Ashton's ballet of the time-honored, rags-to-riches tale in which a girl marries her dream prince incorporates magical Petipa-style classical choreography, fairy variations representing the four seasons, a pas de quatre as well as the lovers' pas de deux, scintillating corps de ballet dances, and a grand entrance for Cinderella, descending the stairs en pointe. For good measure, Ashton himself danced one of the Ugly Sisters.

IN CONTEXT

Myths, legends, and fairy tales, including the tale of Cinderella, have formed the basis of many ballets. The most popular version, called *Cinderella, or the Little Glass Slipper*, was published by Charles Perrault in the late 17th century. In the early 19th century, several ballets based on this story of Cinderella were staged, including ones in London and Vienna.

The first notable production was created in 1893 by Russian imperial choreographer Marius Petipa, together with Lev Ivanov and Enrico Cecchetti, for the Mariinsky Theater, St. Petersburg. The ballet was set to the music of Baron Boris Fitinhof-Schell. This was the first ballet that Pierina Legnani performed in Russia. This version, however, eventually fell from the repertoire and its choreography did not survive.

Choreographer Frederick Ashton had toyed with the idea of creating a full-length ballet for some years. In 1948, having heard about the Soviet versions of *Cinderella* to Prokofiev's score (Rostislav Zakharov choreographed one for the Bolshoi in 1945, and Konstantin Sergeyev recrafted it for the Kirov (Mariinsky) Ballet the following year), Ashton decided to create his own production to the same music. This was Ashton's first three-act ballet, and he completed it in six weeks. Many wartime restrictions had been lifted, so the ballet could be fully realized.

Ashton was inspired by Petipa and his ballets in the creation of *Cinderella*: "I always return to Petipa over everything," he explained. He would often watch ballets such as *The Sleeping Beauty* for inspiration, which he referred to as "having a private lesson." Ashton laced Russian imperial grace and delicacy with a robustly British flavor. He chose to have the stepsisters played by men, en travesti (dressed as women). This decision gives a markedly British pantomime dame feel to the production, and they are often the characters that steal the show. The stepsisters were first danced by Ashton in a famous double act with Australian dancer, actor, and choreographer Robert Helpmann, one of the stars of Sadler's Wells Ballet. Ashton also decided to cut the Prince's round-

▲ **Birmingham Royal Ballet, 2017**
Jenna Roberts as Cinderella and William Bracewell as the Prince dance in David Bintley's *Cinderella* at the Mayflower Theatre, Southampton, UK.

> What I wanted to express above all in the music for *Cinderella* was the poetic love of Cinderella and the Prince, the birth and flowering of that love, the obstacles in its path, and finally the dream fulfilled.
>
> SERGEI PROKOFIEV, 1945

▲ Moira Shearer, Sadler's Wells Ballet, 1948
The star of Ashton's original production, Moira Shearer dances in spirited style with her broom as a makeshift partner.

the-world search for Cinderella, which featured in Prokofiev's full-length score and in the Russian versions.

Ashton had intended to create the role of Cinderella for Margot Fonteyn, but an injury led him to cast Moira Shearer (star of the film *The Red Shoes*) with Michael Somes as her Prince. The ballet was a huge success, and became the company's Christmas production for several years. The Australian Ballet revived Cinderella in 1972 with both Ashton and Helpmann again dancing their roles of the stepsisters with aplomb. The production was refreshed by The Royal Ballet in 2003, and included Anthony Dowell and Wayne Sleep as the stepsisters opposite Alina Cojocaru as Cinderella.

More recent versions

Since Ashton's production, many other choreographers have used Prokofiev's score as a basis for a reimagining of *Cinderella*. In 1986, Rudolf Nureyev created a production for the Paris Opéra Ballet set in Hollywood in the 1930s, with the Fairy Godmother embodying a film producer who discovers Cinderella. Matthew Bourne created a version of *Cinderella* in 1997, set in London during the Blitz, while Jean-Christophe Maillot's 1999 version for Les Ballets de Monte Carlo had Cinderella in bare feet and focused as much on her mother, reincarnated as the Fairy, as on the girl herself. In 2002, Alexei Ratmansky's first full-length work was a production of *Cinderella* for the Mariinsky Ballet. He reworked his quirky, surrealist reimagining in 2013 for The Australian Ballet.

David Bintley staged *Cinderella* for Birmingham Royal Ballet in 2010, setting the first act in the grimiest of kitchens with viciously bullying stepsisters followed by a chilling scene of midnight striking. He won a Classical Choreography Award for the work. Christopher Wheeldon's revival for Dutch National Ballet in 2012, replete with cinematic stage effects, earned him the prestigious Benois de la Danse Prize.

▲ Ugly Sisters, The Royal Ballet, 2010
Luke Haydon and Wayne Sleep dance as Cinderella's stepsisters. The British pantomime element contrasts with the fairytale romance.

Alina Cojocaru (1981–)

Romanian dancer Alina Cojocaru was highly acclaimed for her role as Cinderella in The Royal Ballet's production of 2003. Critics described her as growing in authority and stature for the ball scene, dancing the ballroom pas de deux with great tenderness, and bringing a radiance to the scenes back in the kitchen. British dancer Jonathan Cope first partnered her as the Prince, followed by Johan Kobborg, her real-life, as well as stage, partner.

STORY LINE Cinderella

Cinderella's two stepsisters are preparing for a ball. Once they leave, an old woman reveals herself as the Fairy Godmother and explains that Cinderella will go, too. Cinderella's rags are transformed, and she leaves for the ball, where the guests dance. The Prince enters, followed by Cinderella. When the clock strikes midnight the magic breaks, and Cinderella flees the ballroom in her rags, leaving a shoe behind. Back in the kitchen, the Prince arrives, looking for the woman whose foot fits the discarded shoe. The sisters try on the shoe but it is far too small. Finally, the Prince sees Cinderella and realizes who she is. The shoe fits perfectly.

SARAH LAMB (CINDERELLA) AND FRANCESCA FILPI (THE FAIRY GODMOTHER IN DISGUISE), THE ROYAL BALLET, 2011

ACT I

PLOT OVERVIEW

In the kitchen of Cinderella's father's house, her stepsisters are sewing a scarf in anticipation of the ball.

The stepsisters and Cinderella's father re-enter just as an old woman comes to the kitchen begging. The stepsisters tell her to leave but Cinderella gives her some bread. In preparation for the ball, a tailor, shoemaker, hairdresser, jeweler, and two dressmakers arrive. Finally, a dancing master enters and tries to teach the sisters to dance.

The old woman reappears and reveals herself as Cinderella's Fairy Godmother.

The Fairy Godmother mimes that Cinderella will go to the ball but must leave by 12 o'clock.

Cinderella is revealed wearing a stunning tutu and in a carriage led by white mice.

THE DANCES

They dance comically with the scarf before it splits in two.

The stepsisters dance a comic pas de trois with the dancing master.

Cinderella dances a solo with her broom as a partner.

Cinderella and her Fairy Godmother share a dance.

The Fairies Spring, Summer, Autumn, and Winter each dance a solo. Finally, they all dance together with the Fairy Godmother.

Fairy Attendants arrive and all dance together.

ACT II

PLOT OVERVIEW

The scene opens at the ball with a jester center stage. The stepsisters arrive comically, and try to join the ball.

The Prince's four friends appear and announce the arrival of the Prince. The Fairy Attendants enter the ballroom, followed by the Season Fairies and their pages.

THE DANCES

The sisters and their suitors dance. Each sister then dances a solo.

Cinderella stands at the t of the stairs. Taking the Prince's hand, she comes dow the last few steps en pointe

ANNA TSYGANKOVA (CINDERELLA) AND MATTHEW GOLDING (THE PRINCE), DUTCH NATIONAL BALLET, 2015

SVETLANA ZAKHAROVA AS CINDERELLA AND MARIA VOLODINA AS THE FAIRY GODMOTHER, BOLSHOI BALLET, 2006

FEDERICO BONELLI AS THE PRINCE, KENTA KURA AS THE JESTER, THE ROYAL BALLET, 2010

> Ashton's *Cinderella* is a story of hope fulfilled, a comedy of contrasting characters, and a classical ballet dense with sensuous movement.
>
> ALASTAIR MACAULAY, 2014

The ball guests re-enter and the ball continues.

FRENCH POSTER FOR *CINDERELLA*

The ball continues and the stepsisters dance and argue with each other.

The clock sounds, and Cinderella must leave. The spell breaks and she flees in her rags, leaving a shoe behind her.

Cinderella and the Prince dance, joined by the Fairy Attendants.

The Prince's four friends each partner one of the Season Fairies. Cinderella and the Prince join in.

Cinderella dances a solo with much intricate footwork.

Cinderella and the Prince dance a grand pas de deux.

ACT III

Cinderella is alone in the kitchen at home.

The stepsisters return from the ball. Cinderella helps them to undress.

The stepsisters dance in their underwear.

The Prince arrives and mimes the story of the ball and the shoe. Each sister tries on the shoe, unsuccessfully. Finally, the Prince sees Cinderella, who drops a shoe. He picks up both shoes and gives them to Cinderella. The shoes are a perfect fit.

The Fairy Attendants and the Fairy Godmother dance, joined by the Season Fairies and their partners.

Cinderella and the Prince enter and dance a final pas de deux.

STEPSISTERS ALAZNE LOPEZ EXTEBARRIA AND GRETEL PALFREY LOOK ON AS MINDI KULASHE (THE PRINCE) TRIES THE SHOE ON DANIELA ODDI (CINDERELLA), ENGLISH NATIONAL BALLET, 2013

The final scene switches from Cinderella's father's kitchen to an enchanted garden, where Cinderella and the Prince dance together under the stars.

WEDDING SCENE WITH MAIA MAKHATELI (CINDERELLA) AND ARTUR SHESTERIKOV (THE PRINCE), DUTCH NATIONAL BALLET, 2015

Les Ballets de Monte Carlo, 2001
Choreographed by Jean-Christophe Maillot, this production of *Cinderella* strips away the traditional design with Ernest Pignon-Ernest's clinical white set.

Galina Ulanova

Dancer ▪ 1910–1988

During World War II, Galina Ulanova rose to the highest tier of the Bolshoi Ballet, becoming Russia's prima ballerina. She is considered by many to be the embodiment of the Soviet school of ballet—her technical capabilities were surpassed only by her passionate devotion to each of the roles she assumed. She had a close artistic relationship with *Romeo and Juliet* composer Sergei Prokofiev, who described her as "the genius of Russian ballet, its elusive soul, its inspired poetry."

▲ **At rehearsal in the 1960s**
Galina Ulanova demonstrates a move to soloist Nina Timofeyeva. Ulanova served as ballet mistress of the Bolshoi Ballet for the last 35 years of her life. Her coaching helped to produce the next generation of great Russian ballerinas.

Galina Ulanova was born to Imperial Ballet producer Sergei Ulanov and dancer Maria Romanova. Immersed from birth in the traditions of Russian ballet, Ulanova spent her early years attending performances and learning basic technique from her mother. At the age of nine, she was accepted by the Leningrad State School of Dance, where she went on to train under Agrippina Vaganova.

Instant stardom

Ulanova's devotion to her art and hard work were quickly recognized. She was given opportunities to perform student roles at the Mariinsky Theater, where her graceful lyricism and intuitive acting set her apart.

Seeing her potential for dramatic interpretation, Vaganova personally coached Ulanova for the lead role in *Swan Lake* as part of her school graduation performance. In the audience was Fyodor Lopukhov, artistic director of the Kirov Ballet, who invited her to join his company. Six months later, Ulanova was cast as Odette/Odile in the Kirov Ballet's full-length production of *Swan Lake*.

Ulanova's debut as the Swan Queen set her career in motion. During the 1930s, she danced leading roles in classics, such as *The Sleeping Beauty* and *Giselle*, as well as numerous roles in new works by Soviet choreographers. In 1934, she originated the role of Maria in Rostislav Zakharov's new production of *The Fountain of Bakhchisarai*, and two years later portrayed Korali in his *Lost Illusions*.

After the overnight success of *Romeo and Juliet* in 1940, composer Sergei Prokofiev wrote two more full-length ballets specifically for Ulanova: *Cinderella* in 1945 and *The Stone Flower* in 1954. He especially admired how she imparted "a depth of expression unheard of in 20th-century ballet" to her roles.

Soviet heroine

With the outbreak of World War II, the Kirov Ballet was evacuated from St. Petersburg to Perm. While there, Ulanova continued to perform, dancing briefly with the Kazakh State Ballet and making stage appearances for military troops and political leaders. As political power shifted to Moscow, the Bolshoi Ballet took precedence over the Kirov. By 1944, word of Ulanova's talent had reportedly reached Stalin and she was summoned to Moscow. Within a year, she was prima ballerina of the Bolshoi Ballet.

At the height of her fame, officials praised Ulanova as a triumphant symbol of the Soviet system. She was awarded numerous accolades for her performances and contributions to the State. Named People's Artist of the USSR in 1951, she also received the Order of Lenin, and the Stalin Prize on four separate occasions. Although she was never overtly political, Ulanova was the only dancer to be named a Hero of Socialist Labor.

When travel restrictions eased during the Cold War, the Bolshoi made its first appearance at London's Royal Opera House in 1956. With Ulanova as leading ballerina, fans lined up for days to secure tickets. Her performances as Juliet and Giselle "hit our sedate Opera House like a tornado" wrote one critic. Her first appearances in New York were met with enthusiasm by critics and audiences alike.

Ulanova continued to perform into her 50s, giving her last show in 1962. She then taught ballet until her death in 1998.

▲ **Playing Juliet, 1951**
Galina Ulanova portrayed the title role in the first full-length version of *Romeo and Juliet* in 1940. The ballet was instantly hailed a masterpiece and Ulanova declared a luminary of Soviet ballet. She played the role many times over the years, as here, at the Bolshoi Theater in Moscow.

KEY WORKS

Odette/Odile, *Swan Lake*, 1929 • Title role, *Giselle*, 1932 Maria, *The Fountain of Bakhchisarai*, 1934 • Korali, *Lost Illusions*, 1936 • Title role, *Romeo and Juliet*, 1940 • Title role, *Cinderella*, 1945 • Katerina, *The Stone Flower*, 1954

TIMELINE

- **December 26, 1909** Born in St. Petersburg, Russia, daughter of Sergei Ulanov and Maria Romanova, both at the Imperial Ballet.
- **1914** Taken by her father to watch her first ballet, *The Sleeping Beauty*, in which her mother dances the Lilac Fairy.
- **1918** Enters the Leningrad State School of Ballet as a boarder due to her parents' frequent touring.
- **1923** Takes up advanced studies under the renowned teacher Agrippina Vaganova.
- **1928** Joins the Kirov Ballet in St. Petersburg, making her debut as Princess Florina in *The Sleeping Beauty*.
- **1932** Dances the title role in *Giselle*, coached by the Kirov's prima ballerina Yelena Liukom.
- **January 23, 1934** In one of the greatest portrayals of her career, debuts as Maria in *The Fountain of Bakhchisarai*.

ULANOVA WEARING HER STALIN PRIZES

- **1941** Awarded the first of four Stalin Prizes (also 1946, 1947, and 1951).
- **1944** Named prima ballerina assoluta of the Bolshoi Ballet. Appears outside Russia for the first time, dancing in Vienna, Austria.
- **1956** Draws international acclaim after performing to sold-out crowds at the Royal Opera House, London.
- **1962** Retires from performing; becomes ballet mistress and coach at the Bolshoi.
- **March 21, 1998** Dies in Moscow after a long illness.

Symphonic Variations

First performed: April 24, 1946 ▪ Venue: Royal Opera House, London ▪ Choreography and story: Frederick Ashton ▪ Music: César Franck

This work was the first ballet that choreographer Frederick Ashton created after serving in the Royal Air Force during World War II. On his return to the world of ballet, Ashton noted that, "there seemed to be a clutter of ballets with heavy stories, and I felt the whole idiom needed purifying." Ashton had listened to Belgian-French Romantic composer César Franck's *Symphonic Variations* during the war, and was inspired to create a new piece.

STORY LINE

Symphonic Variations is a one-act plotless ballet. The six solo dancers remain on stage throughout the piece. The choreography, while based in classical technique, is abstract and uses pure movement rather than depicting a narrative.

Originally, Frederick Ashton had planned an elaborate ballet with many dancers based on the theme of the four seasons. These ideas fell by the wayside during a two-month postponement while principal dancer Michael Somes recovered from an injury. Instead, a stripped-back, pure ballet emerged. Ashton took away the corps de ballet, using just principal dancers. He described the resulting ballet as "a kind of testament."

◀ **Original lineup, 1946**
Margot Fonteyn, Pamela May, and Moira Shearer cluster around Michael Somes like Apollo's muses in a tender passage. *Symphonic Variations* opens with only the women on the stage, with the men, which included Henry Danton and Brian Shaw in the original cast, joining them soon after.

▼ **The Royal Ballet, 2017**
Left to right, James Hay, Yasmine Naghdi, Vadim Muntagirov, Marianela Nuñez, Tristan Dyer, and Yuhui Choe dance in Ashton's abstract ballet.

The ballet premiered in 1946 with a star-studded cast that included the Sadler's Wells Ballet's (now The Royal Ballet) three leading ballerinas, Margot Fonteyn, Moira Shearer, and Pamela May, accompanied by Michael Somes, Brian Shaw, and Henry Danton. The company had taken up its new permanent home in the Royal Opera House just two months before and had opened with an opulent revival of *The Sleeping Beauty*—a welcome escape for audiences in a country that had just emerged from World War II. In complete contrast, *Symphonic Variations* is marked by its serenity—a tangible peace offering after the chaos of war.

Artistic collaboration

The sets for *Symphonic Variations* were provided by Ashton's 11-ballet, long-time collaborator Sophie Fedorovitch, a designer born in Russia (now in Belarus), who had immigrated to the UK in 1920.

Symphonic Variations proved a challenge both for Ashton and Fedorovitch, as they needed to make sure that the six dancers and the accompanying set would have an impact on the large Royal Opera House stage, even to the very back of the vast auditorium. The greenish-yellow color of the backdrop was inspired by sunshine that the choreographer and designer saw through the trees when cycling in Norfolk, UK. Ashton recalled: "One day we came up a hill and suddenly there was the most marvelous glade, filled with sunshine, and this had the most terrific effect on us. I said, 'This is the color it's got to be'." The resulting backdrop created an arresting setting for Ashton's pure balletic choreography, which continues to receive critical acclaim around the globe.

▶ **Simple ensemble**
The costume worn by Vadim Muntagirov, seen here with Marianela Nuñez, repeats the black lines of the strikingly colored backdrop.

NEWARK PUBLIC LIBRARY
121 HIGH ST.
NEWARK, NY 14513

The Four Temperaments

First performed: November 20, 1946 ▪ Venue: Central High School of Needle Trades, New York ▪ Choreography: George Balanchine ▪ Music: Paul Hindemith

Unlike anything its first audience and critics had ever seen in ballet before, *The Four Temperaments* was an unprecedented step in choreographic history that signaled the beginning of a new artistic era. Creating an original, visually and emotionally powerful language that reimagined classical moves, Balanchine established a modern, distinctively American style of dance, and a work that was to define the New York City Ballet company.

STORY LINE

A non-narrative, abstract ballet, *The Four Temperaments* interprets a piece of music (comprising a theme and four variations) based on the ancient Greek concept of the four "humors." In a healthy body, these humors are in balance. When one humor dominates, however, it dictates a person's temperament or personality—making them melancholic (gloomy and pensive), sanguine (headstrong and passionate), phlegmatic (unemotional and passive), or choleric (bad-tempered and angry).

In 1946, George Balanchine and impresario Lincoln Kirstein founded a small ballet troupe—the Ballet Society (later renamed New York City Ballet). Performed as part of the troupe's opening program, *The Four Temperaments* marked a milestone in Balanchine's development of a new American neoclassical style of ballet. Its experimental choreography, which distorted and accentuated classical lines, launched a new language of dance, and displayed moves that were to become Balanchine's signature style: attitude derrières folding at sharp 90-degree angles, classical positions accented with forward pelvic thrusts, and flexed feet and hands.

A fresh approach

Not initially intended for dance, the score had been commissioned originally from composer Paul Hindemath in 1940 as a short piece of chamber music for Balanchine to play on his piano at home and with friends. Balanchine liked it so much that six years later he used it as a basis for *The Four Temperaments*, in which he tried to distill the essence of the music into a new style of choreography.

This focus on the abstract interpretation of emotion through dance was also reflected in the evolving costumes for the ballet. In the original designs, artist Kurt Seligmann had tried to personify the four personality types themed in the music. However, the cumbersome outfits, which featured elaborate spiky and veiled headpieces, obscured the choreography, hindered the movement of the dancers, and eventually proved too complicated for Balanchine's taste.

▲ **Iconic choreography**
Hieroglyphic arm movements became a signature Balanchine move—part of his development of a new, and strikingly original, language of dance.

When Balanchine restaged *The Four Temperaments* in 1951 for New York City Ballet, he stripped away the sets and costumes with a minimalist veracity that exposed the brilliant speed and precision of his choreography in its most pure and energized form. This iconic "black and white" version of the ballet—with female dancers in black leotards and white tights, and the men in white tops and black leggings—set a style that was to become an established Balanchine aesthetic and is the version that continues to be performed worldwide today.

◀ **The Royal Ballet, 2006**
Darcey Bussell and Carlos Acosta perform in *The Four Temperaments* at the Royal Opera House, London.

▶ **Simplified costumes**
The complicated outfits originally designed for the ballet were quickly replaced by simple practice clothes that focused attention on the choreography.

Symphony in C

First performed: October 11, 1948 ▪ Venue: New York City Center ▪ Choreography: George Balanchine ▪ Music: Georges Bizet

Culminating in a spectacular finale with the entire cast of 52 dancers on stage in a sea of glittering white tutus, *Symphony in C* is an exhilarating representation of Bizet's music through dance. Each of the ballet's four movements corresponds choreographically to the four sections of Bizet's symphony. One of Balanchine's most popular works, this "black and white ballet" demonstrates that even without a story line, a ballet can be a triumph.

STORY LINE

This ballet is plotless.

Allegro Vivo Virtuoso footwork abounds. There are no in-between positions, and precise tendus sharpen changes in direction.

Adagio Soft port de bras, floating bourrées, and elegantly held leg extensions complement the poetic oboe melody. Comparable to a scaled-down version of Act II of *Swan Lake*, this section inspired Suzanne Farrell to become a ballerina.

Allegro Vivace This, the most energetic movement, has bouncing choreography with plenty of pliés and nonstop relevés, while the leading ballerina soars on and off the stage in jumps, supported by her partner.

Second Allegro Vivace Gallops en pointe and fast whip turns feature in the fourth movement, which runs into the grand finale.

While in Paris as guest ballet master at the Paris Opéra Ballet, George Balanchine choreographed *Le Palais de cristal*, which would later become known as *Symphony in C*. As the work was intended to be a tribute to the Paris Opéra Ballet, Balanchine thought it best to select music from a French composer. His friend Igor Stravinsky suggested the little-known work *Symphony in C Major* by Georges Bizet. Composed in 1855 when Bizet was just 17 years old, the manuscript had never been published and was only discovered in a conservatory library in 1933. Upon hearing the score, Balanchine took just two weeks to choreograph the ballet.

In 1947, *Le Palais de cristal* debuted at the Théâtre National de l'Opéra to great acclaim. Like many of Balanchine's works, it did not follow any particular narrative. Instead, he structured the four movements of the ballet around different precious gemstones. Emeralds, Rubies, Black Diamonds, and Pearls were represented in the colors of the costume design—a concept Balanchine revisited in *Jewels*.

The following year, Balanchine returned to New York and restaged the work for his own American troupe. He made significant changes to the choreography, eliminated the color scheme, simplified the sets, and renamed the work. *Symphony in C* was presented as the grand finale of New York City Ballet's first official performance.

◀ **New York City Ballet, 2012**
Each movement has a principal male dancer and ballerina. Here, Sara Mearns dances the second movement, the Adagio, with Jonathan Stafford.

▲ **Deutsche Oper, Berlin, 1994**
Bettina Thiel and Michael Rissmann take the lead in Balanchine's abstract ballet. Typically, the stage setting is simple, so focus is on the choreography.

▶ **The Royal Ballet, 2010**
The costume design by Anthony Dowell follows Balanchine's monochromatic color scheme. Rupert Pennefather partners Marianela Nuñez.

Frederick Ashton

Choreographer ▪ 1904–1988

Founding choreographer of The Royal Ballet, Frederick Ashton established the "English style" in ballet through lyrical, elegant, technically challenging, yet playful, works. He subtly included his signature sequence, the "Fred Step," in many of his ballets, often tucked away in the moves of the corps de ballet or a minor character. With every step he told a story, and each story was unique. He produced over 100 works in his lifetime, many of which are performed all over the world today.

▲ **Choreographic signature**
Lynn Seymour and Anthony Dowell rehearse with Frederick Ashton for *A Month in the Country*. The ballet includes a clear Fred Step sequence of arabesque, fondu, coupé, petit développé, pas de bourrée, and pas de chat as the duo exit the stage arm in arm.

The quintessentially English choreographer's story began in Ecuador, where Ashton's father was vice-consul at the British Embassy. The family soon moved to Peru, and it was here that Ashton decided he wanted to enter the ballet world after seeing Anna Pavlova, who became his lifelong idol, give a mesmerizing performance.

At the age of 14, Ashton was sent to boarding school in the UK. He hated it. Instead of studying, he spent his teenage years watching ballet. His conventional family—his father George especially—disapproved of his aspiration to become a dancer. When, in 1924, George killed himself, Frederick's brothers received most of the inheritance, and Frederick was left poor but free to pursue his dream.

Dancing and early career

Aged 20, Ashton took ballet lessons with Léonide Massine. When Massine left for the Ballets Russes, he recommended Ashton to study with Marie Rambert, who was short on male dancers, and so taught him for free. It was Rambert who spotted Ashton's talent for choreography. With her encouragement, he debuted as a choreographer in *Tragedy of Fashion* (1926).

In 1928, Ashton left for France to join the Ida Rubinstein Ballet as a dancer, where he worked with the company's chief choreographers Léonide Massine and Bronislava Nijinska. The following year, Ashton returned to London to work for Rambert, as well as for the newly formed Camargo Society and other theatrical ventures. His social life was equally busy, filled with lavish parties held by aristocratic friends in the ballet world.

Gradually, Ashton made his name as a choreographer, and early notable works include *Capriol Suite* (1930) and *Façade* (1931). In 1931, he began working for Ninette de Valois' new company, the Vic-Wells Ballet (later The Royal Ballet). *Les Rendezvous*, which premiered in December 1933 at the Sadler's Wells Theatre, was Ashton's first major work for the Vic-Wells Ballet. The one-act ballet had no plot, but was a series of playful, flirtatious dances in a park, which showcased the technical mastery of its leading stars, the feather-light Alicia Markova and lively Stanislas Idzikowsky.

Choreographic strength

In 1935, Ashton was appointed resident choreographer of the Vic-Wells Ballet and stayed with the company for 35 years, although World War II temporarily interrupted his career, when he was called up for service with the Royal Air Force. At the end of the war, the company moved to its current home, the Royal Opera House in Covent Garden. Ashton's first work there was *Symphonic Variations* (1946), an abstract one-act ballet.

Ashton's first full-length ballet, just two years later, was *Cinderella*. Departing from classic Russian productions, he injected comedy in British pantomime style with the introduction of the Ugly Sisters, one of whom he played himself. Many of Ashton's best-known and later works were choreographed for Margot Fonteyn, including *Sylvia* (1952) and *Ondine* (1958).

Ashton's final full-length ballet was *La Fille mal gardée* in 1960. Inspired by the Suffolk countryside he loved, this was his most English ballet, charmingly including a Lancashire clog dance and a maypole dance scene. He retired in 1970, but continued to choreograph until his death.

▲ **Rehearsing an iconic role**
Rudolf Nureyev (left) rehearses with Frederick Ashton for *Marguerite and Armand*. This was the ballet that cemented the dancing partnership of Margot Fonteyn and Nureyev. Although Ashton did not originally conceive the work with Nureyev in mind, the title roles became synonymous with the two dancers and only they danced the ballet in their, and Ashton's, lifetimes.

KEY WORKS

Façade, 1931 • *Les Rendezvous*, 1933 • *Symphonic Variations*, 1946 • *Cinderella*, 1948 • *Scènes de ballet*, 1948 • *Sylvia*, 1952 *La Fille mal gardée*, 1960 • *Two Pigeons*, 1961 • *Marguerite and Armand*, 1963 • *The Dream*, 1964 • *Enigma Variations*, 1968 • *A Month in the Country*, 1976 • *Rhapsody*, 1980

TIMELINE

- **September 17, 1904** Born in Ecuador to George Ashton and Charlotte Fulcher.
- **1907** Family moves to Lima, Peru, after the birth of his sister, the fifth child.
- **1917** Decides to pursue a career in dance, after seeing Anna Pavlova perform.
- **1918** Sent to school in the UK, and sees ballets in London, including performances by Isadora Duncan and Pavlova.
- **1924** Father dies; takes ballet lessons with Léonide Massine, then with Marie Rambert.
- **1926** Debuts as a choreographer in *Tragedy of Fashion* for Marie Rambert.
- **1928** Joins Ida Rubinstein's company in France as a dancer.
- **1929** Returns from France to London, resuming work as a dancer and choreographer for Rambert.
- **1935** Appointed resident choreographer at the Vic-Wells Ballet (now The Royal Ballet), founded by Ninette de Valois.
- **1948** Produces *Cinderella*, his first full-length ballet.
- **1961** Choreographs *La Fille mal gardée*.
- **1962** Knighted by Elizabeth II.
- **1963** Appointed director of The Royal Ballet as a successor to Ninette de Valois.
- **1970** Retires from The Royal Ballet, replaced by Kenneth MacMillan.
- **1980** Produces last major work, *Rhapsody*.
- **August 19, 1988** Dies in Suffolk, England.

AS AN UGLY SISTER (RIGHT), 1965, IN *CINDERELLA*

Scènes de ballet

First performed: February 11, 1948 ▪ Venue: Royal Opera House, London ▪ Choreography and story: Frederick Ashton ▪ Music: Igor Stravinsky

This groundbreaking ballet employed classical techniques and traditions to new effect and focused on abstract shapes and formal, geometric designs rather than plot. With a hard-edged score by Igor Stravinsky, featuring complex, irregular rhythms, and graphic costumes by a young French artist, the ballet promoted a more modern, neoclassical style of dance. Choreographed by Frederick Ashton, it was one of his favorite works.

STORY LINE

This one-act, non-narrative ballet makes use of classic (i.e., pure) ballet techniques to create abstract patterns and graphic effects over 20 minutes. A ballerina, male partner, four male soloists, and a corps de ballet of 12 women perform pas de deux, principal solos, group dances, and an ecstatic finale.

Its choreographer, Frederick Ashton, explained, "I wanted to do a ballet that could be seen from any angle—meaning anywhere could be front, so to speak. So I did these geometric figures that are not always facing front—if you saw *Scènes de ballet* from the wings, you'd get a very different but equally good picture."

Scènes de ballet was devised by choreographer Frederick Ashton as a follow-up to his hugely successful *Symphonic Variations* of 1946. Keen to build on the public's affection for this work, and the growing appetite for a more modern style of dance, Ashton created *Scènes de ballet* along the same lines. The ballet premiered with Margot Fonteyn and Michael Somes in the principal roles.

Abstract design

The ballet was conceived as an homage to the 19th-century classicist Marius Petipa, with Ashton reinterpreting the emotional and technical facets of classical ballet in a new abstract form. Ashton became fascinated with geometric floor patterns for the dancers, and used these to create a ballet that could be viewed from all angles.

The work had an astringent, detached quality—which was in marked contrast to the gentle lyricism of the earlier *Symphonic Variations*—and was danced to a sharp, acerbic score by Igor Stravinsky, which had been composed in 1944 for a Broadway revue.

The ballet's set (a green-gray viaduct) and dramatic, graphic costumes were designed by André Beaurepaire, but disagreements with Ashton made for a tense collaboration. In January 1948, Ashton noted the difficulty of working through "all [the ballet's] problems, not the smallest of which has been Beaurepaire." The final costumes—modernist reworkings of traditional tunics and tutus—however, proved to be a triumph.

◀ **Iconic costume**
Sarah Lamb (2011) wears the striking tutu design, pearl bracelets, and chokers originally created for Margot Fonteyn by André Beaurepaire.

▲ **Royal Opera House performances**
Moira Shearer at the Royal Opera House, London, 1948. The ballet has been performed here nearly 200 times.

Later productions

Stravinsky's 1944 score, which specified 11 different dances to match each section of the music, has been used by various choreographers. In 1972, John Taras used the score to create a new version of *Scènes de ballet* for New York City Ballet at the New York State Theater. The score was also used in 1999 by Christopher Wheeldon, in a work for students from the School of American Ballet. The Royal Ballet has revived Ashton's original work numerous times at the Royal Opera House, most recently in 2014.

▶ **Debut production**
Margot Fonteyn, Michael Somes, and members of the Sadler's Wells Ballet perform *Scènes de ballet* at the Royal Opera House, London, 1948.

Alicia Markova

Ballerina, choreographer, director, and teacher ▪ 1910–2004

Famed for her exceptional buoyancy and flawless technique, Alicia Markova was the UK's first prima ballerina, and became the first British ballerina to dance the lead role in *Giselle*. Despite changing her surname to one that sounded Russian, Markova continued to believe not only in British ballet, but in ballet being non-elitist, dancing in many unconventional venues, and introducing the dance form to audiences all over the UK and the rest of the world.

▲ **Demonstrating a pose**
In this image from 1965, Markova is seen showing a position to dancer Carol Moon (left), while being lifted by Hans Meister, during her time at the Metropolitan Opera Ballet in New York.

Born in London and named Lilian Alicia Marks by her Irish-Jewish parents, there was seemingly little resemblance between "little Lily" and the great ballerina she became. She was a fragile child and suffered weak legs, but it was due to her condition that she started dancing, after her doctor suggested taking dance lessons to strengthen her legs. As an adult, she remained petite, which contributed to the unique lightness in her dancing; her steps never made a sound on stage.

Child Pavlova

Markova made her professional debut in 1920 at the age of 10 in the pantomime *Dick Whittington*. She quickly became known as the "Child Pavlova," and was described by the *Daily Telegraph* as "a very accomplished ballerina in the miniature."

While taking lessons in London at Princess Seraphine Astafieva's prestigious Russian dance academy, her talents were spotted by Sergei Diaghilev, impresario of the Ballets Russes. Although she was only 13, he offered her a position at the Ballets Russes. She joined in Monte Carlo shortly after turning 14. This is when Diaghilev changed her surname to Markova.

Markova spent her teenage years at the Ballets Russes, absorbing and observing the works of some of the most extraordinary names in ballet history, whether through lessons with Enrico Cecchetti or getting costumes designed by Henri Matisse. Dancer Ninette de Valois took her under her wing, and she worked intensely with the young George Balanchine. Composer Igor Stravinsky was very fond of her, even conducting orchestras for her rehearsals. Shortly after the end of the 1928–1929 season at the Ballets Russes, Diaghilev offered the 18-year-old Markova the lead in *Giselle*. Tragically, Diaghilev died the same year and the Ballets Russes collapsed.

Ambassador for British ballet

Returning to the UK, Markova became the muse of Frederick Ashton, an emerging dancer and choreographer. Their first collaboration was Dryden's *Marriage à la Mode* in London, which received great acclaim. She became the perfect ambassador for British ballet, working for Marie Rambert, who had set up the UK's first dance company—the Ballet Club—as well as for the Camargo Society, which promoted British talent.

In 1931, Markova joined the Vic-Wells Ballet, becoming the first British prima ballerina, and in 1934, the first to dance the lead in *Giselle*. The following year, she set up a new ballet company with her dance partner Anton Dolin, which toured the UK for two years, promoting and performing ballet to non-elite audiences.

In 1938, Markova joined the Ballet Russe de Monte Carlo, successor to the Ballets Russes, traveling to New York with the company at the outbreak of World War II. She stayed with the company until 1941 when she joined the Ballet Theatre, where she was reunited with Dolin. Together they re-formed the Markova-Dolin company and toured internationally.

After the war, Markova and Dolin returned to the UK, and in 1950, founded the Festival Ballet (today's English National Ballet). After retiring from the stage in 1963, Markova was appointed director of the Metropolitan Opera Ballet in New York, where she lectured and taught.

▲ **Grace of a swan**
Alicia Markova holds an elegant pose from her role as Odette/Odile in Tchaikovsky's *Swan Lake* at the Vic-Wells Ballet's premiere in 1934. It was the first time the ballet had been performed in the UK in full.

KEY WORKS

Dancer: *Marriage à la Mode*, 1930 • *Les Sylphides*, 1931 • *Les Rendezvous*, 1933 • *Giselle*, 1934 • *Swan Lake*, 1934 • *The Nutcracker*, 1934 • *Romeo and Juliet*, 1942 • *The Sleeping Beauty*, 1948

TIMELINE

- **December 1, 1910** Born Lilian Alicia Marks in London, to Alfred and Eileen Marks.
- **1920** Debuts at the age of 10 in the pantomime *Dick Whittington*.
- **1921** Offered a specially written part by Sergei Diaghilev for his production of *The Sleeping Princess*. Illness prevents her debut.
- **1924** Joins the Ballets Russes in Monte Carlo, aged 14.
- **1926** Dances her first major role, the Nightingale in *Le Chant du Rossignol*.
- **1930** Begins working with Frederick Ashton, starring in *Marriage à la Mode*.
- **1931** Joins de Valois' new company, the Vic-Wells Ballet (now The Royal Ballet).
- **1934** Dances the lead role in the first-ever production of *Giselle* in the UK.
- **1935** Sets up the Markova-Dolin company with dance partner Anton Dolin.
- **1938** Joins the Ballet Russe de Monte Carlo and follows the company to the US.
- **1950** Returns to the UK and co-founds the Festival Ballet with Dolin.
- **1958** Receives a CBE.
- **1963** Retires from performing and is made a dame. Appointed director of the Metropolitan Opera Ballet in New York.

MARKOVA APPEARS ON THE COVER OF *THE DANCING TIMES*, 1940

- **1971** Becomes a professor at the University of Cincinnati Conservatory of Music.
- **December 2, 2004** Dies in a hospital in Bath the day after her birthday, aged 94.

AMERICAN BALLET

Synonymous with all that is best in American ballet, New York City Ballet is fresh, vital, and forward-thinking, with its own distinctive brand of artistry—athletic and contemporary. In 1934, a pivotal year for ballet in the US, Russo-Georgian dancer and choreographer George Balanchine came to the country at the behest of philanthropists Lincoln Kirstein and Edward Warburg. They wanted him to found a major classical ballet company that would be truly American, but able to rival anything offered in Europe.

Balanchine agreed but, following the philosophy of his own training at the Imperial Ballet School in Russia, started by creating a school. The first enterprise was staffed by many Russian emigrant dancers and teachers. Out of this grew American Ballet (the first Balanchine company, 1935), and Ballet Caravan (1936). In tandem, another US ballet company was in the making. American dancer and dramatist Lucia Chase, together with several colleagues, was also on a quest to create a home-grown ballet company. She founded Ballet Theatre in 1939, which, by 1957, had become known as American Ballet Theatre. It is still one of the world's leading classical ballet companies.

In 1948, Balanchine's company gave its first public performance (of his *Orpheus*) at the Center Theater of the New York City Center of Music and Drama, and shortly afterward changed its name to New York City Ballet. From 1950, its prestige grew with many foreign tours. It relocated to its present home, Lincoln Center for the Performing Arts, in 1964. The company has an extremely wide repertoire, and performs during the summer months at the Saratoga Performing Arts Center in Saratoga, New York.

> I don't want people who want to dance, I want people who have to dance.
>
> GEORGE BALANCHINE

***Architecture of Dance*, 2010** ▶
Spanish architect Santiago Calatrava, known for his seemingly airborne structures, collaborated with New York City Ballet to produce gravity-defying sets for their 2010 spring season of new choreography.

George Balanchine

Choreographer ▪ 1904–1983

One name stands head and shoulders above all others in American ballet: George Balanchine, or "Mr. B" as everyone called him. Balanchine created over 200 ballets, and choreographed for Broadway, vaudeville, opera, film, television, and even the circus: in total 425 works. Through the School of American Ballet, and ultimately New York City Ballet, he single-handedly created the distinctive American style, and choreographed some uniquely stateside ballets.

▲ **Bringing music to life**
Dancers from the New York City Ballet perform Balanchine's *Agon* at the London Coliseum in 2008. Consisting of a series of dance routines without a plot, the choreography presents Stravinsky's composition in form and movement.

The son of a composer, Georgi Balanchivadze was born in 1904 in St. Petersburg, where later he studied at the city's Imperial Ballet School and Conservatory of Music. He choreographed his first piece, *La Nuit*, in 1920, and in 1923 he helped to establish the avant-garde Young Ballet troupe, which drew disapproval from Russian authorities due to its experimental style. On tour in Europe the following year, Balanchine and three others refused to return to Russia, instead defecting to the West, joining Sergei Diaghilev's Ballets Russes.

The American dream

Balanchine choreographed many ballets for Diaghilev, most notably *Apollon Musagète* (1928), commonly known as *Apollo*, which even Balanchine regarded as the crucial turning point in his artistic life. With its roots in classicism, but with 19th-century decoration—large sets, tutus, and intricate narratives—stripped away, Balanchine emphasized technique and imbued his choreography with elements of jazz, the Charleston, and even acrobatics.

Lincoln Kirstein, a wealthy American ballet aficionado, had a dream: to create a new distinctive American ballet. In Balanchine, he saw how this could be realized and invited him to the US. However, when first approached by Kirstein, Balanchine knew that his American ballet plan would not work without a solid base. His famous reply was, "But first, a school," which led to the formation of the School of American Ballet in New York in 1934.

Balanchine's first creation for the school was *Serenade* in 1934. Full of poetic yearning, in the opening gesture each dancer stands with one arm raised, seeming appropriately aspirational. Balanchine's ballets were not always well-regarded initially, and his and Kirstein's first company, The American Ballet, survived for only three years. The pair persevered, and their new group, American Ballet Caravan, was taken on a tour of South America in 1941, before they formed Ballet Society in 1946, and then the New York City Ballet in 1948.

Balanchine was involved in every aspect of their company, where he preferred the title of ballet master. One of his famous quotes is that ballet "… is a woman," and he had several muses: Tamara Geva, Vera Zorina, Maria Tallchief, and Tanaquil Le Clercq, all of whom he married, and Suzanne Farrell. While only some personified the notion of the "Balanchine ballerina" (long-legged, thin, and cool), they danced in his style—with attack and energy, streamlined clarity, fast footwork, big extensions, and full turnouts.

The great collaborator

Balanchine's extensive musical education allowed him to explore and dissect a score in great detail, and to collaborate closely with composers, notably Stravinsky, to whose music he choreographed 39 ballets. His range was enormous, with highlights including his modernist masterpieces, *The Four Temperaments* (1946), *Agon* (1957), and *Stravinsky Violin Concerto* (1972). Plotless and usually performed in simple practice clothes against a plain backdrop, they are the essence of his belief that the perfect meeting of movement and music is an end in itself. Balanchine's best-known work, however, is his 1954 staging of *The Nutcracker*, which the company has performed every year since for its Christmas season in New York.

> He changed the way we look at dance. Very few people in the history of any art have that kind of impact.

EDWIN DENBY, DANCE CRITIC, 1983

▲ **Dance rehearsal**
George Balanchine (left) and Arthur Mitchen rehearse for a performance of Balanchine's *The Four Temperaments* in 1969. The ballet featured four variations: melancholic; sanguinic; phlegmatic; and choleric.

KEY WORKS

Le Chant du Rossignol, 1925 • *Apollo*, 1928 • *Serenade*, 1934
Orpheus, 1948 • *The Nutcracker*, 1954 • *Agon*, 1958
Monumenum pro Gesualdo, 1960 • *Don Quixote*, 1965

TIMELINE

- **January 22, 1904** Born Georgi Melitonovich Balanchivadze in St. Petersburg to a family of musicians.

- **1914** Learns ballet at the Imperial Ballet School, St. Petersburg, making his first stage appearance later that year as a Cupid in *The Sleeping Beauty*.

- **1921** Joins the corps de ballet of the Mariinsky Theater Ballet Company, where he later stages his composition, *Enigmas*.

- **1924** While touring in Europe, joins Diaghilev's Ballets Russes in Paris. Following a knee injury, serves as choreographer and ballet master for the next five years.

BALANCHINE ON THE COVER OF *LIFE INTERNATIONAL* MAGAZINE, 1965

- **1933** Sets up his own ballet company, Les Ballets, in Paris.

- **1934** After traveling to the US at the invitation of Lincoln Kirstein, founds the School of American Ballet in New York.

- **1935** His touring company, the American Ballet, becomes the resident ballet of New York's Metropolitan Opera. Balanchine becomes ballet master.

- **1948** Co-founds the New York City Ballet, becoming its artistic director.

- **1962** Returns to the Soviet Union, touring with the New York City Ballet to great acclaim.

- **1972** Stages the New York City Ballet's first festival, a celebration of the life and work of Igor Stravinsky.

- **1983** Receives the Presidential Medal of Freedom, the highest civilian honor awarded in the US. Dies later that year, on April 30, in New York.

Agon

First performed: December 1, 1957 ▪ Venue: City Center of Music and Drama, New York ▪ Choreography: George Balanchine ▪ Music: Stravinsky

Considered by many to be Balanchine at his best, *Agon* is an uncompromising, modernist ballet that has thrilled audiences ever since its premiere. Devoid of plot, characters, costumes, or set, it is a pure, physical representation of human intimacy and tension that defies interpretation or analysis. It was designed to stretch the boundaries of ballet, and continues to do so, remaining part of the repertoire of many leading companies to this day.

STORY LINE

Agon has no plot and consists of 12 dances divided into four sections—three dances apiece. The curtain rises to reveal four men standing upstage with their backs to the audience, which is also how the ballet ends.

The middle section starts with two pas de trois, with choreography that finds new rhythms and expression, while recalling what has already been seen. The Saraband for a solo male has been called Cubist, while the Galliarde for two women is neoclassical. The Bransle Simple is a canon for two men, while castanets add Spanish flavor to the Bransle Gay for the female solo.

One courtly element remains, a formal bow at each change. *Agon* is unconventional, yet the pas de deux still forms the heart of the ballet.

Following the success of *Orpheus* in 1948, Lincoln Kirstein (cofounder of the School of American Ballet) and Balanchine were eager to collaborate with Stravinsky on a new ballet, which, alongside *Apollo*, would form the third part of a trilogy. After rejecting several subjects, Stravinsky was finally inspired by a manual of 17th-century French court dances by François de Lauze.

Stravinsky and Balanchine frequently worked very closely but never more so than with *Agon*, in which their music and choreography became intrinsically entwined. Together, they drew up a detailed initial sketch that set out the ballet's structure as well as details of the instrumentation, including precise timings of movements. As *Agon* developed, the de Lauze manual came to be almost the only thing French about the ballet, just as the title, which means contest or struggle, was the only thing Greek.

Pushing boundaries

Stravinsky wrote the score at a time when he had a growing interest in 12-tone music, which is gradually revealed as the ballet progresses. Closely complementing Balanchine's choreography, Stravinsky's score for the larger ensemble pieces employed a full orchestra. For the solos, duets, and trios, he used smaller chamber ensembles, often with unique combinations of instruments.

Agon has 12 pieces of music and is a ballet for 12 dancers wearing practice clothes, and set against a plain backdrop. Balanchine wrote, "It is all precise, like a machine, but a machine that thinks." The choreography was designed to be as unconventional and challenging as the score. For the dancers, it was often difficult to perform, and for the audience it could be uncomfortable to watch. Sexual tension is often present; in one lift, a female dancer performs a front-facing split, which was particularly graphic for the period. In contrast, there are also moments of tenderness, the man carefully guiding or placing the woman's feet and legs.

In keeping with the unorthodox choreography and score was the political element of the ballet. The original cast featured Diana Adams and Arthur Mitchell in a mixed-race pairing that made a timely statement in the social climate of the US in the late 1950s, which further underlined the ballet's modernity.

▶ **Visual tension**
American dancers Wendy Whelan and Albert Evans of the New York City Ballet perform at the London Coliseum in 2008.

Boléro

First performed: January 10, 1961 ▪ Venue: Théâtre Royal de la Monnaie, Brussels ▪ Choreography: Maurice Béjart ▪ Music: Maurice Ravel

Commissioned by Russian actress and dancer Ida Rubinstein, *Boléro* was first choreographed as a ballet by Bronislava Nijinska in 1928. It was an exercise in movement and drama, and while innovative, it is Béjart's version that is known today. Against Ravel's sensual score, Béjart's stripped-back choreography has a raw, mechanical quality, mirroring the lead dancer's vulnerability at the center of a restless crowd.

▲ **Role reversal**
Argentinian dancer Jorge Donn performs the lead role, surrounded by men reaching toward him in unison, at the Palais des Congrès de Paris in 1988.

▼ **Taking the lead**
French dancer Sylvie Guillem dances for a circle of admirers in *Boléro* with the Paris Opéra Ballet in 1986. It later became her defining role.

Béjart recreated *Boléro* in 1960 for his muse, Duška Sifnios, a ballerina in his company, Ballet du XXe Siècle. While he retained the essence of Nijinska's original ballet, Béjart pared back the choreography to simple, repetitive movements, leaving an elemental core of raw emotion expressed through rhythm. The startling, almost non-choreography centers around a dancer on a tabletop, surrounded by seated men, who gradually become involved in the movement as it intensifies. The ballet climaxes with the union of the dancer and men on the table.

Béjart's interpretation of *Boléro* has been restaged many times since. In 1979, male dancer Jorge Donn took the role of the principal dancer, becoming the first male to do so. His performance was used by French filmmaker, Claude Lelouch, in the 1981 art house film, *Les Uns et les Autres.*

One of the best-known performances of Béjart's *Boléro* was by Sylvie Guillem of the Paris Opéra Ballet, at the London Palladium in 1990. Assisted by a group of 40 male dancers, she captivated the audience in what is widely regarded as her finest performance. Perhaps fittingly, it was this ballet that Guillem chose to mark her retirement from the stage, her final performance being *Boléro* in Yokohama, Japan, in 2014.

STORY LINE

Boléro is a plotless ballet consisting of a single act. In Nijinska's original version, set in an Andalusian tavern, a Gypsy Woman is encouraged to dance on a tabletop by a group of men. Center-stage, she dances slowly at first, her movements becoming quicker and more intense as the music builds. As she dances, it triggers a sensual reaction amongst the men watching her.

Following a duet, the ballet reaches its climax when the woman is thrown from the table and caught by the surrounding men. In Béjart's version, the ballet ends with the dancer and men together on the table.

Maurice Béjart

Dancer, choreographer, and director ▪ 1927–2007

One of the most avant-garde choreographers of the 20th century, Maurice Béjart was the controversial director of the Ballet du XXe Siècle. Noted for flamboyant theatricality, Béjart treated dance as spectacle, fusing classical and modern movement with diverse musical styles and themes. Béjart saw ballet as popular art and set out to attract those that classical ballet missed, staging large works in unorthodox spaces. His approach had popular appeal, but critics sniped at what they saw as sensationalism.

▲ ***Ballet for Life***
Dressed in costumes designed by Gianni Versace and accompanied by the Cologne Philharmonic, Béjart Ballet Lausanne perform at the 28th Cologne Summer Festival in Germany. Béjart's 1997 work is set to music by Queen and Mozart.

Béjart first discovered a talent for expressive choreography during a tour of Sweden with the Cullberg Ballet in 1949, prompting him to set up Les Ballets de l'Etoile, (later Le Ballet-Théâtre de Paris) on his return to France. In Paris, Béjart pioneered the use of electronic and multimedia compositions, especially *musique concrète* (produced by the combining and manipulation of sound), which he saw as having a vast range of choreographic possibilities. Writing about *Symphonie pour un homme seul* (1955), critic Arnold Haskell noted the cohesion between gesture and rhythm, calling it "a work of brutal, hallucinatory power."

Béjart's first great triumph came with *The Rite of Spring* (1959) for the Théâtre Royal de la Monnaie in Brussels. Without classical steps and with groups of 50 dancers as a single writhing mass, it was novel for its time. After its rapturous reception, he formed the Ballet du XXe Siècle (later Béjart Ballet Lausanne) in the city the following year.

Leading men

Béjart had a huge effect on male dance. He drew guest stars like Vladimir Vasiliev, Richard Cragun, and Rudolf Nureyev for whom he created *Songs of a Wayfarer* (1971). While Béjart choreographed solos for women, including the modern-dance inspired *Isadora* (1976) for Maya Plisetskaya, he preferred men for his ensembles. In a 1983 interview, he joked that his ideal company would have 40 male dancers and five ballerinas. A male corps is most associated with *Boléro* (1961). The solo role was created for a woman, first performed by Plisetskaya. The soloist is elevated on a platform while 40 dancers undulate to Ravel's climactic rhythm, in what Béjart saw as a primitive, spiritual ritual.

Béjart continued to develop his concept of "totaltheater"—bringing together words, music, dance, and direction—in productions such as *Ninth Symphony* (1964). Based on text by the German philosopher Nietzsche, it is a vast realization of Beethoven's masterpiece, with 50 dancers, an orchestra, choir, and audience participation. Another success was *The Firebird* (1970). Danced to a Stravinsky suite rather than a full ballet score, the allegory of revolution, idealism, and rebirth features men in the lead roles.

Cultural diversity

Béjart was exposed to Eastern philosophy by his father, French-Senegalese philosopher Gaston Berger, and developed an interest in Asian philosophy. He was also inspired by traditional art and admired Japanese theater. As his taste for cultural diversity grew, he created works such as *Golestan* (1973), based on a poem by 13th-century Persian poet Sa'adi and set to Iranian music, and *Kabuki* (1986), about samurai honor, with the suicide of 47 samurai at its finale.

Among the most famous of Béjart's later works is his disorienting version of *The Nutcracker* (1998), in which a boy suffers Freudian nightmares as he strives to reconnect with his mother.

Béjart died in 2007 while working on *Round the World in 80 Minutes* but his artistic philosophy continues to be followed today at the Rudra Béjart School in Lausanne, Switzerland, which he established in 1992. The school's two-year course in classical and modern techniques, traditional dances, and Kendo ensures a very Béjartian blending of artistic expression.

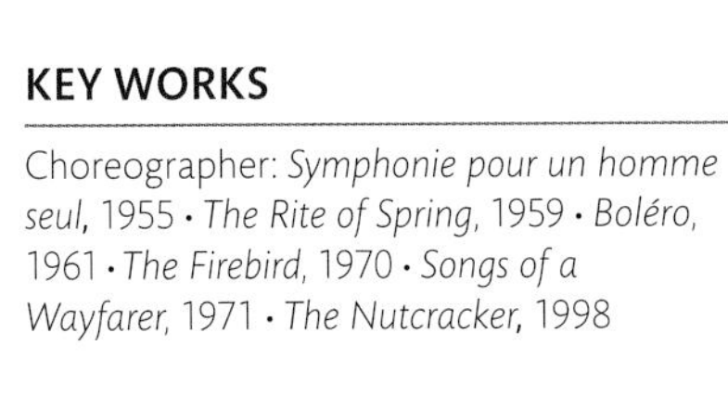

KEY WORKS

Choreographer: *Symphonie pour un homme seul*, 1955 • *The Rite of Spring*, 1959 • *Boléro*, 1961 • *The Firebird*, 1970 • *Songs of a Wayfarer*, 1971 • *The Nutcracker*, 1998

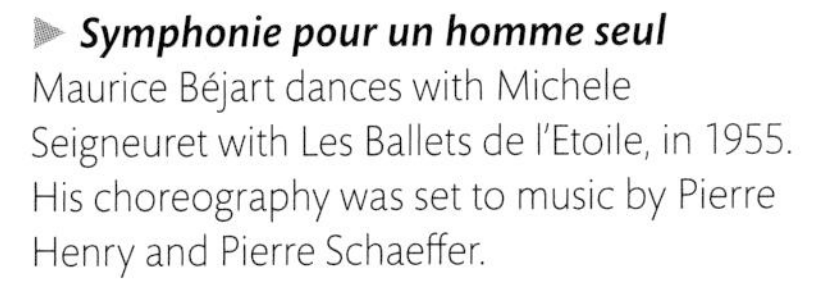

▶ ***Symphonie pour un homme seul***
Maurice Béjart dances with Michele Seigneuret with Les Ballets de l'Etoile, in 1955. His choreography was set to music by Pierre Henry and Pierre Schaeffer.

TIMELINE

- **January 1, 1927** Born Maurice-Jean Berger in Marseilles, France, son of philosopher Gaston Berger.
- **1938** Begins dance lessons on medical advice to improve his slight physique.
- **1945** Assuming the pseudonym Béjart, debuts at Marseille Opéra before moving to Paris Opéra later that year.
- **1947** Dances in London for Mona Inglesby's International Ballet company.
- **1954** Following military service and a period of ill health, founds Les Ballets de l'Etoile in Paris.
- **1955** Creates *Symphonie pour un homme seul*, a ballet set to the experimental electronic *musique concrète* of French composer Pierre Henry.
- **1960** Sets up Ballet du XXe Siècle in Brussels, pioneering modern ballet and drawing dancers of international fame.
- **1961** Directs the opera *Tales of Hoffmann*, a genre he explores over the next decades.
- **1987** Moves his company from Brussels to Lausanne, Switzerland, renaming it the Béjart Ballet Lausanne, Switzerland.
- **1992** Establishes his Rudra School and workshop in Lausanne.
- **1998** Stages *The Nutcracker*, featuring its original choreographer Marius Petipa as one of the principal characters.
- **2003** Sets up Compagnie M as a platform for young dancers from around the world to hone their craft.
- **November 22, 2007** Dies in Lausanne.

BÉJART BALLET LAUSANNE DANCERS PERFORM AT INTERNATIONAL FESTIVAL OF ARTS, 2016

Liebeslieder Walzer

First performed: November 22, 1960 ▪ Venue: City Center of Music and Drama, New York ▪ Choreography: George Balanchine ▪ Music: Johannes Brahms

One of Balanchine's most charming and subtle works, *Liebeslieder Walzer* is a two-part ballet set to 33 waltzes by Johannes Brahms, with lyrics based on poems by Friedrich Daumer and Johann Wolfgang Goethe. As Balanchine's choreography explores the waltz, four couples dance out their affections for one another, with each dance showing a different aspect of love. The setting is 19th-century Vienna, where Brahms spent much of his life.

STORY LINE

Liebeslieder Walzer is an exploration of the waltz, with vocals sung entirely in German.

Act I The dancers perform 18 waltzes set to Brahms's Opus 52 (1869), their unique personalities emerging in a drawing room scene as the couples embrace and whisper, kiss, and gesture privately.

Act II While the men still wear tails, the women appear in long Romantic tutus and pointe shoes, performing 14 waltzes set to Brahms's Opus 65 (1874) in a starlit garden.

The words of the final song, written by Goethe, are left to the singers. The dancers return in their original costumes simply to listen to the waltz. That is all, "because they should be listened to in silence," said Balanchine.

Inspired by Brahms's *liebeslieder walzer* ("love songs") for piano and voices, Balanchine created a neoclassical ballet masterpiece of the same name in 1960. In response to concerns at the length of the piece—nearly an hour long—Balanchine explained, "I felt I had to do the dances, set to this music."

Unusual in that it was choreographed to the human voice, *Liebeslieder Walzer* features four couples accompanied onstage by two pianists and four singers. The staging and atmosphere reflect the social dance of mid-19th-century Vienna, beginning with the men wearing evening dress in midnight blue, with tails, ivory waistcoats, white gloves, and patent leather shoes. The women wear long gowns of pale silk, with lace gloves, petticoats, and heels.

The first act is intimate in nature, and was originally set in a drawing room. Each couple dances two pas de deux, and there are also group dances with playful partner changes. There is even a brief dispute over partners in a section with three pas de trois. When not dancing, the dancers sit and watch.

Lit by the stars, the setting and mood of the second act are more theatrical. The songs and dances vary in texture, while the ballroom steps have a balletic flavor. As the dancers are still for the final waltz, the words "You try in vain to portray how misery and happiness alternate to a loving heart" could be seen to be Balanchine's comment on his own choreography.

▲ **Ashley Bouder and Tyler Angle, 2012**
A 1984 redesign transposed the opening act from a private drawing room to an opulent ballroom salon complete with chandeliers.

◀ **Tyler Angle and Jennie Somogyi, 2015**
Elegant gowns and Romantic tutus designed by Karinska, New York City Ballet's resident costumer, are central to the ballet's identity.

> In the first act, it is the real people who are dancing. In the second act, it is their souls.
>
> GEORGE BALANCHINE

Revelations

First performed: January 31, 1960 ▪ Venue: Kaufmann Concert Hall, New York ▪ Choreography and story: Alvin Ailey ▪ Music: Howard Roberts

This modern and expressive ballet is danced to the spirituals remembered by choreographer Alvin Ailey from his childhood at church in the southern United States—*Revelations* is an emotive expression of African-American cultural heritage. An international sensation thanks to its theme of lives driven by faith, grief, hope, and joy, it quickly became the signature piece of Ailey's eponymous dance company, a status it has maintained to this day.

◀ **Sculptural attire**
Ves Harper's decor and costumes enhance the rhythmic, swirling dance sequences that typify the choreography, as performed by Jacqueline Green.

Created at the brink of the Civil Rights Movement in the US, this work has been performed around the world since its premiere, and has gone on to become the world's most widely seen modern ballet.

Telling the story of African-American Christian faith and the rise from slavery, Ailey drew inspiration for the work from his childhood growing up in Texas and the Baptist church—what he calls his "blood memories." The ballet has a strong Christian message, and features uplifting black spirituals, sung sermons, and gospel songs. The choreography is highly varied, with vibrant group dances and intimate solo pieces.

In its original form, the ballet was planned to consist of 10 sections lasting over an hour but it was later reduced to three sections, lasting 35 minutes in total.

Beginning with dejection, the ballet charts man's spiritual journey from baptism, moving through religious despair to regeneration, and finally culminating in jubilation.

Evolutionary staging

In the initial stagings, Ailey used a live choir to sing the 10 spirituals that accompany the ballet, but it proved too expensive to tour. Reluctantly, recorded music was used for the many national and international tours that followed. Later, Ailey wanted to drop *Revelations* from the repertoire but audiences complained.

More than 50 years on, many dancers have given their own interpretations of the various roles. On European tours, the ballet is always performed last, as several encores are often requested. By the time the joyous finale "Rocka My Soul in the Bosom of Abraham" is reached, audiences are usually standing and clapping, roused by the infectious music and energy of the dancers.

STORY LINE

There are three sections to the piece and each suite of dances consists of several religious spirituals.

Pilgrim of Sorrow The first section is set in the earliest time, showing man trying to get up out of the ground. The earthy brown colors of the costumes reflect this image.

Take Me to the Water The second part of the ballet deals with the purification rite of baptism. In this section, the dancers are dressed in pale blue and white.

Move, Members, Move The final section represents the happiness surrounding the gospel church congregation, where earth tones, yellow, and black are used.

▶ **Holy joy**
Though just 29 when he created it, Ailey imbued his work with the depths of human emotion, from heartfelt grief to holy joy.

Jerome Robbins

Dancer and choreographer ▪ 1918–1998

The first major American choreographer of the 20th century, Jerome Robbins enjoyed unprecedented success, creating over 60 ballets, and playing a leading role in the development of the American Ballet Theatre and the New York City Ballet. He was equally successful on Broadway and collaborated on some of the world's most popular musicals, including *West Side Story* (1957) and *Fiddler on the Roof* (1964). His work for stage and screen earned him many awards, including five Tony awards.

▲ **Jerome Robbins**
With a notebook in hand, Robbins tries out some dance steps in 1959, shortly after setting up his own ballet company, Ballets U.S.A. Robbins was always keen to promote American ballet talent, and took his company on a successful European tour.

Born Jerome Wilson Rabinowitz, Jerome Robbins spent his early childhood in Manhattan, until his family moved to New Jersey in the 1920s. His talent for dance was evident as a teenager, and after briefly studying chemistry, he took up an apprenticeship with Senia Glück-Sandor and Felicia Sorel at the Dance Center in New York. There, with Sandor's encouragement he studied classical ballet intensely, and also modern, Spanish, and Asian dance.

He progressed quickly, and was soon performing professionally on Broadway and in ballets. In 1940, he joined the newly established Ballet Theatre, working his way up from the corps de ballet to soloist, and won acclaim for his performance of the tragic puppet in *Petrushka* under his new name, Robbins.

Instant success

In 1944, Robbins choreographed his first ballet, *Fancy Free*, about three sailors on shore leave in New York. Combining classical ballet and modern theater, it had a uniquely American theme. For its musical score, Robbins collaborated with Leonard Bernstein—then an unknown composer. The ballet proved highly popular, and Robbins became an overnight sensation, receiving two dozen curtain calls at its premiere.

Fancy Free was later turned into the musical, *On the Town*, and helped to establish Robbins on Broadway. He continued to create ballets, such as *Interplay* (1945) and *Facsimile* (1946), as well as a series of musicals, including *Billion Dollar Baby* in 1946.

In 1949, Robbins joined George Balanchine's newly founded New York City Ballet. Although he retired from performing in the mid-1950s, he continued as a choreographer, producing *The Cage* (1951), a haunting tale of a female-dominated world, and *The Concert* (1956), a comical depiction of the fantasies of a concert audience.

Personal crisis

During the 1950s and the heightened tensions of the Cold War, suspected Communist sympathizers were accused across the US, and Robbins was called to testify before the House Un-American Activities Committee. Threatened with public exposure of his sexuality, after three years of resistance, he confessed to having previously been a Communist, and named eight other members. While this saved his career, many refused to forgive him, and the incident left him riddled with guilt.

In 1958, Robbins took leave from the New York City Ballet, and formed his own company, Ballets U.S.A, to promote American ballet. It lasted until 1961. He then returned to the Ballet Theatre in 1965 with *Les Noces*—featuring four grand pianos, soloists, percussionists, and a full chorus accompanying the dancers on stage, the production was hugely popular.

After spending three years exploring experimental theater with his project, American Theatre Lab, Robbins returned to the New York City Ballet in 1969 as resident choreographer. With a new sense of direction, his pieces became more abstract and classical, as seen in such works as *Dances at a Gathering* (1969) and *In G Major* (1975). Robbins became ballet master in 1972, then associate artistic director in 1983. He retired from the company in 1990, but continued to take on individual projects until his death.

▲ **On the road to stardom**
Shortly after this picture was taken on the set of *High Button Shoes*, c.1947, Robbins went on to win his first Tony Award for Best Choreography in 1948. By the age of 30, he had already achieved great success as a dancer and choreographer.

KEY WORKS

Choreographer: *Fancy Free*, 1944 • *Afternoon of a Faun*, 1953 • *The Concert*, 1956 • *Les Noces*, 1965 *Dances at a Gathering*, 1969 • *In the Night*, 1970 *Brandenburg*, 1997

TIMELINE

- **October 11, 1918** Born Jerome Wilson Rabinowitz in New York.
- **1936** Through his sister Sonia, who had danced professionally with Irma Duncan, begins an apprenticeship at the Glück Sandor–Felicia Sorel Dance Center.
- **1940** Joins the Ballet Theatre, New York, where he plays his breakthrough role three years later as the puppet in *Petrushka*.
- **1944** Choreographs and performs in his first ballet, *Fancy Free*.
- **1949** Joins the New York City Ballet as dancer and choreographer.
- **1958** Sets up dance company Ballets U.S.A. to promote American ballet.

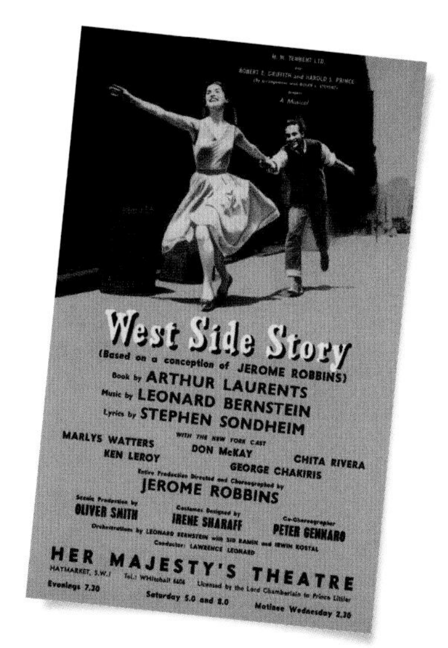

1958 THEATER POSTER FOR *WEST SIDE STORY*, CHOREOGRAPHED BY ROBBINS

- **1966** Sets up the American Theatre Lab to explore experimental musical theater, dance, and drama.
- **1969** Returns to the New York City Ballet as resident choreographer.
- **1970** Enters a creative period in which he produces work in a diverse range of styles, including *In the Night* (1970), *The Goldberg Variations* (1971), and *Watermill* (1972).
- **1972** Becomes ballet master of the New York City Ballet.
- **1983** Becomes the associate artistic director of the New York City Ballet.
- **1990** Retires from the New York City Ballet, and continues to work on individual choreographic projects.
- **July 29, 1998** Dies in New York.

La Fille mal gardée

First performed: July 1, 1789 ▪ Venue: Grand Théâtre de Bordeaux ▪ Choreography and story: Jean Dauberval ▪ Music: Popular French pieces

Audiences today are most familiar with the 1960 version of *La Fille mal gardée* choreographed for The Royal Ballet in London by Frederick Ashton, but the work dates back to the 18th century. The bucolic tale of a widow's hopes for her daughter to make a good match was an immediate hit, accessible to the widest possible audience with its charming mesh of plot and dance, characters and comedy.

IN CONTEXT

French author Charles Maurice, in his book *Histoire Anécdotique du Théâtre*, recounts how Dauberval glanced in the window of a glazier's shop and saw: "a crude coloured print depicting a village youth fleeing from a cottage, with an angry old woman throwing his hat after him, while a peasant girl shed tears. At the end of a very short interval, the ravishing ballet *La Fille mal gardée* was evolved." With its believable human emotion, conflict, and light-heartedness, the work was in stark contrast to the measured steps and stiffly formulaic bucolic stereotypes of previous ballets. It had its greatest success in Russia, called *Useless Precautions*. In the UK, it was sometimes named *The Wayward Daughter* but now normally goes under its French title of *La Fille mal gardée*.

The first performance of *La Fille mal gardée* was on July 1, 1789, at the Grand Théâtre de Bordeaux, less than two weeks before the French Revolution officially began. With its elements of pantomime and happy ending, it had instant appeal. There have since been many interpretations both musically and choreographically, but they all retain the original story.

The music for the original work consisted of 55 popular French pieces. However, when Dauberval took the ballet to London in 1791, the orchestra complained, so the music was changed. Later versions used music by Ferdinand Hérold, in 1828; Peter Ludwig Hertel, in 1864; and Pavel Feldt, in a Russian version in 1937. For the 1960 Ashton production, John Lanchbery studied earlier versions, from which he created the music score that is familiar to audiences today.

Ashton's *Pastoral Symphony*

Frederick Ashton was encouraged to make his version, which he called "my poor man's *Pastoral Symphony*," by Tamara Karsavina, who had danced the role of Lise in St. Petersburg in an 1885 revival by Lev Ivanov. She recalled a mime scene in Act II, in which Lise dreams of becoming a mother to several children,

▼ Ashton's Royal Ballet production of 1960
Nadia Nerina dances Lise with Alexander Grant as her mother's choice of suitor, Alain, sandwiching David Blair as her beloved Colas.

▲ **Leap of love**
Mathias Heymann performs as Colas at the Opéra Garnier, Paris, in 2009. British cartoonist Osbert Lancaster's stage designs brightened this most English and witty of Ashton's ballets.

not knowing that her beloved Colas is watching her. She counts out the imaginary children, smacking one's bottom, rocking another to sleep, and singing to a third. Ashton included the sequence, in what is now one of the ballet's most appealing scenes. Other entertaining moments include ribbon cat's cradles, clog and maypole folk dances, and corn-cutting.

Reviving the original

Of the many versions of *La Fille mal gardée* that have been made, the 1989 revival of the original production by Ballet du Rhin, a French company from Mulhouse in Alsace, was particularly interesting. The steps, costumes, and footwear were as authentic as possible. It was restaged by dance historian Ivo Cramer from the original notation held at Stockholm, where it had been performed in 1812. During the picnic scene, the dancers rushed to the front of the stage and sang a song in support of the revolution, just as in Bordeaux 200 years earlier.

▶ **Loving couple**
Francesca Hayward as Lise and Marcelino Sambé as Colas embrace before their ribbon dance in Act I, Scene 1, of The Royal Ballet's 2016 production.

Yuri Grigorovich (1927–)

Among many revisions to the choreography of *La Fille mal gardée* were those of Yuri Grigorovich for the Bolshoi Ballet in 1993. His production retained the uplifting charm of Ashton's choreography. Grigorovich is considered the outstanding Russian choreographer of the 20th century. To celebrate his 90th birthday early in 2017, the Bolshoi Theatre showed all his ballets during January and February, including *The Nutcracker* and *Swan Lake.*

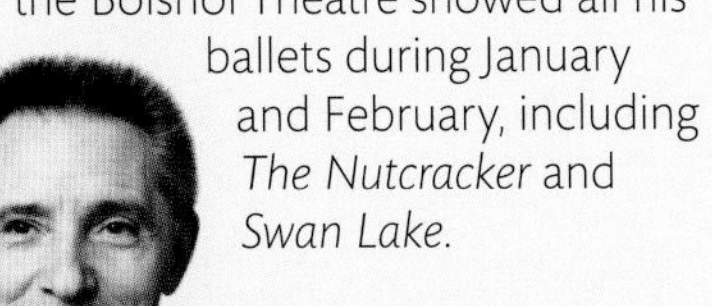

STORY LINE La Fille mal gardée

While nominally set in 18th-century France, Frederick Ashton's exuberant version of this ballet (1960) includes a giddy whirl of ribbons, sunny Suffolk harvest scenes, English folk dances, and a burlesque character, Widow Simone, traditionally played by a man. Widow Simone hopes to arrange a marriage between her only daughter, Lise, and Alain, the simpleton son of a wealthy vineyard owner. However, Lise is in love with the young farmer, Colas. After much comic tribulation, the love triangle is resolved.

SARAH LAMB AS LISE, 2005

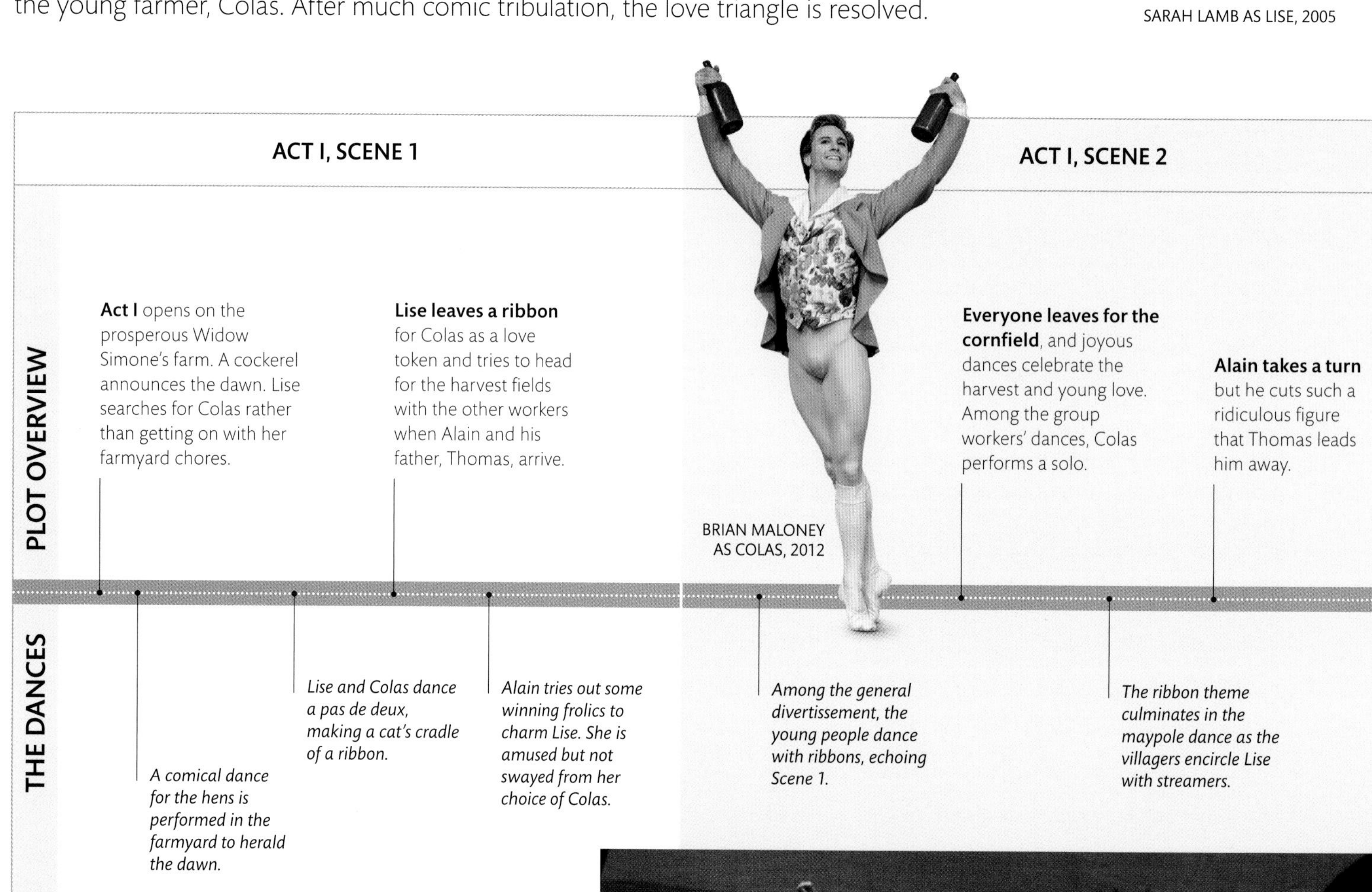

BRIAN MALONEY AS COLAS, 2012

ACT I, SCENE 1

PLOT OVERVIEW

Act I opens on the prosperous Widow Simone's farm. A cockerel announces the dawn. Lise searches for Colas rather than getting on with her farmyard chores.

Lise leaves a ribbon for Colas as a love token and tries to head for the harvest fields with the other workers when Alain and his father, Thomas, arrive.

THE DANCES

A comical dance for the hens is performed in the farmyard to herald the dawn.

Lise and Colas dance a pas de deux, making a cat's cradle of a ribbon.

Alain tries out some winning frolics to charm Lise. She is amused but not swayed from her choice of Colas.

ACT I, SCENE 2

PLOT OVERVIEW

Everyone leaves for the cornfield, and joyous dances celebrate the harvest and young love. Among the group workers' dances, Colas performs a solo.

Alain takes a turn but he cuts such a ridiculous figure that Thomas leads him away.

THE DANCES

Among the general divertissement, the young people dance with ribbons, echoing Scene 1.

The ribbon theme culminates in the maypole dance as the villagers encircle Lise with streamers.

PAUL KAY AS THE COCKEREL IN THE CHICKEN DANCE, 2012

MAYPOLE DANCE, HAMBURG BALLETT, 2004

> There exists in my imagination a life in the country …, a leafy pastoral of perpetual sunshine …

FREDERICK ASHTON ON HIS VISION FOR *LA FILLE MAL GARDEE*

ALINA COJOCARU AS LISE, THE ROYAL BALLET, 2010

EVA EVDOKIMOVA (LISE) AND VLADIMIR GELVAN (COLAS), DEUTSCHE OPER, BERLIN, 1978

ACT II

Back at the farm, Simone sets Lise to work while she dozes. The farm workers arrive with the cornsheaves and Simone leaves to sign the marriage contract for Lise and Alain with Thomas.

Lise and Colas are declaring their love when they hear Simone approaching. Lise hides Colas in her bedroom. Alain opens the door to claim his bride and finds Lise in an embrace with Colas.

Widow Simone is persuaded to perform a clog dance. After initial reluctance, she takes up the dance with aplomb.

A thunderclap sounds and a sudden storm sends everyone running for shelter at the end of Act I.

Ashton includes his hallmark "Fred Step" (a lilting sequence that travels first one way and then the other) into the corps de ballet.

Colas and Lise attempt a dance over the locked door.

Alain gets the last laugh, creeping back to claim his signature prop, an umbrella.

WILLIAM TUCKETT AS WIDOW SIMONE WITH CLOG DANCERS, 2010

Widow Simone senses something is going on and sends Lise to her room to prepare to sign the marriage contract. Unbeknown to Simone, Colas is hiding in Lise's bedroom …

Lise and Colas plead with Simone, who eventually concedes, and the farm workers arrive for a happy finale dance.

LISE AND COLAS DANCE TOGETHER, DEFYING THE BARRIER OF A DOOR, 2007

Paris Opéra Ballet, 2007
Farm workers prepare for the day's harvest in a bucolic dance, complete with scythes, near the beginning of *La Fille mal gardée*.

Nadia Nerina

Dancer and choreographer ▪ 1927–2008

As a teenager in 1945, Nadia Nerina sailed from South Africa to the UK, where she went on to dance an array of roles as principal dancer and later guest artist at what is now The Royal Ballet. Renowned for her versatility and virtuosity, she defined the role of Lise in *La fille mal gardée*. Technically flawless, expressive, and full of charm, in an interview in 1969, Nerina said, "I believe you have to conquer technique, and be above it, as it were, before you can express yourself as an artist."

▲ **In rehearsal**
Nadia Nerina and dance partner David Blair are given coaching advice by the celebrated French ballerina Yvette Chauviré in London in 1963.

Nerina began dancing at a young age in Durban, when her doctor suggested ballet to help strengthen a twisted ankle. She also learned drama. She was offered a generous scholarship to move to the UK as an actress but chose ballet over acting. She initially trained with Marie Rambert and then with the Sadler's Wells School, before joining the Sadler's Wells Theatre Ballet (now Birmingham Royal Ballet) in 1947.

Nerina made her solo debut as Spring Fairy in Frederick Ashton's *Cinderella* in 1948, after quickly progressing from the corps de ballet. She took the lead role in the same ballet in 1951, and was made principal dancer the following year.

Roles in comedy and tragedy

Although many critics agree that Nerina's style was most suited to comedic roles, her training in drama gave her a diverse range of expression, be it in *Les Sylphides*, *The Firebird*, or *Giselle*. In 1954, Ninette de Valois's new production of *Coppélia* featuring Nerina and David Blair, with whom she often danced, received much acclaim. Nerina also starred in darker ballets, including Kenneth MacMillan's *Noctambules*, in 1956, and in 1963, the lead role in Robert Helpmann's *Elektra*.

The most celebrated moment in Nerina's career came in 1960 when Ashton, who at the time was almost solely creating ballets for Margot Fonteyn, choreographed *La fille mal gardée* for Nerina. She was partnered with Blair, and danced the role of Lise with exquisite and expressive speed, lightness, and charm. Ashton may have choreographed the part, but it was Nerina who made the delightful role of Lise her own. In the same year, she became the first dancer at the company to be invited to perform for both the Bolshoi and the Kirov Ballet, winning acclaim for her acrobatic performances in *Swan Lake* and *Giselle*.

Troublesome partnerships

Nerina was at the height of her career, and was set to succeed Fonteyn whose retirement was expected. In 1962, The Royal Ballet anticipated the debut of Dane Erik Bruhn, in partnership with Nerina, to be their most exciting event of the year. Yet unexpectedly, Fonteyn's popularity resurged in the same year after she and Rudolf Nureyev danced *Giselle*. The partnership became a sensation, and Fonteyn did not retire for another decade. Nerina therefore never gained the same kind of stardom as Fonteyn.

Nerina also partnered Nureyev, and though they were well matched in performances, they clashed offstage. Nureyev was in a romantic relationship with Bruhn, but he felt overshadowed by Nureyev and lost his confidence. To make matters worse, Nureyev critiqued Bruhn's dance rehearsals with Nerina, which undermined him further. Seeing how this affected Bruhn's performance, Nerina would angrily ask Nureyev to leave, increasing the animosity between them.

In one performance of *Giselle*, Nureyev stunned his audience by inserting 16 entrechats-six, a jump where the legs are crossed rapidly three times in mid-air. In retaliation, Nerina inserted 32 entrechats-six in her performance in *Swan Lake*, fully aware that Nureyev would be watching.

In 1965, Nerina became a guest artist at The Royal Ballet, allowing her to perform around the world. She toured extensively in Europe and the US, as well as South Africa before retiring in 1969.

◀ ***Cinderella*, 1951**
Nerina performing the title role in Ashton's production of *Cinderella* at The Royal Ballet while Moira Shearer was indisposed. She was later praised by critics for the "adorable spontaneity" of her interpretation. She had previously danced in the ballet in a role created for her in 1948.

KEY WORKS

Dancer: The Faded Beauty, *Noctambules*, 1956 • Mazurka and Valse, *Les Sylphides*, 1948 Princess Aurora, *The Sleeping Beauty*, 1953 Swanilda, *Coppélia*, 1954 • Title role, *Giselle*, 1956 • Title role, *The Firebird*, 1956 • Title role, *Sylvia*, 1959 • Lise, *La fille mal gardée*, 1960 Title role, *Elektra*, 1963

TIMELINE

- **October 21, 1927** Born Nadine Judd in Bloemfontein, South Africa.
- **1939** Begins studying ballet in Durban with Eileen Keegan and Dorothea McNair, who encourage Nerina to train in the UK.
- **1944** Her mother dies; focuses more on drama than ballet as an outlet for grief.
- **1945** Moves to London and begins training with Marie Rambert.
- **1947** Joins the Sadler's Wells Theatre Ballet, and renames herself Nadia Nerina (Nerina being her mother's name, after a South African flower).
- **1948** Dances her first solo as Spring Fairy in *Cinderella*.
- **1952** Appointed principal dancer of the Sadler's Wells Theatre Ballet.
- **1953** Dances the lead role of Princess Aurora in *The Sleeping Beauty*.
- **1956** Marries banker Charles Gordon. Dances The Fading Beauty, an aging woman who regains beauty under hypnosis, in *Noctambules*.

Royal Opera House
COVENT GARDEN
HOUSE MANAGER . JOHN COLLINS

THE ROYAL OPERA HOUSE, COVENT GARDEN LIMITED
GENERAL ADMINISTRATOR . DAVID L. WEBSTER
in association with the Arts Council of Great Britain
presents
THE ROYAL BALLET
Director: NINETTE DE VALOIS
Associate Director and Principal Choreographer: FREDERICK ASHTON
Musical Director: HUGO RIGNOLD
Conductors: JOHN LANCHBERY EMANUEL YOUNG
Choreographers for the current season include:
JOHN CRANKO KENNETH MACMILLAN
in the first performance by the Royal Ballet of

La Fille Mal Gardée

BALLET IN TWO ACTS
Music by FERDINAND HEROLD
freely adapted and arranged by John Lanchbery from the 1828 version
Choreography by FREDERICK ASHTON
Scenery and costumes by OSBERT LANCASTER
with
COVENT GARDEN ORCHESTRA
Leader: Charles Taylor
on
THURSDAY, 28th JANUARY, 1960

PROGRAM COVER, WORLD PREMIERE OF *LA FILLE MAL GARDEE*, 1960

- **1960** Dances Lise in *La fille mal gardée*, a role to which she is perfectly suited.
- **1965** Made guest artist of The Royal Ballet, enabling her to dance worldwide for other companies.
- **1969** Retires from performing.
- **2008** Dies at the age of 80 in Beaulieu-sur-Mer, France.

CHINESE BALLET

Noted for their exceptional clarity of technique, Chinese dancers can be found in ballet companies worldwide. Yet ballet in China is only a few generations old. Its development is a reflection of the country itself, first importing Russian ideas before realizing its own national style, and recently opening up and incorporating contemporary techniques as it adapts to modern tastes. Shanghai Ballet has been particularly prominent in its contemporary approach to classical work.

Ballet in China truly began in 1954 with the opening of what is now the Beijing Dance Academy, led by Dai Ailian, known as the "mother of Chinese ballet." Five years later, what is now the National Ballet of China was formed as the school's Experimental Ballet Company.

From the beginning, Dai combined Western ballet with Chinese cultural elements to form something unique, an approach that continues to this day. Among the best-known early examples are two revolutionary ballets, now regarded as Chinese classics: *The Red Detachment of Women* (1964), about an oppressed young farmworker who joins a women's unit of Communist fighters to defeat a local tyrant; and *The White-Haired Girl* (1965). More recent examples include *Raise the Red Lantern* (2001), a tragic story of a woman sold into marriage, and *The Peony Pavilion* (2008), a colorful melodrama about first love that switches between dream and reality. Both works combine ballet with traditional Chinese arts and costumes.

Companies increasingly collaborate with artists abroad. The National Ballet of China even worked with Akram Khan, the British choreographer trained in the classical Indian dance of Kathak, on the culture-crossing *Bahok* (2008). Chinese ballet companies often tour overseas and foreign choreographers are invited to come and work in China.

> Our country is now rising in the world, and our ballet company would like to go with it.
>
> ZHAO RUHENG, ARTISTIC DIRECTOR OF THE NATIONAL BALLET OF CHINA 1994–2009, 1998

***The White-Haired Girl* (1965)** ▶
Performed by the Shanghai Dance Academy, the ballet tells the story of a peasant girl who flees to the mountains to escape a despotic landlord. There is a happy ending when her fiancé is reunited with her, now white-haired and with her clothes in tatters. Part-musical, part-ballet, the songs are familiar to everyone raised in 1960s China.

Marguerite and Armand

First performed: March 12, 1963 ▪ Venue: Royal Opera House, London ▪ Choreography: Frederick Ashton ▪ Music: Franz Liszt ▪ Story: Alexandre Dumas *fils*

A triumph on its premiere, which received 21 curtain calls, this ballet was only ever danced by Margot Fonteyn and Rudolf Nureyev during their lifetimes. Although not originally conceived with Nureyev in mind, *Marguerite and Armand* became a dramatic vehicle for their world-famous partnership, cementing the dancers' onstage magnetism and showcasing their intense talent for portraying character and emotion.

STORY LINE

In 19th century Paris, the beautiful courtesan Marguerite lies dying of consumption. In a series of flashbacks, she revisits memories of a passionate love affair with a young man. We see Marguerite's first meeting with Armand; her life with him in the countryside after leaving Paris and the duke, her former protector and lover; and Armand's despair when Marguerite leaves him at the behest of his disapproving father, eager to protect his son's reputation. In the final scenes, Armand's father reveals that he was to blame for Marguerite's unexplained desertion, and Armand rushes to her apartment where he is tragically reunited with Marguerite on her deathbed. She dies in his arms.

... performances of heart-wrenching intensity ... see the dancer become the dance.

LUKE JENNINGS ON TAMARA ROJO AND SERGEI POLUNIN IN *MARGUERITE AND ARMAND*, 2013

Based on the story of Marguerite Gautier, the protagonist of *La Dame aux Camélias* by Alexandre Dumas *fils,* Frederick Ashton wrote *Marguerite and Armand* for Margot Fonteyn, who at 43 had been considering retiring from dance. Casting Rudolf Nureyev after his arrival in London in 1961, the ballet established an intense partnership that reinvigorated Fonteyn's career and elevated Nureyev's.

Put together in just 15 rehearsals over two weeks, the ballet's tragic story played to each dancer's strengths. Nureyev was well known for his fiery temperament, while Fonteyn had a calm disposition—contrasting personalities that worked brilliantly on stage. Their magnetic relationship gave the story an added poignancy and intimacy, as well as a heightened sense of realism. Fonteyn and Nureyev went on to perform the ballet over 50 times, most frequently at the Royal Opera House, London, with their last performance in 1977.

Music and design

Ashton chose the music for *Marguerite and Armand*—Liszt's Piano Sonata in B minor—after hearing it on the radio one evening. In a quirk of synchronicity, he later discovered that the character of Marguerite Gautier was based on a real woman, Marie Duplessis, who had love affairs with both Liszt and with Alexandre Dumas *fils*.

The simple sets by Cecil Beaton used the bed on which Marguerite lies dying as a constant theme, and a gilded cage–like structure, symbolizing Marguerite's trapped but privileged life. His designs for the costumes were more Romantic and elaborate, with Victorian-themed shirts, jackets, and dresses. The costumes proved unpopular with Nureyev, however, who tore the collar off his jacket, then cut off its tails during the ballet's dress rehearsal, angry that they were getting in the way of his dancing and feeling that they made his legs look short.

Rebirth of the ballet

The roles of Marguerite and Armand became so synonymous with Fonteyn and Nureyev that no one else performed the ballet while they, or Frederick Ashton, remained alive. After their deaths, Sylvie Guillem finally danced the role of Marguerite at the Royal Opera House, London, in 2000. Other ballerinas have followed suit, including Tamara Rojo and the Bolshoi Ballet's Svetlana Zakharova in 2013 (both with Sergei Polunin as Armand), and Alessandra Ferri and Zenaida Yanowsky in London in 2017.

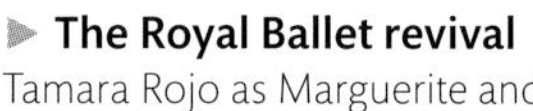

▶ The Royal Ballet revival Tamara Rojo as Marguerite and Sergei Polunin as Armand, performing at the Royal Opera House, London, in 2013.

▶ Margot Fonteyn with Rudolf Nureyev The passionate dress rehearsal for Ashton's original production of the ballet in 1963 was attended by 50 members of the press.

Margot Fonteyn

Dancer ▪ 1919–1991

The most famous dancer of her generation, Margot Fonteyn dominated British ballet for more than four decades, and was admired around the world. For many, she was considered the perfect ballerina; the one against whom everyone else was measured. On and off stage she had an aura, supreme grace and charm, and a captivating smile. She became not only the face of The Royal Ballet in London—where she spent her entire career—but an icon, her celebrity extending far beyond ballet.

▲ **The perfect pairing**
Fonteyn and Nureyev receive bouquets following their debut pairing in the title roles of MacMillan's *Romeo and Juliet* at The Royal Ballet, London, in 1965. On its first night, the ballet received 43 curtain calls, taking over 40 minutes.

From the age of four, Fonteyn (born Margaret Hookham) studied ballet, encouraged by her half-Irish, half-Brazilian mother. After moving with her family from the UK to China aged eight, six years later her mother traveled with her to London to pursue a career in ballet. There, she joined the Vic-Wells Ballet School, and made her professional debut the following year as a snowflake in *The Nutcracker* with Vic-Wells Ballet.

In 1935, dancer Alicia Markova left the company, and its director, Ninette de Valois, turned to Fonteyn. At the age of 16, she danced her first principal role, Odette/Odile in *Swan Lake*, and soon became the company's leading dancer. When the company relocated to the Royal Opera House in 1946, Fonteyn danced Aurora in *The Sleeping Beauty* on the opening night—she was a revelation.

Public adoration

Fonteyn had an appealing, unaffected personality, and her slight but strong physique was perfect for ballet. As a dancer, she was exceptional, and as an actor, she brought her roles to life. Such was her presence, that even when standing still, eyes gravitated toward her. Unsurprisingly, Fonteyn became a British favorite, and when the company visited New York in 1949, she captured American hearts, too, becoming the first ballerina to make the cover of *TIME* magazine.

Fonteyn's life was as dramatic away from the stage as it was on it. While she had several affairs, only one love endured, Roberto (Tito) Arias, son of the then president of Panama. They met in 1937, and although she was smitten, their lives kept them apart until 1953, when they met again in New York. They married in Paris in 1955, after which he was made Panamanian ambassador in London. Fonteyn once wrote, "In Tito's company, I felt complete."

Made a dame in 1956, Fonteyn's diplomatic and dancing worlds were largely kept apart until 1959 when Arias, with Fonteyn at his side, sailed into Panama harbor on a boat full of guns and men. The attempted revolution failed. Arias escaped but Fonteyn was arrested and held briefly in jail.

The Nureyev years

At the age of 42, Fonteyn's retirement seemed imminent, until she danced with Rudolf Nureyev in *Giselle* in 1962—they received 23 curtain calls. Despite their differences off-stage, they were a perfect match on it, and became widely seen as the greatest ballet partnership ever. There was even speculation that their relationship extended beyond dancing. Partnering Nureyev extended Fonteyn's career by more than 15 years, and they were seen as the ideal pairing in many ballets, notably Kenneth MacMillan's *Romeo and Juliet* (1965) and Frederick Ashton's *Marguerite and Armand* (1963).

Fonteyn continued to perform until her 60th birthday, largely in order to pay for medical care for Tito, who had been paralyzed in an attempted assassination in Panama in 1964. Upon her retirement, The Royal Ballet (as it was called by then) named her prima ballerina assoluta, the only dancer in the history of the company to hold the title. She then moved to Panama to be with her husband. Virtually penniless, Fonteyn spent her last years nursing her beloved Tito on their remote farm. She wrote that it was the happiest time of her life.

▲ **Defining role**
Fonteyn, seen here in 1951, first professionally danced the role of Odette/Odile from *Swan Lake* as a child. Through her pairing with Nureyev, she became synonymous with the role and ballet.

KEY WORKS

Aurora, *The Sleeping Beauty*, 1946 • Agathe, *Les Demoiselles de la Nuit*, 1948 • Title role, *Daphnis and Chloë*, 1951 • Title role, *L'Ondine*, 1958 • Title role, *Giselle*, 1962 • Title role, *Marguerite and Armand*, 1963 • Odette/Odile, *Swan Lake*, 1965

TIMELINE

- **May 18, 1919** Born in Reigate, she later attributes her musical ability to her half-Irish, half-Brazilian mother.
- **1923** Attends dance classes run by Grace Bosustow in Ealing, London, aged four.
- **1928** Her father's job moves the family to China, after a spell living in the US.
- **1931** Inspired by seeing Alicia Markova in *Les Sylphides* during a visit to London.
- **1933** Returns to the UK and auditions for the Vic-Wells School, dancing her first solo a year later in *The Haunted Ballroom.*
- **1935** Dances her first principal role, Odette/Odile in *Swan Lake.*
- **1946** Stars in *Symphonic Variations*, the first ballet created by Frederick Ashton for the Sadler's Wells Ballet in London.
- **1955** Marries Dr. Roberto Arias, son of the former president of Panama.
- **1959** Starts being billed as a guest artist by The Royal Ballet, allowing her to accept invitations from other ballet companies.
- **1962** Begins her dance partnership with Rudolf Nureyev, inspiring a renaissance in her dancing and career.
- **1964** Her husband, Tito, is shot by a colleague, leaving him paralyzed.

1960 LOBBY CARD SHOWING FONTEYN IN *THE FIREBIRD* AT THE ROYAL BALLET, LONDON

- **1975** *Margot Fonteyn: Autobiography* is published.
- **1979** Given the unique title prima ballerina assoluta by The Royal Ballet, London, following a gala held to mark her 60th birthday.
- **1989** Following many years of ill health, her husband Tito dies.
- **February 21, 1991** Dies of cancer in hospital in Panama.

The Dream

First performed: April 2, 1964 ▪ Venue: Royal Opera House, London ▪ Choreography: Frederick Ashton
Music: Felix Mendelssohn, arranged by John Lanchbery ▪ Story: William Shakespeare

This one-act ballet is adapted from William Shakespeare's *A Midsummer Night's Dream*, a tale of fairy mischief set in a magical forest. The roles of the noble Oberon, the sprightly Puck, and the comical Bottom are much coveted by male dancers.

▲ **The Royal Ballet premiere, 1964**
Antoinette Sibley, as Titania, dances with Anthony Dowell, as Oberon. Sibley was admired for her ability to emulate a half-wild creature.

STORY LINE

Four Athenians experiencing romantic turmoil flee to the forest. Deep in this forest, Oberon, king of the fairies, quarrels with his queen, Titania. To punish her, Oberon sends his fairy Puck to find a magic flower. Its juice makes the victim fall in love with the first living thing seen on awakening. Oberon plans to humiliate Titania by contriving a monstrous being to be present when she awakes.

A group of country workmen comes into the forest. Puck gives one of them, Bottom, the head of a donkey. In this guise, he dances en pointe to imitate hooves—most unusual for a male dancer. Enchanted Titania, upon waking, is smitten with the donkey-headed Bottom.

Meddling again, Oberon moves to the four Athenians who open the ballet and are now asleep. Puck squeezes the flower over the wrong eyelids, causing further complications.

Choreographer Frederick Ashton created *The Dream* for two Royal Ballet dancers: the graceful, perfectly proportioned Antoinette Sibley and Anthony Dowell, elegant and long-limbed. *The Dream* was first shown in 1964 as part of The Royal Ballet program commemorating the 400th anniversary of Shakespeare's birth, in a triple bill with Kenneth MacMillan's *Images of Love*, and Robert Helpmann's *Hamlet*. Across the globe, Graeme Murphy (now a famous choreographer) gave another memorable performance, dancing Puck at The Australian Ballet's premiere in 1969.

Ashton wished to convey narrative through action and dance—in just 50 minutes, the entire story unfolds, and a happy resolution is reached. He cleverly interspersed the comic scenes with innovative dance movements and a minimum of mime.

As in Shakespeare's original, the ballet opens on four young Athenians, Hermia and Lysander, and Helena and Demetrius. All four are caught up in a state of turmoil and star-crossed love, and have fled in anguish to the forest outside Athens, where the fairy story takes place.

The enchanting score by Mendelssohn (first written in 1826 and added to in 1842) enhances every scene with its light, ethereal quality. *The Dream* remains extremely popular worldwide, and is one of Ashton's best-known works.

▼ **The source of the quarrel**
Oberon (Steven McRae) and Titania (Roberta Marquez) quarrel because she will not give him her changeling boy (Enrique Ngbokota) as an attendant, in this Royal Ballet production of 2012.

▶ **Magnanimous Oberon, 2014**
Eventually, Oberon (danced by Steven McRae) resolves the mischief caused by the magic flower. Everyone is freed from their enchantment and restored to their rightful partner.

Rudolf Nureyev

Dancer and choreographer ▪ 1938–1993

Born onboard a train on the Trans-Siberian railway, it was clear from the start that Nureyev was destined to go places, and, to the frustration of Soviet authorities, his direction was to the West. From humble beginnings, he grew to be a star of the Russian ballet, before making his "leap to freedom" and becoming one of the world's most famous male dancers. He was also one half of ballet's most celebrated partnership, dancing with Margot Fonteyn until she retired 18 years later.

▲ **Man of the moment**
Photographed here during the 1960s after defecting to the West, Nureyev soon became the center of attention both on stage and in his private life. His striking personality and looks made him a favorite in high society circles.

Born en route to where his father, Hamit, was stationed with the Red Army in Russia, Nureyev was the youngest of four children. The family was very poor, but once Nureyev started school aged five, his mother, Farida, was able to work. Although their living conditions were harsh, Farida managed to buy a single ticket to the ballet, and smuggled in her children to see *Song of the Cranes*. Nureyev was captivated and his destiny decided.

As a child, Nureyev showed talent during folk dance classes at school and, following a recommendation, began taking ballet lessons—despite his father's disapproval. At 15, Nureyev began training professionally at the newly opened ballet studio attached to the local theater, and started to earn money as an extra, quickly progressing to the corps de ballet. Nureyev then auditioned for the Bolshoi Ballet Academy, as well as the Kirov's Vaganova Academy, and although accepted by both, he chose Vaganova.

The Kirov years

At Vaganova, Nureyev joined a class taught by the militaristic Valentin Ivanovich Shelkov but the two clashed violently. When Nureyev asked the school's artistic director, Nicolai Ivanovsky, if he could move to Alexander Pushkin's class instead, Shelkov tried to get him expelled. Ivanovsky granted Nureyev's wish, however, and he soon became Pushkin's star pupil. As training intensified, the fervent dancer became increasingly temperamental, and often had emotional outbursts. Only Pushkin could calm him at such times, and their relationship deepened as Pushkin became something of a father figure to him. With Pushkin's guidance, Nureyev grew into a magnificent dancer, and upon graduation in 1958, he joined the Kirov Ballet as a soloist. Following his debut in *Laurentia* (1958), alongside Natalia Dudinskaya, Nureyev became an instant sensation in the Soviet Union.

Leap to freedom

While dancing with the Kirov in Paris in 1961, Nureyev escaped from his KGB bodyguards and defected—the first of many dancers to do so. Almost immediately he began dancing for the Grand Ballet du Marquis de Cuevas.

The same year, Nureyev was invited by Margot Fonteyn to dance at an annual fund-raising gala. Nureyev had dreamed of dancing with Fonteyn since he was a child, but when he approached her, she declined. Instead, he performed *Poème tragique*, a solo made especially for him by Frederick Ashton, which stunned the audience, and saw him offered a place at The Royal Ballet as a principal dancer.

In 1962, Nureyev, then 23, got his wish when he was paired with Fonteyn, 42, in *Giselle*. This marked the beginning of their celebrated partnership and lifelong friendship. Nureyev remained with The Royal Ballet until 1970, where he succeeded as both a world-class performer and as a choreographer.

Nureyev became director of the Paris Opéra Ballet in 1983, and set about reviving the company with new dancers, new productions, and improved studios. Although he became ill the following year, he continued to work. His final choreographic work was a production of *La Bayadère* (1992). At its premiere, he astonished the audience by appearing at the curtain call. Supported on each side, it proved to be an emotional farewell.

▲ **Made for two**
Nureyev and Margot Fonteyn dance at the press call for The Royal Ballet's production of *Pelléas et Mélisande* in 1969. The ballet tells of the couple's pursuit of an impossible love, portrayed with heartrending sincerity by the famous duo.

KEY WORKS

Dancer: *Laurentia*, 1958 • *Poème tragique*, 1961
Albrecht, *Giselle*, 1962 • Armand, *Marguerite and Armand*, 1963 • Prince Siegfried, *Swan Lake*, 1966
The Sleeping Beauty, 1975

> For me, purity of movement wasn't enough. I needed expression, more intensity, more mind.
>
> RUDOLF NUREYEV

TIMELINE

- **March 17, 1938** Born in Siberia, Russia, the son of a political officer in the Red Army.
- **1945** Resolves to be a dancer after seeing the ballet *Song of the Cranes* at his local theater in Ufa, the Bashkir capital.
- **1953** Having studied ballet under local teachers who recognized his potential, leaves school and earns money for his family by working as a theater extra in Ufa.
- **1955** Gains a place on a ballet tour of Moscow after mastering a folk-dance solo meant for another dancer.
- **1955** Courted by the Bolshoi Ballet school—with whom he auditions while in Moscow on tour—Nureyev instead enters the Vaganova Academy in St. Petersburg.
- **1958** Joins the Kirov Ballet after graduating and makes his debut partnering ballerina Natalia Dudinskaya.
- **1959** Dances outside the Soviet Union for the first time, at the International Youth Festival in Vienna, Austria.
- **1961** While on tour in Paris, evades his KGB minders and seeks asylum in France.
- **1962** Begins an enduring partnership and friendship with Margot Fonteyn at The Royal Ballet in London.
- **1979** Stages the one-act ballet *Manfred* at the Paris Opéra Ballet.
- **1983** Becomes artistic director of the Paris Opéra Ballet, then principal choreographer six years later.
- **January 6, 1993** Dies in Paris aged 54.

POSTER FOR *VALENTINO* (1977), ONE OF THE FEW FILMS IN WHICH NUREYEV STARRED

A Midsummer Night's Dream

First performed: January 17, 1962 ▪ Venue: New York City Center ▪ Choreography: George Balanchine ▪ Music: Mendelssohn ▪ Story: William Shakespeare

Although Balanchine is best known for his one-act non-narrative ballets, he also made some enthralling longer story works. He had an enduring fondness for Shakespeare's tale of lovers' mishaps. Having been an elf in a Mikhailovsky Theater production of the play as a child in St. Petersburg, as an adult, he still remembered many of the lines, and liked to say that he knew the play "better in Russian than a lot of people know it in English."

STORY LINE

Act I As Frederick Ashton later did in *The Dream* (1964), Balanchine bypasses the first part of Shakespeare's play and takes the audience directly to a scene of leafy boughs. The story follows Shakespeare's tale of tangled relationships—of the fairy royals and two hapless mortal couples—with their idiotic quarrels, forest chases, and makings-up, all orchestrated with magic from gleeful and impish Puck.

Act II Opening with Mendelssohn's familiar Wedding March, Act II is built around a triple marriage celebration for the two hapless couples, and for Theseus, Duke of Athens, and Hippolyta.

▼ **Titania and Bottom**
When Oberon gives Titania (here, danced by Uliana Lopatkina for The Mariinsky Ballet) a magic potion, she falls in love with Bottom (Dimitri Vedeneev) even though he appears as an ass. In Act I they dance a tender pas de deux.

The first wholly original full-length work that George Balanchine choreographed in the US, *A Midsummer Night's Dream* quickly became a repertory staple. It grew partly out of New York City Ballet seeking a spring production that would bring the same family appeal, roles for children, and healthy box office as his *The Nutcracker*. *A Midsummer Night's Dream* seemed a good choice, although Balanchine never hid the fact that what interested him most was Mendelssohn's music. Indeed, choreographer Jacques d'Amboise said that he had experimented with the score in a now forgotten outdoor performance as early as 1943.

The composer's Overture and Incidental Music for *A Midsummer Night's Dream* only ran to about an hour, so Balanchine scoured Mendelssohn's catalogue for additions, finally selecting a number of extra overtures, a nocturne, an intermezzo, and an excerpt from Symphony No. 9. Unlike the Shakespeare play, and in a reversal of most ballets that shift between the real and fairy or supernatural worlds, Balanchine anchors the work in the forest realm of Oberon and Titania, king and queen of the fairies. The story, which is largely condensed into Act I, is all told with a light touch, but very much through dance not mime. Balanchine demonstrates the many permutations of the love relationship in a series of pas de deux. He shows cloying embraces, distraught pleadings, and resistance to unwanted attention. Tellingly, Oberon and Titania never dance together but perform celebratory solos for their admiring retinues. When Titania does find a partner, it is Bottom.

▲ **Act I, New York City Ballet, 1964**
The forest scene is soon filled with busy, buzzing bugs, butterflies, and fairies, many played by children. Edward Villella (center) dances Oberon.

In Act II, Balanchine largely puts the story to one side. Instead, he focuses on the formal dancing and divertissements, all with perfect etiquette, recalling Marius Petipa and Imperial St. Petersburg. The ballet comes to a climax in the intricate and slow divertissement pas de deux that represents ideal, untroubled love.

Song of the Earth

First performed: November 7, 1965 ▪ Venue: Württembergische Staatstheater, Stuttgart ▪ Choreography and story: MacMillan ▪ Music: Gustav Mahler

A ballet in one act of several movements, danced to Gustav Mahler's *Das Liede von der Erde* ("Song of the Earth"), this work is about the bittersweet joys of life, and ultimately, death—not as a menacing and dreadful figure, but as an inevitability, a participant and companion in all human activity. Austere but ultimately uplifting, *Song of the Earth* is often considered one of Kenneth MacMillan's most successful ballets.

◀ **Star cast, 2007**
In this Royal Ballet production, Carlos Acosta danced the Messenger of Death with Darcey Bussell as the Woman.

Kenneth MacMillan's *Song of the Earth* took several years to be realized. MacMillan had been wanting to choreograph a piece to the symphonic song cycle of Gustav Mahler for some time. In 1959, when he proposed the work to the board of the Royal Opera House, Covent Garden, they told him that the music was unsuitable for ballet. The board also rejected a renewed proposal in 1965, despite the overwhelming success of MacMillan's *Romeo and Juliet*. Rebuffed, he offered the concept to his friend John Cranko at the Stuttgart Ballet in Germany, who received the idea warmly.

Framework of Mahler's song cycle

Gustav Mahler's song cycle was indeed a challenge. The songs, sung in German, take for their lyrics loose translations of Chinese poems from the 8th-century Tang Dynasty. The poems are reflections of human joys and sorrows, and the ultimate inevitability of death. Mahler himself had suffered the sorrow of losing a child, and expressed in this song cycle something of the transient and fleeting quality of life.

John Cranko allowed MacMillan to choose the dancers at Stuttgart that he felt would best interpret the concept he wanted to put into dance. Ray Marra, Marcia Haydée, and Egan Marsden were his first cast in the original production and took the roles of the Man, the Woman, and the shadowy masked figure who is the Messenger of Death or the Eternal One. MacMillan's choreography combined neoclassical, abstract, and Asian movements. Positions and body lines are unconventional, angular, and sweeping by turn, matching Mahler's music and bringing a suggestion of hope and renewal at the end.

Following the ballet's huge success in Stuttgart in 1965, MacMillan was asked to mount the work for The Royal Ballet after all, where it received an equally rapturous response.

STORY LINE

The Drinking Song of Earthly Sorrow The Man dances happily with five friends, carefree and very much alive; but he is claimed by the Messenger of Death.

The Lonely One in Autumn The Woman and three girls dance with partners. The Woman is left wistfully with the Messenger of Death, but not yet claimed.

Several songs Youthful enjoyment, passion, and happiness are the themes. Girls dance and pick flowers; young men carouse.

The final section This sequence of almost 30 minutes brings together the Man, the Woman, and Death, who claims them.

▶ **Premiere in London, 1966**
Despite previously rejecting MacMillan's proposal, The Royal Ballet later produced *Song of the Earth* with, left to right, Marcia Haydée as guest artist, Donald MacLeary, and Anthony Dowell.

Lynn Seymour

Dancer and choreographer ▪ 1939–

Born Berta Lynn Springbett in Canada, Seymour moved to London alone in 1954 to take up a scholarship at the Sadler's Wells Ballet School. It was a big step for a 15-year-old to make, but it paid off, and a successful career followed her training. As a dancer, she was acclaimed for her passionate and expressive style, and also for her acting ability. Her private life was no less colorful, and by returning to the stage after having children, she challenged the expectations of how ballet dancers lived.

▲ **Unlikely partners**
Lynn Seymour and Frank Frey rehearse their roles in MacMillan's production of *Swan Lake* for the Deutsche Oper in Berlin in 1969. The dancers were chosen by MacMillan for their contrasting styles.

Upon graduating from the Sadler's Wells Ballet School, Seymour joined the Sadler's Wells Theatre Ballet, The Royal Ballet's touring arm. It was here that choreographer Kenneth MacMillan first saw her, which he recalled in 1980, "I first saw Lynn Seymour as a member of the corps de ballet ... I was immediately impressed by her freedom of movement, which was unlike that of any other member of the company."

In 1958, MacMillan cast Seymour as the Adolescent in *The Burrow*, after which she soon became his muse. MacMillan admired Seymour's skill as a dancer and actor, and in 1960 he cast her as the Bride in his *Le Baiser de la fée*, and in 1961 as the Girl in Frederick Ashton's *Les Deux Pigeons*.

Shattered dreams

Seymour's biggest break came in 1965, when MacMillan created the role of Juliet for her in his new production of *Romeo and Juliet*. Impressed at her realism on stage, MacMillan made Seymour/Juliet the driving force behind the ballet. The production created for Seymour and her young fellow dancer, Christopher Gable, was set to propel the young couple to stardom. Seymour wrote later, "My life was dedicated to the ballet ... Juliet was a priceless gift from Kenneth ... the classical heroine of the theatre was the culmination of all my fantasy roles as a dancer."

Unfortunately for Seymour and Gable, US impresario and The Royal Ballet's tour manager, Sol Hurok, was insistent that the established stars Margot Fonteyn (then aged 46) and Rudolph Nureyev dance at the US premiere. Despite MacMillan's protests, the management of The Royal Ballet capitulated, and altered the London casting to match. Seymour and Gable were dropped to fourth cast—a devastating blow for the young dancers. Years later, Seymour recalled that "Romeo (*Romeo and Juliet*) broke hearts and shattered my life."

After Juliet

The year after *Romeo and Juliet*, Seymour left The Royal Ballet to join the Deutsche Oper, Berlin, where MacMillan was artistic director. It was there that he created *Anastasia* for her, premiering it as a one-act work in 1967, then as a three-act piece for The Royal Ballet in 1971.

Returning to The Royal Ballet in the early 1970s as a guest artist, Seymour created the roles of Isadora Duncan in Frederick Ashton's *Five Brahms Waltzes in the Manner of Isadora Duncan* in 1975, and Natalia Petrovna in *A Month in the Country* in 1976. Macmillan once again found a muse in Seymour for the creation of her 1978 role of Mary Vetsera in *Mayerling*.

From 1978–1980, Seymour became ballet director at the Bavarian State Opera in Munich. She retired as a dancer in 1981, but occasionally appeared as a guest performer with various companies in the years that followed. Then, between 2006–2007, she became artistic director of the Greek National Opera Ballet.

Seymour married three times and had three children, overturning the received conventions of ballerinas, as it was very unusual for them to have children and to return to the stage at this time. One of the most dramatic dancers of her era on stage, too, such is Seymour's dancing legacy that The Royal Ballet School gives an annual Lynn Seymour Award for Expressive Dance.

Lynn Seymour is a great dancer, a great artist.

KENNETH MACMILLAN, 1980

KEY WORKS

Adolescent, *The Burrow*, 1958
Girl, *The Invitation*, 1960 • Bride, *Le Baiser de la fée*, 1960 • Young Girl, *Les Deux Pigeons*, 1961
Juliet, *Romeo and Juliet*, 1965
Anna Andersen, *Anastasia*, 1967
Five Brahms Waltzes in the Manner of Isadora Duncan, 1975
A Month in the Country, 1976

◀ **Unrequited love**
Gable and Seymour perform the title roles of MacMillan's *Romeo and Juliet*. Despite not performing in the premiere, Seymour declared, "Juliet was mine."

TIMELINE

- **March 8, 1939** Born in Alberta, Canada, daughter of a dentist.
- **1954** Having studied dance in Vancouver, Canada, Seymour moves to London and joins the Sadler's Wells Ballet School.
- **1958** Dances in *The Burrow* by Kenneth MacMillan, with whom she goes on to have a lasting relationship as his muse.
- **1958** Tours Australia with her first classic role of Odette/Odile in *Swan Lake* with the Sadler's Wells Theatre Ballet.
- **1959** Becomes a principal dancer at The Royal Ballet, London.
- **1961** Begins a celebrated partnership with British ballet dancer Christopher Gable.
- **1962** Marries British dancer Colin Jones, but the couple divorce soon after.
- **1965** Instrumental in developing the role of Juliet in MacMillan's *Romeo and Juliet*, but Margot Fonteyn performs at its US premiere.
- **1966** Takes up the role of prima ballerina at Deutsche Oper in West Berlin, under MacMillan's directorship.

LYNN SEYMOUR PICTURED DURING REHEARSALS FOR *LES DEUX PIGEONS*, 1961

- **1973** Choreographs her first ballet, *Night Ride*, for The Royal Ballet Choreographic Group.
- **1978** Becomes ballet director of the Bavarian State Opera, Munich.
- **1981** Retires from dancing, but continues as an occasional ballet coach.
- **1996** Returns from retirement to star as the decadent queen in *Swan Lake* at Sadler's Wells.
- **2006** Becomes artistic director of the Greek National Opera Ballet.

Monotones

First performed: March 24, 1965 ▪ Venue: Royal Opera House, London ▪ Choreography: Frederick Ashton ▪ Music: Erik Satie, orchestrated by Claude Debussy and Alexis Roland-Manuel

Originally just over three minutes long, this ballet was devised as a program-filler for The Royal Ballet's annual Benevolent Fund Gala held at the Royal Opera House in London in 1965. It immediately stunned the audience, but its short length—though perfect for a gala—was unsuitable for a normal repertoire. As a result, Ashton extended the work a year later, and created a diptych of modernist choreography.

◀ The Royal Ballet, 2013
Yasmine Naghdi, Tristan Dyer, and Emma Maguire perform a series of controlled movements in *Monotones I* at the Royal Opera House, London.

STORY LINE

A one-act plotless ballet originally in one part for three dancers, later extended to two parts with six dancers.

The first part—a pas de trois for two men and one woman dressed in white—relies on synchronous coordination and control in one long, constantly evolving, supported adage. The fluid movement of the dancers conceptualize beings on the moon, moving at a slow pace and gazing into space. The extended second part—another pas de trois—features two women and one man dressed in green, who represent beings of the earth with movements that are heavier and more grounded.

Inspired by Russian and American scientists visiting space, Frederick Ashton wanted to create a ballet that reflected "how people might move on the moon." At its gala premiere, *Monotones* stole the show. Its three dancers—Vyvyan Lorraine, Anthony Dowell, and Robert Mead—captured the spirit of the piece, as well as the imagination of the audience. All three were dressed alike in close-fitting white unitards, their hair covered in matching studded caps, reminiscent of astronauts' space suits.

Having admired the work of French composer Erik Satie for a long time, Ashton chose his *Trois Gymnopédies* for the score. The ballet provided the perfect pairing of movement and music. The slow, pulsating, almost hypnotic quality of the score was echoed by the sinuous and continuous movements of the dancers. They intertwined, moved in unison, separated, and then came together again, but always at a calm, serene pace. *Monotones* was a sensation because of its complete lack of sensationalism.

Extending the work

The ballet proved to be so popular that Ashton decided to expand it. His new choreography—a second pas de trois to Satie's *Trois Gnossiennes*—echoed, but did not entirely replicate, the original piece.

The first version became known as *Monotones II*, while the second, though created later, was *Monotones I*. The reworked ballet of both parts was presented at the Royal Opera House on April 25, 1966, and featured the original dancers alongside Antoinette Sibley, Georgina Parkinson, and Brian Shaw, who danced *Monotones I*. Satie's *Préludes d'Eginhard* was included as an overture, resulting in a piece of almost 11 minutes.

The ballet premiered in the US in 1974 with the Joffrey Ballet. It was also danced by Zenaida Yanowsky, Iñaki Urlezaga, and Edward Watson at the joint gala of The Royal Ballet and Bolshoi in Moscow in 2003. *Monotones* is still very popular.

◀ Rehearsal with Ashton in 1965
The three original dancers Anthony Dowell, Vyvyan Lorraine, and Robert Mead were perfectly matched in physique and technique. They danced as "heavenly bodies" in futuristic white costumes.

▶ The Royal Ballet, 2015
The lime green costumes seen in *Monotones I* represent the organic earth and are worn by the terrestrials.

Peter Wright

Dancer and choreographer ▪ 1926–

As a dancer, choreographer, teacher, and company and television director, Peter Wright has worked with most of the ballet greats of the second half of the 20th century in a career spanning more than 70 years. His productions of the classics, true to the original yet appealing to today's audiences, are among the most popular works in the repertories of ballet companies worldwide. In recognition of a lifetime of outstanding achievement in dance, he has had numerous awards conferred upon him.

▲ ***The Nutcracker*, 2017**
To celebrate Wright's 90th birthday, Birmingham Royal Ballet put on his *Nutcracker* production. Here, Maureya Lebowitz, Gabriel Anderson, and Kit Holder perform the Spanish dance in Act II.

Wright's passion for ballet first took hold while he was a teenager at boarding school. Although his professional debut as a soldier in *The Green Table* in 1943 was in a modern, expressionist vein with the Ballets Jooss, he felt the call of classical ballet and worked to improve his technique in the late 1940s and '50s, studying with Vera Volkova and taking classes alongside Margot Fonteyn and Frederick Ashton. He performed with several companies including Metropolitan Ballet, St. James Ballet, and Sadler's Wells Theatre Ballet, interrupting his time with the latter for a second spell with Jooss.

In 1959, Wright was appointed ballet master to the Sadler's Wells Opera and teacher at The Royal Ballet School. When Sadler's Wells decided to abandon the opera ballet, he left to become freelance, working in theater and for the BBC, including as ballet master on a production of *The Sleeping Beauty*, with Fonteyn and Michael Somes (1959). Wright was about to join the BBC full time, when, in 1962, John Cranko invited him to Stuttgart to take up a post as ballet master. It was a turning point in his career.

Career takes off in Stuttgart

Wright had already had choreographic success with *A Blue Rose* (1957) for Sadler's Wells Theatre Ballet and *The Great Peacock* (1958) for the Edinburgh International Ballet. However, it was in Stuttgart that he blossomed, creating several one-act ballets including *The Mirror Walkers* (1963), *Designs for Dancers* (1964), and *Namouna* (1967). Wright's first production of *Giselle* (1966) was a huge success, as were his interpretations of other classics: *The Sleeping Beauty*, for the Cologne Opera Ballet, then for The Royal Ballet (both 1968); *Coppélia* (1975) for The Royal Ballet Touring Company, revised for Birmingham Royal Ballet (BRB, 1995); and *Swan Lake* (1981) for Sadler's Wells Royal Ballet. His stagings of *The Nutcracker* for The Royal Ballet (1984, 1999) and BRB (1990) were highly popular, the latter with its growing Christmas tree creating a spectacular transformation scene.

Dramatic realism

Wright's classics invariably stay faithful to the original, while keeping the story and presentation fresh enough for modern audiences. He is adamant that the classic ballets belong to a specific period and that is where they should remain; contemporary settings and modern dress are not for him. Key to his success is dramatic realism—telling the story clearly and credibly with strong characterizations. For Wright, the narrative must make sense. For example, he insists that Giselle kills herself since, if she just died of a broken heart she would not be buried in unhallowed ground.

Back from Stuttgart, Wright returned to the BBC, The Royal Ballet, then Sadler's Wells Royal Ballet, later overseeing the company's relocation to Birmingham in 1990, when it became BRB. Wright considers establishing the company in its new home as his greatest achievement. He turned the company into a major force with a repertoire of classics, new works, and revivals of 20th-century masterpieces including *The Green Table* and *Choreartium*.

Wright had to step down in 1995 after developing myasthenia gravis (a muscle disease), but as director laureate he has retained strong links with the company and his ballets. He received the UK Critics' Circle De Valois Award in 2004.

▲ ***Coppélia* in rehearsal**
Peter Wright rehearses Alain Dubreuil and Marion Tait at the Royal Opera House, Covent Garden, London in 1979. This interpretation of *Coppélia* is highly acclaimed, as is his later 1995 revision for Birmingham Royal Ballet.

KEY WORKS

Choreographer: *A Blue Rose*, 1957 · *The Mirror Walkers*, 1963 · *Giselle*, 1966 · *Namouna*, 1967 · *The Sleeping Beauty*, 1968 · *Coppélia*, 1975 · *Swan Lake*, 1981 · *The Nutcracker*, 1984

TIMELINE

- November 25, 1926 Born to a stern Quaker father who prohibited his dancing so he ran away from his boarding school.
- 1942 Sets his sights on a ballet career after seeing *Les Sylphides* at the Edinburgh International Ballet with his mother.
- 1943 Joins Ballets Jooss, run by German choreographer Kurt Jooss, the father of a school friend, as an apprentice.
- 1949 Admitted to de Valois' Sadler's Wells Theatre Ballet, but returns to Ballets Jooss, now in Germany, two years later.
- 1954 Marries British ballerina and actress Sonya Hana.
- 1955 Invited to run a new Sadler's Wells Opera Ballet.
- 1957 Choreographs his first ballet, *A Blue Rose*, performed by the Sadler's Wells Theatre Ballet.
- 1961 Joins the Stuttgart Ballet as teacher and ballet master, with the company's new director John Cranko.
- 1964 Guest director on *Ballet Class*, a television ballet for the BBC.
- 1966 Returns to London with his family, as associate to The Royal Ballet directors.
- 1977 Appointed director of Sadler's Wells Royal Ballet, supervising the transition to Birmingham Royal Ballet in 1990.
- 1994 Awarded a knighthood.
- 1995 Retires from the role of director at the Birmingham Royal Ballet due to illness; becomes the company's director laureate.
- 2016 His autobiography *Wrights & Wrongs: My Life in Dance* is published.

AUTOBIOGRAPHY *WRIGHTS & WRONGS* (2016)

Onegin

First performed: April 13, 1965 ▪ Venue: Stuttgart State Theater ▪ Choreography: John Cranko ▪ Music: Tchaikovsky ▪ Story: Alexander Pushkin

Cranko's output was prodigious, and he left a particularly rich repertoire of story ballets. Standing tall among them is the powerful, richly emotional dance-drama, *Onegin*. His definitive masterpiece, it is one of the finest narrative ballets of the 20th century, and remains in demand by companies and audiences alike worldwide. As a ballet it has everything: tragedy and drama, comedy in the second act, but most of all, finely drawn characters of great depth.

STORY LINE

Act I Tatiana is infatuated with world-weary city aristocrat Onegin, after being introduced by her sister Olga's fiancé, Lensky. She writes him a passionate love letter.

Act II At Tatiana's birthday ball, Onegin tears up her letter and offends Lensky, resulting in a duel. In the ensuing pistol fight he unwittingly kills his friend and flees, full of remorse.

Act III Meeting Tatiana again years later, Onegin realizes he spurned the only woman who ever truly loved him. But it is too late—now married to Gremin, whom she loves, Tatiana rejects him.

Based on Pushkin's 1833 novel, *Eugene Onegin*, Cranko's magnum opus is a human drama in the vein of *Romeo and Juliet*. Like Juliet, Tatiana is a role many ballerinas will confess they most want to dance. Portraying Tatiana's development from country girl to a sophisticated society woman needs huge dramatic sensibility and technical finesse.

Onegin took time to come to fruition. Cranko first had the idea when creating dances for Tchaikovsky's opera *Eugene Onegin* at Covent Garden in 1952. But when he pitched his idea, the Royal Opera House objected to adapting the great composer's opera music for ballet.

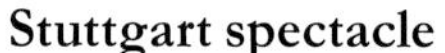

Stuttgart spectacle

After moving to Stuttgart Ballet, Cranko tried again but the management there would also not allow the score to be used. Cranko then turned to Kurt-Heinze Stolze to arrange music from other Tchaikovsky pieces. While audiences hailed the result, some critics did not. The music caused further controversy, this time over discarding the opera score.

Cranko tells the story almost entirely through dance. The hearty ensemble dances are full of Russian-flavored steps, lively polonaises, and genteel promenades. The solos say much about character and mood. At the ballet's heart, though, are the powerful pas de deux. None is more intense than the letter-writing scene, when the young Tatiana dances a duet with her dream image of Onegin. With soaring lifts and throws, it vividly depicts her wild, romantic imagination. More restrained, but if anything more beautiful, is the farewell pas de deux that portrays Tatiana's hesitation in the face of the returned Onegin's confessed feelings.

▲ **Modern reinterpretation**
Onegin was recreated for its first showing at the Royal Opera House in 2001, featuring Tamara Rojo as Tatiana and Christopher Saunders as Gremin.

▶ **Supporting characters**
Cranko's choreography is noted for the intricate sequences danced by all four lead roles, including Olga and Lensky—danced by Akane Takada and Vadim Muntagirov in 2015.

◀ **Leading ballerina**
For the 1965 premiere, the role of Tatiana was danced by principal ballerina Marcia Haydée, pictured here with Richard Cragun as Onegin in a later production.

John Cranko

Director and choreographer ▪ 1927–1973

Responsible for what *The New York Times* called "Stuttgart's ballet miracle," John Cranko turned the Stuttgart Ballet into an international force. A powerhouse of ballet, the choreographer and director also played a leading role in ballet companies in London, Paris, and New York. As a choreographer, Cranko was prolific, and produced a varied catalog of works encompassing high drama, comedy, and storytelling. Today, his spirit lives on in the Stuttgart company, his school, and his ballets.

▲ **Stars of Stuttgart**
Prima ballerina at Stuttgart Ballet, Marcia Haydée sits next to Cranko to watch Richard Cragun, "a prince of the ballet world," rehearse. Following Cranko's death in 1973, Haydée replaced him as the company's director until 1995.

Cranko's early dance education mainly took place at the University of Cape Town, where in 1945, he choreographed his first ballet, *The Soldier's Tale*, for the Cape Town Ballet Club. The following year, he moved to the Sadler's Wells Ballet School in London and joined the Sadler's Wells Theatre Ballet.

In 1946, Cranko's restaging of *Tritsch-Tratsch* was enough for the company's director, Ninette de Valois, to encourage him to pursue a career in choreography. After successes in 1949 with *Sea Change*, *Children's Corner*, and *Beauty and the Beast*, he retired as a dancer to become resident choreographer of Sadler's Wells Theatre Ballet, aged only 23.

Among the many well-known short ballets he choreographed in the years that followed are the Gilbert and Sullivan ballet *Pineapple Poll* (1951) and his comedic *The Lady and the Fool* (1954). In 1957, Cranko choreographed his first full-length ballet, *The Prince of the Pagodas* (1957). It was the first three-act British ballet with a specially commissioned score, composed by the celebrated Benjamin Britten, but it received mixed reviews.

On the international stage

Cranko was soon playing a leading role in other major ballet companies around the world, namely Paris Opéra Ballet, New York City Ballet, and London's Ballet Rambert. At Sadler's Wells (by now renamed The Royal Ballet) Cranko began to feel frustrated by the presence of Frederick Ashton and Kenneth MacMillan, which limited his own choreographic opportunities.

In 1959, Cranko finally decided to leave London and joined the Stuttgart Opera. There, following a successful run of *The Prince of the Pagodas* for Stuttgart Ballet in 1960, Cranko was first appointed guest choreographer, then ballet director the following year.

The polar opposite of many dictatorial directors of the time, there was no doubt Cranko was in charge but he was also well-liked and had warm relationships with his dancers. He soon set about building the company and expanding its repertory. The group he assembled included Richard Cragun, Birgit Keil, Marcia Haydée (who became his muse), and Egon Madsen. He would later make the symphonic ballet *Initials R.B.M.E* (1972) in recognition of them.

A storyteller and more

Part of Cranko's success came with his ability to tell stories in ways that appealed to audiences, and his understanding of what worked theatrically. While his Stuttgart breakthrough came with *Romeo and Juliet* (1962), it was *Onegin* (1965) that was his most highly acclaimed work. Featuring large dance ensembles of contrasting styles in each act, it was set to a score created by Kurt-Heinz Stolze from Tchaikovsky's less familiar works.

Ever eager to encourage new talent, in 1966 Cranko persuaded the company's ballet master, Peter Wright, to allow young choreographers from Stuttgart's Noverre Society to showcase their work with the company. While still with Stuttgart Ballet, in 1968 Cranko also became chief choreographer of the Bavarian State Opera Ballet, spreading his influence yet further. He left the post in 1971, the same year that he finally decided to establish his own ballet school. While Cranko died two years later, his school continues to prosper to this day.

He sees the dance as drama and even more as storytelling.

CLIVE BARNES, *THE NEW YORK TIMES*, 1971

▲ **Sadler's Wells rehearsal, 1951**
Resident choreographer John Cranko and fellow South African ballerina Maryon Lane watch Pauline Harrop rehearse an enchaînement. Although he was utterly focused in his work, Cranko developed an informal, relaxed approach with dancers.

KEY WORKS

Choreographer: *Pineapple Poll*, 1951 • *The Lady and the Fool*, 1954 • *Cranks*, 1955 • *The Prince of the Pagodas*, 1957 • *Onegin*, 1965 • *Taming of the Shrew*, 1969 • *Carmen*, 1971 • *Initials R.B.M.E*, 1972

TIMELINE

- **August 15, 1927** Born in Rustenburg, near Johannesburg, South Africa.
- **1944** Joins the University of Cape Town Ballet School, having studied privately with Marjorie Sturman.
- **1946** Set to Strauss's polka of the same name, *Tritsch-Tratsch* becomes the first of his performances to receive critical acclaim.
- **1946** Moves to London to dance at the Sadler's Wells Ballet School.
- **1949** Achieves popular acclaim with *Beauty and the Beast.*
- **1950** Becomes resident choreographer at Sadler's Wells Theater Ballet.
- **1958** La Scala Theater Ballet in Milan, Italy, performs Cranko's production of *Romeo and Juliet.*
- **1960** Works with the Stuttgart Ballet as guest choreographer, and is made the company's ballet director the following year.
- **1963** Influenced by Frederick Ashton, choreographs a theatrical staging of *Swan Lake.*
- **1967** Tours South America with the Stuttgart Ballet, to considerable acclaim.
- **1968** Becomes principal choreographer of the Bavarian State Opera Ballet, a post he holds until 1971.
- **1969** The Stuttgart Ballet's season at the New York Metropolitan Opera raises the international profile of German ballet.
- **1971** Establishes a ballet school in Stuttgart, renamed the John Cranko Schule in 1974 after his death.
- **June 26, 1973** Dies mid-flight returning to Stuttgart following a successful US tour.

AMERICAN BALLET THEATRE PERFORMING CRANKO'S *ONEGIN* IN NEW YORK IN 2012

METROPOLITAN OPERA HOUSE

The vibrant centerpiece of New York's Lincoln Center, the Metropolitan Opera House ("the Met") is the oldest and largest opera house in the US. Home to the Metropolitan Opera Company and, since 1977, annual host to American Ballet Theatre, the building stages over 200 performances each year with leading artistes from around the globe. The Met was founded in 1883, and originally located in New York's Garment District on 39th Street. It was moved for technical and staging reasons to Lincoln Center in 1966. The new Metropolitan Opera House officially opened on September 16, 1966, with the world premiere of Samuel Barber's *Antony and Cleopatra*, directed by Franco Zeffirelli and choreographed by Alvin Ailey. In a rare 1986 appearance, then American Ballet Theatre artistic director Mikhail Baryshnikov and Paris Opéra ballet director Rudolf Nureyev performed together at the Met for a fundraising gala.

On display in the interior foyer and visible from the outside plaza are two large murals created for the space by early modernist artist Marc Chagall. Dual cascading staircases also feature in the lobby's decor as well as 11 crystal sputnik chandeliers. The 32 chandeliers that hang throughout the Met were donated by Austria in gratitude for the US's help rebuilding the Vienna State Opera House after World War II.

The stage is exceptionally deep and is fitted with hydraulic elevators and rigging systems for staging the most complex of productions. With 14 floors (five of which are underground), the range of facilities within the Met make it one of the best-equipped performance spaces in the world.

> The new Met wanted to be a symbol of the space age.
>
> JAMES BARRON, *NEW YORK TIMES*, 2008

Outside plaza—approaching the Met ▶
Designed by architect Wallace Harrison, the exterior facade consists of five concrete arches backed by glass and bronze panels.

AMERICAN BALLET THEATRE
Welcome To Josie Robertson Plaza
Lincoln Center
Welcome To Josie Robertson Plaza
Josie Robertson Plaza
Lincoln Center
Welcome To Josie Robertson Plaza

Jewels

First performed: April 13, 1967 ▪ Venue: New York State Theater ▪ Choreography: George Balanchine ▪ Music: Gabriel Fauré, Stravinsky, and Tchaikovsky

The ballet *Jewels* represents the essence of choreographer George Balanchine's oeuvre, combining the French, American, and Russian influences that echoed across his life and career. Balanchine selected emeralds, rubies, and diamonds as the premise of his glittering new production. It became one of his most celebrated works and was praised for its magnificent concept and sustained inspiration.

George Balanchine was inspired to create his triptych, *Jewels*, by the beautiful gemstones he saw in the window displays of the jewelers Van Cleef & Arpels on his daily walk down Fifth Avenue in New York.

Considered to be the world's first full-length abstract ballet, *Jewels* had no self-evident plot, but Balanchine linked its three parts with his choreography. A monumental and artistic innovation, *Jewels* moved ballet away from the classic fairytale narratives of the past to focus solely on the relationship between the music and movements. Each piece is color coded in backdrop and costume to the relevant gemstone.

▲ **Original New York City Ballet cast, 1967**
Patricia McBride (left) played the gemstone Ruby; Violette Verdy (seated) and Mimi Paul, Emeralds; and Suzanne Farrell, Diamond.

STORY LINE

To define each of the three gemstones/ movements in *Jewels*, Balanchine chose musical scores by composers working in different veins, and Karinska created costumes to suit each era.

Emeralds Set to the work of French Romantic composer Gabriel Fauré, the ballerinas wore swishing tulle skirts.

Rubies The music of Russian minimalist Igor Stravinsky was paired with modern, petal flap skirts that flared at the hips.

Diamonds Classic white tutus were chosen to match Tchaikovsky's music.

Three-part ballet

The first piece, *Emeralds*, gracefully evokes the sophisticated and romantic style of 1920s Paris and hearkens back to Balanchine's tenure in France working with the Ballets Russes. He created the work for French ballerina Violette Verdy, whose elegant port de bras exemplified the refined arm movements of the French school of ballet. His choreography for *Emeralds* at first follows classical protocol, but becomes more nuanced with delicate lyricism as the ballet progresses.

In contrast to *Emeralds'* romantic dreaminess, the choreography for *Rubies* follows with punchy vigor. Inspired by the jazzy New York culture Balanchine experienced upon his arrival in the US in the 1930s, *Rubies* epitomizes many of the neoclassical elements for which the choreographer is famous. Inverted passés, hip swings, and flexed feet are all playfully incorporated as dancers bounce on and off the stage in quirky asymmetrical patterns. Set to Stravinsky's *Capriccio for Piano and Orchestra*, *Rubies* is a good example of Balanchine's talent for bringing this composer's work to brilliant visual fruition on stage.

While *Rubies* testifies to Balanchine's flair for the avant-garde, *Diamonds* looks back to classical ballet and is a reminder of Balanchine's affection for the imperial elegance of his Russian roots. Twelve couples polonaise around the stage, changing patterns with large sweeping movements, reminiscent of Balanchine's more formal works such as *Ballet Imperial* and *Theme and Variations*. With a large cast of 34, *Diamonds* is a fitting grand finale.

Jewels was an overnight success in 1967. Today, it continues to be one of the most loved and frequently performed works in Balanchine's repertoire.

◀ **Royal Ballet production, 2007**
Alina Cojocaru and Rupert Pennefather dance the *Diamonds* section of *Jewels* at the Royal Opera House, Covent Garden, London. *Diamonds* is the most classically oriented of the three pieces.

▶ **Rubies, 2017**
Sarah Lamb and Steven McRae dance in The Royal Ballet's 50-year celebratory revival of George Balanchine's inspired ballet.

Anastasia

First performed: June 25, 1967 ▪ Venue: Deutsche Oper, Berlin ▪ Choreography: MacMillan ▪ Music: Bohusla Martinů ▪ Story: Based on Anna Anderson

Best-known in its 1971 three-act version, Kenneth MacMillan's *Anastasia* began life four years earlier in Berlin as a one-act ballet that told the story of a woman rescued from drowning in a canal in the city in 1920. Calling herself Anna Anderson, the diagnosed schizophrenic claimed to be Grand Duchess Anastasia, youngest daughter of Czar Nicholas II, and sole survivor of the 1918 massacre of the Romanov family at Ekaterinburg.

STORY LINE

Act I The ballet begins at an Imperial family summer picnic in 1914. The arrival of a telegram brings news of the outbreak of war.

Act II The action shifts to St. Petersburg in 1917 and Anastasia's coming-of-age party at the Imperial Palace. The celebrations end abruptly when the ball is invaded by armed revolutionaries and the family are led away.

Act III The story fast-forwards another three years. In the asylum where Anderson has been incarcerated, she watches silent films of her supposed past. She sees her happiness and her lover, but also tragedy and firing squads.

MacMillan found Anderson's story compelling, with its "theme that has sometimes appeared in my work before: the outsider figure." With Lynn Seymour as Anderson, and set to Martinů's hallucinatory and other-worldly Sixth Symphony (written when he himself was recovering from a head injury), MacMillan dug into the nightmare that was the woman's memories. Whether they were real or imagined, he left for the audience in Berlin to decide.

On his return to London as director of The Royal Ballet, MacMillan decided to make Anderson/Anastasia's story the subject of a full-length work by adding two prequel acts that went back in time to the princess's youth. For the new acts, MacMillan opted for Tchaikovsky's First and Third Symphonies, both roughly contemporary with the events depicted. The Berlin ballet became the third act.

It was Seymour's idea that the youngster's playful character in Act I could best be established by having her enter on roller skates, wearing a sailor suit. There is an illusion of peace and joy as she dances with some sailor cadets.

Among the formal dances that appear in Act II is a pas de deux for the Czar's ex-mistress—Mariinsky ballerina Mathilde Kschessinska—and her partner (danced in 1971 by Antoinette Sibley and Anthony Dowell). The glitter of the ballroom contrasts with the revolutionary discontent and slogans visible outside. Act III ends unresolved but Anderson never doubted her own identity—though, in 1994, DNA tests determined that she was, in fact, Franziska Schanzkowska, a Polish factory worker. That knowledge has not altered the ballet's appeal, however, and it remains one of MacMillan's most poignant works.

▲ **Lynn Seymour with David Wall, 1971**
Kenneth MacMillan created the ballet for Lynn Seymour as Anastasia/Anderson. The ambitious London version met a mixed reception.

▼ **The final act, 2016**
Natalia Osipova plays a crop-haired, dowdy Anderson for Act III of this Royal Ballet production. Here, memories are confused and past, present, and different realities intermingle.

▶ **Viviana Durante, 1996**
Durante took the lead role in this Royal Ballet production, dancing with Adam Cooper in the ballroom scene in Act II.

Spartacus

First performed: December 27, 1956 ▪ Venue: Kirov Theater, Leningrad ▪ Choreography: Leonid Yakobson ▪ Music: Khachaturyan ▪ Story: Nikolay Volkov

The three-act ballet *Spartacus* is a Soviet work on a huge and impressive scale. Armenian composer Aram Khachaturyan wrote the score in 1954, and was awarded a Lenin Prize for his work. The plot is based on a slave insurrection under the leadership of the gladiator Spartacus during the time of the Roman Empire. *Spartacus,* using the later choreography of Yuri Grigorovich, remains a staple of the Bolshoi Ballet today.

STORY LINE

Act I Spartacus and his wife Phrygia have been captured by Crassus and brought to Rome. The couple are separated: Phrygia to join Crassus's harem and Spartacus to be a gladiator. After being made to kill a friend, Spartacus incites the other captives to revolt.

Act II Spartacus gathers his rebels into an army. He finds Phrygia at Crassus's villa. Spartacus and Crassus duel; Spartacus wins but refuses to kill Crassus.

Act III Disgraced, Crassus rallies his army to find and kill Spartacus. They surround and defeat Spartacus and his diminished troops. Spartacus is killed, and Phrygia mourns.

This ballet was first staged in 1956 by the Kirov Ballet, Leningrad (the Soviet names for the Mariinsky Ballet, St. Petersburg). Choreographer Leonid Yakobson used a cast of more than 200 dancers, in Roman-style sandals, and dispensed with pointe work completely. While not a great success at the time, the Mariinsky Ballet revived this version in 2010, and it remains in their repertoire.

Spartacus at the Bolshoi

In 1958, *Spartacus* was staged at the Bolshoi Theater, Moscow, with choreography by renowned folk and character dance choreographer Igor Moiseyev. Ten years later, the Bolshoi put on a new production, this time with choreography by artistic director and former dancer Yuri Grigorovich. This production propelled *Spartacus* into the public eye and received great acclaim. *Spartacus* showcased Soviet ballet and, despite its revolutionary theme, the Soviet authorities approved of the work.

When discussing the creation of the ballet years later, Grigorovich explained: "My objective was to concentrate attention not on the everyday aspect of things, nor historical or ethnographic truth, but on the significance of the dramatic conflicts, the eternal struggle against violence, and aspiration for freedom." The male-dominated ballet was full of drama and virtuoso technique.

Spartacus was first performed in Western Europe in 1969 when the Bolshoi Ballet toured to London. The work was an immediate sensation, as outside Russia the ballerina largely reigned supreme and such pyrotechnic leaps and lifts had not been seen before. *Spartacus* became the Bolshoi Ballet's calling card and the company performed it, or at least excerpts of it, wherever they went. It became hugely popular for its sheer scale and bombastic style both within and outside Russia.

Perhaps the most famous and certainly the youngest man to dance the leading role was Irek Mukhamedov. In 1981, after winning a major ballet competition aged 21, he was invited to join the Bolshoi Ballet as a soloist. Here, Mukhamedov became Grigorovich's favorite dancer and first choice for the title role of *Spartacus.*

▲ **Adagio from Act I, 2008**
Natalia Bessmertnova plays Phrygia and Irek Mukhamedov dances as Spartacus. Even after the end of Soviet rule, *Spartacus* remains in demand.

◀ **Captive heroes, 1970**
Vladimir Vasiliev as Spartacus and Natalia Bessmertnova as Phrygia are taken in chains of slavery to Rome.

▶ **Irek Mukhamedov as Spartacus, 1990**
The final, brutal moments of the ballet show Spartacus held aloft by the Roman legionnaires, impaled on the point of their spears.

Kenneth MacMillan

Dancer and choreographer ▪ 1929–1992

Born to a family with little interest in the arts, Scotsman Kenneth MacMillan discovered ballet while evacuated to Nottinghamshire during World War II. He became a leading choreographer of his generation, creating 10 full-length and more than 70 one-act ballets. Rather than showing the academic, decorative side of ballet, he explored his characters' psychological motivations with sometimes raw exposés of real life. Even his more abstract ballets have hints of plot and character.

▶ **MacMillan the dancer**
MacMillan practices steps from *Daphnis and Chloe* at the Royal Opera House, London, in 1951. He had an elegant classical style as a dancer, but stage fright nudged him into choreography.

MacMillan's association with The Royal Ballet began when he joined Ninette de Valois' Sadler's Wells Ballet School aged 15 on a full scholarship, having forged a letter from his father requesting an audition. He was soon a member of the Sadler's Wells Ballet. A notable actor-dancer, he suffered from severe stage fright, so was encouraged to try choreography. His *Somnambulism* (1953) and *Laiderette* (1954) for de Valois' new Choreographers Group were well received, but he really came to attention with *Danses Concertantes* (1955).

New, postwar approach

MacMillan's works are often about people at odds with the world. A prevailing theme is a lonely, rejected central character, which reflected his own background: he was not close to his father, was told not to discuss his mother's epilepsy, and had to keep his dancing a secret. That, and growing up in wartime, gave him a bleak outlook on life and relationships.

Of MacMillan's early ballets, *The Burrow* (1958) dealt with a group of oppressed people living in terror of "the knock on the door," while *The Invitation* (1960) pushed ballet into new territory with its graphic depiction of a rape. He created both for his muse Lynn Seymour.

MacMillan invariably started ballets with the main duet—the best known is the balcony pas de deux in *Romeo and Juliet* (1965), for Seymour and Christopher Gable. MacMillan was not pleased when, for commercial reasons, the Royal Opera House board insisted Rudolf Nureyev and Margot Fonteyn were the first-night cast and leads in the 1966 film of the work. Tensions rose again later that year, when the board objected to the use of Mahler's music for *Song of the Earth* (1965), and so MacMillan instead created it for Stuttgart Ballet. Instantly a success, it was in The Royal Ballet's repertory the following May, but the damage was done. He left for Berlin and the directorship of the Deutsche Oper Ballet, taking Seymour with him. It was not a happy experience, though, as he felt isolated.

Back to London

In 1970, MacMillan returned to London to direct The Royal Ballet. He expanded *Anastasia* into a three-act ballet (1971) and created *Manon* (1974), both dividing opinion. However, a rare light-hearted ballet, *Elite Syncopations* (1974), to music by Scott Joplin, and *Requiem* (1976), made in Stuttgart after a Royal Opera House refusal, were immediately successful.

MacMillan resigned as director in 1977, but remained as choreographer, first creating *Mayerling* (1978), a study of the tormented Crown Prince Rudolf of Austria and his suicide pact with his mistress. His short ballets of the period are also dark: *My Brother My Sisters* (1978) features a disturbed family, *Playground* (1979) is set in a mental hospital, and *Valley of Shadows* (1983) includes scenes in a concentration camp. His final full-length ballet, *The Prince of the Pagodas* (1989), starred the fast-rising Darcey Bussell. *The Judas Tree* (1992), his last work, a tale of betrayal and sexual violence featuring Viviana Durante, proved one of his most controversial.

KEY WORKS

Choreographer: *Somnambulism*, 1953 • *Danses Concertantes*, 1955 • *Romeo and Juliet*, 1965
Anastasia, 1971 • *Manon*, 1974 • Mayerling, 1978
Isadora, 1981 • *The Prince of the Pagodas*, 1989
The Judas Tree, 1992

▲ **In rehearsal with Lynn Seymour**
Kenneth MacMillan was highly inventive with movement, which was for him a way to express psychological motivation, as here, not an end in itself. He never abandoned classical technique but would drop it if the drama justified it.

TIMELINE

- **December 11, 1929** Born in Dunfermline, Scotland, where he learns Scottish dancing.

- **1935** Family moves to Great Yarmouth, England, where he learns tap and performs at talent shows on the seaside town's pier.

- **1940** His grammar school is relocated to Nottinghamshire after Great Yarmouth is regarded as a target for German air raids in World War II. He learns ballet there.

- **1942** His mother, Edith MacMillan, dies while he is at school in Nottinghamshire.

- **1945** Joins the Sadler's Wells Ballet School, London.

- **1946** Founder member of Ninette de Valois' Sadler's Wells Ballet, a junior dance company. His father, William, dies.

- **1949** Dances the role of Florestan in *The Sleeping Beauty* in New York.

- **1952** Joins a small dance group under John Cranko in a bid to combat stage fright.

- **1955** Becomes resident choreographer for the Sadler's Wells Theatre Ballet.

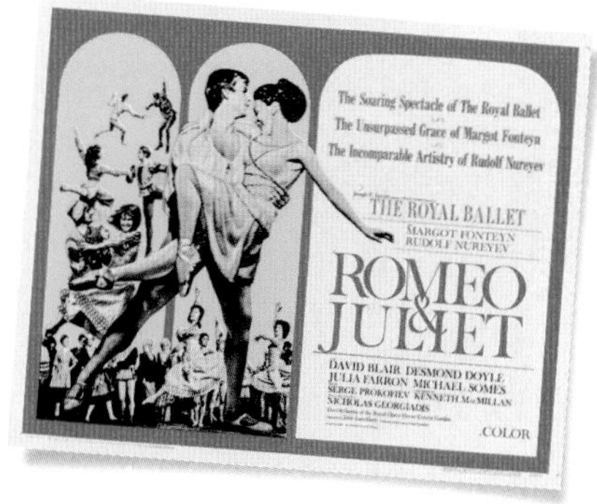

FILM POSTER OF *ROMEO AND JULIET* (1966)

- **1956** Creates *Noctambules*, his first work for The Royal Ballet in London.

- **1965** Creates *Romeo and Juliet*, then *Song of the Earth*—a non-representational, plotless work—for the Stuttgart Ballet.

- **1970** Becomes director of The Royal Ballet, London, after four unhappy years at the Deutsche Oper Ballet in West Berlin.

- **1973** Marries artist Deborah Williams.

- **1984** Becomes artistic associate of American Ballet Theatre, New York.

- **October 29, 1992** Dies of a heart attack while backstage at the Royal Opera House.

SYDNEY OPERA HOUSE

One of the world's most recognizable buildings, Sydney Opera House sits like a ship in full sail on a narrow spit of land projecting into Sydney Harbour. It has seven art companies in residence, including the Opera Australia and The Australian Ballet, and its performances have an annual audience of two million. Containing not one but seven performance spaces, the building was designed by 38-year-old Danish architect Jørn Utzon in a 1956 international competition. Utzon, who had never been to Sydney, studied maritime maps of the area to get a sense of the landscape, and drew inspiration from Kronborg Castle near his home in Hellebaek, immortalized as Elsinore in Shakespeare's *Hamlet*. This Renaissance castle on a promontory between Denmark and Sweden helped Utzon to imagine Bennelong Point on the other side of the world.

Utzon was never to see his extraordinary vision realized. In 1966, amid controversy over engineering difficulties and cost overruns, he resigned from the project, leaving Australia shortly afterward. The team of architects and engineers that continued the work were faced with many problems. Utzon had designed curved and sweeping structures that had never yet been built, so construction processes had to be continually invented to make the building possible. It was opened by Queen Elizabeth II in 1973.

> The sun did not know how beautiful its light was until it was reflected off this building.
>
> LOUIS KAHN, AMERICAN ARCHITECT

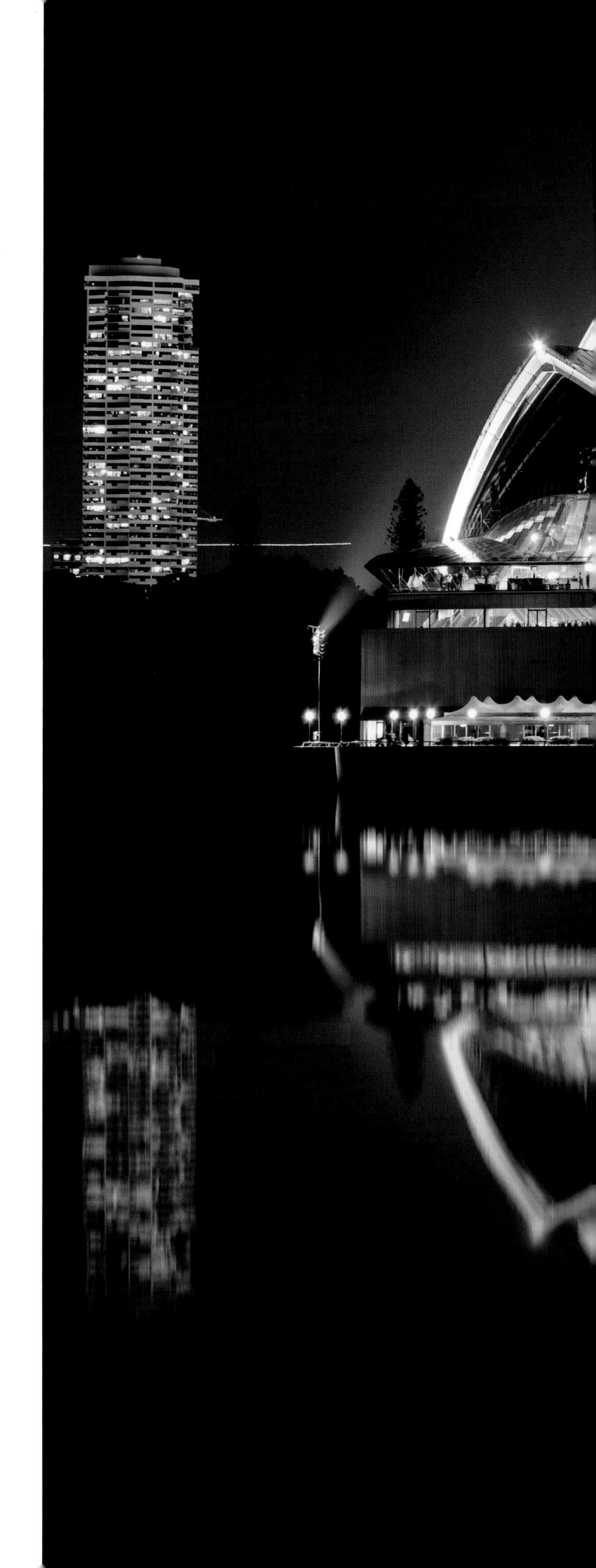

Icon of Australian culture ▶
Sydney Opera House is one of the world's busiest performing arts centers, presenting more than 2,000 shows a year. The Australian Ballet regularly performs there.

Manon

First performed: March 7, 1974 ▪ Venue: Royal Opera House, London ▪ Choreography: Kenneth MacMillan ▪ Music: Jules Massenet ▪ Story: Abbé Prévost

When it premiered in 1974, *L'Histoire de Manon* (generally known as *Manon*) met with mixed critical reviews, largely due to its adult themes and the amoral nature of the character Manon herself. However, despite MacMillan's ballet showing the dark side of humanity and the underbelly of society all interwoven with sex and money, the public appeared to love it instantly. The work quickly became a key piece in The Royal Ballet's repertoire.

STORY LINE

Act I Manon is on her way to enter a convent when her brother, Lescaut, attempts to sell her to the highest bidder. Manon meets Des Grieux and falls in love. When Lescaut tries to sell her to Monsieur G.M., Manon and Des Grieux run away to Paris. Lescaut finds Manon and she agrees to become G.M.'s mistress.

Act II G.M. catches Des Grieux trying to cheat him at cards. Manon and Des Grieux make their escape during a fight. G.M. finds them, and Manon is detained and Lescaut killed.

Act III Manon is sentenced to a penal colony in New Orleans. Des Grieux accompanies her and eventually they escape together. Manon dies, exhausted, in the arms of Des Grieux.

▲ **Viviana Durante as Manon**
MacMillan wanted to create a large-scale operatic-style ballet that provided extensive roles for all ranks of dancers. Durante was a principal dancer of The Royal Ballet when she danced as Manon in 1995.

▼ **The Royal Ballet, 1974**
Antoinette Sibley was the first ballerina to dance as Manon alongside Anthony Dowell as Des Grieux.

Kenneth MacMillan's idea for *Manon* came from Abbé Prévost's 1731 novel *L'Histoire du Chevalier des Grieux et de Manon Lescaut.* He was also influenced by the Puccini and Massenet operas based on Prévost's story. Composer and former Ballets Russes dancer Leighton Lucas provided the score—an adaptation and arrangement of Massenet's works, though not from his opera *Manon*, but from a selection of his incidental music, orchestral suites, and other opera.

Greek stage and costume designer Nicholas Georgiadis designed the set, having already designed several of MacMillan's ballets, including *Romeo and Juliet* and *Song of the Earth.* For *Manon*, he made use of the 18th-century setting to portray both the sumptuous and impoverished sides of the story. Dance writer Jann Parry considered his designs to be a reflection of the "precarious division between opulence and degradation" with "the stench of poverty ever-present."

The ballet opened in 1974 with dancers Antoinette Sibley and Anthony Dowell in the leading roles, and David Wall as Lescaut. Despite criticism from the press regarding the unpleasant story and characters, *Manon* proved a success on its opening night, with the audience giving it a standing ovation.

As with *Romeo and Juliet*, MacMillan used a series of pas de deux to show the development of love between the main characters. He left the role of Manon open to interpretation, and ballerinas who have tackled this role since Sibley include Viviana Durante, Sylvie Guillem, and Natalia Makarova. Beyond The Royal Ballet, *Manon* has been reproduced by companies around the world including American Ballet Theatre and The National Ballet of Canada.

▶ **The Royal Ballet, 2009**
Tamara Rojo and Carlos Acosta dance in a production of *Manon* at the Karl Marx Theater in Cuba. Rojo's disheveled appearance in Act III indicates the dramatic change to the heroine.

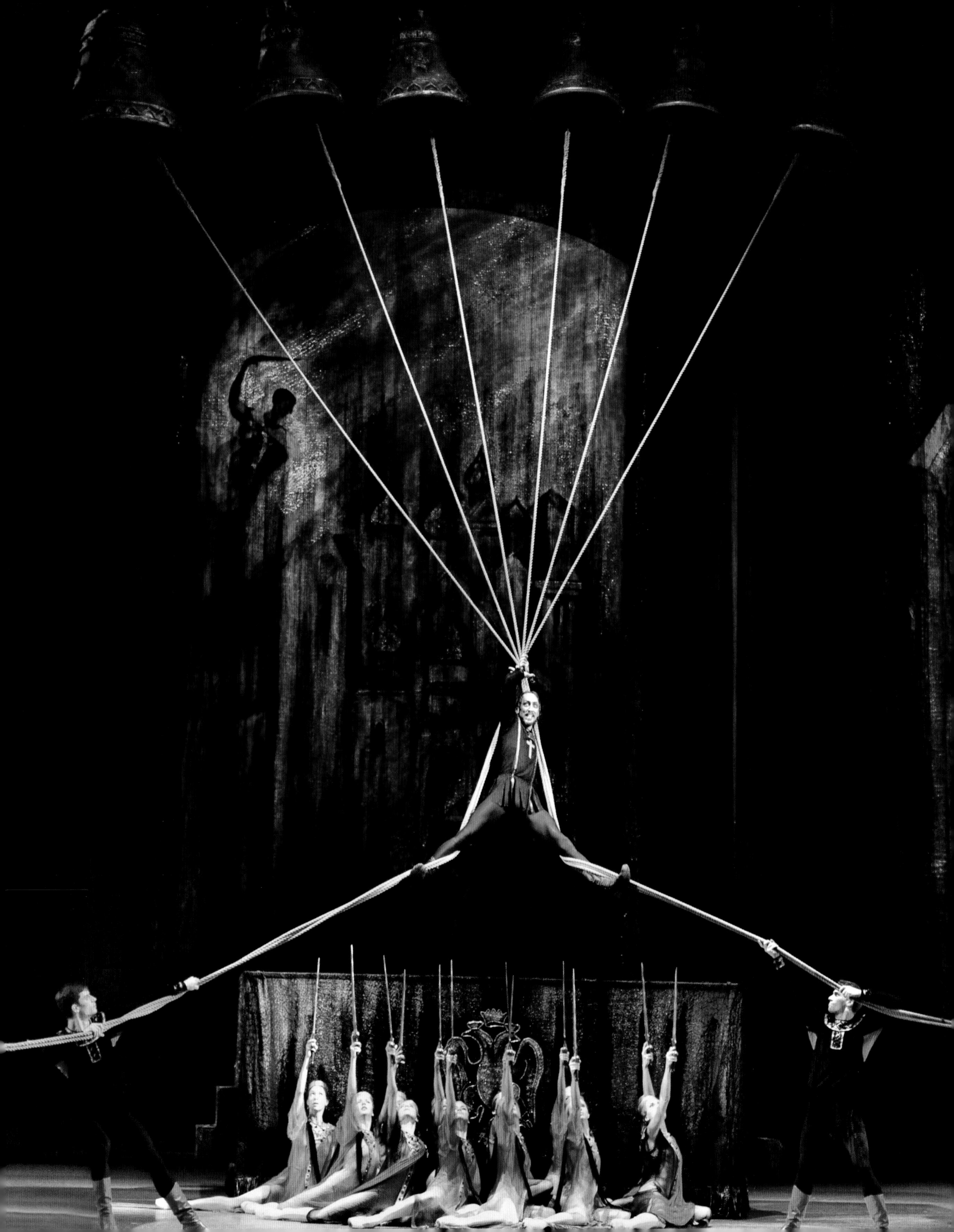

Ivan the Terrible

First performed: February 20, 1975 ▪ Venue: Bolshoi Theater ▪ Choreography and story: Yuri Grigorovich ▪ Music: Sergei Prokofiev

Set to the strident score that Prokofiev originally composed for Sergei Eisenstein's 1944 film of the same name (and its sequel), Grigorovich designed this ballet to be more in tune with the music than with historical facts. In dealing with themes of love, death, cruelty, and insanity—and running for over two hours—this dramatic ballet is bleak and epic in equal measure. However, it was widely acclaimed upon opening and is still performed to this day.

◀ Moscow debut
Yuri Vladimirov and Natalia Bessmertnova as Ivan and Anastasia during the debut performance of *Ivan the Terrible* at the Bolshoi Theater in 1975.

Telling the tale of the tortured Russian tyrant, with its forbidding score, large ensemble, and extended duration, Grigorovich's *Ivan the Terrible* is a ballet of Soviet dimensions. While the production was acclaimed following its Bolshoi premiere in 1975, many were also alarmed at its apparent underlying political message that "the end justifies the means"—that brutality can be justified. Grigorovich defended the work, stating "My conception was based primarily on music, not on something else."

The score for the ballet was adapted by composer Mikhail Chulaki from the music created by Sergei Prokofiev for Sergei Eisenstein's two-part film, *Ivan the Terrible* (1944, 1958), supplemented with further pieces by Prokofiev, including his Russian Overture. The ingenious and imposing set was designed by the Bolshoi's chief designer, Simon Virsaladze. Featuring three vertical illuminated cylinders that opened and closed, each portrayed a different setting—Ivan's world being the central cylinder. The set also featured a series of bell ropes hung across the stage, which were pulled between acts to punctuate the plot. Like the strings of a puppet, they symbolized control and feature in the ballet's dramatic climax when Ivan becomes ensnared as a result of his manipulations.

◀ Ivan ensnared
Ivan, danced by Pavel Dmitrichenko with the Bolshoi Ballet in 2012, finds himself trapped by the web of intrigue and manipulation that he has spun, symbolized by the bell ropes.

Grigorovich's choreography is robust and muscular, and given the ballet's long duration, the lead role, who is on stage almost throughout, demanded a dancer of considerable stamina and presence. For this, the choreographer turned to Yuri Vladimirov, who had won acclaim for his role as Spartacus in Grigorovich's ballet of the same name six years earlier. For Ivan's wife, Anastasia, Grigorovich cast his own wife, Natalia Bessmertnova.

West meets East

During the Cold War, Soviet ballets rarely left the country, but following *Ivan the Terrible*'s 1975 Moscow debut, the Bolshoi toured the US with the ballet that same summer, then performed in Paris the following year. It was eventually also staged in Germany, Czechoslovakia, and the UK.

In 1990, *Ivan the Terrible* was dropped from the Bolshoi's repertoire, although it was revived by other choreographers, including in 2004 by Mikhail Tchoulaki. After more than 20 years, the ballet finally returned to the Bolshoi in 2012, revived by Grigorovich himself.

STORY LINE

Act I Ivan proclaims himself Czar of all the Russias, which displeases the Boyars (the old Russian aristocracy), who believe some of them have a greater claim to the throne. Further unrest follows after Ivan chooses Anastasia—with whom Kourbski, a Boyar, is in love—to be his bride. Having battled foreign invaders, Ivan returns to Anastasia but quickly falls ill. The Boyars conspire to take over but Ivan unexpectedly recovers.

Act II The Boyars, including Kourbski, prepare a poisoned chalice for Ivan, but Anastasia drinks from it and dies. The Boyars flee, and a grieving Ivan seeks revenge. He uses his secret police, the Oprichniki, to find and massacre every Boyar. Still grieving for Anastasia, and haunted by his own demons, Ivan is driven insane by the actions he has brought about.

▼ Grigorovich returns
Mikhail Lobukhin and Svetlana Zakharova perform a tender scene as Ivan and Anastasia in Grigorovich's revival of *Ivan the Terrible* for the Bolshoi Ballet in 2012.

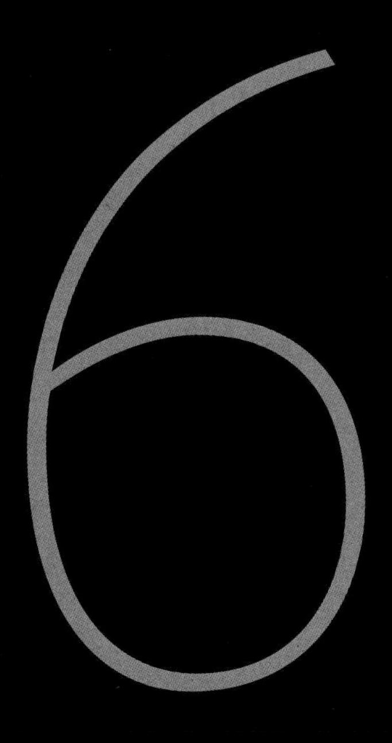

BALLET TODAY

(1975–present)

Ballet today 1975–present

With many ballet companies now successfully established, and their modern repertoires finding eager audiences, the mid-1970s marked a new period of confidence in ballet. While aspects of contemporary ballet, which fuses modern dance and classical ballet, had been developed earlier in the 20th century, the style really took off during the last three decades. Following the trails blazed by earlier choreographers, such as Vaslav Nijinsky, Michel Fokine, and George Balanchine, their artistic descendants were more eager than ever to stamp their own unique marks by challenging ballet conventions, exploring new themes, and reinterpreting ballet for modern audiences.

One of the first works in the emerging genre of contemporary ballet was Twyla Tharp's *Push Comes to Shove* (1976), which featured a seemingly illogical medley of contemporary and classical choreography and music, yet worked brilliantly. William Forsythe further challenged the accepted norms of ballet audiences with works of deconstructed classicism such as *Steptext* (1985), and Jiří Kylián reconstructed classical ballet moves into startling new forms, and raised eyebrows by staging bare-breasted ballerinas in his *Bella Figura* (1995).

With confidence also came bravery. Many choreographers staged innovative plotless pieces, often exploring human emotion through movement, and challenging story ballets also emerged that ventured into previously taboo areas. Most notably, Kenneth MacMillan continued to shocked audiences with his dark, psychological ballets, *Mayerling* (1978) and *The Judas Tree* (1992), with themes of murder, suicide, and sexual violence, expressed through a combination of classical and contemporary styles.

Choreographers continued to tackle the classics, too, restaging, rechoreographing, and redesigning for new generations of dancers and audiences. One of the most influential of these reinterpretations came in 1995, with Matthew Bourne's retelling of *Swan Lake*. Although it retained Tchaikovsky's celebrated score, it featured a corps de ballet of male swans, replacing the familiar feminine elegance with strident masculinity.

In the 21st century, contemporary and classical techniques now commonly sit alongside one another. Established ballet institutions, such as The Royal Ballet and New York City Ballet, strike a balance, employing contemporary choreographers, such as Wayne McGregor, and staging new story ballets by the likes of Christopher Wheeldon, alongside popular Romantic and classical ballets. Through global media, national companies have become internationally renowned, and their dancers, such as Tamara Rojo, Roberto Bolle, Misty Copeland, and Marianela Nuñez, are now worldwide stars.

A Month in the Country

First performed: February 12, 1976 ▪ Venue: Royal Opera House, London ▪ Choreography: Frederick Ashton ▪ Music: Chopin ▪ Story: Ivan Turgenev

Master choreographer Frederick Ashton had toyed with the idea of a ballet based on Russian playwright Ivan Turgenev's play *A Month in the Country* since the 1930s. The single-act ballet that emerged some 40 years later was one of the last he created for The Royal Ballet, and features a complex domestic narrative centered around a series of nuanced pas de deux, set to the stirring music of Frédéric Chopin, arranged by John Lanchbery.

STORY LINE

The ballet is set in the grandeur of a Russian country house, and portrays the interplay of thwarted passions and societal constraints on the family who live there. A young tutor, Beliaev, has been employed to teach Natalia's son, Kolia. Natalia is the bored, unfulfilled wife of the wealthy landowner, Yslaev. Although she already has an admirer, Rakitin, she falls in love with her son's tutor despite knowing that her ward, Vera, and maid, Katia, also have feelings for him. Eventually all is revealed as Vera invites the household to witness the couple's illicit embrace. Beliaev is dismissed and Natalia is left alone with her shame. The ballet ends with Beliaev entering to return the rose that Natalia had given him.

▼ **Domestic drama**
Karen Kain and Robert Conn evoke Natalia and Baliaev's emotional entanglement in rehearsal for The National Ballet of Canada's 1995 staging.

Choreographed after his retirement from The Royal Ballet, London, Ashton dedicated his new ballet "to the memory of Sophie Fedorovitch and Bronislava Nijinska, Chopin's compatriots and my mentors." This reflected the influence that Fedorovitch, his leading design collaborator for many years, and ballerina, choreographer, and teacher, Nijinska, had on him.

The ballet is set in 1850 at around the time that Turgenev wrote the original script, as opposed to the 1870s when the play was first performed. Ashton and designer, Julia Trevelyan Oman, chose the 1850s for the ballet's setting, as they felt that the fashions of this period would be more easily adapted for dancing.

Ashton had previously considered pieces by Tchaikovsky, among other Russian composers, before he finally decided on Chopin for the score. Once this decision was made, his next task was to turn the five-act play of the same name into a ballet. To do this, Ashton used a series of pas de deux to convey the story and move the plot, which consists of just eight characters, forward.

Signature sequence

Ashton placed a choreographic signature now known as the "Fred Step" in nearly all of his ballets. Consisting of a sequence of an arabesque, fondu, coupé, petit developpé, pas de bourée, and pas de chat, it is one of the most famous motifs in ballet. Of all of Ashton's ballets, it is particularly noticeable in *A Month in the Country*. The sequence is performed by Natalia and her admirer Rakitin as he leads her into the garden.

Since its premiere at The Royal Ballet in 1976—featuring Lynn Seymour and Anthony Dowell in the lead roles of Natalia and Beliaev—*A Month in the Country* has been performed by most leading companies around the world.

▲ **Elegant setting**
Ashton's 1976 production—with Lynn Seymour and Anthony Dowell in the lead roles—featured opulent designs by Oman that richly conveyed the splendor of a Russian country house.

▶ **Modern staging**
The single-act classic is a frequent fixture for The Royal Ballet. Seen here are Alexandra Ansanelli and Jonathan Howells in a 2008 production.

> As always, Ashton found inspiration in the talents of his dancers.
>
> DAVID VAUGHAN, DANCE HISTORIAN

Push Comes to Shove

First performed: January 9, 1976 ▪ Venue: Uris Theater, New York ▪ Choreography: Twyla Tharp ▪ Music: Joseph Lamb and Franz Joseph Haydn

Blending traditional ballet with jazz and modern dance, and using a score that mixed ragtime with the classical music of Haydn, Twyla Tharp pushed the boundaries in *Push Comes to Shove* to create the ultimate crossover work, and a new form of contemporary ballet. A witty, energetic romp, it epitomized her eclectic style and unconventional practice—forcing dancers and audiences to challenge both their expectations and their limitations.

STORY LINE

The light-hearted, almost plotless work is built around three main characters—two women and one man—and their interaction, supported by a corps de ballet.

Prelude A man jokes around with a bowler hat, strutting and preening.

Movement I Two women—a vamp and an *ingénue*—join the man and vie for attention.

Movements II and III The threesome is joined by the corps de ballet.

Movement IV The cast engage in an increasingly energetic dance, which ends in a dramatic freeze-frame climax.

Created for American Ballet Theatre in 1976, *TIME* magazine called the premiere of *Push Comes to Shove*, "the most important dance event of the year." With Mikhail Baryshnikov, who had recently defected from the Soviet Union, in the male role, choreographer Twyla Tharp developed a new and innovative form of contemporary American ballet, combining classical moves with modern dance, jazz, and vaudeville-style slapstick to playful effect.

Having formed her own company—Twyla Tharp Dance—in 1966, Tharp was already beginning to make a name for herself with crossover works that used a distinctive mixture of genres. Another unconventional trademark was her choice of accompaniment, which varied from using only the sounds uttered by the dancers in some works, to unexpected combinations of classical, jazz, and pop music. The musical accompaniment for *Push Comes to Shove* was no exception, featuring a surprising mix of ragtime, by composer Joseph Lamb, and Franz Joseph Haydn's Symphony No. 82.

While an unlikely mixture of music and dance styles, Tharp made it work. In the ballet's prelude, Baryshnikov was in his element dancing to a piece of Lamb ragtime—coy and provocative by turns, making a gesture here and a turn of the head there, then suddenly launching into a burst of pyrotechnical virtuosic dance.

Running at just over 20 minutes, the ballet marked the beginning of a long and successful artistic partnership between Tharp and Baryshnikov—Tharp acting as artistic associate at the American Ballet Theatre in the 1980s, while Baryshnikov was its artistic director.

▼ **Symmetrical lines**
Sona Kharatian, Brooklyn Mack, and the corps de ballet from the Washington Ballet Company rehearse *Push Comes to Shove* in February 2012.

Forgotten Land

First performed: April 4, 1981 ▪ Venue: Grosses Haus, Stuttgart ▪ Choreography: Jiří Kylián ▪ Music: Benjamin Britten

Exploring the universal themes of the fragility of life, loss, relationships, and how these are mirrored in nature, the choreography for *Forgotten Land* was driven by the spirit of Benjamin Britten's *Sinfonia da Requiem* and inspired by a painting by Edvard Munch. Powerfully emotional and visually striking, the ballet established Jiří Kylián's unique choreographic style and his reputation as one of the most innovative modern choreographers.

▲ **Royal Ballet of Flanders, 2015**
The costumes, originally designed in 1981 by John McFarlane, echo the women (and stages of life) in Munch's painting *The Dance of Life* (1899), which also influenced the ballet's content.

▼ **Powerful forces**
Kylián's choreography attempted to portray the push and pull of the forces that govern life, with dancers recreating the ebb and flow of waves.

Produced for the Stuttgart Ballet in 1981, *Forgotten Land* showed Jiří Kylián's innovative use of an abstract, expressive form of choreography suited to portraying life's broad themes and emotions. The ballet's aesthetics and subject matter were inspired by Edvard Munch's painting *The Dance of Life*, which portrays a woman dancing near the sea at three different stages of her life—as an innocent girl in white, a passionate lover in red, and as an older woman reflecting on her younger self dressed in black.

The powerful choreography was developed as a direct response to Benjamin Britten's *Sinfonia da Requiem*—which echoed the themes of Munch's painting in its concerns with relationships, the passage of time, loss, vulnerability, and the fragility of life.

Melding traditional ballet moves with the fluidity of contemporary dance, the choreography made use of strong angular shapes softened with classical touches, such as beautifully pointed feet and turned out leg extensions. Kylián also used elements from folk dance to build tension, and to balance contrasting harmonious and hostile movements.

Well-received by critics and audiences, the Stuttgart Ballet's 1981 performance in London won a West End theater award for outstanding achievement. The ballet continues to be performed worldwide as one of Kylián's most important works.

STORY LINE

Forgotten Land uses the sea as a metaphor for the rhythms of life, and as a backdrop for an exploration of relationships, loss, and memory. The ballet begins with six pairs of dancers, their backs to the audience, walking slowly toward an abstract seascape. The only sound is the wind howling (a recording of Kylián's own breathing). Tension mounts, and a series of vigorous ensemble sections follow, each with an emotional pas de deux to match the score—intense in the first movement (*Lacrimosa*, "weeping"); explosive in the second (*Dies Irae*, "God's wrath"); and quiet and reflective in movement three (*Requiem Aeternum*, "eternal rest").

William Forsythe

Dancer and choreographer ▪ 1949–

Forsythe grew up in the US in the 1950s and '60s with rock 'n' roll. This is naturally reflected in his choreography, which he once described as "ballet with a funk influence." While appreciating ballet's history, Forsythe also believed it should be of the present with an eye on the future—that choreographers must move on and see what is possible. The 26 minutes of pulsing dance in *In the Middle, Somewhat Elevated* (1987) announced his arrival on the ballet scene very loudly indeed.

▲ ***The Vertiginous Thrill of Exactitude***
Marianela Nuñez and Steven McRae dance in The Royal Ballet's 2017 production of William Forsythe's 1996 work. Eleven minutes long, the piece is considered to be one of the most demanding modern short ballets.

Forsythe had no formal dance training until his late teens. In the early 1970s, he danced with Joffrey Ballet II before joining John Cranko's Stuttgart Ballet in 1973—many of whose dancers went on to become celebrated choreographers. Later appointed Stuttgart's resident choreographer, Forsythe created his first full-length work, *Orpheus* (1979), and began to develop his own dynamic vision of ballet. In 1984, he was appointed artistic director of Ballet Frankfurt, turning it into one of the most innovative companies in the world.

In 1987, Forsythe electrified the ballet world with *In the Middle, Somewhat Elevated*. He saw this piece as being the central act of his full-length *Impressing the Czar* (1988), which explores the decline of civilization with a first act that includes auctioning off cultural treasures and a third that sees the cast, dressed as schoolgirls, hurtling around the stage in drunken revelry.

Technically complex work

Forsythe's approach is often referred to as deconstruction, but he always insists it is not his intention to destroy or dismantle ballet, more to reveal aspects not previously acknowledged. He frequently turns classical dance and devices inside out. He shifts alignment and emphasizes transitions rather than positions, all giving his dance a unique drive. Movement is magnified and changed, sometimes pulling the body off its vertical axis with specific body parts isolated: legs may be extended in excess of 180 degrees. Everything is precise and detailed. Forsythe rarely abandons pointe work for long, but has produced pieces with dancers in socks, heavy boots, and even slippers.

Forysthe plays on the stage space and audience sight lines, too. *Slingerland* (1989) and *Limb's Theorem* (1990) are both designed so those sitting high up and to the sides see aspects invisible to those sitting in the center. In *Kammer/Kammer* (2000), moving partitions segment the stage and sometimes hide dancers who are seen instead on large video screens. In *Artifact* (1984), he uses a trapdoor from which the head and torso of the "Other Person" appear. *White Bouncy Castle* (1999) was performed in a giant bouncy castle, with the audience inside, too.

Forsythe continued to challenge ballet's structures and traditions in works such as *The Loss of Small Detail* (1991); *Herman Schmerman* (1992), named after a phrase taken from Carl Reiner's comedy film *Dead Men Don't Wear Plaid*; and *The Vertiginous Thrill of Exactitude* (1996). He often took control of other aspects of production, too, including designing costumes and lighting himself. Aurally, Forsythe admired Dutch composer Thom Willems' hard, percussive, industrial sounds, but also made use of other unconventional soundscapes.

The Forsythe Company

After Ballet Frankfurt closed in 2004, Forsythe established The Forsythe Company. He had always been eager for his dancers to participate actively in the creative process, often giving them a set of conditions from which they would mold short sequences of dance that he could then manipulate. With his new ensemble, he took this further, presenting works directed and edited in real time, making every show different. Forsythe stepped down from directing in 2015, and is now a professor of choreography.

▲ **Scene from *Artifact* (1984)**
The Royal Ballet of Flanders dances *Artifact* in 2011 at the Opera Berlioz in Montpellier, France. In this ballet, Forsythe has the curtain crash down several times, disrupting the continuity of the viewing and revealing a new formation every time it rises.

KEY WORKS

Choreographer: *Urlicht*, 1976 • *Dream of Galilei*, 1978 • *Orpheus*, 1979 • *In the Middle, Somewhat Elevated*, 1987 • *Herman Schmerman*, 1992 • *Three Atmospheric Studies*, 2005 • *Sider*, 2011

TIMELINE

- **December 30, 1949** Born in New York.
- **1969** After learning dance under Nolan Dingman and Christa Long while studying drama in Florida, enrolls at the Joffrey Ballet School in New York.
- **1971** Dances with Joffrey Ballet II, the company's junior troupe.
- **1973** Dances with Stuttgart Ballet; made resident choreographer five years later.
- **1979** Begins to express his own vision of dance in his unconventional work *Orpheus*, which jars with the norms of classical ballet.
- **1980** Works as a freelance choreographer for companies including Munich State Opera Ballet, Netherlands Dance Theater, Ballet Frankfurt, and the Paris Opéra Ballet.
- **1984** Becomes director of Ballet Frankfurt, a position he holds for 20 years.
- **1994** In partnership with the Karlsruhe Center for Art and Media, develops a computer-based teaching tool.
- **1999** Awarded Commandeur des Arts et Lettres by the French government.
- **2000** Marries American dancer and long-time collaborator Dana Caspersen.
- **2004** Leaves Ballet Frankfurt after public funding is withdrawn, setting up his own troupe, The Forsythe Company.
- **2005** His new company debuts with *Three Atmospheric Studies.*
- **2009** Sets up Motion Bank, an online tool for creating collaborative digital scores. Receives his third Laurence Olivier Award.

YES, WE CAN'T REHEARSAL, 2012

- **2015** Becomes professor at the Glorya Kaufman School of Dance, Los Angeles.
- **2018** Choreographs *Playlist (Track 1, 2)* for the English National Ballet.

Mayerling

First performed: February 14, 1978 ▪ Venue: Royal Opera House, London ▪ Choreography: Kenneth MacMillan ▪ Music: Franz Liszt ▪ Story: Gillian Freeman

A shockingly dark and powerful ballet that many consider to be MacMillan's greatest work, *Mayerling* is based on the true story of the murder-suicide of Crown Prince Rudolf of Austria-Hungary and his 17-year-old mistress, Mary Vetsera. A tragic event that had far-reaching effects on Europe's ailing monarchies, MacMillan's intention was to explore the social, political, and personal pressures that might have driven the prince to such desperate measures.

STORY LINE

Act I At his wedding ball, Prince Rudolf flirts with his new sister-in-law, unhappy with his arranged marriage to Princess Stephanie. That night, he threatens his bride with a revolver.

Act II Rudolf and Stephanie visit a tavern in disguise, but Stephanie leaves in disgust. Rudolf is entertained by his mistress before a police raid causes them to hide. Mary Vetsera is established as his next mistress, and is later smuggled into his apartment.

Act III At a shooting party, Rudolf's unstable behavior is evident. Mary and Rudolf later make a suicide pact. The ballet ends at the hunting lodge at Mayerling, where Rudolf shoots Mary and, finally, himself.

▼ Original pairing
MacMillan choreographed the parts of Mary Vetsera and Crown Prince Rudolf for Lynn Seymour and David Wall, pictured here during rehearsals in 1978.

Kenneth MacMillan resigned from his position as artistic director of The Royal Ballet in 1977, because he wanted to focus his efforts more fully on choreography. However, he remained the company's principal choreographer until 1992. *Mayerling* was one of his first works following his resignation, and was his fourth full-length ballet.

MacMillan commissioned a scenario from Gillian Freeman, and John Lanchbery orchestrated a selection of pieces by Franz Liszt to create the score. The resulting ballet is long and extremely complex, with multiple characters and plot intrigues.

Demanding role

MacMillan had planned to cast Anthony Dowell as Prince Rudolf, but an injury meant that the role was created for David Wall. A highly demanding role, the male lead is rarely off stage as he drives the narrative forward through a series of pas de deux with the five different women in Prince Rudolf's life. *Mayerling* was arguably the first British ballet to have such a demanding and classical role for the principal male.

The ballet premiered on Valentine's Day in 1978, and received a standing ovation. *Mayerling* had its New York premiere in 1983, performed by The Royal Ballet at the Metropolitan Opera House. Initially, it was not planned to be included in the touring repertoire, but MacMillan threatened to withhold all his ballets if it was not staged.

Tragedy in the wings

Mayerling has been revived several times by The Royal Ballet, and it was during the last act of the opening night of the 1992 staging that Kenneth MacMillan died backstage from a heart attack. His death was announced following the end of the performance; the audience was asked to leave the Royal Opera House in silence.

A fixture of The Royal Ballet, *Mayerling* has also been performed by the Royal Swedish Ballet, Vienna State Opera Ballet, and Hungarian National Ballet. In 2017, Houston Ballet became the first American company to present the work in North America.

► Tragic couple
Irek Mukhamedov and Viviana Durante dance the lead roles during a 1992 production of *Mayerling* at The Royal Ballet, London.

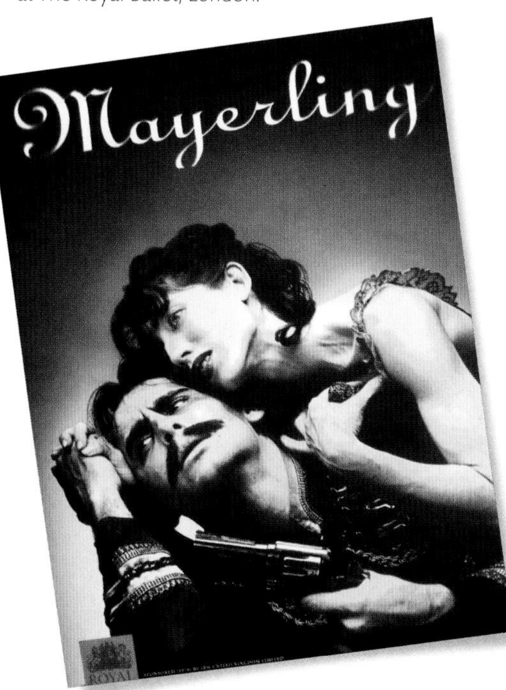

► Theater poster
This poster for The Royal Ballet's 1994 staging of *Mayerling* depicts Leanne Benjamin as Mary Vetsera and Zoltan Solymosi as Prince Rudolf.

Mikhail Baryshnikov

Dancer, choreographer, and actor ▪ 1948–

Born in the then Soviet-occupied Latvia, Mikhail Baryshnikov became one of the most celebrated dancers of the Kirov Ballet during the 1960s and '70s, until defecting to Canada in 1974. As a dancer, he was acclaimed for the precision of his movements and for his ability to prolong dramatic leaps, which mesmerized audiences. He also found success as a choreographer and as an actor, being nominated for an Academy Award for his role in the 1977 ballet-centered film, *The Turning Point*.

▲ **At the New York City Ballet**
Performing in Jerome Robbins' ballet, *Other Dances*, in 1980, Baryshnikov dances with Soviet-Russian-born ballerina Natalia Makarova. The pair danced together numerous times.

The most famous Soviet dancer of the day, one minute Baryshnikov was signing autographs following the last performance of his tour in Toronto in 1974, and the next he was running toward Canadian government officials who granted him asylum.

Baryshnikov started life in Riga, Latvia, raised by his father, a Soviet army officer, and his mother, who worked in a fashion studio. At the age of 9, his mother began taking him to ballet lessons, and, aged 12, he was accepted into Riga's opera ballet school. Following his mother's death, Baryshnikov joined Vaganova, the ballet school of the Kirov Ballet in Leningrad.

Training with Pushkin

At Vaganova, the young dancer became Alexander Pushkin's most exciting pupil since Rudolf Nureyev. At the age of 17, Baryshnikov's technique was already exceptional, and he progressed swiftly. In 1966, when he joined the Kirov Ballet, he was immediately made soloist, despite the Kirov tradition of dancers starting in the corps de ballet. He debuted in the Peasant pas de deux in *Giselle* the following year, and quickly became the most popular Soviet dancer. Two ballets, *Gorianka* (1968) and *Vestris* (1969), were created especially for him.

The Soviet Union kept a watchful eye on Baryshnikov as he grew more and more famous, as they could not afford to lose yet another gifted dancer to the West, after suffering several damaging defections. While Baryshnikov saw leaving his country as the only option to further progress his career, he respected his colleagues, and also did not want to place his relatives under official scrutiny. When he made the difficult decision to defect in 1974, he told his lawyer that he would not escape before dancing the final performance of the tour.

New York, new life

During the same year as his defection to the West, Baryshnikov joined the American Ballet Theatre, New York, as a principal dancer, staying for four years. As well as showcasing his dancing abilities, it also revealed his talent as a choreographer with his restagings of *The Nutcracker* and *Don Quixote*.

Baryshnikov left the company in 1978 to dance under George Balanchine at the New York City Ballet, debuting as Franz in *Coppélia* the following year. He also began to dance in contemporary pieces, and in 1979, took the lead role in *Opus 19: The Dreamer*, created for him by Jerome Robbins. However, Baryshnikov's career at the New York City Ballet was often frustrated by ill health. In 1980, aged 32, he was invited back to the American Theatre Ballet as its artistic director—a role he held until 1989.

While at the New York City Ballet, Baryshnikov had established a dance foundation in 1979 (the Baryshnikov Dance Foundation) in order to promote and support other artists. In 1990, he cofounded White Oak Dance Project, the touring company of his foundation, featuring mainly older dancers and choreographers. Baryshnikov continued to run and dance with the company until 2002, before establishing the Baryshnikov Arts Center in New York in 2005, where he is artistic director. The center provides space and support for artists of all disciplines, and showcases local and international dance, music, and theater.

◀ **Hollywood dream**
Baryshnikov is seen here rehearsing his role in Twyla Tharp's ballet *When Push Comes to Shove.* It was staged at the Hollywood Bowl in 1979 and was commissioned especially for Baryshnikov.

I do not try to dance better than anyone else. I only try to dance better than myself.

MIKHAIL BARYSHNIKOV

KEY WORKS

Dancer: Lead role, *Gorianka* (1968) • Lead role, *Vestris* (1969) • Peasant, *Giselle* (1972) • Franz, *Coppélia* (1978) • Lead role, *Opus 19: The Dreamer* (1979) • Choreographer: *The Nutcracker* (1976) *Don Quixote* (1978)

TIMELINE

- **January 27, 1948** Born in Riga, Latvia—then part of the USSR—to Russian parents.
- **1960** Enters Riga's opera ballet school at the age of 12.
- **1964** Joins Vaganova ballet school, the training school for the Kirov Ballet in Leningrad, where he becomes a pupil of ballet master, Alexander Ivanovich Pushkin.
- **1966** Wins the gold medal at the Varna International Dance Competition in Bulgaria, a feat he repeats three years later at the First International Ballet Competition in Moscow.
- **1967** Joins the Kirov Ballet as a soloist.
- **1974** Granted asylum in Canada while on tour in Toronto. Joins the American Ballet Theatre in New York.
- **1977** Stars in the film *The Turning Point*, winning a nomination for an Academy Award for Best Actor in a Supporting Role.
- **1978** Joins George Balanchine's New York City Ballet, but his time is curtailed by a heart attack and injury.

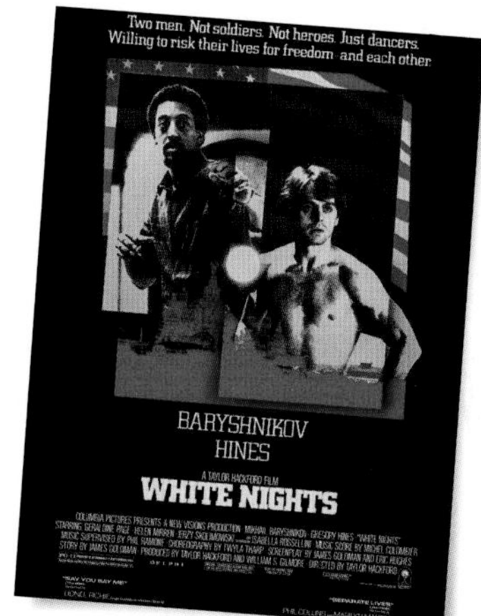

POSTER FOR THE 1985 FILM *WHITE NIGHTS*, WHICH STARRED BARYSHNIKOV

- **1980** Rejoins the American Ballet Theatre as principal dancer and artistic director.
- **1989** Makes his Broadway debut in *Metamorphosis*, a play by Steven Berkoff.
- **1990** Cofounds the White Oak Dance Project—a modern-dance touring company.
- **2005** Founds the Baryshnikov Arts Center in New York.
- **2017** Granted citizenship by the Republic of Latvia for his services to Latvian culture.

BALLET METHOD

Different schools (countries) teach different techniques and favor a particular style, known as ballet method. French ballet is soft, light, quick, and elegant, using épaulement (precise shoulder placement). Students at the Paris Opéra also learn the traditional court dances of Louis XIV. English ballet demands technical exactitude, épaulement, and quick footwork. It is more lyrical than French style, especially in Ashton and de Valois' works. Russian ballet (called the Vaganova method after teacher Agrippina Vaganova) is more passionate, and very athletic. It looks strong and virile, with showy tricks, especially for the men, and uses arm movements as an integral part of the dynamics. Italian ballet is powerful and virile for male dancers, too, but it is also characterized by soft arm lines held below the shoulder level, fluid movement, and épaulement. The Italian teaching system, the Cecchetti method, is named after the great ballet master Enrico Cecchetti. Danish dance, synonymous with choreographer Bournonville, is technically challenging with speedy, intricate footwork and strong elevation, performed in an understated way and with great clarity. All these schools teach the traditional principles of classical ballet, which uses highly specific positions of the arms, feet, legs, and head.

Ballet style changes over time as well as place. Romantic ballet evolved at the beginning of the 19th century, when pointe work and the long white tulle skirt came to be associated with the ballerina. It gave way to pure classical ballet, and imperial Russian classics such as *The Nutcracker.* Neoclassical ballet started in the 1920s, and was exemplified in the works of George Balanchine. It fuses classical steps and movements with pared-down, fluid use of arm and body lines. Contemporary ballet is based on more natural movement and body dynamics, while still using classical principles of weight transference.

[The dancer's] body is simply the luminous manifestation of the soul.

ISADORA DUNCAN, 1920

◀ ***Live*, Hans van Manen, Dutch National Ballet, 2001**
Van Manen draws on classical ballet and American modern dance. *Live* was the first video ballet, revolutionary in its method when it premiered in 1979. The camera operator tracks the dancer's (here, Sabine Chaland) every move, projecting close-ups, from lyrical arm movements to beads of sweat to the straining of a pointe-shoe ribbon, onto a vast screen.

Sylvie Guillem

Dancer and choreographer ▪ 1967–

A force of nature with seemingly supernatural physicality, French dancer Sylvie Guillem earned herself the nickname "Mademoiselle Non" early in her career for her refusal to conform to the repertoire. However, the reward for this approach came whenever Guillem took to the stage, where her extraordinary coordination and quality of motion was spectacular. First dancing with the Paris Opéra, then The Royal Ballet, Guillem went on to become one of the world's finest contemporary dancers.

▲ **The power to pose**
Dancing in Maurice Bejart's *Tribute to Versace*, Guillem holds her leg vertically in her trademark six o'clock position. Such was her strength as a dancer that Guillem could hold this pose almost effortlessly for several seconds.

Born in a working-class suburb of Paris, Sylvie Guillem was the only daughter of her motor-mechanic father, and her mother, a gymnast. At the age of 11, while part of the French Junior Olympic gymnastic squad, Guillem was picked for a year-long exchange with the Paris Opéra ballet school. As much as she disliked the discipline of ballet class, this shy, uncommunicative girl felt transformed as soon as she stepped on stage.

At 16, Guillem joined the Paris Opéra corps de ballet and three years later came under the artistic direction of Rudolf Nureyev. Theirs was a fiery relationship but their differences disappeared when on stage. She recalled, "When we danced together we were one person."

Guest choreographer at Paris Opéra, William Forsythe also recognized Guillem's talent, notably her ability to express ideas, and created the lead role of *In the Middle, Somewhat Elevated* (1987) for her. However, after five years as an étoile, Guillem felt frustrated by the company's level of control over her and left.

Chasing freedom

Guillem joined The Royal Ballet, London, where she was soon at odds with the company's leading choreographer, Kenneth MacMillan. Perceived as being distant and aloof, she kept to her dressing room and was emphatic about her choice of roles and where she performed. Her rationale was that to be part of the group "you have to play under your abilities."

Although singular in her approach, Guillem trained relentlessly with the male dancers, developing the unrivaled height of her double flips, and what was to become her trademark, her leg raised vertically in the six o'clock position.

Company director at The Royal Ballet, Anthony Dowell, recognized the dramatic sensibility that underpinned Guillem's physicality, and sought to utilize it by frequently casting her "against type" in delicate, vulnerable roles.

Finding freedom

Guillem began to explore contemporary dance, collaborating with groundbreaking choreographers and dancers. Her first success came in 1995, when she won acclaim for *Evidentia*, a film linking modern choreography with avant-garde film work. Many new projects followed, notably in 2002 when she persuaded Swedish choreographer, Mats Ek, to stage his modernist version of *Carmen* at The Royal Ballet, with herself dancing the lead role—a cigar-smoking temptress.

In 2003, Guillem collaborated with renowned contemporary choreographer, Russell Maliphant, in *Broken Fall*, and again two years later in *Push*. Dancing fearlessly in both, she moved with such fluidity that she seemed almost boneless. Guillem left The Royal Ballet in 2007 and became an associate artist at Sadler's Wells Theatre, favoring its more eclectic program. This included Akram Khan's *Sacred Monster* (2006), infused with classical South Indian Khattak and contemporary dance.

At the age of 50, Guillem embarked on her farewell world tour, entitled *Life in Progress*. The tour ended in Japan with a production of Maurice Béjart's *Bolero*, in which dancers in a clock formation counted down to midnight, and to the end of her career. There would be no more dancing for Guillem because to go downhill would be unbearable. "I did it the way I wanted. All those years the best I can be," she said.

Technical perfection is insufficient. It is an orphan without the true soul of the dancer.

SYLVIE GUILLEM

TIMELINE

- **February 23, 1965** Born in Paris, France, into a working-class family.
- **1977** After excelling at gymnastics under her mother's tuition, enters the school of the Paris Opéra Ballet.
- **1981** Joins the corps de ballet at Paris Opéra, winning a gold medal at the Varna International Ballet Competition in 1983.
- **1983** Makes her first solo appearance, dancing the part of the Queen of the Dryads in *Don Quixote*, staged by Rudolf Nureyev.
- **1987** Dances the lead role in William Forsyth's *In the Middle, Somewhat Elevated*, a new work created around her.
- **1988** Dances the title role in *Giselle*, partnering Nureyev in The Royal Ballet's 50th birthday celebration for the Russian star.
- **1989** Leaves Paris Opéra, becoming a permanent guest artist with The Royal Ballet, London.
- **2003** Collaborates with contemporary dance choreographer Russell Maliphant, appearing in *Broken Fall* with the Balletboyz at the Royal Opera House, London.
- **2006** Leaves The Royal Ballet and is made an associate artist of Sadler's Wells Theatre.
- **December 31, 2015** Retires from the stage after touring around the world in her farewell show, which features works by her long-time collaborators Ek, Forsythe, Khan, and Maliphant.

▶ ***Marguerite and Armand*, 2000**
When Sylvie Guillem and Nicolas Le Riche took the title roles in this ballet, they were the first to do so since Fonteyn and Nureyev. Guillem, with her powerfully athletic style of dancing, proved that the ballet was not untouchable.

KEY WORKS

Dancer: Lead role, *In the Middle, Somewhat Elevated*, 1987 • Title role, *Giselle*, 1988 • Title role, *Manon*, 1991 • Title role, *Romeo and Juliet*, 1992 Title role, *Carmen*, 2002 • Female lead role, *Broken Fall*, 2003 • Female lead role, *Sacred Monsters*, 2006

Steptext

First performed: January 11, 1985 ▪ Venue: Teatro Municipale, Reggio Emilia, Italy ▪ Choreography: William Forsythe ▪ Music: Johann Sebastian Bach

An enormously engaging, if sometimes disconcerting exercise in deconstructed classicism, William Forsythe's *Steptext* is a ballet for one woman and three men, consisting of a collection of pas de deux and solos to an edited recording of the Chaconne from Bach's *Partita No.2 in D minor.* It was created for the Italian company, Aterballetto, although the core material emerged from what Forsythe called "a compression of the two pas de deux" from Act II of *Artifact* (1984), his first evening-length ballet as director of Ballet Frankfurt.

STORY LINE

This ballet has no storyline. The curtain rises on an unlit stage as the audience walks in, and dancers freely stroll on and off. Two men in black improvise in the near-darkness. A woman briefly improvises, then stands stage front gazing at the audience—implying she is trying to communicate something.

In the middle of the work, the house lights go up, then down again, and the ballet appears to restart. Various pas de deux begin, with the dancers frequently changing partners. The ballet ends with the dancers walking backward, facing the audience, into the darkness behind them.

Forsythe had long been challenging the perceived conventions and wisdoms of ballet prior to creating *Steptext*, with works such as *Artifact* (1984), his homage and critique of the world of ballet. In *Steptext*, however, he sought to thwart the audience's entire expectations of how a ballet should be performed, structured, and even presented. The result was to deconstruct ballet into what Forsythe called "musical, decorative, and choreographic suspensions." In *Steptext*, he not only plays with expected dance phrasing, using unexpected combinations of steps and other movements, but also questions and contravenes almost every convention of the theater.

From the very beginning, *Steptext* seeks to surprise the audience, with the curtain rising as they take their seats. As the ballet starts, partially visible dancers seemingly stroll on and off the dimly lit stage as they please. In near-silence, save for a few snatches of Bach's sliced-up score, the woman improvises—the duration of which varies between performances—before stopping to stare at the audience. The house lights then come up again, before the ballet resumes.

The centrality of dance

Throughout the ballet, the dancers' movements are angular and geometric, exclusively initiated by shoulders, elbows, or wrists, as Forsythe demonstrates that dance does not have to involve legs or feet. Unlike in many modern ballets, the dancers' faces are intently expressive, conveying emotions of anger, sadness, and resentment, especially when they are dancing in pairs. While moments in the duets may suggest some sort of story, Forsythe is adamant: *Steptext* is simply an expression of a voracious desire to dance.

Forsythe's staging also breaks with convention, with the score fragmented, and unexpected lighting changes. Even the extent of the performance area itself seems undefined, as dancers disappear into areas of darkness, then reappear. Forsythe intends to give the idea that the dance continues whether visible or not—and sometimes steps can still be heard in the darkness. As such, it can be seen as Forsythe's message about the enduring presence of dance.

◀ **Complex movements**
Dancers from St. Petersburg's Mariinsky Ballet perform *Steptext* at Sadler's Wells Theatre in London in 2008.

In the Middle, Somewhat Elevated

First performed: May 30, 1988 ▪ Venue: Palais Garnier, Paris ▪ Choreography: William Forsythe ▪ Music: Thom Willems

Widely considered to be William Forsythe's most famous work, and still in demand by companies worldwide, this piece was originally created as the central section of a three-part work, *Impressing the Czar.* Its quirky name is derived from the position of part of the set, a pair of golden cherries, which were suspended above the stage as described.

◀ **Making their names**
Dancers Sylvie Guillem and Manuel Legris perform one of the many challenging holds from *In the Middle, Somewhat Elevated* at the Théâtre des Champs-Elysées in Paris in 1988.

This is a ballet of extravagant athleticism. The extended and accelerated ballet positions set in the ballet's tight theme-and-variations structure, and the power of its solos, duets, and ensemble sections, are electrifying.

The atmosphere of the ballet is charged, and the dance is visceral. Striding on and off the stage with purpose, the dancers possess an air of arrogance, joining and leaving the fray seemingly whenever it suits them and prowling around the stage as they command the space. While in most ballets the dancers face the front, in this work they face all directions, causing the audience focus to constantly change.

In the Middle, Somewhat Elevated features many duets but any ideas of the Romantic pas de deux are quickly dispelled. Couples clasp hands tightly as they move into off-center balances, and position their limbs to 180 degrees and beyond. Throughout, the steps take real physical power and almost violence to perform.

The atmosphere is further magnified by Thom Willems' relentless, throbbing, industrial score. It drives the dancers ever onward and sends shudders through the theater, adding to the ballet's impact.

Breaking new ground

In 1987, *In the Middle, Somewhat Elevated* was ballet in a new light. The first cast included Sylvie Guillem, Laurent Hilaire, Isabelle Guérin, and Manuel Legris, who Forsythe warmly described as his "wunderkinder"—the ballet made international stars of them all.

Agnès Noltenius, former Frankfurt Ballet dancer and now répétiteur for Forsythe's work, said in 2015, "After this emblematic piece, classical ballet was not the same any more." People were inspired and thrilled by *In the Middle, Somewhat Elevated* in 1987—they still are.

STORY LINE

This ballet has no story line. It begins with two dancers entering the stage from the dimly lit rear, and performing a duet. A soloist enters to dance, and the pair leaves. In turn, the soloist is replaced on stage by another pair. And so the ballet continues, with dancers entering and leaving the stage, all performing excerpts from the main sequence.

The ballet has no dramatic climax; instead the dancers simply return to the stage at the end of the piece.

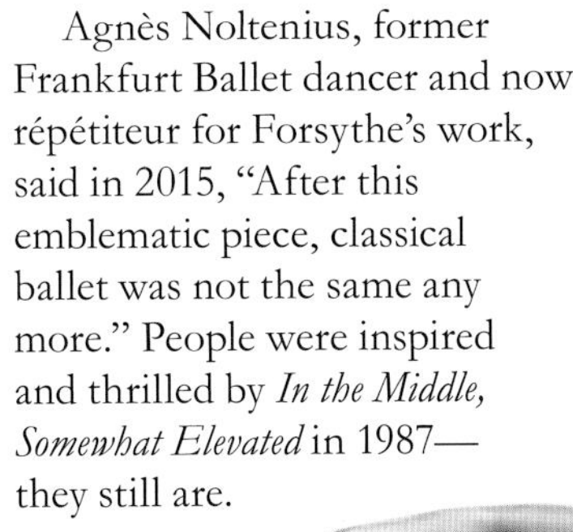

▼ **Intense performance**
Members of The Australian Ballet perform *In the Middle, Somewhat Elevated* at the Sydney Opera House in 2016, demonstrating the intense physicality of the choreography.

Darcey Bussell

Dancer and television dance show judge ▪ 1969–

Tall and willowy, the athleticism, grace, and sensitivity of Bussell's dancing was quickly spotted as a student. Aged just 20, she became the youngest-ever principal dancer at The Royal Ballet in London, where she spent her entire career. In her 20 years with the company, Bussell performed more than 80 roles, 17 of which were created for her. She also appeared with leading ballet companies around the world, and became one of the most famous dancers of her generation.

▲ **Perfect pairing**
Performing in George Balanchine's *Apollo*, Bussell dances with Carlos Acosta at the Royal Opera House in London in 2007, the same year that she retired from the company.

Born in London, and briefly living in Australia, Bussell spent her remaining childhood in London with her mother, an actress and model, and her adoptive father, an Australian dentist. Although Bussell began taking ballet classes at age five, it was not until she was studying at the Arts Educational School that she really discovered an aptitude for ballet. Her first performance as a stork "on one leg a lot" was, however, something of a letdown.

Bussell auditioned for The Royal Ballet School at the age of 13, which was late compared to other students, and struggled to catch up with her peers for the first year. However, when selections were made for senior school, she was one of only five chosen from her class of 20. Bussell trained and studied hard, and in 1986, she won a cash prize at the Prix de Lausanne, which she spent on training with Rudolf Nureyev in Monte Carlo.

Rising star

In 1987, Bussell joined Sadler's Wells Royal Ballet, and performed her first solo—the Lilac Fairy in *The Sleeping Beauty*—the following year, which was well received. The same year, oblivious to the intense interest in her talent, she found herself being plucked from the Sadler's Wells company at the request of choreographer Kenneth MacMillan to join The Royal Ballet in a major new work. MacMillan had noticed her athletic dancing style, and had resolved to create the role of The Princess Rose for her in his production of *The Prince of the Pagodas*. At its London premiere in 1989, Bussell was astounded to be suddenly promoted to principal dancer. As a Royal Ballet principal, Bussell was superlative in roles that used her height and physical strength but longed to prove herself in those traditionally reserved for dainty, petite dancers.

Height of success

In 1991, Bussell was cast as the heroine in MacMillan's *Manon*, and was partnered with Irek Mukhamedov. Frustratingly for Bussell, their physical incompatibility became apparent during rehearsals, and she was replaced two weeks before the opening by the petite Viviana Durante. A year later, however, Bussell was again cast as Manon, this time with Zoltan Solymosi, a tall Hungarian guest artist. Her sensual, provocative performance was described as "mesmeric." A further display of Bussell's versatility came in 1997, when she was given the role of 14-year-old Juliet in MacMillan's *Romeo and Juliet*. Dancing with touching fragility, one reviewer described it as "breathtaking, one of the finest Juliets ever."

After marrying and having children, Bussell switched to become guest principal at The Royal Ballet, until she retired in 2007. For her final role, she chose MacMillan's *Song of the Earth*, and later described being overwhelmed by "relief and loss" during her final curtain call. Any regrets were soon laid to rest, however, when Bussell came out of retirement to lead a troupe of 300 dancers in a "Spirit of the Flame" dance at the closing ceremony of London's 2012 Olympic Games—the same year she became a judge on the BBC's *Strictly Come Dancing* show and was elected as President of the Royal Academy of Dance. Recognizing her services to dance, Bussell was made a Dame Commander of the Order of the British Empire in 2018.

▲ **Striking a pose**
With her elegant stature and natural grace, Bussell has modeled for some of the world's most famous photographers, including Mario Testino and Lord Snowdon. This image was taken by acclaimed British photographer Anthony Crickmay.

KEY WORKS

The Prince of the Pagodas, 1989 • *Winter Dreams*, 1991
Romeo and Juliet, 1997 • *La Bayadère*, 1998 • *Variations*, 2000
In the Middle, Somewhat Elevated, 2001 • *Sylvia*, 2004
Manon, 2005 • *Song of the Earth*, 2007

TIMELINE

- **April 27, 1969** Born in London.
- **1983** Having studied dance at the Arts Educational School, joins The Royal Ballet Lower School in London.
- **1986** Appointed lead dancer in a school production at the Royal Opera House in London, and wins the Prix de Lausanne in Switzerland later that year.
- **1989** Becomes principal dancer at The Royal Ballet at the age of 20, the youngest in the history of the company.
- **1993** Makes her first guest appearance at the New York City Ballet in a pas de deux from *Agon*.
- **1995** Awarded an OBE in the Queen's New Year Honours List.
- **1997** Marries Australian Angus Forbes. Becomes guest principal at The Royal Ballet.
- **1998** Guests with the Mariinsky Ballet in St. Petersburg in *La Bayadère*.
- **2004** Dances in The Royal Ballet's new production *Sylvia* by Léo Delibes.
- **2006** Awarded a CBE in the Queen's Birthday Honours List.

BUSSELL AND ROBERTO BOLLE DANCE *LES RENDEZVOUS* AT THE ROYAL BALLET, 2000

- **2007** Retires from the stage with a final performance of *Song of the Earth* at the Royal Opera House.
- **2012** Comes out of retirement to lead an ensemble of more than 300 dancers in the closing ceremony of the Olympic Games in London.

Falling Angels

First performed: November 23, 1989 ▪ Venue: AT&T Danstheater, The Hague ▪ Choreography: Jiří Kylián ▪ Music: Steve Reich

Forming part of Jiří Kylián's collection of six surrealist and minimalist works known as the "Black and White" ballets, *Falling Angels* explores different facets of the feminine psyche with gravity and lightheartedness. An homage to female dancers, it is about performers and the art of performing—the spirit, confidence, flair, and humor that they have, but also their hidden vulnerabilities and inferiority complexes.

STORY LINE

The ballet begins with eight women walking forward and stepping into their own square of light. Beams of light and lighted spaces change throughout the piece to separate dancers from the group for solos or duets, or to bring them back together. All dancers stay on the stage for the duration of the work. The choreography is driving and insistent, with continual use of repeated phrases.

Demonstrating their will for perfection, the dancers move in unison for most of the ballet, as if part of a chorus. Expressing their wish to break out and be free, individuals or pairs of dancers sometimes split off and move differently as they succumb to events and temptations, such as ambition, seduction, pregnancy, motherhood, self-awareness, birth, and death, that upset the perfect state. The other dancers often seem to lose energy until the complete ensemble reforms.

For *Falling Angels,* Jiří Kylián combined neoclassical lines with grounded modern movements to create a short, 16-minute work that is interspersed with quirky choreographic interludes. The eight female performers, dressed in simple black leotards, present a study of two opposing aspects of being a dancer—the need for discipline, and the desire for freedom—as well as the influence of life events and emotional states.

▲ **Teatro de la Zarzuela, Madrid**
A dancer from the National Dance Company of Spain performs a typically gestural move in *Falling Angels* in 2013.

Belonging versus independence

In a visual power play between belonging and independence, the dancers move anonymously within tight lines and rigid formations, only to break out of the pack in eccentric and frenzied moments of liberation. The stark lighting design, which dissects the stage into geometric areas, reinforces these moments of group versus independent action. Gesture plays an important role—hands are placed over mouths or faces indicating excitement, nervousness, or shock; fingers are wagged at those who break away. The movements become increasingly flirtatious, with moments of humor as the women appear to play peek-a-boo, wave, blow kisses, smile, swing hips, and pull their leotards away from their bodies.

Inspired by ceremonial ritual music from Ghana, accompaniment is provided by the relentless, repetitive rhythms and shifting phases of Drumming Part 1 by Steve Reich. Played on four bongos, the piece uses "phasing"—where a phrase is repeated on two or more instruments in steady but different tempi, causing them to gradually shift out of unison before coming back together. Molding the choreography, these rhythms echo the universal theme and thrust of the work—the struggle between the need to belong and our desire for independence.

◀ **Unpredictable movement**
In *Falling Angels,* moments of classicism merge with sharp percussive moves; beautiful lines meet with distortions such as flexed feet and splayed palms.

Bella Figura

First performed: October 12, 1995 ▪ Venue: AT&T Danstheater, The Hague ▪ Choreography: Jiří Kylián ▪ Music: Lukas Foss, Giovanni Battista Pergolesi, Alessandro Marcello, Giuseppe Torelli, and Antonio Vivaldi

Hailed as a masterpiece that fuses contemporary and classical ballet, *Bella Figura* is one of Kylián's best-loved works. The Italian title has a double meaning—"beautiful form" and "to put on a brave face"—referencing the ballet's tension between artifice and truth, and its exploration of the concept of performance in life and art. Aesthetically bold, it uses striking costume design, subtle lighting, and clever staging to conjure a unique vision.

▲ **Paris Opéra Ballet**
Dancers—some in the striking unisex long red skirts—perform a scene from *Bella Figura* during a rehearsal at the Palais Garnier, Paris, 2016.

Despite being created in just four weeks, this one-act, 30-minute, neoclassical ballet continues to mesmerize and challenge audiences with its evocative choreography and striking costumes. Kylián described *Bella Figura* as "like standing on the edge of a dream. The moment in which dream intrudes into our lives and life into our dreams—this is the point of my curiosity." The dreamlike quality is enhanced by devices such as the curtain coming down just as the ballet has started. Certainly nothing is quite what you anticipate in this imaginative world—the dancers change and evolve, and panels of black fabric screen, envelop, and expose figures whose sinuous movements constantly interact in ways that are often unexpected. At one point, dancers catch a descending curtain and embrace it in outstretched arms before vanishing beneath it.

Laid bare

Central to the ballet is a section in which both male and female dancers wear full red skirts, their upper bodies naked. Seen by some as startling and rather daring, Kylián used this visually dramatic device to question ideas of masquerade and the nature of artifice versus truth or reality.

The accompaniment to the ballet also plays with concepts of performance. The Baroque pieces create a sense of courtly formality that is undercut by the dancers' costumes and choreography. The work begins and ends in silence, with only the slight sounds from the dancers' movements creating a kind of whisper that stirs the imagination. It is this intoxicating blend of dream and reality, the visible and the invisible, that has made *Bella Figura* one of Kylián's most enduring works, and why it is so widely performed today.

STORY LINE

This non-narrative ballet creates a series of striking images set to Baroque pieces. With the house lights still on, nine dancers get into position, then freeze as a curtain falls. Curtains continue to be used to change the performance space in different ways—opening fully to show the whole stage, creating small frames and viewing holes, enclosing, and even wrapping around the dancers. Sequences involve duets, trios, and quartets, with the dancers changing costumes between scenes. The ballet ends with male-female duets flanked by blazing fire pits on either side of the stage.

It is a "parable" on the relativity of sensuality, beauty, and aesthetics in general.

JIRI KYLIAN, 2007

▼ **Striking aesthetics**
The pared-down, ethereal quality of the ballet is intensified by the spare, lightly costumed dancers and the use of dramatic lighting.

Jiří Kylián

Dancer, choreographer, and artistic director ▪ 1947–

"I don't mind if people don't understand my work because, actually, I don't understand it myself and I never did," Jiří Kylián told an interviewer in 2008. True or not, there are few choreographers with such a reach as the Czech-born dance-maker, who will be forever associated with Nederlands Dans Theater (NDT), the company he directed and molded for 24 years. Crossing the dance spectrum, his work is performed by ballet and contemporary dance companies worldwide.

▲ ***Doux Mensonges* ("Sweet Lies"), 1999**
Kylián rehearses Nicolas Le Riche and Delphine Moussin of the Paris Opéra for his ballet about the public and hidden faces of love. While Kylián often explores life in his work, he is private about his own.

Born in Prague, Kylián studied ballet there before joining The Royal Ballet School in London on a scholarship in 1968. A year later, he joined John Cranko's Stuttgart Ballet, becoming one of the many successful choreographers to pass through the company. He almost never got there, however. Prior to taking up his new post, Kylián returned to his homeland for a holiday. While there, Warsaw Pact forces invaded the country, and the day after he had left for Stuttgart, the border with the West was closed. In 1975, Kylián was appointed artistic co-director at Nederlands Dans Theater (NDT), then sole artistic director at the company two years later.

Unique direction

Although Kylián's dance changed over time, it always bridged classical and modern techniques. He first came to international prominence in 1978 with *Sinfonietta*, set to music by fellow Czech, Leoš Janáček. Like many of his earlier works, it is non-narrative yet dramatic, featuring subtle references to folk dance. It is often viewed as a celebration of his origins, yet Kylián claims it is about freedom in general.

More landmark works followed including *Symphony of Psalms* (1978), *Soldiers' Mass* (1980), a powerful all-male piece about the futility of war, and *Forgotten Land* (1981), an exploration of memories, events, and people that over time are lost or forgotten.

Ever on the lookout for new inspirations, Kylián produced several works after attending an aboriginal dance event in Australia. Taken by the way that the aboriginals saw dance as a window into the past, and how it engaged and crossed generations, in 1983 he created *Stamping Ground* and *Dream Time*. Both works feature strong hints of loneliness and sorrow, as almost half-human, half-animal forms are twisted into unusual positions.

Open to interpretation

Kylián's work at NDT steadily became more abstract and surreal, and his dance increasingly featured symbols, metaphors, and double meaning. In 1989, he created a light-hearted homage to female dancers, *Falling Angels*, which also explored the opposing forces they face: discipline and freedom; belonging and independence; and their desire for perfection and what thwarts their efforts. In contrast, his companion work, *Sarabande* (1990), looks at stereotypes of masculinity and what it means to be a man.

Among Kylián's best-known works from this time is the humorous *Petite Mort*, which he created in 1991 to mark the bicentenary of Mozart's death. Set to the composer's music, it is about the world as a place where nothing is sacred, and where brutality, aggression, sexuality, and foolishness are routine.

Perhaps influenced by his time with Cranko, Kylián encouraged creativity in others, too. NDT's regular choreographic workshops became a breeding ground for many future successful choreographers, including present NDT directors Paul Lightfoot and Sol León. Kylián also set up NDT 2, for dancers aged 17–22, and the short-lived NDT 3, for those over 40.

In 1999, Kylián retired as artistic director but stayed on as a choreographer for a further 10 years. Still exploring new avenues, he has since produced a number of short films, such as *Car Men* in 2006.

KEY WORKS

Choreographer: *Viewers*, 1973 • *Sinfonietta*, 1978 *Symphony of Psalms*, 1978 • *Forgotten Land*, 1981 *Stamping Ground*, 1983 *Dream Time*, 1983 • *Petite Mort*, 1991 • *Arcimboldo*, 1995

◀ **Reaching out**
Maria Seletskaja and Teun van Roosmalen perform Kylián's *Forgotten Land* with the Royal Ballet of Flanders in 2015. The work laments how things and people are forgotten with the passing of time.

... you cannot dance classical technique with perfection. So you have to adapt the technique to your abilities ...

JIRI KYLIAN

TIMELINE

- **March 21, 1947** Born in Prague, Czechoslovakia, to parents Vaclavnker, an economist, and Marketa, a former dancer.

- **1956** Enters the School of National Ballet in Prague.

- **1962** Accepted into the Prague Conservatory and choreographs two works of his own, *Nine Eighths* and *Quartet*.

- **1967** Joins The Royal Ballet School, London, thanks to a British Council scholarship.

- **1968** Offered a place at the Stuttgart Ballet by its director John Cranko, whom he meets during his time in London.

- **1973** After a visit to Stuttgart, the Nederlands Dans Theater (NDT) invites Kylián to choreograph for the company.

- **1975** Creates *Return to a Strange Land* in tribute to Cranko, a year after the death of the Stuttgart Ballet's enigmatic director.

- **1975** Made artistic co-director—along with Hans Knill—of NDT, then becomes sole artistic director two years later.

- **1978** Choreographs *Sinfonietta*, which is internationally recognized, raising the profile of NDT worldwide.

- **1978** Sets up a proving ground for young dancers, NDT 2, sister company to the NDT.

- **1991** Founds NDT 3 for dancers aged 40 and over, completing his ideal of the "three dimensions of a dancer's life."

- **1999** Retires as artistic director of NDT, but remains with the company as a choreographer for the next 10 years.

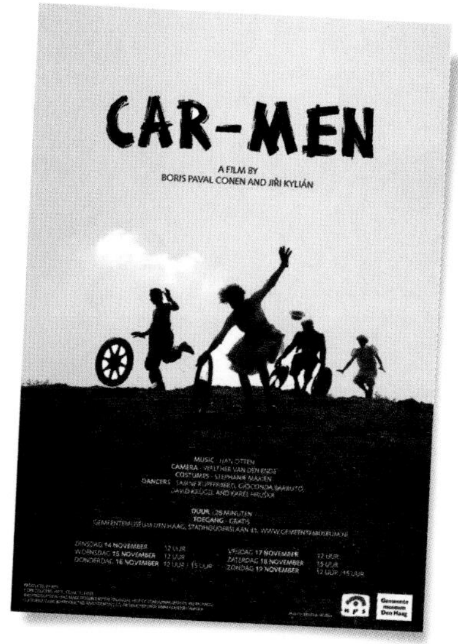

POSTER FOR KYLIÁN'S FILM, *CAR MEN*, WHICH HE COLLABORATED ON IN 2006

Petite Mort

First performed: August 23, 1991 ▪ Venue: Kleines Festspielhaus, Salzburg ▪ Choreography: Jiří Kylián ▪ Music: Wolfgang Amadeus Mozart

A master interpreter of emotional dynamics, Jiří Kylián explores human intimacy, the relationship between life and death, and eroticism in *Petite Mort*. Delving into complex relationship themes, the ballet navigates sexual encounters using his characteristically provocative and witty modern balletic style. The work forms part of Kylián's group of six "Black and White" ballets—abstract pieces linked by their similar use of props, sets, and tone.

STORY LINE

The ballet is choreographed for six women, six men, and six fencing foils, which at times substitute for dance partners. The men manipulate their foils in a show of potency, before a giant sheet swoops forward and retracts to reveal six women. The men run to them, and a series of synchronized group dances and individual pas de deux follow as the partnerships are symbolically consummated. Cutouts of Baroque dresses are used as props by the women, creating a playful element.

◀ **English National Ballet, London, 2013**
Kylián's trademark use of a bare stage and minimal costumes focuses attention on the dramatic shape, motion, and sensuality of the dancers.

Kylián's choreographic career surged in the late 1970s when he became artistic director of the Nederlands Dans Theater. *Petite Mort* is the 46th ballet he created for the Dutch company and is one of the most widely performed works in his repertoire.

The term petite mort, or "little death," is generally used to mean orgasm. In his notes on the ballet, Kylián commented, "It may be so that in the moment of pleasure (or in the moment of potentially creating a new life) we are reminded of the fact that our lives are of a relatively short duration, and that death is never too far from us." The complexity of these relationships—between death and ecstasy, endings and beginnings, light and darkness—form the life force of the work.

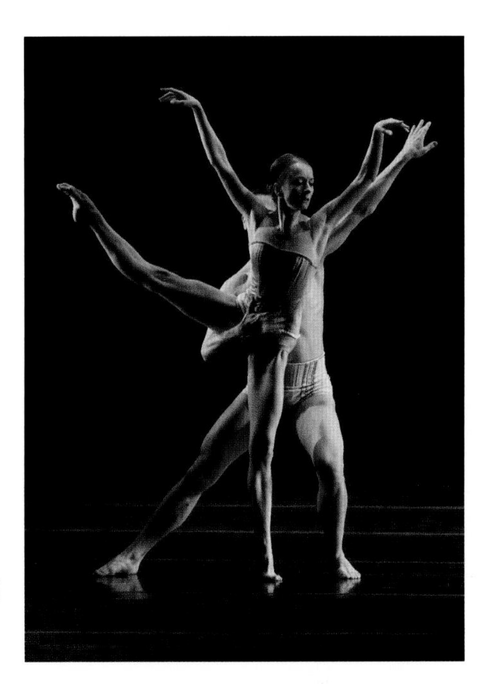

▲ **Dramatic lighting**
Kylián's use of light and shade is an integral part of the work—heightening suspense and intensity, and highlighting the spare lines of the choreography.

Strength and vulnerability

Petite Mort premiered in 1991 as part of the Salzburg Festival. To honor the city's most famous musical resident, Kylián based the ballet on two slow movements from Mozart's piano concertos No. 21 and No. 23. Kylián intentionally singled these out from the concerto's fast-paced movements, leaving them, in his words, "as mutilated torsos" to reflect that he was "living and working as part of a world where nothing is sacred." The duality of strength and vulnerability of *Petite Mort* underpins Kylián's choreography—classical lines contrast with angular, more modern shapes; moments of stillness are followed by intense action; and sensuality vies with the spiritual. In the six duets, a constant interplay between supporting and being supported creates an intriguing and ever-shifting equilibrium where it is rarely clear who is the guiding force. At their own distinct pace, each couple merges into a single entity—Kylián's ultimate depiction of the dynamics of intimacy.

◀ **Powerful props**
Daria Klimentova and James Streeter in *Petite Mort*, 2013. Props and dancers become inseparable in the ballet, with fencing foils acting as surrogate partners, and as symbols of power and sexuality.

> ["Mort"] is the most faithful companion we have, from the dawn of our existence to the end.
>
> JIRI KYLIAN, 2007

Viviana Durante

Dancer, actor, choreographer, teacher, and model ▪ 1967–

Widely considered to be one of the greatest dramatic performers of her generation, English-trained, Italian ballerina Viviana Durante was just 21 when she became The Royal Ballet's youngest principal dancer. She has won many awards since, including Dancer of the Year in four countries, and is renowned for her expressive "liquid arms" and elegant, prolonged balances. Durante also understands the need to act a part rather than simply dance it, which has won her many leading roles.

▲ **Boundless talent**
Durante dances in the first revival of *Anastasia* with The Royal Ballet in 1996. Of Durante's performance in the title role, Jenny Gilbert of the *Independent on Sunday* said, "the immaculate dancer proves also to be Durante the unsurpassable actress."

Born in Rome, Durante began ballet lessons aged six at the Teatro dell'Opera di Roma. She was spotted by ballerina Galina Samsova and taken to The Royal Ballet School, London, at the age of 10. There she experienced classes with world-class directors and dancers, and first appearances with the corps de ballet. At the age of 17, Durante joined The Royal Ballet; at 19 she became a soloist, and at 21 a principal dancer.

MacMillan and Durante

Durante's rise to stardom began backstage at a Royal Ballet production of *Swan Lake,* where having performed her pas de trois in Act I, she was suddenly asked to stand in for the principal dancer, Maria Almeida, who had injured her foot. Durante had never danced the lead role before, but she put on her tutu to finish Act III, practiced Act IV in the interval, and was whispered through the final duets by her leading man. She received a standing ovation and a media frenzy duly followed.

Already celebrated for her technique, Durante caught the eye of Royal Ballet choreographer, Kenneth MacMillan. In addition to her petite frame, long dark hair, small face, and expressive eyes, she could act, and had the ability to bring her roles to life.

MacMillan first partnered Durante with Russian Irek Mukhamedov in *Manon*, leading critics to quickly draw comparisons between the pair and other legendary partnerships, namely Fonteyn and Nureyev. Durante performed many works under MacMillan in the five years that they worked together, culminating in her most challenging role in the controversial *The Judas Tree*. In this allegory of Christ's betrayal, Durante played a provocative lone female who is gang raped and murdered. The work won a Laurence Olivier Award and earned her an individual Olivier nomination.

In 1992, while dancing in MacMillan's revival of *Mayerling*, Durante sensed a change in the atmosphere in the theater. During the performance, MacMillan had left his seat in the auditorium and died from a heart attack in a corridor backstage. When the ballet finished, the director came on stage to announce MacMillan's death, and the audience left silently.

International acclaim

Durante's masterful technique and talent as a dance-actress gave her an unusually broad range, and she danced nearly every leading role in The Royal Ballet repertoire. She created many new roles, including Wayne McGregor's first classical choreography, and won more than a dozen awards, including the London *Evening Standard* Ballet Award at the age of 21.

In 2001, she parted ways with The Royal Ballet and danced with other leading companies around the world, including American Ballet Theatre in New York, La Scala Ballet in Milan, and Tetsuya Kumakawa's K-Ballet in Japan. More recently, Durante has danced, acted, and choreographed for film and stage, and has been a juror of major ballet awards, including the Prix de Lausanne, in Switzerland.

In 2009, Durante married the British writer, Nigel Cliff, and gave up dancing and its associated travel in order to raise their son. She now coaches for The Royal Ballet, sharing her extraordinary dramatic skills with a new generation of dancers.

▲ ***Giselle*, The Royal Ballet, 1996**
Durante danced the leading role in *Giselle* many times. She was an ideal choice to portray the character's transition from happy village girl to tragic heroine betrayed in love.

KEY WORKS

Dancer: Title role, *Manon*, 1991 • Irina, *Winter Dreams*, 1991 • Mary Vetsera, *Mayerling*, 1992 • The Woman, *The Judas Tree*, 1992 • Title role, *Giselle*, 1995 • Title role, *Anastasia*, 1996 • Nikiya, *La Bayadère*, 1998

TIMELINE

- **May 8, 1967** Born in Rome, Italy.
- **1973** Begins her dance training at the Teatro dell'Opera di Roma.
- **1977** Joins The Royal Ballet School, London, after being spotted by Russian ballerina Galina Samsova in Rome.
- **1984** Wins the Prix de Lausanne.
- **1984** Graduates to The Royal Ballet, becoming a soloist two years later and a principal dancer within five years.
- **1988** Flourishes under The Royal Ballet's resident choreographer Kenneth MacMillan, partnering leading man Irek Mukhamadov.
- **1992** Works with MacMillan to create her searing role in *The Judas Tree*.
- **1995** Stars as Princess Aurora in The Royal Ballet's production of *The Sleeping Beauty*.
- **1999** Joins American Ballet Theatre in New York as a principal dancer.
- **2001** Becomes the leading ballerina for K-Ballet in Tokyo, Japan, a company set up by Tetsuya Kumakawa.

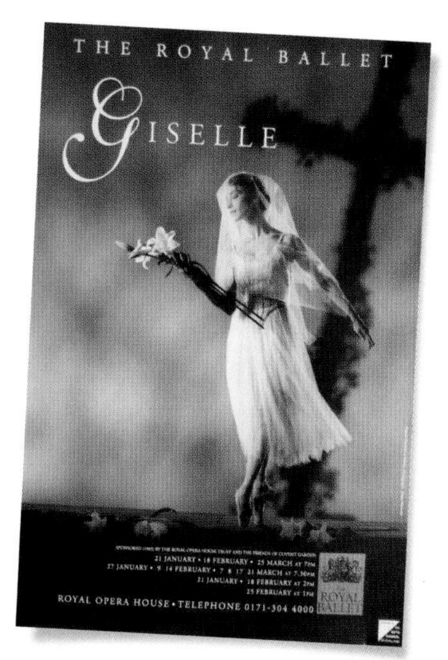

THEATER POSTER FOR DURANTE IN *GISELLE*

- **2010** Forms Viviana Durante Company, choreographing *Lamentoso* at the Edinburgh Festival.
- **2011** Sits on the jury at the Prix de Lausanne, a role she repeats five years later.
- **2016** Returns to The Royal Ballet to coach a revival of Kenneth MacMillan's *Anastasia*.
- **2018** Stages *Kenneth MacMillan: Steps Back in Time* at the Barbican Pit, London.

The Judas Tree

First performed: March 19, 1992 ▪ Venue: Royal Opera House, London ▪ Choreography and story: Kenneth MacMillan ▪ Music: Brian Elias

This one-act ballet references the biblical betrayal story of the Kiss of Judas, which leads directly to the arrest of Jesus Christ and his later crucifixion. Placed in a modern setting, the cast of 13 men and one mysterious woman, suggesting the Mary Magdalene figure, enacts the last hours of the life of Jesus. *The Judas Tree* was Kenneth MacMillan's final ballet and remains his most controversial work.

STORY LINE

The one woman in *The Judas Tree* is unnamed on the cast list, although she is called Mary in the notes of MacMillan and British composer Brian Elias. At some points, she appears demure, wrapped in a veil; but underneath she is scantily clad, her behavior overtly sexual and provocative.

The behavior of the Woman arouses the men to sexual violence, especially when she appears to favor one—the Jesus figure—over all the others. As he struggles to protect her from attack, he is grabbed by the Foreman (Judas) and roughly kissed. This is the sign that triggers an explosion of violence: gang rape, murder, and suicide. At the end, the spirit of the Woman remains as a witness to the fallibility of man.

▶ **The Royal Ballet, 2017**
Lauren Cuthbertson and Thiago Soares star in this production at London's Royal Opera House.

The title of the ballet comes from the common name of a tree that produces purple-red flowers along its branches before the leaves come out in spring. In Christian folklore, these flowers represent drops of Judas's blood, spilled when he hanged himself in remorse for having betrayed Jesus.

Contemporary set, timeless theme

MacMillan and composer Brian Elias were both inspired by biblical stories of betrayal and guilt, but also by more contemporary events. This fusion of past and present is evident in the set, designed by Scottish painter Jock McFadyen, in which the tree is represented by the then newly completed Canary Wharf tower in London's Docklands. The Mary figure is modeled on a woman in one of McFadyen's paintings of London's East End, viewed against a graffiti-covered background. The 13 men are a gang of construction workers, overseen by the Foreman, who is revealed to be the Judas figure.

For all its horrific violence, *The Judas Tree* is not a work that abandons hope. The soul of the Woman is unconquerable; in a way, she triumphs over all. In its early performances, the ballet was frequently interpreted as a degrading exploitation of a woman's sexuality. In more recent years, however, it has been interpreted in a more figurative, less literal way.

▲ **Setting the scene**
Performing with the The Royal Ballet in 2010, Leanne Benjamin dances as the Woman alongside Edward Watson as the Foreman's friend. The stark backdrop reflects the brutality of the work.

MacMillan created *The Judas Tree* for three Royal Ballet dancers: Irek Mukhamedhov, Viviana Durante, and Michael Nunn. Durante matched Mukhamedhov perfectly, and the two went on to dance together in a partnership spanning a decade. They both left The Royal Ballet in 2001, as did Michael Nunn, who went on to found the all-male dance company, BalletBoyz.

MacMillan's final ballet was frequently controversial and *The Judas Tree* is no exception. Even more than 25 years later, it still has the power to shock audiences.

▶ **The original production, 1992**
Viviana Durante dramatically conveys the provocative nature of the Woman's role in this highly charged hold with Irek Mukhamedhov, dancing as the Foreman/Judas.

David Bintley

Dancer and choreographer ▪ 1957–

A major figure in British ballet, David Bintley is best known as the artistic director of Birmingham Royal Ballet (BRB). He is arguably the most distinguished and versatile ballet choreographer working in the UK today, and a strong champion of the heritage of The Royal Ballet. He has curated BRB's collection of classics as well as choreographing popular ballets with a comic touch such as *Beauty and the Beast*, darker tales—notably *Edward II*—and abstract creations including *E=mc²*.

▲ **David Bintley rehearses in London**
Bintley started his career as a dancer at Sadler's Wells, with notable interpretations of the Ugly Sisters in *Cinderella*, Alain and Widow Simone in *La Fille mal gardée*, Bottom in *The Dream*, all by Frederick Ashton, and the lead in *Petrushka*.

Bintley's talent for choreography was clear early on. Shortly before joining The Royal Ballet School at 16, Bintley made a version of *The Soldier's Tale*, to the Stravinsky score, with 51 dancers aged 6 to 16. His first professional commission, at 19, was *The Outsider* (1978), a ballet that dealt with the themes of prostitution and murder, and premiered at the Birmingham Hippodrome. By 1983, he had produced his first major narrative ballet, *The Swan of Tuonela* (1982), and had become resident choreographer of Sadler's Wells Royal Ballet. Three years later, he took the same role at The Royal Ballet, where triumphs include "*Still Life" at the Penguin Café* (1988), a series of light-hearted dances on the serious theme of endangered species; and *Hobson's Choice* (1989), a cheery retelling of Harold Brighouse's tale of northern folk.

Traditions of British ballet

In 1995, Bintley returned to his first company, now Birmingham Royal Ballet (BRB). Here, as artistic director, Bintley shaped the company, building a repertoire rooted in British ballet in which his own creations sit comfortably. His tribute to British dance legacy, particularly Frederick Ashton, came in *Tombeaux* (1993), while British history and culture were explored in his other works: Morris dance in "*Still Life*", Lancashire clog dancing in *Hobson's Choice*, and English country dancing in *Far from the Madding Crowd* (1996).

Ever appreciative of what will please, more lighthearted, humorous ballets have been staged in Birmingham, including *Beauty and the Beast* (2003), *Cyrano* (2007), *Sylvia* (2009), *Cinderella* (2010)—unusual for its barefoot heroine in Act I—and *The Tempest* (2016). Bintley has a darker side, too, as seen in *Edward II* (1995), a violent story of homosexuality and struggle for power in medieval England, originally made for Stuttgart Ballet. Bintley also created his first work in Birmingham at this time, *Carmina Burana* (1995), a tale of morality, temptation, and corruption.

Exploring different types of ballet

In 2015, Bintley went from ballet stories to the story of ballet and its beginnings with the award-winning *The King Dances*, a piece about the Sun King, Louis XIV, created using Baroque-style dance of the period. He also presented a television documentary on the subject, a follow-up to an earlier film about British ballet in wartime, *Dancing in the Blitz* (2014).

However, Bintley's work is not limited to narrative ballets. Besides *Tombeaux*, more abstract pieces include *Allegri diversi* (1987) and *The Seasons* (2001), plotless responses to Rossini and Verdi respectively. He can be serious and spiritual, too, as in *The Protecting Veil* (1998). More recently, with composer Matthew Hindson, he explored the worlds of physics in *E=mc²* (2009) and sports in *Faster* (2012). Commissioning scores from relatively unknown composers, at least in ballet terms, has become a feature of his work.

Bintley has created several ballets set to jazz (his father loved jazz), including *The Nutcracker Sweeties* (1996) and *The Shakespeare Suite* (1999), two witty ballets to the music of Duke Ellington, and *Take 5* (2007) to that of Dave Brubeck. He made *Aladdin* in 2008 for the National Ballet of Japan, and in 2010 was appointed their artistic director, a post he held for four years, dividing his time between Tokyo and Birmingham.

▲ ***Carmina Burana*, 2015**
Birmingham Royal Ballet perform what is now Bintley's signature piece. This ballet tells the story of three troubled seminarians, and is set to the music of Carl Orff, who based the oratorio on a manuscript of medieval poems.

KEY WORKS

Choreographer: *The Swan of Tuonela*, 1982 • *"Still Life" at the Penguin Café*, 1988 • *Tombeaux*, 1993 • *Carmina Burana*, 1995 *Edward II*, 1995 • *Far From the Madding Crowd*, 1996 • *Beauty and the Beast*, 2003 • *E=mc²*, 2009 • *Cinderella*, 2010 • *Faster*, 2012

TIMELINE

- **September 17, 1957** Born near Huddersfield, West Yorkshire.
- **1961** Experiences the thrill of the stage at a village Sunday-school concert.
- **1973** Joins The Royal Ballet Upper School, London, after choreographing Stravinsky's *The Soldier's Tale*.
- **1976** Graduates to Sadler's Wells Royal Ballet, London, later Birmingham Royal Ballet (BRB)—a company he returns to throughout his career.
- **1978** Encouraged by director Peter Wright, choreographs *The Outsider*.
- **1983** Appointed resident choreographer at Sadler's Wells Royal Ballet.
- **1986** Takes the position of resident choreographer at The Royal Ballet, London.
- **1995** Moves to BRB as director, staging the hugely popular *Carmina Burana*.
- **2001** Awarded CBE for services to dance.
- **2004** BRB launches the Ballet Hoo! project, offering dance training to 200 disadvantaged young people.
- **2005** Britain's top independent ballet school, Elmhurst, moves to Birmingham to act as a feeder school for BRB.
- **2009** Creates *E=mc²* about physics.
- **2010** Becomes artistic director of the National Ballet of Japan.

PERFORMANCE OF *E=MC²* (2009)

- **2015** Celebrates 20 years at the BRB by staging *Carmina Burana* and a new work, *The King Dances*.
- **2018** Announces his resignation from BRB from July 2019.

Matthew Bourne's Swan Lake

First performed: November 9, 1995 ▪ Venue: Sadler's Wells Theatre ▪ Choreography: Matthew Bourne ▪ Music: Pyotr Ilyich Tchaikovsky
Story: Possibly Vladimir Begichev and Vasily Geltser

A bold reinterpretation of one of classical ballet's most cherished works, Matthew Bourne's *Swan Lake* is a contemporary dance spectacle that stretched the boundaries of modern ballet when it premiered more than 20 years ago. Renowned for transferring the role of the swans from graceful female ballet dancers to muscular, bare-chested men, Bourne's production is shot with themes of identity, lack of freedom, and psychological torment.

Set to Tchaikovsky's celebrated score, *Swan Lake* is probably the world's most famous ballet—every major ballet company has a version based on Julius Reisinger's 1877 choreography. In the 20th century, several new versions were produced, notably a 1987 Swedish production by Mats Ek set in the 1940s.

Into this rich heritage entered Matthew Bourne's contemporary dance/theater company, Adventures in Motion Pictures, with the goal of updating the classic ballet for late-20th-century audiences. Bourne turned the original story and staging of *Swan Lake* on its head, making sweeping changes that upset traditionalists but made the ballet a hit with wider audiences. It played to full houses and brought in a section of the public who would not have gone to watch ballet on stage previously.

Swans reborn

Bourne's most radical change was to choreograph the part of the swans for male dancers, transposing the Odette/Odile role into a muscular swan leader who morphs into a seductive, leather-clad man. Seeking inspiration for his choreography, Bourne spent hours watching swans in London parks. He observed that they were often ungainly on the ground, but powerful nevertheless. When creating the choreography, Bourne also made his swans flock menacingly in a manner reminiscent of scenes from the Hitchcock thriller, *The Birds*.

A late starter in dance terms—he did not start training until he was aged 22—Bourne studied for a degree at the Laban Centre for Movement and Dance in London. While there, he created witty pieces for fellow students, many of whom continued to dance with him.

Bourne's early work had been designed for small stages, so moving from studio theaters to the large venues that came to show *Swan Lake* was something that he and his dancers had to adapt to. Today, while a global success, Bourne continues to update his work, and to adapt the choreography throughout its runs.

▲ **Paris premiere**
This 2005 poster advertises the Paris premiere of Bourne's *Swan Lake* at Théâtre Mogador, where it opened to huge acclaim.

STORY LINE

Act I A Prince takes his new girlfriend to a ballet. After finding his girlfriend was paid to accompany him, he resolves to kill himself.

Act II Just as the Prince is about to drown himself in a park lake, a bevy of swans appears. Recognizing the leading swan from his dreams, he abandons his suicide attempt.

Act III During a debauched ball at the palace, a black-leather-clad stranger flirts with all the women, including the Prince's mother, the Queen. Attracted to the stranger himself, the Prince feels jealousy toward the women.

Act IV Confined to an asylum, the Prince dreams of swans, only for the leading swan to rise out of his bed. As the other swans attack the Prince, the leading swan gives his life in a failed attempt to save him. The Queen finds her dead son and collapses in grief.

◀ **Laid bare**
Bourne's choreography wrenched a classic tale out of the hallowed ballet canon and thrust it into contemporary dance, with dancers wearing pointe shoes for only one scene of the entire show.

▶ **Pared-back costumes**
The swan costumes consist of trousers with leaf-shaped soft fabric sewn onto them, giving the appearance of feathers. The bare-chested dancers are adorned with white body paint.

John Neumeier

Dancer and choreographer ▪ 1942–

The second-longest serving artistic director in the world (after Alicia Alonso), John Neumeier has led Hamburg Ballet for over four decades. A powerful artistic voice in European ballet, he has created more than 150 ballets that, while preserving tradition, have a dramatic contemporary framework. Neumeier has a unique aesthetic and narrative style, and believes that it is the psychological motivation of characters that is always the most important part of a story.

◀ ***Nijinsky*, 2012**
Neumeier's second ballet on Nijinsky is shown at the Stanislavsky and Nemirovich-Danchenko Moscow Academic Music Theater. It depicts the dancer's life in flashbacks.

Neumeier first started dancing with the Sybil Shearer Company in Chicago in 1960. After training in Copenhagen and London, he moved to Germany in 1963 to join Stuttgart Ballet, having been spotted by Marcia Haydée, the company's prima ballerina. It was here that Neumeier began to choreograph.

Only six years later, he was appointed director of Frankfurt Ballet, where he quickly caused a stir with reinterpretations of *Romeo and Juliet* and *The Nutcracker* (both 1971), the latter evading direct references to Christmas. He moved north again in 1973 to become artistic director and chief choreographer of Hamburg Ballet which, according to dance writer Horst Koegler, was then "sunk in sheer mediocrity." Neumeier turned the company into a major force, creating the Hamburg Ballet Festival and establishing the School of the Hamburg Ballet. In 1996, he became ballettintendant, a uniquely German position that equates to general director.

Choreographic inspirations

Best known for his adaptations of literary classics, Neumeier successfully transforms them into modern works without losing their essence. He has drawn inspiration from texts as diverse as Alexandre Dumas' *Lady of the Camellias* (1978), Henrik Ibsen's *Peer Gynt* (1989), and Leo Tolstoy's *Anna Karenina* (2017).

Although applauded in mainland Europe, Neumeier's deconstruction and modernizing has not always traveled well. A huge success in the US, though, was *The Little Mermaid*, a co-production with San Francisco Ballet in 2010, originally created in 2005 for the Royal Danish Ballet. Essentially about someone willing to renounce her own beauty and world for love, Neumeier also exposed the dark psychology and tragedy in the story.

Away from literature, a continuing source of fascination for Neumeier is dancer Vaslav Nijinsky, reflected in his three biographical ballets: *Vaslav* (1979); *Nijinsky* (2000); and *Le Pavillon d'Armide* (2009), which references Fokine's ballet of the same name. Since 1975, Neumeier has concluded each Hamburg season with a five-hour gala dedicated to the dancer.

Looking to the future

While his focus is very much on Hamburg Ballet, Neumeier also works with other major companies worldwide. Notably, he created *Sounds of Empty Pages* for the Mariinsky Ballet in 2001, becoming the first Western choreographer for about 100 years to create a ballet for the company.

In 2011, Neumeier founded Germany's first National Youth Ballet, who present a mostly contemporary repertoire in schools, museums, and retirement homes. For his contribution to the arts, Neumeier received the prestigious Kyoto Prize in 2015.

▲ **Dramatic choreography**
Neumeier always focuses on expressing the drama in a narrative. "There is no point in a story that is told artfully but that does not reach the heart," he once told a Japanese interviewer.

KEY WORKS

Choreographer: *Romeo and Juliet*, 1971 • *The Nutcracker*, 1971 *Third Symphony of Gustav Mahler*, 1975 • *Lady of the Camellias*, 1978 • *Saint Matthew Passion*, 1981 • *The Little Mermaid*, 2005

TIMELINE

- **February 24, 1942** Born in Milwaukee, WI.
- **1953** Discovers the story of Vaslav Nijinsky at 11 years of age, reading Anatole Bourman's *The Tragedy of Nijinsky* (1936).
- **1960** Dances with the Sybil Shearer Company in Chicago while a student of English literature and theater studies at Marquette University, Milwaukee.
- **1961** Graduates, then continues his dance training under Vera Volkova in Copenhagen, Denmark, and at The Royal Ballet School in London.
- **1963** Joins John Cranko's Stuttgart Ballet, where he becomes a soloist and develops his choreographic lexicon.
- **1969** Appointed director of the Frankfurt Ballet.
- **1973** Joins the Hamburg Ballet as artistic director and chief choreographer, founding the Hamburg Ballet Festival a year later as an annual finale to each ballet season.
- **1978** Oversees the creation of the School of the Hamburg Ballet, which soon becomes a feeder school to the senior company.

SCENE FROM NEUMEIER'S *SONG OF THE EARTH*, HAMBURG STATE OPERA, 2016

- **1996** Appointed general manager of the Hamburg State Opera.
- **2006** Wins the Nijinsky Award for Lifetime Achievement.
- **2006** Establishes the John Neumeier Foundation to house dance artifacts.
- **2011** Sets up the National Youth Ballet in Hamburg, Germany, a touring company for eight young aspiring dancers.
- **2015** Wins the Kyoto Prize for contributions to the arts and philosophy.

上海大劇院
SHANGHAI GRAND THEATRE

SHANGHAI GRAND THEATRE

Designed by French architect firm Arte Charpentier and opened in 1998, the Shanghai Grand Theatre in the People's Square is one of the city's landmark buildings. Its exterior is a contemporary interpretation of some key elements of Chinese culture. The ground plan is based on a square, representing the earth, while the upturned arc of the roof depicts the heavens.

The building is home to three theaters. Decked out in warm red and gold, the main auditorium is the 1,631-seat Lyric Theater, used to stage ballet, Chinese and Western opera, classical music, musicals, and large-scale drama. Major ballet companies that have performed on its stage include The Royal Ballet, Birmingham Royal Ballet, the Mariinsky Ballet, and Dutch National Ballet. On the west side of the complex, the 575-seat walnut-toned Buick Theater is used to present chamber music and small and mid-scale drama, and provides a home for many arts education activities. On the fifth floor, there is an experimental Studio Theater that seats up to 300.

The almost 2,392 yd² (2,000 m²) lobby stands five floors high. Its black and white marble floor has patterns shaped like piano keys and an abstract ear and eye. Above hangs the Blue Danube, an Austrian-made crystal chandelier more than 8 yd (7 m) tall and 3 yd (3 m) wide with over 300 lights.

> The history of ballet in China is not long ... We did not replicate the West. Chinese ballet tells its own stories.
>
> ZHAO RUHENG, ARTISTIC DIRECTOR, NATIONAL BALLET OF CHINA 1994–2009

◀ **Symbol of cultural emergence**
The Shanghai Grand Theatre combines Eastern and Western elements. At night, light installations against the glass facade of the exterior make it resemble a crystal palace.

Wayne McGregor

Choreographer ▪ 1970–

Long noted for his challenging contemporary dance choreography, Wayne McGregor thrilled the ballet world with his work *Chroma* for The Royal Ballet, London, in 2006. It was only his second main-stage work (after *Qualia*, 2004), but led to his appointment as the company's first resident choreographer since Kenneth MacMillan. Given McGregor's non-ballet background, it was initially seen as a risky decision by the then director, Monica Mason, but her choice proved to be an inspired one.

▲ **Telling tales**
Sarah Lamb performs the title role in McGregor's *Raven Girl* for The Royal Ballet in 2015. A modern-day fairytale, it is the choreographer's first story ballet, about a half-raven/half-girl who longs to fly.

Growing up in Stockport, UK, McGregor studied dance at Bretton Hall College, part of the University of Leeds, and at the José Limón dance school in New York. After graduating in 1992, aged 22, he was promptly engaged by John Ashford as resident choreographer with the London Contemporary Dance School—the first in the role not to have studied or taught at the school. The same year, McGregor also founded Random Dance (now Studio Wayne McGregor), the conduit for his creative output, and Company Wayne McGregor, his own ensemble through which he developed his unique style.

Finding inspiration

McGregor worked tirelessly developing his style, producing works for his own company and for venues across the UK. From the very beginning, his pieces were usually devoid of a plot or characters, and incorporated different forms of choreography and movement, combined with experimental visuals, sound, and technology. As he has said, for him, collaboration with visual designers, sound designers, and composers is equally important. It is a process of give and take, where things are made in parallel, and everyone is on equal terms. The result is one object, one art work, not two or more.

While McGregor initially focused on contemporary dance, he produced his first en pointe piece in 1997 for former New York City Ballet dancer Antonia Francheschi, performed at the Saatchi Gallery in London. His connection with classical ballet came three years later when he asked The Royal Ballet dancer Viviana Durante if he could create a piece for her. The result was the duet, *Fleur de Peux*, which was McGregor's first choreography for the ballet company. The following year, McGregor was commissioned directly by the company, and produced *Symbiont(s)*. With a jagged electronic score, it featured dancer Edward Watson, who went on to perform in most of McGregor's subsequent works.

Finding acclaim

As his reputation grew, McGregor's company was invited to take up a residency at Sadler's Wells Theatre in London in 2001. Five years later, he achieved critical acclaim with his sensual, one-act ballet, *Chroma*, produced for The Royal Ballet. It was typical of his work, in which the movement is dramatic and hyperextended, as the dancers are pushed to physical extremes. That same year, McGregor was appointed resident choreographer by the company.

Further successes followed, including *Infra* (2008), staged under a giant LED backdrop; *Limen* (2009), described by McGregor as a meditation on "thresholds of life and death, darkness and light, reality and fantasy"; the award-winning ballet triptych *Woolf Works* (2015), inspired by the works of writer Virginia Woolf; and *Yugen* (2018).

Underpinning McGregor's success is his belief that choreography is about thinking with the body, that "dance is a cognitive act, not a physical act." He is now heavily in demand away from his own company and The Royal Ballet. Recent years have seen him directing movement for theater and film, including *Harry Potter and the Goblet of Fire* (2005), and music videos, such as the Grammy-nominated *Lotus Flower* for Radiohead.

▲ **Seeking perfection**
Dancers Calvin Richardson (left) and Edward Watson (center) of The Royal Ballet rehearse with McGregor (right) for his 2016 production of *Obsidian Tear.*

KEY WORKS

Sulphur 16, 1998 • *Symbiont(s)*, 2000 • *Qualia*, 2004 *Chroma*, 2006 • *Infra*, 2008 • *Limen*, 2009 • *Raven Girl*, 2013 • *Woolf Works*, 2015 • *Obsidian Tear*, 2016

TIMELINE

- **March 12, 1970** Born in Stockport, UK.
- **1982** After his dance tutor encourages him to improvise his own steps, begins to give lessons to other children.
- **1988** Begins studying dance at Bretton Hall, dance school of the University of Leeds.
- **1992** After graduating, founds his own dance company, Random Dance, and becomes choreographer in residence for the London Contemporary Dance School.
- **1998** Blends dance, multimedia, and digital technology in his cutting-edge piece, *Sulphur 16*, at Random Dance.
- **2001** Invited to bring his dance troupe to Sadler's Wells Theatre, London, as the new theater's first resident company.
- **2006** Appointed resident choreographer at The Royal Ballet, the first contemporary-dance specialist to hold the post.
- **2007** *Chroma* wins an Olivier award for best new dance production.
- **2011** Awarded a CBE in the Queen's New Year's Honours list.

MELISSA HAMILTON AND JONATHAN WATKINS PERFORM IN *INFRA* IN 2008

- **2014** Appointed as professor of choreography at London's Trinity Laban Conservatoire of Music and Dance.
- **2017** *Autobiography*, a new work based on a digital algorithm derived from computer sequencing of McGregor's own DNA, debuts at Sadler's Wells Theatre.

Tryst

First performed: May 18, 2002 ▪ Venue: Royal Opera House, London ▪ Choreography: Christopher Wheeldon ▪ Music: James MacMillan
Story: Christopher Wheeldon

Inspired by the beauty of the Scottish Highlands and set to music by Scottish composer James MacMillan, *Tryst* was British choreographer Christopher Wheeldon's first work for The Royal Ballet. The piece centers around a slow, powerful pas de deux—the lovers' tryst—first danced by Darcey Bussell and Jonathan Cope. Abstract but full of expression, *Tryst*'s pas de deux is an inspired and multi-layered piece of choreography.

STORY LINE

Tryst has no precise plot, and just one act. In choreography of neoclassical abstraction, the busy urban lives of city dwellers are juxtaposed with the huge spaces and silences of open countryside.

The ballet begins with a female dancer alone on stage and expands to four couples and an ensemble of 12 dancers. At times the choreography is busy and crowded, with 20 bodies moving in patterns as intricate and finely tuned as downtown New York City traffic. Set amongst these, the slow pas de deux, with its expressive movements and fully elongated limbs, is a thing of beauty.

The idea for *Tryst* evolved while Christopher Wheeldon was driving through the Scottish Highlands in 2001, listening to the James MacMillan piece of the same name. Wheeldon was touched not only by "the serenity and beauty of the middle part of the music, but also by the shifting colors of the landscape of the Scottish Highlands." The resulting critically acclaimed work, *Tryst*, strived to create a contrast between this soaring beauty and tranquility and "the idea of a very urban civilization, a very contemporary, angular city like New York—and how, as human beings, we need to escape to nature from these urban existences." A huge gray screen, onto which blurry splashes of color are projected, dominates designer Jean-Marc Puissant's set, representing the ever-changing Highlands skies. The tryst itself begins with a bar of pale light across the stage and a transition to dreamy, faintly familiar folk melodies in the score.

Modern choreography

The dancers negotiate odd phrases and difficult timing, twisting their hands into knots, rapidly changing direction, and responding physically to the blasts of brass instruments that slice the air, representing urban culture. In contrast, the slow but dramatic pas de deux evokes mountains and vast open spaces.

This central pas de deux, influenced by the Scottish feel of the MacMillan score, was first interpreted by The Royal Ballet dancers Darcey Bussell and Jonathan Cope. These two dancers, with their long limbs and athletic style of dance, were perfectly suited to the piece. After seeing the pair perform together in a 2007 production, an *Independent* dance critic wrote, "They fold and unfold into each other; individual steps have less impact than the sight of these dancers flowing from shape to shape." To help prepare later dancers taking on the duet, Wheeldon used Zeus and Aphrodite coming together as a metaphor, and asked them to imagine that wings were growing from their backs as they stretched out their arms.

MacMillan had not had dance in mind when he composed Tryst in 1989, but, pleased by the collaboration, he worked with Wheeldon on a new score for a New York City Ballet premiere, *Shambards,* in 2004. MacMillan also conducted The Royal Ballet's 2010 revival of *Tryst.*

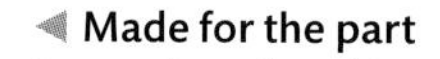

◄ **Made for the part**
Darcey Bussell and Jonathan Cope danced *Tryst*'s iconic pas de deux for the last time in Bussell's farewell performance at Sadler's Wells in 2007.

Chroma

First performed: November 16, 2006 ▪ Venue: Royal Opera House, London ▪ Choreography: Wayne McGregor ▪ Music: Joby Talbot and Jack White, The White Stripes ▪ Story: Wayne McGregor

When *Chroma* was first performed at London's Royal Opera House in 2006, it brought together the unlikely union of minimalist architecture, a garage rock band from Detroit, and the top tier of British ballet. The fast-paced, 25-minute work choreographed by Wayne McGregor both embraced and departed from classical ballet traditions, and has since become a paragon of contemporary ballet.

◀ **Premiere performance**
Chroma was first staged by The Royal Ballet at London's Royal Opera House in 2006, as part of a triple bill. Dancer Eric Underwood displays the fierce intensity of the piece.

STORY LINE

A short piece danced by five couples, *Chroma* is an exploration of the human body and how it communicates extreme thoughts and emotions. In terms of movement, it is a head-first plunge into a world where contorted spines, creaturesque postures, and extreme extensions are the norm. The dancers explore the boundaries of ballet technique in a series of interwoven group sequences, contrasting pas de deux and a vigorous male trio. Demanding an incredible range of movement and stamina from the cast, the work is set against a stark backdrop that leaves the dancers' every move exposed.

At the time of *Chroma*'s creation, Wayne McGregor was something of a ballet outsider, focusing on experimental projects that engaged people from a wide range of artistic genres and scientific disciplines to create dance that he described as "intimately plugged into the world we live in today." The ballet's initial concept, movements, and stylized positions were drawn from his academic research, which explored dance concepts with neuroscientists from Cambridge University. McGregor described *Chroma* as an investigation into what happens when the human form exists in the absence of color.

Ballet rocks

Staying true to his collaborative nature for *Chroma*, McGregor combined rock music from The White Stripes with minimalist sets by British architect John Pawson and costumes by German designer Moritz Junge. The band did not perform live at the premiere; instead three of their songs, "The Hardest Button to Button," "Aluminum," and "Blue Orchid," were rearranged by Joby Talbot for a 35-piece orchestra and combined with Mozart and Tchaikovsky interludes to complete the ballet's score. Pawson's set placed the sculpted lines of the dancers within a modern, crisp, white-washed box, which featured a square portal at the rear to allow dancers to step in and out of the work via a raised platform. Junge's costumes, with loosely fitted bodices in varying shades of flesh tones accented with faint pastel and gray tints, visualized McGregor's belief that "color evokes certain emotions—when you see flesh tones, you see something innately human."

As with the music, the choreography mixes both classical and modern as balletic and contemporary dance create a captivating duality. *Guardian* dance critic Judith Mackrell wrote, "the tension between chaos and minimalism, anarchy and classicism, ratchets up to thrilling extremes."

Chroma was instantly popular with audiences and critics, winning the Laurence Olivier Award for Best New Dance Production and The Critics' Circle National Dance Award in 2007. Seen as a major contribution to the evolution of modern ballet, *Chroma* has been restaged by leading dance companies around the world, including San Francisco Ballet, Bolshoi Ballet, National Ballet of Canada, and Dutch National Ballet.

▶ **Extreme emotion**
Clad in flesh tones, Federico Bonelli and Sarah Lamb dance a pas de deux in The Royal Ballet's 2006 premiere of *Chroma*.

Carlos Acosta

Dancer, choreographer, and ballet company director ▪ 1973–

Cuban dancer Carlos Acosta is celebrated for his unparalleled strength, grace, and ability to communicate the sheer joy of dancing to his audiences. In the decades since he won the Prix de Lausanne in 1990—beating 126 dancers from 20 countries at the age of 16—Carlos Acosta has become the most acclaimed male dancer of his age, drawing comparisons with Nureyev and Baryshnikov, but with an athleticism and emotional intensity that are all his own.

▲ ***La Bayadère*, 2009**
As Solor, Acosta leaps with characteristic power and panache in this The Royal Ballet production. His work with Paris Opéra, the Bolshoi, American Ballet Theatre, and UK's English National Opera and The Royal Ballet has injected new energy into the world of ballet.

Born in the poor neighborhood of Los Pinos, Havana, Carlos Junior ("Yuli") Acosta lived with his two sisters and Spanish mother, Maria. His truck-driver father Pablo, who was 20 years Maria's senior and had eight other children, maintained an iron grip on his family, especially on Yuli.

Years before, Pablo Acosta had watched "parasol ladies" twirling across a cinema screen and become enchanted with ballet. When he learned that the city ballet school offered free meals and a route to the Cuban National Ballet, he mapped out a future for his son in dance.

Young Yuli preferred soccer. At his audition, he pretended to dribble a ball to music, but his perfect proportions and precise movement won him a place. He hated getting up at 5am for the long bus rides to school and, after weeks of playing truant and nearly missing a key performance, he was expelled. However, Pablo's determination and Yuli's irrefutable talent secured him a place at an arts boarding school in Pinar.

Coming along in leaps and bounds

On a trip to see the Cuban National Ballet, Yuli had an epiphany as he watched dancer Alberto Terrero defying gravity with his leaps. Yuli began to work hard and graduated with the highest possible scores in his exams before joining the National Ballet School in Havana. There, his teacher, Ramona de Sáa, spurred him on to win his first major awards: the Prix de Lausanne and the Paris grand prix.

Acosta joined the corps de ballet in the Cuban National Ballet but was soon invited to dance as a principal with the English National Ballet. Far from home in London, the 18-year-old made his debut in the Polovtsian Dances from *Prince Igor*, then appeared in *Cinderella*, *Le Spectre de la rose*, *Les Sylphides*, and *The Nutcracker*. After an ankle injury, Acosta limped home to the Cuban National Ballet and a country in economic meltdown after the collapse of its Soviet Bloc support. He was soon restored to his peak under the direction of Alicia Alonso but, like most Cuban workers, he was earning a pittance.

The flying Cuban

Acosta's move to the Houston Ballet in 1993 brought him wealth and global recognition, and the opportunity to develop new roles with Ben Stevenson. After five years with the company, in 1998, "the flying Cuban" became the first-ever black principal dancer in The Royal Ballet. As principal guest artist, he made numerous international appearances and tours, appearing in the US, Russia, the Netherlands, Chile, Argentina, Greece, Japan, Italy, Germany, France, and Australia. His seasons with American Ballet Theatre brought audiences of black Americans to the Metropolitan Opera House to see him perform in *Swan Lake*. "Nobody who looks like me had ever played the roles I danced," he said.

Acosta retired after 17 years with The Royal Ballet and his final performance was his own sizzling reinterpretation of *Carmen*. Now he enjoys family life in the UK, has plans for a new Cuban dance academy, and works with his own Havana-based company Acosta Danza. In 2017, their first shows burst into life with a mix of ballet, contemporary dance, hip hop, and flamenco—everything that Acosta's heritage has to offer.

Carlos had a rare wow factor—he had fiery sex appeal, and incredible technical ability.

DARCEY BUSSELL ON CARLOS ACOSTA DURING AN INTERVIEW

◀ **George Balanchine's *Apollo***
Acosta takes on the lead role in this The Royal Ballet production in 2013. Excerpts from this ballet were incorporated into Acosta's farewell gala performance at the Royal Albert Hall in 2016, alongside parts from other works by Balanchine, MacMillan, Ashton, and Fokine.

KEY WORKS

Dancer: Prince, *The Nutcracker*, 1993 Albrecht, *Giselle*, 1994 • Title role, *Apollo*, 2002 • Romeo, *Romeo and Juliet*, 2006 Crown Prince Rudolf, *Mayerling*, 2013 Choreographer: *Tocororo – A Cuban Tale*, 2003 • *Don Quixote*, 2014

TIMELINE

- **June 2, 1973** Born in Havana, Cuba, the youngest of 11 children in a poor family.
- **1982** Begins to learn ballet at a state-funded school, later enrolling at the National Ballet School of Cuba.
- **1989** Dances internationally for the first time, performing in Italy and Venezuela.
- **1990** Wins the gold medal at the Prix de Lausanne, the grand prix at the fourth biennial Concours International de Danse de Paris, the Vignale Danza prize in Italy, and the Frédéric Chopin prize.
- **1991** Graduates from the Cuban National Ballet School, joining London's English National Ballet as principal dancer.
- **1993** Debuts in *The Nutcracker* as principal dancer at the Houston Ballet, US.
- **1995** Given a Dance Fellowship by the Princess Grace Foundation in New York.
- **1997** Creates the role of Frederick in *Dracula*, a new work by Ben Stevenson, director of the Houston Ballet.
- **1998** Joins The Royal Ballet as principal dancer, becoming principal guest artist five years later.
- **2003** Creates the semi-autobiographical *Tocororo—A Cuban Tale*, which debuts at the Sala Garcia Lorca in Havana.
- **2007** Wins the Laurence Olivier award for outstanding achievement in dance. His autobiography, *No Way Home*, is published.
- **2011** Creates the Carlos Acosta International Dance Foundation to restore the School of Ballet in Havana.
- **2012** Combines dance with drama in a role in the film *Day of the Flowers*.
- **2016** Retires from the stage; directs his company Acosta Danza, which debuts at the Gran Teatro Alicia Alonso in Havana.

DAY OF THE FLOWERS, 2012

CHINA'S ARTS CENTER

Known colloquially as the Egg or Water Drop, the National Centre for the Performing Arts (NCPA) on Chang'an Avenue in Beijing rises like an island out of its surrounding artificial lake and green space. Designed by French architect Paul Andreu and opened in 2007, the futuristic-looking building sits immediately to the west of Tiananmen Square and the Great Hall of the People, and near the Forbidden City. Andreu's aim was to acknowledge the nearby traditional Chinese architecture by complementing the red walls of the ancient buildings and letting the NCPA melt into its surroundings rather than stand out from them.

At the heart of the building is the red and gold 2,416-seat Opera House, which regularly receives top international and national ballet and contemporary dance companies, as well as staging opera and other large-scale shows. A venue for large classical and national music performances, the slightly smaller Concert Hall is home to a 6,500-pipe organ, believed to be the largest of its kind in China. A smaller third theater is used for traditional Chinese opera, drama, and national song and dance, while a fourth, smaller still, is multifunctional.

The four theaters sit under a huge 50yd (46m) high titanium-plated dome divided by a curved glass curtain. During the day, light flows through the glass roof. At night, people and events within can be seen from outside. A lounge on the top level affords spectacular views of the city.

> My purpose is to do something original. I can only hope that it disturbs in a positive way.
>
> PAUL ANDREU, ARCHITECT OF THE NCPA

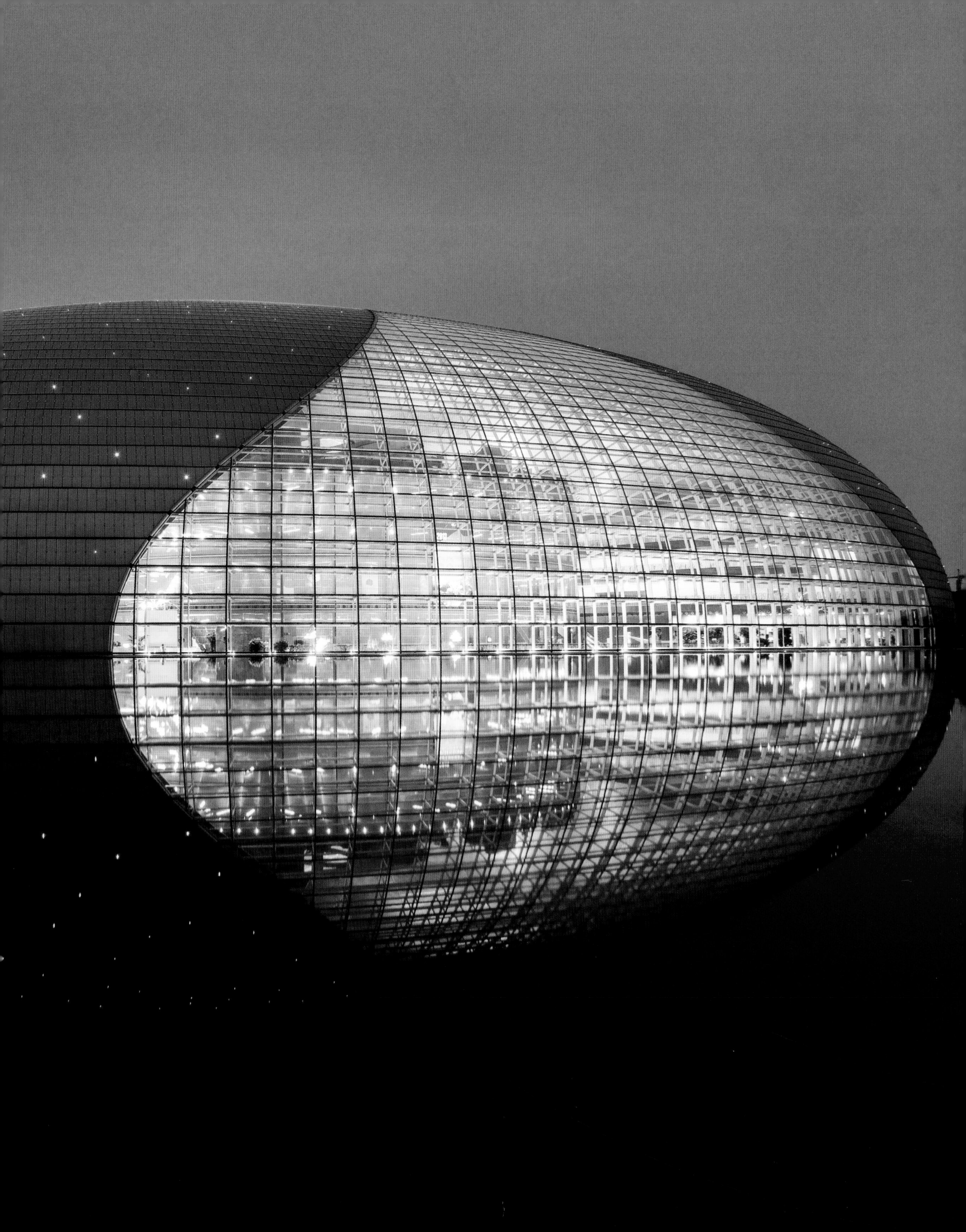

Alice's Adventures in Wonderland

First performed: February 28, 2011 ▪ Venue: Royal Opera House, London ▪ Choreography: Christopher Wheeldon ▪ Music: Joby Talbot ▪ Story: Lewis Carroll

The Royal Ballet's first full-evening narrative ballet commissioned for more than a decade, *Alice's Adventures in Wonderland* was a co-production with The National Ballet of Canada. Its reception showed that choreographer Christopher Wheeldon had fulfilled his intention to "make a ballet that would encourage people to come in and enjoy themselves, and then, God forbid, come back." The original production was reworked into three acts in 2012.

STORY LINE

Act I At a garden party in 1862, Lewis Carroll turns into the White Rabbit. Alice follows him into Wonderland, where she finds a series of bizarre characters, including Jack (the Knave of Hearts), the Duchess, and the Cheshire Cat.

Act II Disoriented, Alice arrives at a tea party hosted by the Mad Hatter. Next, she meets an exotic Caterpillar before finding herself in a garden filled with dancing flowers.

Act III The Queen and the Duchess begin a croquet game with flamingos for mallets and hedgehogs for balls. Jack is put on trial for stealing tarts, and all the characters of Wonderland come together. The whole court collapses and Alice wakes in 2011, with Jack.

Based on Lewis Carroll's well-known 1865 children's story, this full-length ballet was a new undertaking for Wheeldon, who was better known for contemporary single-act abstract works. While the episodic nature of the original tale makes it complicated to translate to a ballet, the result is a very 21st-century piece that is wildly imaginative and eye-catching, and full of colorful characters.

Fantastical inventions

Wheeldon created the role of Alice for British ballerina Lauren Cuthbertson, while her love interest Jack, the Knave of Hearts, was created for Ukrainian ballet dancer Sergei Polunin.

Wheeldon included several "in jokes" in the ballet, including a parody of the famous Rose Adagio from *The Sleeping Beauty*, performed by the Queen of Hearts and four terrified partners. One of the story's iconic characters, the Mad Hatter, was created for principal dancer Steven McRae who—as well as being a classical dancer—is a trained tap dancer.

Bob Crowley's designs for the production included a plethora of imaginative special effects, including illusions, lighting, and projection. One of the most notable was his design for the Cheshire Cat, which relied on puppetry that allowed the mysterious creature to appear and vanish at will.

Wheeldon's production was not the first balletic interpretation of Carroll's work. In 1986, The National Ballet of Canada premiered *Alice*, choreographed by Glen Tetley. English National Ballet staged a production based on Carroll's story in 1995, choreographed by Derek Deane, and Shawn Hounsell created *Wonderland* for the Royal Winnipeg Ballet in 2011.

Wheeldon's ballet proved hugely popular, and has become the most successful adaptation to date. It has been staged frequently by The Royal Ballet and The National Ballet of Canada, as well as being restaged by the Royal Danish Ballet, Royal Swedish Ballet, and The Australian Ballet.

▲ **Graphic approach**
This 2011 promotional poster mimics Bob Crowley's anarchic costumes and special effects, with Alice flanked by the Mad Hatter and the Queen of Hearts.

◀ **Romantic lead**
Wheeldon's production departs from Lewis Carroll's original by casting Jack, the Knave of Hearts—danced here by Vadim Muntagirov in 2014—as a romantic partner for the teenage Alice.

▶ **Dazzling dramatics**
Alexander Campbell plays the unhinged Mad Hatter, whom Wheeldon cast as a tap-dancing eccentric, in The Royal Ballet's 2013 production of *Alice's Adventures in Wonderland*.

In this Style 10/6

Tamara Rojo

Dancer and artistic director ▪ 1974–

As a child, becoming a successful dancer was simply not enough for Tamara Rojo—even then she aspired to run her own dance company in order to have the broadest possible influence on the art form. Born into a family of political activists, and named after Che Guevara's last lover, struggle and revolution is in Rojo's blood. As a dancer, she won popular acclaim and broke box office records, and as an artistic director she is finding exciting new ways to broaden the appeal of ballet.

▲ **Tamara Rojo as Mexican artist Frida Kahlo**
Tamara Rojo performs as Frida Kahlo in *Broken Wings*, part of the *She Said* production she commissioned as artistic director for the English National Ballet in 2015. It was the first role Rojo had ever danced that had been choreographed by a woman (Annabelle Lopez Ochoa).

Although born in Canada, Rojo moved to her parent's native Spain when she was just an infant, and she started to learn ballet there at the age of five. Aged 11, she joined the Real Conservatorio Profesional de Danza Mariemma in Madrid as a full-time pupil of Víctor Ullate and Karemia Moreno. After graduating from the conservatory at 16, Rojo began her professional career the following year with the Ballet de la Comunidad de Madrid, under the direction of her former teacher, Ullate.

In 1994, Rojo won the Gold Medal at the Paris International Dance Competition, where the judges included Natalia Makarova, Vladimir Vasiliev, and Galina Samsova. Impressed by her obvious talents, Samsova, artistic director of the Scottish Ballet, offered her a contract. At this time Rojo spoke no English, but as she wryly commented "neither did they." Just a year later, she spoke English fluently.

London calling

Rojo was invited to London by Derek Deane in 1997 to join the English National Ballet to create the role of Juliet in his new version of *Romeo and Juliet*. Within six months she was promoted to principal dancer, and went on to break attendance records for her performance of Clara in *The Nutcracker* at the London Coliseum.

In 2000, Rojo resolved to join The Royal Ballet in London, where she was willing to take "any role." Fortunately for her, Viviana Durante left the company later that year, and Rojo was engaged as a principal dancer. There, despite suffering a strained ankle herself, she was soon replacing an injured Darcey Bussell in *Giselle* to great acclaim. Further successes followed, as did injuries, the latter notably in 2002, when she suffered a burst appendix during a performance. Typical of her determination, however, she was back on stage a week later.

Methodical approach

Rojo is often described as a passionate dancer. While her father initially thought that she was too analytical to become an artist, it is her meticulous approach to researching her roles that earned her a reputation for bringing characters to life and making them believable—drawing on her own experiences, rather like a method actor. This, combined with her incredible technique, saw Rojo receive over a dozen international awards for her work with The Royal Ballet, including the 2012 Laurence Olivier award for Best New Dance Production.

By 2012, Rojo was ready to undertake a new creative direction and left The Royal Ballet to join the English National Ballet, as both its artistic director and lead principal dancer. Having dreamed as a child of running a ballet company, she immediately set about transforming it. As she said at the time, "I hope to inspire a whole new generation of dancers that will in turn become teachers, choreographers, and managers themselves."

Since taking the reins, Rojo has been true to her word, and has staged many groundbreaking productions, including *She Said* in 2015, which highlighted the work of female choreographers. The following year she staged Akram Khan's *Giselle*. Set in a 21st-century migrant community, it is an example of how she is creating ballet that is relevant to a new generation of ballet audiences.

◀ **Tamara Rojo and Federico Bonelli**
Performing at The Royal Ballet in 2011, Tamara Rojo and Federico Bonelli perform *Requiem*, Kenneth MacMillan's tribute to his friend and fellow choreographer, John Cranko.

KEY WORKS

Dancer: Juliet, *Romeo and Juliet*, 1997 • Clara, *The Nutcracker*, 2000 • Mary Vetsera, *Mayerling*, 2004 Odette/Odile, *Swan Lake*, 2008 • Title role, *Snow White*, 2008 • Nikiya, *La Bayadère*, 2009 • Artistic director: *Giselle*, 2011 • *Le Corsaire*, 2013 • *Lest We Forget*, 2014 • *She Said*, 2016

TIMELINE

- **May 17, 1974** Born in Montreal, Canada, but is taken to live in Spain, aged just four months, by her Spanish parents.
- **1979** Takes ballet lessons at the Victor Ullate School in Madrid, Spain.
- **1985** Starts to study ballet full-time at the Real Conservatorio Profesional de Danza Mariemma in Madrid.

TAMARA ROJO AND AKRAM KHAN IN *LEST WE FORGET: DUST*

- **1991** Joins Victor Ullate's Ballet de la Comunidad de Madrid, simultaneously continuing her education at night school.
- **1994** Wins the Paris International Dance Competition at the age of 20.
- **1996** Joins the Scottish Ballet, where she plays a host of leading classical ballet roles.
- **1997** Joins the English National Ballet (ENB), London, and resolves to one day direct the company.
- **2000** Becomes a principal at The Royal Ballet, London.
- **2012** Becomes artistic director and lead principal dancer of the ENB. Introduces My First Ballet, a workshop for children aged three to seven to take part in ballet.
- **October 2013** Stages her first production for the ENB, *Le Corsaire*, performed to acclaim at Milton Keynes.
- **2016** Awarded a CBE in the Queen's New Year's Honours list for services to ballet.
- **April 2016** Presents *She Said*, a triple bill of works choreographed by women at Sadler's Wells, London.

The Winter's Tale

First performed: April 10, 2014 ▪ Venue: Royal Opera House, London ▪ Choreography: Christopher Wheeldon ▪ Music: Talbot ▪ Story: Wheeldon and Talbot

"Christopher Wheeldon rises to the challenge of translating Shakespeare into dance, creating one of [the] most fully achieved story ballets to be staged at Covent Garden in years," wrote critic Judith Mackrell of this tragi-comic tale of false accusations, mistaken identity, rejection and reunion, a dash of magic, and a bear—the latter created by Basil Twist, who made the special effects for *Alice's Adventures in Wonderland.*

STORY LINE

Act I King Polixenes is staying at his friend Leontes' court in Sicilia. Leontes suspects his wife Hermione of infidelity with Polixenes. Hermione gives birth to a daughter, whom Leontes orders to be abandoned. Hermione collapses, apparently dead. Baby Perdita is left in Bohemia, and rescued by a shepherd.

Act II In Bohemia, 16 years later, Perdita is in love with Florizel, Polixenes' son, disguised as a shepherd. The couple flee to Sicilia.

Act III Leontes helps the couple, and Perdita's true identity is revealed. Father and daughter are reunited, and Perdita and Florizel marry. They visit the statue of Hermione, which comes to life.

◀ **Jealous anguish**
Edward Watson as Leontes claws at his wife Hermione, danced by Lauren Cuthbertson, in choreography reminiscent of Kenneth MacMillan's *Mayerling.*

The same artistic team that created *Alice's Adventures in Wonderland,* Christopher Wheeldon, composer Joby Talbot, and designer Bob Crowley, tackled a new ballet in 2014, based on the play *The Winter's Tale.* Choreographers have often turned to Shakespeare for inspiration. *Romeo and Juliet, A Midsummer Night's Dream, The Taming of the Shrew, The Tempest,* and even *Othello* and *Hamlet* have all formed the basis for ballets.

Written near the end of Shakespeare's career, *The Winter's Tale* is often viewed as a problematic play as it contains elements of tragedy, comedy, and romance. The story also involves time lapses, disguised characters, and perhaps the most famous stage direction ever: "Exit, pursued by a bear."

Narrative drive

When asked in an interview for The National Ballet of Canada why he looked to Shakespeare for inspiration, Wheeldon replied: "Well, he wrote good stories! Of course, the beauty of the language is what draws people to want to stage them and read them, but he also wrote terrific plot lines—that's why I chose *The Winter's Tale.*" Despite the play's idiosyncrasies, the resulting work is widely agreed to be a masterful modern narrative ballet.

Wheeldon closely followed the play's plot. The ballet, like the play, shifts abruptly from wintry Sicilia to spring in Bohemia, where villagers engage in robust and radiant dancing with the bucolic charm of Frederick Ashton's *La fille mal gardée.* Bob Crowley helped the transition from jealousy to the joys of spring—his large, flowering green tree dominated the stage in Act II, contrasting sharply with the cold severity of the stage sets for Act I.

Wheeldon and his collaborators also chose to place some of the musicians in Act I and II onstage and integrate them in the action—something rarely seen in ballet, but which works well in this piece. The ballet opened in 2014 and, like *Alice's Adventures in Wonderland,* was a co-production between The Royal Ballet and The National Ballet of Canada.

▶ **The Royal Ballet, 2014**
Wheeldon created the ballet for British dancers Edward Watson and Lauren Cuthbertson (seen here as Leontes and Hermione). The second act was dominated by Sarah Lamb as Perdita and Steven McRae as Prince Florizel.

▼ **Act II in spring**
After the chilly Sicilian winter of Act I, the curtain goes up in Act II to reveal Crowley's enormous tree hung with talismans, to the accompaniment of a musician playing the bansuri (Indian flute) on stage. The dancing becomes fluid and joyful in contrast to the contorted writhings of Act I.

Christopher Wheeldon

Dancer and choreographer ▪ 1973–

One of the few modern-day ballet choreographers to make a significant impact in both Europe and the US, Christopher Wheeldon once described his intention when choreographing as "To paint music, to show the complexity and the layers of music through the movement." As a true advocate of the art, he also firmly believes that ballet should be accessible to all, and has produced a catalog of highly imaginative works that combine British theatricality with the precision of George Balanchine.

▲ The Royal Ballet, 2014
Wheeldon (rear) leads Edward Watson, principal dancer at The Royal Ballet, London, through the role of Leontes in his ballet, *The Winter's Tale*, based on Shakespeare's play. The ballet opened in 2014 and proved a great success.

Brought up by his theater-loving parents in Yeovil, Somerset, Wheeldon was first attracted to ballet after watching a film of Frederick Ashton's comedic *La fille mal gardée*. He later admitted to having been particularly taken by the dancing chickens. After learning ballet locally from the age of eight, Wheeldon joined The Royal Ballet School in London three years later. It was there, after noticing Wheeldon's fledgling talent for choreography, that Kenneth MacMillan encouraged him to practice it at every opportunity. He did just that, and received several accolades for his efforts including, in 1990, the school's most important choreography prize, the Ursula Moreton Choreographic Award.

Going stateside

In 1991, Wheeldon joined The Royal Ballet, and while recovering from a twisted ankle the following year, he traveled to New York. Once settled, and suitably healed, he got permission to take classes with New York City Ballet, and was soon invited to join the company. While there, he continued to develop his choreography, and received critical acclaim in 1996 for *Danses Bohémiennes* for the School of American Ballet.

Wheeldon retired from dancing in 2000 but remained with New York City Ballet, first as artist-in-residence, then resident choreographer, both positions created for him. His first ballet, *Polyphonia* (2001), met with outstanding reviews, as did his *Variations Sérieuses* the same year. In her review of the latter, *The New York Times* critic Anna Kisselgoff wrote, "No ballet choreographer of his generation can match his imaginative use of the classical vocabulary."

Although resident at New York City Ballet, Wheeldon was not tied exclusively to the company. As his reputation grew, he was increasingly asked to produce work for other leading ballet companies.

A man in demand

Wheeldon created his first short ballet for London's The Royal Ballet in 2002—*Tryst,* a collaboration with Scottish composer, James MacMillan. This was followed two years later by a full-length production of *Swan Lake* for Pennsylvania Ballet, then in 2006, he was back at The Royal Ballet with *DGV: Danse à Grande Vitesse*.

In 2007, Wheeldon produced *Hamlet* for the Bolshoi Ballet, becoming the first British choreographer to stage a new work for the company. This was also the year that he established his own ensemble, Morphoses/The Wheeldon Company, with dancer Lourdes Lopez. He left New York City Ballet the following year. In its first three years, his new company produced 33 ballets, including *Electric Counterpoint* (2008) for The Royal Ballet, before his resignation in 2010.

Working freelance, in 2011 Wheeldon produced his acclaimed *Alice's Adventures in Wonderland* for The Royal Ballet, the company's first newly commissioned full-length ballet in over 10 years. More praise followed three years later with his staging of *The Winter's Tale*, by which time he was the company's artistic associate.

Beyond ballet, Wheeldon has also worked in theater, choreographing and directing *An American in Paris* in 2014, which earned him the 2015 Tony Award for Best Choreography. His portfolio even extends to working on films, including *Center Stage* (2000), *Ballets Russes* (2005), and *The Sleeping Beauty* (2008).

The mystery of Christopher Wheeldon deepens. Yes, he's the most talented of the younger ballet choreographers—indeed, where's the competition?

ROBERT GOTTLIEB, EDITOR

◀ **Seeking perfection**
Rehearsing for a performance of Michel Fokine's *The Firebird* (1910) in 1999, Wheeldon dances with Boston Ballet principal dancer, Adriana Suarez.

KEY WORKS

Choreographer: *Slavonic Dances*, 1997
Polyphonia, 2001 • *Variations Sérieuses*, 2001
Alice's Adventures in Wonderland, 2011 • *The Winter's Tale*, 2014 • *Strapless*, 2016 • *The Nutcracker*, 2016 • *Corybantic Games*, 2018

TIMELINE

- March 22, 1973 Born in Yeovil, son of an engineer and a physical therapist.
- 1981 Takes lessons at the East Coker Ballet School, moving to The Royal Ballet School in London three years later.
- 1990 Wins The Royal Ballet School's Ursula Moreton Choreographic Award.
- 1991 Enters The Royal Ballet, London, after winning the Prix de Lausanne with a solo of his own creation.
- 1993 Joins New York City Ballet, becoming soloist five years later.
- 2000 Retires from dance to concentrate on choreography.
- 2004 Creates *Swan Lake* for the Pennsylvania Ballet, blending traditional and modern choreography.
- 2007 Establishes Morphoses/The Wheeldon Company as a vehicle for his own productions.
- 2010 Resigns from his company, preferring to work freelance instead.
- 2011 Creates *Alice's Adventures in Wonderland* for The Royal Ballet, London.
- 2012 Collaborates with Alastair Marriott on the closing ceremony of the London Olympic Games.
- 2012 Becomes artistic associate of The Royal Ballet in London.
- 2016 Made an OBE in the Queen's New Year's Honours List.
- 2016 Creates *The Nutcracker* for the Joffrey Ballet, Chicago, transposing this classic work to a new setting.

SARAH LAMB PERFORMS WHEELDON'S *ELECTRIC COUNTERPOINT* IN LONDON

UPDATING THE CLASSICS

As ballet technique and audience tastes have altered over the years, so, too, have ballet's classics. By bringing new elements to traditional works, companies have been able to revive classics and introduce audiences to contemporary innovative ballets while at the same time honoring iconic works.

From the choreography and the score to the costumes and the set, any aspect of a classic can be reworked to make it accessible to a different audience. *Giselle* is a prime example, and in 1984, Frederic Franklin staged a version—known as *Creole Giselle*—for Dance Theater of Harlem, shifting the setting to a Louisiana sugar plantation in the 1840s. While some critics considered this ballet to be secondary to the original, many viewed it as a great accomplishment with its inclusion of an entirely African American cast, rarely seen in a production of a classic. In a similar vein, Graeme Murphy re-imagined *The Nutcracker* in 1992 for The Australian Ballet, adapting the narrative to include the story of the heritage of ballet in Australia, while still maintaining the magic of the original tale.

The 21st century is seeing yet more experiments with tradition. Matthew Bourne, who has completely re-imagined all of Tchaikovsky's masterpieces, turned to *The Sleeping Beauty* in 2012. With the inclusion of vampires and fairies, Bourne's revival has been described as an "exuberant re-imagining" and transports the audience to different times, starting in the fin de siècle period through to the Edwardian era and finishing in the modern day.

Companies, directors, and choreographers can meet with resistance when updating classic ballets. Tamara Rojo, director of English National Ballet, nonetheless views reinvigorating as essential, and said she would like "the repertoire [to be] consistently revived with a new vision and artistic direction that, sometimes, makes works wonderfully relevant and new."

> [For a classic ballet] to stay important and relevant to the next generation it has to adapt, it has to evolve.
>
> AKRAM KHAN

English National Ballet, 2016 ▶
Alina Cojocaru and Isaac Hernandez perform in Akram Khan's *Giselle*, which moves the action to an industrial setting and sees workers toiling behind an ominous wall.

Other key figures

Organized chronologically from 1800 to the present day, this directory gives a brief overview of additional individuals who have made an important impact in ballet. Many of these are dancers who went on to become teachers, directors, and choreographers.

August Bournonville

1805–1879

DANCER AND CHOREOGRAPHER

Born in Copenhagen, Denmark, into a family of dancers and choreographers, August Bournonville went on to become director of the Royal Danish Ballet. After studying with his father, celebrated dancer Antoine Bournonville, August traveled to Paris to train with Auguste Vestris. He performed at the Paris Opéra and in London, before returning to Denmark. Bournonville joined the Royal Danish Ballet as soloist and choreographer. Although his style was influenced by his training in Paris, Bournonville developed a distinct Danish style of ballet: clean, controlled, and classical. His choreography is notable for the equal prominence it gives to male and female dancers at a time when the role of the ballerina was most celebrated.

KEY WORKS: (Choreographer) *La Sylphide*, 1836; *Napoli*, 1842; *A Folk Tale*, 1854

▲ MICHEL FOKINE AND TAMARA KARSAVINA IN *THE FIREBIRD*, 1910

▽ Michel Fokine

1880–1942

DANCER AND CHOREOGRAPHER

Fokine joined the Imperial Ballet School at the Mariinsky Theater in his native St. Petersburg in 1889, at the age of nine. He was a talented dancer, but also an avid artist, and his broad interest in the visual arts profoundly influenced his choreography. In 1905, he created a solo, *The Dying Swan*, for Anna Pavlova. The dance encapsulates Fokine's desire for fluidity of movement and stylistic accuracy in ballet.

Fokine choreographed for Sergei Diaghilev's Ballets Russes from 1909 until 1914, when World War I made touring in Europe increasingly difficult and audiences were diminished. Fokine moved to Sweden in 1918 and later to the US, where he founded the American Ballet in New York in 1924. His works form a significant part of the repertoire of 20th-century ballet.

KEY WORKS: (Choreographer) *The Dying Swan*, 1905; *Les Sylphides*, 1909; *The Firebird*, 1910; *Petrushka*, 1911

Sergei Prokofiev

1891–1953

COMPOSER

Original in his musical talent and naturally gifted, Prokofiev was plucked by his mother from a countryside childhood in Sontsovka, Ukraine, and enrolled at the age of 13 at St. Petersburg's prestigious conservatory, where he studied musical theory and composition. Inspired by modernist trends in painting, theater, and poetry, Prokofiev was an avid innovator, and initially found success in his homeland. As opportunities dwindled in Russia following the revolution, he was permitted to travel to the West, where he rekindled contact with Sergei Diaghilev in Paris, having first met the impresario in 1914. There, in 1921, he produced his first ballet, *Chout*, for the Ballets Russes, which he followed with his one-act ballets *Le Pas d'acier* (1926) and *The Prodigal Son* (1928).

After a string of triumphant symphonies, concerti, and operas, Prokofiev reached the pinnacle of his ballet career with his reworked score for Leonid Lavrovsky's *Romeo and Juliet* in 1940.

KEY WORKS: *Romeo and Juliet*, 1940; *Cinderella*, 1945; *The Stone Flower*, 1954

Bronislava Nijinska

1891–1972

DANCER AND CHOREOGRAPHER

After training at the Imperial Ballet School in St. Petersburg, Nijinska danced with the company from 1908. She then joined the Ballets Russes, where she performed alongside her brother, Vaslav Nijinsky, and helped him with his choreography. Nijinska went on to create her own works and Diaghilev invited her to choreograph for the Ballets Russes beginning in 1921. At the outbreak of World War I, she moved to the US, where she opened a ballet school and choreographed for various companies.

KEY WORKS: (Choreographer) *Les Noces*, 1923; *Les Biches*, 1924

Kurt Jooss

1901–1979

BALLET MASTER AND CHOREOGRAPHER

Born in Germany, Jooss had an avid interest in dance as a child, and although he had received little previous training, aged 18 he became a student of Rudolf Laban—whose theories later came to underpin modern dance. In 1924, Jooss became ballet master at the Municipal Theater of Münster, and established his own company, Neue Tanzbühne. As the company's choreographer, Jooss often collaborated with the composer, Frederick Cohen, and they produced many important works together, notably *The Green Table* in 1932. With Hitler's rise, Jooss moved to Dartington Hall in the UK, where he continued to choreograph and teach.

KEY WORKS: (Choreographer) *The Green Table*, 1932; *The Big City*, 1932; *The Seven Heroes*, 1933

Antony Tudor

1908–1972

DANCER AND CHOREOGRAPHER

Born William Cook, Tudor worked in London as an office clerk before seeking a career in ballet. After seeing the Ballets Russes perform, in 1928 he joined Marie Rambert's school, paying his way by working for the school and also playing the piano. After studying different dance forms from around the world, Tudor produced his first significant ballet in 1936, *Jardin aux Lilas*.

In 1940, he moved to New York as resident choreographer at Ballet Theatre. He then created works for the New York City Ballet, but later became a teacher and directed different companies.

KEY WORKS: (Choreographer) *Jardin aux Lilas*, 1936; *Pillar of Fire*, 1942; *Echoes of Trumpets*, 1963

▲ ALICIA ALONSO IN THE LEAD ROLE OF *GISELLE* IN 1947

△ Alicia Alonso

1921–

DANCER AND CHOREOGRAPHER

Born Alicia Martínez, Alonso grew up in Havana, Cuba, and studied ballet at the Sociedad Pro-Arte Musical. Aged 16, she married fellow dancer, Fernando Alonso, and moved to New York, where she trained at the School of American Ballet. In 1940, she joined Ballet Theatre but began to be troubled by the poor eyesight that was to plague her later career.

In 1943, she danced the lead in *Giselle*, one of her celebrated roles. Soon recognized for her dramatic and precise technique, she became the company's principal dancer three years later.

Alonso founded her own ballet company in Cuba in 1948, though it struggled financially and closed in 1955. She also toured with various companies, but returned to Cuba after Fidel Castro's rise to power, and founded the Cuban National Ballet in 1959.

KEY WORKS: (Dancer) *Giselle*, 1943; *Carmen* 1967

Maya Plisetskaya

1925–2015

DANCER AND CHOREOGRAPHER

Plisetskaya was born into a Jewish family in Moscow. Her father, once hailed a Soviet hero, was arrested in Stalin's purges and executed. After her mother was sent to a Gulag camp, Plisetskaya joined the Bolshoi Ballet aged nine, which became her home.

When Galina Ulanova retired in 1960, Plisetskaya became prima ballerina, and epitomized the company's spirit with her raw and unpretentious dancing. After touring with the Bolshoi in 1959, she became a global superstar.

Despite her fame, Plisetskaya was constantly monitored by the KGB, and she expressed her political struggles through her work. Soviet leader Nikita Khrushchev lauded her as a great example of Soviet artistic success—the dancer who did not defect. She continued to perform on stage well into her 60s.

KEY WORKS: (Dancer) *Swan Lake*, 1957; *The Dying Swan*, 1957

Maria Tallchief

1925–2013

DANCER AND CHOREOGRAPHER

Born in Oklahoma, Tallchief began studying ballet at the age of three. Her family moved to Los Angeles, where Tallchief trained with Bronislava Nijinska, who instilled a love of ballet in the 12-year-old. When she was 17, she moved to New York to dance with the Ballet Russe de Monte Carlo under choreographer George Balanchine.

When Balanchine moved to work with the Paris Opéra Ballet in 1946, Tallchief joined him. The pair then returned to New York, and to what is now Balanchine's New York City Ballet, and Tallchief became its first prima ballerina. She left the company in 1960 and retired from dancing six years later. In 1981, Tallchief set up the Chicago City Ballet with her sister, which ran until 1987.

KEY WORKS: (Dancer) *The Firebird*, 1949; *The Nutcracker*, 1954

Moira Shearer

1926–2006

DANCER AND ACTRESS

Born in Scotland, Shearer spent her early childhood in Northern Rhodesia, where she first studied dance. Her family returned to the UK in 1936, where she trained under Nicholas Legat, before studying at Sadler's Wells School until 1939. Shearer later joined Sadler's Wells Ballet. While she had a successful classical dancing career, Shearer is best known for starring in the film, *The Red Shoes* (1948), which popularized ballet in the UK and the US.

KEY WORKS: (Dancer) *The Sleeping Beauty*, 1946; *Symphonic Variations*, 1946; *Cinderella*, 1948; *The Red Shoes*, 1948 (film)

▲ ROBERT JOFFREY AT A SUMMER WORKSHOP, 1961

△ Robert Joffrey

1930–1988

DANCER AND CHOREOGRAPHER

Born in Washington to an Afghan father and Italian mother, Joffrey first studied ballet in Seattle at the age of nine. He later moved to New York, where he trained at the School of American Ballet, before joining the Paris Opéra Ballet under Roland Petit, making his debut there in 1949. Returning to New York, Joffrey founded his own school, the Joffrey Ballet School, in 1953.

With a background in modern dance as well as classical ballet, Joffrey blended different dance styles in his works. In 1954, he founded the Robert Joffrey Ballet Concert (later the City Center Joffrey Ballet, then the Joffrey Ballet), staging works by leading choreographers, as well as his own. His style of choreography proved hugely influential and perfectly reflected the youthful vitality of the period.

KEY WORKS: (Choreographer) *Pas des Déesses*, 1956; *Gamelan*, 1962; *Postcards*, 1980

Alvin Ailey

1931–1989

DANCER AND CHOREOGRAPHER

Ailey was born in Texas but at the age of 11 moved to Los Angeles, California, where he decided to pursue a career in dance. In 1949, Ailey joined the school of Lester Horton's Dance Theater—the only mixed-race dance school in the US at the time—where he studied several forms of dance, including ballet, jazz, and Native American dances. After Horton's sudden death in 1953, Ailey briefly became the company's artistic director, aged just 22, choreographing and directing its performances.

In 1954, Ailey traveled to New York, where he appeared in a number of Broadway shows, before founding his own company, the Alvin Ailey American Dance Theater, in 1958. With an ensemble of just seven all-black dancers, it staged its debut performance the same year, premiering Ailey's own work, *Blues Suite*.

Reflecting his early training, Ailey's energetic choreography incorporated many dancing styles, and often drew inspiration from the music of his childhood in the south. Extremely prolific, Ailey created 79 original ballets.

KEY WORKS: (Choreographer) *Blues Suite*, 1958; *Revelations, 1960*

Hans van Manen

1932–

DANCER AND CHOREOGRAPHER

Born in Amsterdam, van Manen first trained at Ballet Recital under Sonia Gaskell, before joining the Netherlands Opera Ballet, aged 19. After a brief stint with the Ballets de Paris, van Manen joined the Nederlands Dans Theater (NDT) as choreographer and artistic director until 1971. After periods with the Dutch National Ballet and NDT, he is now resident choreographer at the Dutch National Ballet. Founded on classical ballet with elements from other dance forms, his work has an austere, voyeuristic quality.

KEY WORKS: (Choreographer) *Feestgericht*, 1957; *Four Schumann Pieces*, 1975; *Live*, 1979

▽ Ekaterina Maximova

1939–2009

DANCER AND CHOREOGRAPHER

Born in Moscow, Maximova trained at the Bolshoi School, before joining the company in 1958. When Galina Ulanova retired from dancing, she coached Maximova throughout her career. Maximova also forged a close partnership with fellow dancer Vladimir Vasiliev, whom she married in 1961.

After leaving the Bolshoi, Maximova danced with many companies around the world, including the Ballet de Marseille, the English National Ballet, and the Joffrey Ballet. She was also a successful actress, gaining fame for her performance in Franco Zeffirelli's 1982 film version of Verdi's *La Traviata*. After retiring from dancing, Maximova worked as a coach at the Kremlin Ballet and the Russian Academy of Theater Arts.

KEY WORKS: (Dancer) *Giselle*, 1958; *The Stone Flower*, 1959; *Cinderella, 1963; The Nutcracker*, 1966; *Spartacus*, 1968

▲ EKATERINA MAXIMOVA AND VLADIMIR VASILIEV DANCE THE LEAD ROLES IN *GISELLE*

Natalia Makarova

1940–

DANCER AND CHOREOGRAPHER

Makarova was born in Leningrad (St. Petersburg) and studied ballet from the relatively late age of 13 at Leningrad Choreographic School (later the Vaganova Academy). In 1956, she joined the Kirov, and soon became prima ballerina. She toured with the company until 1970, when she defected while in London.

Already well known for her classical roles, she was eager to embrace more contemporary choreography after her defection. Audiences were drawn to her emotive, supple, and tender style of dance. She returned to the Kirov in 1989 for a final performance before retiring from dance.

KEY WORKS: (Dancer) *Giselle*, 1961; *Swan Lake*, 1970

▷ Vladimir Vasiliev

1940–

CHOREOGRAPHER AND DANCER

Vasiliev grew up in Moscow, where he studied at the Bolshoi School from the age of seven. He eventually joined the company in 1958, becoming principal dancer the following year. His dance partner, and fellow principal, was former classmate, Ekaterina Maximova. They were a dancing sensation and became global stars following the Bolshoi's triumphant tour to New York in 1959. They married in 1961, and despite their international fame, they remained in Russia.

As a dancer, Vasiliev was renowned for his physical strength and charisma, which embodied the spirit of the Bolshoi during the 1980s. Following the departure of Yuri Grigorovich, Vasiliev became director of the company in 1995, until he was fired under the orders of Russian president, Vladimir Putin, in 2000. Vasiliev continues to work as a choreographer, with projects in Italy, Brazil, and China.

KEY WORKS: (Dancer) *Spartacus*, 1968

▲ VLADIMIR VASILIEV AS SPARTACUS AT THE BOLSHOI THEATER IN 1968

Twyla Tharp

1941–

DANCER AND CHOREOGRAPHER

Born in Indiana, Tharp learned different dance styles in her youth, before being tutored in New York by choreographer and dancer Martha Graham. In 1965, she founded Twyla Tharp Dance, and began to create her own work, pushing the boundaries of modern dance and ballet.

To date, Twyla Tharp has choreographed some 160 works, including four ballets, and has also worked in television and film, including *Hair* (1979) and *Amadeus* (1984).

KEY WORKS: (Choreographer) *Push Comes to Shove*, 1976

Suzanne Farrell

1945–

DANCER

Farrell was born in Cincinnati, Ohio, and in 1960 won a scholarship to the School of American Ballet. There, George Balanchine fell in love with her, casting her in the leading role in many of his ballets.

In 1965, Farrell's career took off when she danced Dulcinea in *Don Quixote*, with Balanchine in the title role. She soon became principal ballerina at the New York City Ballet, her many performances including a classically cool Diamonds in the original cast for *Jewels*.

Farrell retired as a dancer in 1989 and became a teacher and coach. In 1993, she started teaching at the Kennedy Center for the Performing Arts and, in 2000, founded the Suzanne Farrell Ballet, disbanded in 2017.

KEY WORKS: *Don Quixote*, 1965; *Jewels*, 1967; *Tzigane*, 1975; *Le Bourgeois gentilhomme*, 1980; *Mozartiana*, 1981

Gailene Stock

1946–2014

DANCER AND TEACHER

Born in Ballarat, Australia, Stock suffered polio as a child and was told she might never walk again. However, the avid dancer was back at ballet class within a few years. Aged 16, she won a scholarship to London's Royal Ballet School, where she studied for a year before returning to Australia to join The Australian Ballet. She toured Europe and North America with the company before moving to Canada, where she danced as a principal with the Royal Winnipeg Ballet and the National Ballet of Canada.

After returning to The Australian Ballet, Stock retired as a dancer in 1978, and turned her attention to teaching and directing at the National Ballet School. In 1999, she was invited to become director at The Royal Ballet School in London, where she oversaw major changes, including the building of new premises next to the Royal Opera House in Covent Garden.

Jorge Donn

1947–1992

DANCER AND CHOREOGRAPHER

Born in Buenos Aires, Argentina, Donn began dancing at the age of four, before studying at the Teatro Colón school. Inspired by Maurice Béjart's Ballet of the Twentieth Century, which toured Argentina, he later joined the company in Brussels and soon became its principal dancer. Throughout his career, Donn worked closely with Béjart, who choreographed roles for him. He later became the company's artistic director, and set up his own enterprise, L'Europa Ballet.

KEY WORKS: (Dancer) *Nijinsky, Clown de Dieu* 1971; *Golestan ou le jardin des roses*, 1973; *Boléro* 1979

▲ YOKO MORISHITA TAKES A CURTAIN CALL WITH THE ZURICH BALLET IN 1980

△ Yoko Morishita

1948–

DANCER

Morishita was born in Hiroshima, Japan, three years after the city was devastated by an atomic bomb. She started ballet at the age of three and moved to Tokyo to train at the Tachibani Ballet School. She joined the Asami Maki Ballet at the age of 16, then moved to the Matsuyama Ballet Company in 1971, where she debuted in *Swan Lake* in 1975. First promoted to principal, then prima ballerina, Morishita was the first Japanese ballet dancer to achieve international success.

During her career she worked with leading ballet stars, such as Nureyev and Fonteyn, which helped her to develop her own flawless technique.

KEY WORKS: *Swan Lake, 1975; Giselle, 1977*

▷ Karen Kain

1951–

DANCER AND DIRECTOR

Born in Ontario, Canada, Kain first took ballet classes to improve her posture and discipline. Aged 11, she began training at the National Ballet School in Toronto, and in 1969 joined the National Ballet of Canada. Within two years, after dancing the lead in *Swan Lake*, she was promoted to principal. During her career she worked closely with Rudolf Nureyev and partnered him many times. She also danced with international companies, including the Bolshoi, Le Ballet de Marseille, the Paris Opéra Ballet, the London Festival Ballet, and the Vienna State Opera Ballet.

After retiring from dance in 1997, Kain continued to work with the National Ballet of Canada as artist-in-residence and was appointed its artistic director in 2005.

KEY WORKS: (Dancer) *Swan Lake*, 1971; *Intermezzo*, 1971; *The Sleeping Beauty*, 1972

Gelsey Kirkland

1952–

DANCER

Born to playwright father Jack Kirkland in Pennsylvania, Kirkland took ballet classes with her sister Johann. Both went on to train at the School of American Ballet in New York, where Kirkland was spotted by George Balanchine, who invited her to join the New York City Ballet aged just 15. In the early 1970s, she was appointed principal and danced the lead in some of Balanchine's creations, including *The Firebird*, which he adapted for her.

In 1974, Kirkland moved to American Ballet Theatre to join Mikhail Baryshnikov. However, over the next 10 years her constant search for perfection drove her to drug addiction and mental health problems. Seeking a new start, Kirkland moved to London in 1984 and joined The Royal Ballet, where she partnered Anthony Dowell to great acclaim.

Kirkland published two frank autobiographies, *Dancing on My Grave* (1986) and *The Shape of Love* (1990), in which she detailed her struggles. Having rebuilt her life and career, Kirkland returned to the US in the early 1990s, and began teaching at the American Ballet Theatre. She also founded the Gelsey Kirkland Academy of Classical Ballet in New York with her husband, fellow dancer and choreographer Michael Chernov.

KEY WORKS: *The Firebird*, 1970; *Giselle*, 1975; *Swan Lake*, 1977; *The Nutcracker*, 1977

▲ KAREN KAIN HOLDS A POSE, 1986

Fernando Bujones

1955–2005

DANCER AND DIRECTOR

Bujones was born into a Cuban family in Miami, Florida. He first learned ballet at Alicia Alonso's Cuban National Ballet in Havana before studying at the School of American Ballet in New York. After joining American Ballet Theatre (ABT), he became the company's youngest principal in 1974, aged 19. That same year, Bujones became the first male American dancer to win a gold medal at the International Ballet Competition in Varna, Bulgaria. He worked closely with Mikhail Baryshnikov while at ABT, although the two became rivals.

After a career as a guest artist at many of the world's leading ballet companies, Bujones retired in 1993. He then became artistic director for Ballet Mississippi and Orlando Ballet.

KEY WORKS: (Dancer) *Don Quixote*, 1970; *Les Patineurs*, 1976; *La Sylphide*, 1977

James Kudelka

1955–

DANCER AND CHOREOGRAPHER

Born in Ontario, Canada, Kudelka trained at the National Ballet School, where he choreographed his own works. He joined the National Ballet of Canada in 1972 and danced with the company until 1981, when he moved to Les Grands Ballets Canadiens.

Kudelka's choreography centers on reworking classics, along with smaller-scale, more abstract works. In 1996, he was appointed artistic director at the National Ballet of Canada, where he remained for 11 years. He continues to teach and direct.

KEY WORKS: (Choreographer) *The Nutcracker*, 1995; *Cinderella*, 2004

▲ REX HARRINGTON AS LEWIS CAROL IN *ALICE*, 1986

◁ Rex Harrington

1962–

DANCER

Born in Ontario, Canada, Harrington went on to study at Canada's National Ballet School before joining the National Ballet of Canada in 1983. He was promoted to principal dancer in 1988, and during his 20-year career with the company, partnered many leading dancers including Ekaterina Maximova, Karen Kain, and Evelyn Hart. As a guest artist, he danced with the Royal Winnipeg Ballet, La Scala Theater Ballet, the San Francisco Ballet, and the Stuttgart Ballet. Although Harrington retired as a dancer in 2004, he remains at the National Ballet of Canada as artist-in-residence. He has also recently forged a successful career in Canadian television.

KEY WORKS: *Don Quixote*, 1986; *Romeo and Juliet*, 1990; *Onegin*, 1990; *The Four Seasons*, 1997

Uwe Scholz

1958–2004

DANCER AND CHOREOGRAPHER

Scholz was born in Jugenheim, Germany, and started music and ballet lessons at the age of four. From the age of 13, he trained at the John Cranko Academy in Stuttgart, where he was taught by Marcia Haydée. She encouraged him to start choreographing—he produced his first piece, *Serenade for 5+1* in 1976—and mentored him throughout his career.

Scholz won a scholarship to study at George Balanchine's School of American Ballet, which he accepted before returning to Stuttgart in 1977 to complete his training. He then joined the Stuttgart Ballet as a dancer and became its resident choreographer three years later.

At the age of 26, Scholz moved to the Zurich Ballet to take the post of artistic director. After six years, he returned to Germany to direct the Leipzig Ballet, where he spent the remainder of his career. Scholz was a prolific choreographer and his work reflected his eclectic taste in music.

KEY WORKS: (Choreographer) *The Red and the Black*, 1988; *Symphonie Fantastique*, 1993; *Great Mass*, 1998

Nicolette Fraillon

1960–

CONDUCTOR

Born in Melbourne, Australia, Fraillon learned to play piano and violin as a child, before studying at the University of Melbourne. In 1984, she trained in conducting at the Hochschule für Musik in Vienna, and made her debut at the Nederlands Dans Theater in 1990. She later became music director and chief conductor at the Dutch National Ballet, and worked with many other European orchestras. Returning to Australia in 1997, Fraillon joined the Australian National University School of Music in Canberra as director, and in 2003 became chief conductor and music director for The Australian Ballet.

Russell Maliphant

1961–

DANCER AND CHOREOGRAPHER

Maliphant was born in Canada but grew up in Cheltenham, Gloucestershire. He studied ballet at The Royal Ballet School in London from the age of 16, before joining The Royal Ballet three years later. After eight years, he left the company in 1988 in order to explore other forms of dance. He collaborated with the dance company DV8, and choreographers including Rosemary Butcher and Laurie Booth. As well as exploring other forms of human movement, including tai chi and capoeira, Maliphant also studied biomechanics, physiology, and anatomy to help inform his choreography. In 1996, he set up the Russell Maliphant Company, where he created his distinctive style, while also producing works for other leading companies.

KEY WORKS: (Choreographer) *Broken Fall*, 2003; *Push*, 2005; *Solo*, 2005

Alessandra Ferri

1963–

DANCER

Ferri was born in Milan and trained at the city's La Scala Ballet School. She later transferred to The Royal Ballet School in London and won a scholarship to continue there. She joined The Royal Ballet in 1980, where she was made principal aged 19. In 1985, she joined Baryshnikov's American Ballet Theatre, where she formed a strong partnership with Julio Bocca. She was a guest artist with the Paris Opéra Ballet and the Mariinsky, and guest principal with La Scala Theater Ballet. She excelled in Kenneth MacMillan's story ballets.

KEY WORKS: *Valley of Shadows*, 1983; *Romeo and Juliet*, 1984; *Woolf Works*, 2015

Wendy Whelan

1967–

DANCER AND CHOREOGRAPHER

Whelan grew up in Louisville, Kentucky, where she began dance lessons aged three. She started training with the School of American Ballet at 14, before eventually moving to New York to study full time. In 1985, Whelan joined the New York City Ballet, where she stayed for 30 years, dancing in Balanchine's creations and working with Jerome Robbins and many other choreographers for whom she originated roles. Her strength and muscularity were well suited to Balanchine's choreography. Whelan also appeared as a guest artist with The Royal Ballet and the Kirov. After retiring as a dancer in 2014, she was appointed an artistic associate with the New York City Center.

KEY WORKS: (Dancer) *The Nutcracker*, 1989; *Labyrinth Within*, 2010; *Restless Creature*, 2012

▲ MISTY COPELAND AT SADLER'S WELLS THEATRE, 2011

Crystal Pite

1970–

DANCER AND CHOREOGRAPHER

Pite grew up in Victoria, British Columbia, where she danced and choreographed from a very young age. She trained with Maureen Eastick and Wendy Green, and choreographed dances for her classmates. In 1988, she joined the Ballet British Columbia, where she created her first professional work the following year, *Between the Bliss and Me*. She left Canada in 1996 to join William Forsythe's Ballett Frankfurt, where she danced on tour and developed choreography with Forsythe.

Pite returned to Canada in 2001, and in 2002 set up Kidd Pivot dance company in Vancouver. She also choreographs for the Nederlands Dans Theater and the National Ballet of Canada, and has worked as associate artist with Sadler's Wells, London.

KEY WORKS: (Choreographer) *Between the Bliss and Me*, 1990; *Double Story*, 2002; *Man Asunder*, 2004; *Lost Action*, 2007; *Dark Matters*, 2009

Tetsuya Kumakawa

1972–

DANCER AND DIRECTOR

Born in Hokkaido, Japan, Kumakawa started ballet aged 10, taking lessons in Sapporo. Aged 13, he entered and won a competition in Tokyo, which encouraged him to focus his training. He won a scholarship to study at The Royal Ballet School and so left Japan, aged 15, for London. A year later, Kumakawa was offered a contract to join The Royal Ballet, and became the company's youngest soloist. The role of the Fool in *The Prince of the Pagodas* was choreographed by Kenneth MacMillan especially for him.

In 1998, Kumakawa left The Royal Ballet, along with five other dancers, and set up a new company, K-Ballet, in Japan. Then in 2003, he established the K-Ballet School.

KEY WORKS: (Dancer) *The Prince of the Pagodas*, 1989; *Don Quixote*, 1993

Ethan Stiefel

1973–

DANCER AND DIRECTOR

Ethan Stiefel was born in Pennsylvania and studied ballet from the age of eight, eventually moving to New York to train at the School of American Ballet. He trained alongside Mikhail Baryshnikov, whose School of Classical Ballet he later danced with. In 1989, Stiefel joined the New York City Ballet, and he was made a principal in 1995. He moved to the American Ballet Theatre in 1997, and worked as a guest artist for various companies, including The Royal Ballet, the Mariinsky, and the National Ballet of Canada.

After retiring as a dancer, Stiefel focused on teaching and directing. He set up Stiefel & Students, a summer workshop for young dancers to train with leading professionals. He also worked as artistic director for Ballet Pacifica, and became dean of the University of California's School of Dance and director of the Royal New Zealand Ballet.

KEY WORKS: (Dancer) *Romeo and Juliet*, 2004; *Don Quixote*, 2007; *Swan Lake*, 2009; (Choreography) *The Nutcracker*, 2009

Roberto Bolle

1975–

DANCER

Born in Piedmont, Italy, Bolle studied ballet from an early age and went to train at the ballet school of La Scala Theater in Milan, aged 12. He joined La Scala Theater Ballet and made his debut in *Romeo and Juliet* aged 20, and was promoted to principal soon after. Bolle left La Scala just a year later to dance with various companies, including The Royal Ballet, the Stuttgart Ballet, and the National Ballet of Canada.

In 2003, Bolle was appointed étoile at La Scala, where he partnered Alessandra Ferri. He joined the American Ballet Theatre as principal in 2009. He has danced many of the famous classical ballets for various companies, including lead roles.

KEY WORKS: *Romeo and Juliet*, 1995; *La Bayadère*, 2006; *Manon*, 2007

◁ Misty Copeland

1982–

DANCER

Copeland was born in Kansas City but grew up in San Pedro, California, where she began studying ballet at the relatively late age of 13. She went on to train at the San Francisco Ballet School, and attended a summer school program with the American Ballet Theatre, for which she had won a scholarship.

In 2001, Copeland joined American Ballet Theatre's corps de ballet, and was promoted to soloist six years later. Following a string of highly acclaimed performances, she was further promoted to principal dancer in 2015, becoming the first African American woman to hold the position at the company.

During her career, Copeland has danced a varied repertoire of classical and contemporary roles, and has frequently worked with choreographer Alexei Ratmansky. Credited with changing the face of ballet, and for diversifying the art form, Copeland was named one of *TIME* magazine's most influential women in 2015.

KEY WORKS: *The Nutcracker*, 2014; *Swan Lake*, 2014; *Romeo and Juliet*, 2015

▽ Marianela Nuñez

1982–

DANCER AND CHOREOGRAPHER

Nuñez was born in Buenos Aires, Argentina, and began her ballet training at the school of Teatro Colón. She joined the company at the age of 14, and danced both in the corps and as a soloist, first touring Argentina and Cuba, then Europe and the US. In 1997, Nuñez joined The Royal Ballet School, then The Royal Ballet a year later. She became a principal in 2002, and went on to perform lead roles in classical and modern ballets. Nuñez received the Olivier Award for Outstanding Achievement in Dance in 2013.

KEY WORKS: (Dancer) *The Sleeping Beauty*, 2011; *Swan Lake*, 2015

▲ MARIANELA NUNEZ DANCES IN *DON QUIXOTE* WITH THE ROYAL BALLET, 2013

Liam Scarlett

1985–

DANCER AND CHOREOGRAPHER

Born in Ipswich, Suffolk, Scarlett began his training at the Linda Shipton School of Dancing. He joined The Royal Ballet School aged 11, where he went on to win the Kenneth MacMillan and the Ursula Moreton Choreographic Awards for his choreography. In 2005, he joined The Royal Ballet and became its first artist in 2008. After retiring as a dancer in 2012, he became The Royal Ballet's first artist-in-residence. Scarlett has choreographed many works for The Royal Ballet, as well as for other companies including New York City Ballet, American Ballet Theatre, and English National Ballet.

KEY WORKS: (Choreographer) *Liebestraum*, 2009; *Asphodel Meadows*, 2010; *Jubilee pas de deux*, 2012; *Frankenstein*, 2016

Steven McRae

1985–

DANCER AND CHOREOGRAPHER

McRae was born in Sydney, Australia, where he took classes in ballet and tap dancing from an early age. He entered dance competitions in Sydney, and in 2002 won the Adeline Genée Gold Medal. The following year, at the Prix de Lausanne in Switzerland, he won a scholarship to The Royal Ballet School. He went to train there, and in 2004 graduated to The Royal Ballet, where he was promoted to principal in 2009. McRae has also appeared as a guest artist with ballet companies worldwide, including American Ballet Theatre and Tokyo Ballet.

KEY WORKS: (Dancer) *Symphonic Variations*, 2005; *Alice in Wonderland*, 2011; *Frankenstein*, 2016; *Swan Lake*, 2017

▲ JUSTIN PECK DURING REHEARSALS IN NEW YORK, 2014

△ Justin Peck

1987–

DANCER AND CHOREOGRAPHER

Peck grew up in San Diego, California, and learned tap dancing as a child. He chose to study ballet at the age of 13 after being inspired by a performance of *Giselle* by American Ballet Theatre. Aged 15, he moved to New York and trained at the School of American Ballet.

Peck joined the New York City Ballet as an apprentice, on invitation from choreographer Peter Martins in 2006, and joined the company's corps de ballet the following year. In 2009, Peck started to work on his own choreography at the New York Choreographic Institute, and has since choreographed many works for the New York City Ballet.

In 2013, Peck was promoted to soloist, then the company's resident choreographer the following year. To date, he has created more than 30 ballets, which are performed by companies all over the world.

KEY WORKS: (Choreographer) *Year of the Rabbit*, 2012; *Everywhere We Go*, 2014

Other key ballets

This directory lists some of the other important works created during the celebrated history of ballet. Upon reception they were acclaimed by critics and audiences alike—for their gripping themes, curious stories, evocative music, and innovative choreography.

▲ VERA FOKINE, MICHEL'S WIFE, IN HER ROLE IN *SCHÉHÉRAZADE*, 1910

△ Schéhérazade

1910

The first work created for the Ballets Russes, *Schéhérazade* was set to a score adapted from Nikolay Rimsky-Korsakov's 1888 symphonic suite of the same name, which itself was inspired by tales from *The Arabian Nights*.

Léon Bakst's vivid Oriental costumes and sets and Michel Fokine's frenzied choreography were combined with a story of mass adultery and murderous vengeance. Set in a Persian harem, Shah Shahriar's favorite wife, Zoebéide, persuades the Chief Eunuch to release her slave lover—first played by a gold-painted Vaslav Nijinsky—and his fellow slaves while the Shah is away. However, Shahriar discovers the ensuing orgy and orders a mass blood-letting to avenge his concubine's infidelity.

The Golden Age

1930

Composer Dmitri Shostakovich's first of three forays into ballet, *The Golden Age* tells the tale of a Russian soccer team in an unnamed Western city. Over the course of three acts, each created by a different choreographer, the team overcomes various perceived enemies of the Communist system, including the Diva, the Agent Provocateur, and the Fascist. Despite suffering match rigging and police harassment, the team succeeds in spreading its revolutionary message—and when the players are unjustly imprisoned by the bourgeoisie, the local workers overthrow their capitalist masters and free their Soviet heroes. Despite its overtly socialist themes, *The Golden Age* was censored by the Stalinist authorities: its choreography was considered to be too Western for Soviet tastes.

▽ The Green Table

1932

A satirical, anti-war comment on the futility of peacemaking, *The Green Table* is the masterpiece of German choreographer Kurt Jooss. Blending formal ballet steps and free-flowing gestures into a form of Expressionistic dance-theater, Jooss's single-act ballet won the 1932 International Choreographic Prize in Paris.

The ballet charts the ruthless toll taken by Death throughout six scenes of war, each presenting a variation of the same theme. The Farewells precedes The Battle, and The Partisan, The Refugees, and The Brothel depict the collateral damage caused by conflict, while The Aftermath reveals the cruel outcome for survivors. The ballet ends as it begins, with a group of diplomats around a green negotiating table, culminating in gunshots and the declaration of war.

Fancy Free

1944

Inspired by *The Fleet's In!*, Paul Cadmus's bawdy painting of sailors on shore leave, *Fancy Free* was the first ballet choreographed by Jerome Robbins, who also danced in its initial showings. Premiered on April 18, 1944, at the Metropolitan Opera House, New York, its boisterous, comedic theme of three off-duty sailors vying for female attention hinted at the popular success that Robbins later achieved, not just in ballet, but in film, musical theater, and Broadway. Although rooted in classical technique, Robbins's choreography is peppered with zany solos and anarchic group dances as the sailors jostle to impress two beautiful girls, descend into fisticuffs, and set off in pursuit as a third female wanders by.

Fall River Legend

1948

Agnes de Mille choreographed for movies, stage musicals, dance theater, and ballet, and her work was distinguished by a close attention to dramatic detail, characterization, and plot.

▲ THE ROYAL BALLET OF FLANDERS PERFORMING KURT JOOSS'S *THE GREEN TABLE* IN 2015

▲ *"STILL LIFE" AT THE PENGUIN CAFE* PERFORMED BY THE ROYAL BALLET AT THE ROYAL OPERA HOUSE, LONDON, IN 1998

Her second ballet, *Fall River Legend*, was commissioned by American Ballet Theatre and had its premiere on April 22, 1948, at the Metropolitan Opera House, New York. Based on the real-life story of Massachusetts spinster Lizzie Borden, who in 1893 was acquitted of the ax-murder of her father and stepmother, it is considered de Mille's finest ballet. Gothic in style, and with a poignant, absorbing narrative, it portrays Borden as a shy, sensitive character hemmed in by small-town attitudes and driven to a murderous act, for which, in a twist from actual events, she is found guilty and hanged.

Dances at a Gathering

1969

Set to 18 pieces of Frédéric Chopin's delicate piano music, and inspired by the Slavic character of the Polish composer's homeland, *Dances at a Gathering* heralded American choreographer Jerome Robbins's return to New York City Ballet after a 13-year absence. Premiering on May 22, 1969, it drew immediate acclaim for its soft, graceful solos, pas de deux, and group dances, and its gentle portrayal of a peasant community. Widely regarded as Robbins's masterwork, it blends classical ballet and folk dance. Every step and gesture is informed by musicality, and a clear sense of camaraderie is shared between the cast of 10 dancers. Robbins described it as without plot or role—rather as a pure expression of a particular time and place through dance.

Leaves are Fading

1975

Antony Tudor's ballets are a form of psychological dance conveyed through pared-back choreography, Classical technique, subtle gesture, and minimal staging. *Leaves are Fading* was one of his last ballets, and marked his return to American Ballet Theatre after an absence of nearly 25 years. It was rapturously received when it premiered on July 17, 1975. Plotless in form, its theme is a woman's autumnal reminiscences of springs past, played out in a series of encounters—some playful, others romantic—in a brown-green sylvan glade, set against Antonin Dvorak's string chamber music. The nuanced, poetic, emotional work reaches its climax in a sequence of pas de deux, with heightening expressions of love passionately shared between successive couples.

△ "Still Life" at the Penguin Café

1988

Created by The Royal Ballet's resident choreographer David Bintley, *"Still Life" at the Penguin Café* masks a moral ecological message behind a seemingly frivolous and entertaining cast of characters from the vulnerable fringes of the natural world. The music of Simon Jeffes was both inspiration for the ballet's subject matter and score to the finished production. Clad in exaggerated masks and costumes, endangered species and human groups shelter from the rain in a café, dancing sometimes clumsily, sometimes poignantly, in styles themselves at risk of being lost from the dance repertoire. Bintley intended the ballet to be humorous but with a serious message of environmental responsibility at its heart.

The Four Seasons

1997

Technically inventive and emotionally literate, Canadian choreographer James Kudelka has created an array of ballets rich in classical steps and modern-dance technique. His aptitude for tackling established composers and classics is clear in *The Four Seasons*—a highly original ballet set to Vivaldi's string concerto that premiered on February 12, 1997, by the National Ballet of Canada. The work tells the story of a man passing through the four stages of life—youth, prime, middle age, and old age—each anchored by a pas de deux with a different ballerina, who personifies each season. Through complex ensemble dances and intricate, quick-paced solos and duets, spring's youthful optimism gives way to the romance of summer. In turn, autumn embodies contentment and the warmth of companionship, leading inevitably to winter's gradual decline and death.

Polyphonia

2001

British choreographer Christopher Wheeldon's breakthrough work, *Polyphonia* is an abstract ballet set to the piano music of György Ligeti. The ballet takes its name from "micropolyphony"—a distinctive compositional style developed by Ligeti, resulting in a dissonant sound described by Wheeldon as a "complex, twisted, layered world." Intricate, elegant, and at times acrobatic choreography is paired with a uniquely intense score, opening with an ensemble piece for the full cast of eight dancers, followed by a series of duets and solos, culminating in a dramatic ensemble dance.

Premiered by New York City Ballet, Wheeldon's emotive work was highly acclaimed, and drew glowing comparisons with the experimental ballets of George Balanchine. In 2001, Wheeldon was awarded the Critics' Circle Award for Best New Choreography for *Polyphonia*, followed by the Olivier Award for Best New Dance Production a year later.

Glossary

Adage (or Adagio) A series of exercises consisting of a succession of slow and graceful movements, which can be simple or complex. Also refers to the opening section of a classical pas de deux, in which the ballerina, assisted by her partner, performs slow movements and enlèvements.

Assemblé A move in which a dancer slides one foot along the floor before pushing off the other leg to raise both legs together in the air. The dancer then lands on both feet in a plié in fifth position.

Ballet d'action A ballet that tells a story, such as *Coppélia*.

Ballet de cour An early form of ballet performed in royal courts, by and for the nobility, during the 16th and 17th centuries, such as *Ballet Comique de la Reine*.

Ballet master/mistress The person in a ballet company whose duty is to give a daily company ballet class and rehearse ballets that the dancers will perform. Ballet masters and mistresses are considered part of an "artistic staff" of a ballet company and usually work very closely with both the director and dancers.

Ballet blanc Any ballet in which the ballerinas traditionally wear long white costumes, such as *Giselle* and *La Sylphide*.

Ballet Russe/Les Ballets Russes de Monte Carlo Following Sergei Diaghilev's death in 1929 and the demise of the Ballets Russes, impresario René Blum formed Les Ballets Russes de Monte Carlo with Colonel W. de Basil in 1932. Blum left the company in 1934, after which time the name underwent changes (Ballets Russes de Colonel W. de Basil, 1934–1937; Covent Garden Russian Ballet, 1938–1939; and Original Ballet Russe from 1939). Blum founded a new company in 1936, Ballets de Monte Carlo, which became Ballet Russe de Monte Carlo in 1938.

Character dance The term used to describe either a style that borrows from traditional folk dance, or dancing a role that requires acting, such as an animal.

Classical ballet A ballet that follows the definitive framework established in the 19th century. Most "story ballets" are regarded as classical ballets, such as *The Sleeping Beauty* and *Swan Lake*.

Coda The concluding segment of a classical performance, or the final dance of the pas de deux, trois, or quatre.

Contemporary ballet A genre that combines aspects of classical ballet—such as the pointing of the toes—with modern dance, which allows for more freedom of movement—for example, the turn-in of the legs rather than the traditional turnout seen in classical ballet.

Corps de ballet The ensemble of a ballet company—the dancers who do not appear as soloists or principals.

Danseur A male dancer.

Danseur, premier A leading male dancer of the company.

Danseuse A female dancer.

Danseuse, première A leading female dancer of the company.

Divertissement A light piece of music for a small group of dancers, often performed as an interlude between acts. It may be added to a ballet to display a dancer's particular talents.

Drambalet A type of ballet, most typically from the Soviet era, staged to deliver a political message, such as Leonid Lavrovsky's *Romeo and Juliet*.

Enlèvement A move in which the male dancer lifts his female partner in a step or pose.

Entrechat A step in which the dancer jumps into the air and rapidly crosses their legs before landing. There are many types, depending on the number of crosses made, and the position of the feet. For example, an entrechat

quatre has four crossings and the dancer lands on both feet; an entrechat cinq has five crossings and the dancer lands on one foot.

Entrée The arrival on stage of a dancer or dancers at the start of a divertissement, or the beginning of a grand pas de deux, when the pair make their entrance.

Épaulement The placement of a dancer's head and shoulders—one shoulder forward, the other back, with the head turned or inclined over the forward shoulder.

Fouetté The whipping movement of the raised foot ahead or behind the supporting foot or a rapid turning of the body from one direction to another.

Grand pas A series of dances that consist of 5–7 elements, including an entrée; grand adage; solo variations, female variations, male variations; and a coda.

Grand pas classique The execution of classical ballet moves dominate in this type of grand pas, rather than contributing to the story of the ballet.

Grand pas d'action This type of grand pas carries the action of the ballet forward by helping to tell a key part of the story.

Impresario The organizer, manager, or director of a ballet or ballet company.

Librettist The writer of a libretto.

Libretto The text used in, or intended for, an extended musical work. It contains all the words and stage directions.

Musique concrète A form of experimental music, which uses natural recorded sounds, such as noises from the environment, to create a musical montage.

Pas A classical ballet step or movement in which weight is transferred.

Pas de deux Two dancers perform a duet of ballet steps.

Pas de deux, Grand A pas de deux that follows a set structure, consisting of five elements: entrée, adage, female variation, male variation, and a coda.

Pas de trois Three dancers perform ballet steps together. Pas de quatre is for four dancers; pas de dix, for 10.

Plié A move in which a dancer bends their knees and then straightens them, performed with a turnout of the feet.

Pointe, en The dancer supports their body weight on the tips of their toes, usually while wearing reinforced pointe shoes.

Port de bras The movement of the arms from one position to another. Also, exercises designed to make dancers' arms move gracefully and harmoniously.

Régisseur The stage manager, particularly in France and Russia, who coordinates the work of the producer, stage technicians, and orchestra, and handles the company finances and tour arrangements.

Répétiteur A person who teaches dancers the steps and movements of a ballet, as it was originally intended by the choreographer.

Romantic ballet The style of ballet produced during the early 19th century, with a focus on storytelling or portraying a mood.

Super Costumed extra on stage, used to enhance setting.

Tableau A large picture on stage that is formed from an artistic grouping or formation of dancers. It is usually an important moment frozen in time, allowing the audience to digest the scene.

Travesti, en The portrayal of a character performed by a dancer of the opposite sex, such as the Ugly Sisters in stagings of Ashton's *Cinderella*, who are typically danced by men.

Variation A solo dance in classical ballet.

Index

Page numbers in **bold** refer to main entries.

A

B

C

D

E

F

G

H

I

J

K

L

Q

R

S

T

U

Z

Acknowledgments

Dorling Kindersley would like to thank the following people for their assistance with this book:

For original photography: Ruth Jenkinson at Ruth Jenkinson Photography; José Alves at Ballet Black and Fumi Kaneko at The Royal Ballet for modeling.

Jennifer Reiter Hand for her review of the contents list as US Consultant.

Rachel Hollings and Kate Shaw at The Royal Ballet.

Mike Markiewicz and Lotte Parmley at ArenaPal, Nicole Cornell at The George Balanchine Trust, Kina Poon at The New York City Ballet, Anna Meadmore at The Royal Ballet School, Sophie Rafalowska-Dunning at Performing Arts Artists Management LLP, Oliver Tobin at Martha Graham Resources, Christopher Nourse at The Frederick Ashton Foundation.

Anna Chiefetz, Michael Clark, Arpita Dasgupta, Richard Gilbert, Ruth O'Rourke-Jones, Victoria Pyke, Jennifer Reiter Hand, Rohan Sinha, and Andy Szudek for editorial assistance; Phil Gamble, Renata Latipova, Anjali Sachar, and Simran Saini for design assistance; Steve Crozier for retouching; Alexandra Beeden for proofreading; and Helen Peters for indexing.

The publisher would like to thank the following for their kind permission to reproduce their photographs:

(Key: a-above; b-below/bottom; c-centre; f-far; l-left; r-right; t-top)

4 Alamy Stock Photo: Andriy Bezuglov (tr). **5 ArenaPAL:** Johan Persson (tr); Asya Verzhbinsky (tl); Royal Academy of Dance (tc). **6 Alamy Stock Photo:** Nikolay Vinokurov (tl, tr). **7 Alamy Stock Photo:** National Geographic Creative (tr). **Getty Images:** Cover / Quim Llenas (tl). **10 Getty Images:** Gemma Levine. **14 Waddesdon Manor:** Imaging Services Bodleian Library © National Trust, Waddesdon Manor / Attributed to Henri Gissey, Scenery Design of Sea Shore for First Watch, 1st Entrée: "Ballet de la Nuit", 1653; Waddesdon (National Trust) Bequest of James de Rothschild, 1957; acc. no. 3666.3.2. (c). **16 Alamy Stock Photo:** Paul Fearn. **17 Alamy Stock Photo:** Art Collection 2 (cra). **ArenaPAL:** Roger-Viollet (crb). **18-19 Getty Images:** Heritage Images / Fine Art Images. **20 ArenaPAL:** Collection Christophel (br). **Getty Images:** API / Gamma-Rapho (bl). **21 Waddesdon Manor:** Imaging Services Bodleian Library © National Trust, Waddesdon Manor / Attributed to Henri Gissey, Scenery Design of Sea Shore for First Watch, 1st Entrée: "Ballet de la Nuit", 1653; Waddesdon (National Trust) Bequest of James de Rothschild, 1957; acc. no. 3666.3.2.. **22-23 Getty Images:** Paris Match / Helene Pambrun. **24 Alamy Stock Photo:** Chronicle (tr); Paul Fearn (cl). **25 Alamy Stock Photo:** Music-Images (cra). **Waddesdon Manor:** Imaging Services Bodleian Library © National Trust, Waddesdon Manor / Attributed to Henri Gissey, Scenery Design with Curieux Watching the Sabbath for Third Watch, 11th Entrée: "Ballet de la Nuit"; Waddesdon (National Trust) Bequest of James de Rothschild, 1957; acc. no. 3666.3.103. (cl). **26 ArenaPAL:** Roger-Viollet / Colette Masson (b). **27 Bibliothèque nationale de France, Paris:** (br). **The New York Public Library:** Jerome Robbins Dance Division, "L'Europe galante". (l). **28 akg-images:** Laurent Cars (cl). **Alamy Stock Photo:** Paul Fearn (tr). **29 Getty Images:** Paris Match / Patrick Jarnoux / Choreography by George Balanchine © The George Balanchine Trust (c). **Penrodas Collection:** (cr). **30-31 akg-images:** Castle Rheinsberg. **32 Alamy Stock Photo:** Art Collection 4 (tr); Florilegius (bl). **33 ArenaPAL:** Roger-Viollet (c). **Getty Images:** Print Collector / Hulton Archive (crb). **34-35 Alamy Stock Photo:** Marco Kesseler. **36 ArenaPAL:** Thompson Theatre Collection (tr). **Bridgeman Images:** Private Collection / The Stapleton Collection (bl). **37 The New York Public Library:** Jerome Robbins Dance Division, "Medée, dans l'opéra de Jason et Medée" (ca); Jerome Robbins Dance Division, "Jason et Médée, Ballet tragique." (br). **38-39 Getty Images:** Mondadori Portfolio / Archivio Angelo Cozzi / Angelo Cozzi. **42 Getty Images:** AFP Photo / Attila Kibenedek. **44 Bridgeman Images:** British Library, London, UK / British Library Board. All Rights Reserved (br). **Getty Images:** DEA / G. Dagli Orti (bl). **45 Bridgeman Images:** Musee des Arts Decoratifs, Paris, France. **46 Alamy Stock Photo:** Paul Fearn (tr). **Getty Images:** Photo Josse / Leemage / Corbis Historical (cl). **47 Alamy Stock Photo:** Paul Fearn (cra). **ArenaPAL:** Fine Art Images / Heritage Images / TopFoto (c). **48-49 Getty Images:** Cindy Ord (b). **48 akg-images:** Paris, Bibliotheque Nationale (cr). **49 Yumiko Europe:** Joris Jan Bos (tl). **Getty Images:** Corbis / Hulton-Deutsch Collection (r). **50 ArenaPAL:** Bill Cooper (bl); Marilyn Kingwill / Choreography: Sir Peter Wright (cl); Johan Persson (br). **Getty Images:** Bettmann (tr); WireImage / Earl Gibson III (bc). **51 Getty Images:** AFP Photo / Attila Kibenedek (bl); Cindy Ord (tl); The Washington Post / Bill O'Leary (tr); Corbis / Robbie Jack / Choreography: Sir Peter Wright (br). **52-53 Getty Images:** Corbis / Robbie Jack / Choreography: Sir Peter Wright. **54 ArenaPAL:** V. Blioh / Sputnik (cl). **SuperStock:** A. Burkatovski / Fine Art Images (tr). **55 akg-images:** Anatolij Fjodorowitsch Gelzer / Moscow, Bakhrushin Museum (c). **Internet Archive:** Adam, Adolphe, 1803-1856; Strube, Gustav, 1867-1953; Dwight, John Sullivan, 1813-1893 / Brigham Young University / Harold B. Lee Library (br). **56-57 Getty Images:** DeAgostini. **58 ArenaPAL:** TopFoto (cl). **Lebrecht Music and Arts:** Leemage (tr). **59 Alamy Stock Photo:** Chronicle (c). **The New York Public Library:** Jerome Robbins Dance Division, "The opera polka" (cra). **60 ArenaPAL:** Roger-Viollet / Colette Masson. **61 Huset Mydtskov. 62 Alamy Stock Photo:** Archive PL (br). **ArenaPAL:** Nigel Norrington (bl). **63 ArenaPAL:** Marilyn Kingwill. **64 ArenaPAL:** Royal Academy of Dance (tr). **The New York Public Library:** Jerome Robbins Dance Division,"The celebrated Pas de quatre composed by Jules Perrot". (bl). **65 Costin Radu Photography:** Royal Danish Ballet (b). **66 Alamy Stock Photo:** Paul Fearn (tr). **ArenaPAL:** Sputnik Images (cl). **67 Alamy Stock Photo:** Paul Fearn (br). **The Metropolitan Museum of Art:** Bequest of Mrs. Harry Payne Bingham, 1986 (c). **68-69 ArenaPAL:** Nigel Norrington. **70 Getty Images:** Ian Gavan (t). **71 Getty Images:** Corbis / Leo Mason (cr); The Asahi Shimbun (cl); Heritage Images / Fine Art Images (bl). **72 Getty Images:** Corbis / Leo Mason (bl); Ian Gavan (tr); TASS (br). **The New York Public Library:** Jerome Robbins Dance Division, "The corsair" (clb). **73 ArenaPAL:** Marilyn Kingwill (br); Nigel Norrington (tl); Sputnik Images (tr). **Getty Images:** Corbis / Leo Mason (bl). **74-75 Elliott Franks. 78 Getty Images:** Jack Vartoogian. **80**

Getty Images: Corbis / Robbie Jack. **81 ArenaPAL:** Sputnik Images (br). **Bridgeman Images:** Tretyakov Gallery, Moscow, Russia / Ryndin, Vadim Fyodorovich (tl). **Getty Images:** David M. Benett (bl). **82 ArenaPAL:** Mander and Mitchenson / University of Bristol (cl); Roger-Viollet / Colette Masson (bl). **Elliott Franks:** (br). **Getty Images:** Cindy Ord (tr). **83 ArenaPAL:** Marilyn Kingwill (tl). **Getty Images:** Corbis / Robbie Jack (cra, br); Linda Vartoogian (bl). **84-85 Getty Images:** AFP / John D Mchugh. **86 Alamy Stock Photo:** Paul Fearn (bl). **Rex by Shutterstock:** Mayette / AP / Choreography by George Balanchine © The George Balanchine Trust (cr). **87 ArenaPAL:** Nigel Norrington. **88-89 4Corners:** Günter Gräfenhain. **90 ArenaPAL:** Royal Opera House / Felix Fonteyn / Choreography: Frederick Ashton © Anthony Russell-Roberts CBE (b). **Lebrecht Music and Arts:** Leemage / Selva (tr). **91 ArenaPAL:** Roger-Viollet / Colette Masson (tr). **Getty Images:** Anthony Barboza (cla). **92 Alamy Stock Photo:** Collection PJ (bc). **ArenaPAL:** Royal Opera House / Tristram Kenton / Choreography: Frederick Ashton © Anthony Russell-Roberts CBE (tr, br); Royal Opera House / Felix Fonteyn / Choreography: Frederick Ashton © Anthony Russell-Roberts CBE (bl). **Getty Images:** Corbis / Robbie Jack (cl). **93 akg-images:** Erich Lessing (tr). **ArenaPAL:** Royal Opera House / Tristram Kenton / Choreography: Frederick Ashton © Anthony Russell-Roberts CBE (c, bl); Johan Persson / Choreography: Frederick Ashton © Jean-Pierre Gasquet (br). **94-95 ArenaPAL:** Roger-Viollet / Colette Masson. **96 ArenaPAL:** Sputnik Images / TopFoto (tr). **Lebrecht Music and Arts:** De Agostini (cl). **97 Bridgeman Images:** Private Collection (cra). **Rex by Shutterstock:** Sovfoto / Universal Images Group. **98-99 Alamy Stock Photo:** Brian Jannsen. **100 Wikimedia:** Imperial Mariinsky Theatre. St. Petersburg / MrLopez2681 (b). **101 ArenaPAL:** Johan Persson (br); Russia's President Vladimir Putin with Ulyana Lopatkina-Sputnik Images (cra). **Getty Images:** AFP Photo / Saeed Khan (tl). **102 Alamy Stock Photo:** Paul Fearn (tr). **ArenaPAL:** Nigel Norrington (bl); Topfoto / Sputnik Images (cr); Diana Zehetner (c). **Getty Images:** TASS / Vyacheslav Prokofyev (br). **103 ArenaPAL:** Royal Opera House / Tristram Kenton (bl); Sputnik Images (tl). **Elliott Franks:** (br). **Getty Images:** AFP / Attila Kisbenedek (tr). **104-105 Getty Images:** Robbie Jack. **106 Alamy Stock Photo:** Interfoto (cl, tr). **107 ArenaPAL:** Sputnik Images / TopFoto. **Getty Images:** De Agostini / A. Dagli Orti (br). **108 Getty Images:** Jack Vartoogian (b). **109 Getty Images:** AFP / Stringer (bl); Roger-Viollet / Lipnitzki; Linda Vartoogian (br). **110 Getty Images:** Corbis / Peter Andrews (bl); Heritage Images / Fine Art Images (tr); TASS / Vyacheslav Prokofyev (cl); Jack Mitchell (bc); Jack Vartoogian (br). **111 ArenaPAL:** Mark Ellidge (tr). **Getty Images:** Corbis / Leo Mason (br); Jack Vartoogian (bl). **TopFoto.co.uk:** SCRSS (tl). **112-113 Andrew Ross:** Birmingham Royal Ballet. **114 Alamy Stock Photo:** Paul Fearn (cl). **ArenaPAL:** Fine Art Images / HIP / TopFoto (tr, br). **115 Getty Images:** Guildhall Library & Art Gallery / Heritage Images (cr). **Penrodas Collection:** (l). **116-117 Getty Images:** Corbis / Robbie Jack. **118 Getty Images:** Corbis / Bojan Brecelj. **119 Alamy Stock Photo:** Heritage Image Partnership Ltd (tr). **Getty Images:** Robbie Jack (b); Los Angeles Times / Carolyn Cole (cla). **120 ArenaPAL:** Royal Opera House / Frank Sharman (tr). **Elliott Franks:** (bl). **Getty Images:** Corbis / Leo Mason (br). **121 ArenaPAL:** Johan Persson (c); Sputnik Images (tr). **Getty Images:** Corbis / Leo Mason (br); ullstein bild / Dagmar Scherf (tl); LatinContent / Jam Media / Juan Villa (bl). **122-123 Alamy Stock Photo:** Nikolay Vinokurov. **124 Alamy Stock Photo:** Courtesy: CSU Archives / Everett Collection (cl). **ArenaPAL:** The Granger Collection (tr). **125 ArenaPAL:** Roger-Viollet. **Rex by Shutterstock:** Museum of London (br). **126-127 ArenaPAL:** Royal Opera House. **128 ArenaPAL:** Royal Opera House / Johan Persson / Choreography: Sir Peter Wright (t). **129 ArenaPAL:** Nigel Norrington (tl); Sputnik Images (bl). **Getty Images:** Corbis / Robbie Jack / Choreography: Sir Peter Wright (br). **130 ArenaPAL:** Nigel Norrington (tr, br); Topfoto / SCRSS (bl). **Getty Images:** Corbis / Robbie Jack / Choreography: Sir Peter Wright (c). **131 ArenaPAL:** Bill Cooper / Choreography: Sir Peter Wright (bl); Mark Ellidge / Choreography: Sir Peter Wright (tl). **Getty Images:** Corbis / Robbie Jack / Choreography: Sir Peter Wright (br); Heritage Images / Fine Art Images (tr). **132-133 Getty Images:** Corbis / Robbie Jack. **134 ArenaPAL:** Performing Arts Images (bl). **Getty Images:** The AGE (br). **135 Getty Images:** John Bryson. **136-137 Alamy Stock Photo:** Everett Collection Inc. **138 Getty Images:** Heritage Images / Museum of London. **139 ArenaPAL:** Topfoto (c). **Getty Images:** Hulton Archive / Claude Harris (br). **142 Getty Images:** Los Angeles Times / Gary Friedman. **144 Alamy Stock Photo:** John Astor (tr). **Getty Images:** Sasha / Stringer (cl). **145 ArenaPAL:** Independent Producers / RNB / Collection Christophel (br). **Getty Images:** Fine Art Images / Heritage Images (cl). **146 ArenaPAL:** Sputnik Images (b). **147 Getty Images:** Bettmann. **148-149 Getty Images:** The Print Collector. **150 ArenaPAL:** (tr). **Getty Images:** Time Life Pictures / Mansell / The LIFE Picture Collection (cl). **151 Alamy Stock Photo:** Chronicle (cr). **Getty Images:** ullstein bild Dtl. / Contributor (c). **152 Getty Images:** Print Collector (cra). **The New York Public Library:** Martha Swope / UNK, "New York City Ballet - "Firebird". / Choreography by George Balanchine © The George Balanchine Trust (bl). **153 Getty Images:** Jack Mitchell / Choreography by George Balanchine © The George Balanchine Trust. **154 akg-images:** © The Estate of Edmund Dulac. All rights reserved. / © DACS 2018 (cl). **Getty Images:** George Hoyningen-Huene / Condé Nast (tr). **155 ArenaPAL:** Royal Academy of Dance (cr). **Getty Images:** Apic / Retired (c). **156 Bridgeman Images:** British Library, London, UK / © British Library Board. All Rights Reserved (cr). **Getty Images:** Popperfoto (bl). **157 ArenaPAL:** Marilyn Kingwill. **158 akg-images:** Erich Lessing (br). **ArenaPAL:** Heritage Image / Fine Art Images (bl). **Getty Images:** DeAgostini (cr). **159 Getty Images:** Bettmann; The Print Collector / Art Media (bl). **160 Alamy Stock Photo:** Linh Hassel / age fotostock (tr). **Getty Images:** Art Media / Print Collector (cl). **161 ArenaPAL:** ullstein bild (cr). **Getty Images:** Hulton-Deutsch Collection / Corbis (c). **162-163 Getty Images:** Sygma / Thierry Orban. **164 Getty Images:** Los Angeles Times / Gary Friedman (t). **165 ArenaPAL:** Roger-Viollet / Boris Lipnitzki (br). **Getty Images:** Corbis / Robbie Jack (c); Jack Mitchell / Martha Graham Dance Company (tl). **166 Alamy Stock Photo:** Sputnik Images (bl). **ArenaPAL:** Clive Barda (cl); Roger-Viollet (tr); Johan Persson (cr). **Getty Images:** Corbis / Robbie Jack (br). **167 Alamy Stock Photo:** Vibrant Pictures (tr). **ArenaPAL:** Royal Academy of Dance (cl). **Getty Images:** Corbis / Robbie Jack (b). **Rex by Shutterstock:** Shutterstock / Alastair Muir (tl, cr). **168-169 Getty Images:** Corbis / Robbie Jack. **170 ArenaPAL:** TopFoto (tr). **Bridgeman Images:** AGIP (cl). **171 Imperial War Museum:** IWM (D 14038) / Ministry Of Information Second World War Official Collection (l). **Rambert Dance**

Company: (cr). **172 Alamy Stock Photo:** Paul Fearn (cra). **ArenaPAL:** Roger-Viollet / Colette Masson (bl). **173 akg-images:** Eric Vandeville / Succession Picasso / © DACS 2018. **174-175 Library of Congress, Washington, D.C.**. **176 ArenaPAL:** Royal Opera House / Tristram Kenton (cr). **Getty Images:** Conde Nast / Cecil Beaton (bl). **177 ArenaPAL:** Linda Rich (b). **178 Alamy Stock Photo:** Everett Collection Historical / Martha Graham in Imperial Gesture, Choreographed by Martha Graham / Martha Graham Dance Company (tr). **ArenaPAL:** TopFoto / Martha Graham in Night Journey, Choreographed by Martha Graham / Martha Graham Dance Company (clb). **179 Bridgeman Images:** Photo © Collection Gregoire / Martha Graham / Martha Graham in Herodiade, Choreographed by Martha Graham / Cris Alexander / Martha Graham Dance Company (crb). **Getty Images:** Stringer / Hulton Archive / Martha Graham in Salem Shore, Choreographed by Martha Graham / Martha Graham Dance Company (c). **180 ArenaPAL:** Roger-Viollet / Choreography by George Balanchine © The George Balanchine Trust. **181 Getty Images:** Robbie Jack / Choreography by George Balanchine © The George Balanchine Trust (br). **Paul Kolnik:** New York City Ballet / Permission: Adrian Danchig-Waring / Ashly Isaacs / Lauren Lovette / Tiler Peck / Choreography by George Balanchine © The George Balanchine Trust (c). **182-183 Getty Images:** ASAblanca / Robert Griffin. **184 Getty Images:** Popperfoto / Choreography: Dame Ninette de Valois © The Royal Ballet School, London (tr). **V&A Images / Victoria and Albert Museum, London:** Choreography: Dame Ninette de Valois © The Royal Ballet School, London (cl). **185 Getty Images:** Sasha / Choreography: Dame Ninette de Valois © The Royal Ballet School, London (c). **Lebrecht Music and Arts:** Choreography: Dame Ninette de Valois © The Royal Ballet School, London / Set Design: Edward McKnight Kauffer (br). **186 ArenaPAL:** Clive Barda (bl). **V&A Images / Victoria and Albert Museum, London:** Gabrielle Enthoven Collection / Choreography by George Balanchine © The George Balanchine Trust (cr). **187 ArenaPAL:** TopFoto / HIP / Fine Art Images / Fine Art Images / HIP / TopFoto / HIP / Fine Art Images / State Museum of Theatre and Music Art, St Petersburg / © DACS 2018 (cl). **Bolshoi Theatre:** Bolshoi Ballet / Damir Yusupov (b). **188-189 Getty Images:** AFP / Damir Yusupov. **190 Paul Kolnik:** New York City Ballet / Choreography by George Balanchine © The George Balanchine Trust (b). **191 Bridgeman Images:** Private Collection (cl). **Getty Images:** Jack Mitchell (bl). **192 ArenaPAL:** Nigel Norrington (bl); Royal Opera House (cr). **193 ArenaPAL:** Nigel Norrington. **194 Alamy Stock Photo:** Everett Collection Inc. **195 Alamy Stock Photo:** Pictorial Press Ltd (br). **196 ArenaPAL:** Performing Arts Images / Photo: Denis de Marney (bl). **V&A Images / Victoria and Albert Museum, London:** (c) Nicholas Georgiadis (cr). **197 Paul Kolnik:** New York City Ballet / Permission: Sterling Hyltin / Gonzalo Garcia / Choreography by George Balanchine © The George Balanchine Trust. **200 ArenaPAL:** Roger-Viollet / Colette Masson. **202 Getty Images:** Corbis / Robbie Jack (t). **203 ArenaPAL:** Royal Opera House / Tristram Kenton / Choreography: Frederick Ashton © Wendy Ellis Somes (bl). **Getty Images:** The LIFE Picture Collection / Gjon Mili (tr). **TopFoto.co.uk:** Johan Persson (br). **204 ArenaPAL:** Marilyn Kingwill (br); Royal Opera House / Tristram Kenton / Choreography: Frederick Ashton © Wendy Ellis Somes (tr). **Getty Images:** Jo Hale (bl). **205 ArenaPAL:** Roger-Viollet (cl); Royal Opera House / Tristram Kenton / Choreography: Frederick Ashton © Wendy Ellis Somes (tl). **Getty Images:** Corbis / Leo Mason (br); Royal Opera House / Tristram Kenton / Choreography: Frederick Ashton © Wendy Ellis Somes (bl). **206-207 ArenaPAL:** Roger-Viollet / Colette Masson. **208 ArenaPAL:** Sputnik Images / TopFoto (cl); SCRSS - Society for Co-operation in Russian & Soviet Studies / Topfoto (tr). **209 ArenaPAL:** SCRSS - Society for Co-operation in Russian & Soviet Studies / Topfoto (crb); ITAR-TASS / Georgy Petrusov / Topfoto. **210 Getty Images:** Baron / Choreography: Frederick Ashton © Wendy Ellis-Somes. **211 ArenaPAL:** Nigel Norrington / Choreography: Frederick Ashton © Wendy Ellis- Somes (bl); Nigel Norrington / Choreography: Frederick Ashton © Wendy Ellis-Somes (br). **212 ArenaPAL:** Johan Persson / Choreography by George Balanchine © The George Balanchine Trust (bl). **NYCB Archive:** Choreography by George Balanchine © The George Balanchine Trust and George Platt Lynes (cr). **213 Getty Images:** Afro American Newspapers / Gado / Choreography by George Balanchine © The George Balanchine Trust. **214 Paul Kolnik:** New York City Ballet / Permission: Tyler Angle / Maria Kowroski / Choreography by George Balanchine © School of American Ballet. **215 ArenaPAL:** ullstein bild / Choreography by George Balanchine © School of American Ballet (cla); Royal Opera House / Choreography by George Balanchine © School of American Ballet (br). **216 ArenaPAL:** Topfoto (tr). **V&A Images / Victoria and Albert Museum, London:** Anthony Crickmay / Choreography: Frederick Ashton © Sir Anthony Dowell CBE (cl). **217 Rex by Shutterstock:** Reg Wilson. **V&A Images / Victoria and Albert Museum, London:** Choreography: Frederick Ashton © Wendy Ellis-Somes (br). **218 ArenaPAL:** Nigel Norrington (bl); Royal Opera House (cr). **219 ArenaPAL:** Royal Opera House. **220 Getty Images:** Jack Mitchell (tr, cl). **221 AF Fotografie:** (br). **Getty Images:** Baron / Stringer (l). **222-223 Paul Kolnik:** New York City Ballet. **224 ArenaPAL:** Nigel Norrington / Choreography by George Balanchine © The George Balanchine Trust (cl). **Getty Images:** Ernst Haas / BALANCHINE is a Trademark of The George Balanchine Trust (tr). **225 Getty Images:** Gjon Mili / The LIFE Premium Collection / BALANCHINE is a Trademark of The George Balanchine Trust (cr). **The New York Public Library:** Martha Swope / Billy Rose Theatre Division, "New York City Ballet "The Four Temperaments". / BALANCHINE is a Trademark of The George Balanchine Trust / Choreography by George Balanchine © The George Balanchine Trust (c). **226 ArenaPAL:** Nigel Norrington / Choreography by George Balanchine © The George Balanchine Trust (br). **227 ArenaPAL:** Roger-Viollet / Colette Masson (cl); Roger-Viollet / Colette Masson / Dancer: Sylvie Guillem (b). **228 ArenaPAL:** ullstein bild (cl). **Getty Images:** Manuel Litran / Paris Match (tr). **229 Getty Images:** Fabrice Coffrini / AFP (br); Lipnitzki / Roger Viollet. **230 eyevine:** Redux / The New York Times / Andrea Mohin / Choreography by George Balanchine © The George Balanchine Trust (cr). **Paul Kolnik:** Dancer: Jacqueline Green / Alvin Ailey American Dance Theater (cl); New York City Ballet / Permission: Tyler Angle / Jennie Somogyi / Choreography by George Balanchine © The George Balanchine Trust (bl). **231 Getty Images:** Jack Mitchell / Alvin Ailey American Dance Theater (br). **232 Getty Images:** Jack Mitchell (tr). **Magnum Photos:** Philippe Halsman (cl). **233 ArenaPAL:** Peter Joslin (cr). **Getty Images:** Archive Photos. **234 Getty Images:** The LIFE Picture Collection / Gjon Mili (b). **235 ArenaPAL:** Royal Opera House / Helen Maybanks / Choreography: Frederick Ashton © Anthony Russell-Roberts CBE (r). **Getty Images:** ullstein bild / Virginia (bl); Corbis / Robbie Jack / Choreography: Frederick Ashton © Jean-Pierre Gasquet (tl). **236 ArenaPAL:** Royal Opera House / Tristram Kenton / Choreography: Frederick Ashton © Jean-Pierre Gasquet (cr, bl); Clive Barda / Choreography: Frederick Ashton © Jean-Pierre Gasquet (tr); ullstein bild / Kujath / Choreography: Frederick Ashton © Jean-Pierre Gasquet (br). **237 ArenaPAL:** Nigel Norrington / Choreography: Frederick Ashton © Jean-Pierre Gasquet (bl); Roger-Viollet / Colette Masson / Choreography: Frederick Ashton © Jean-Pierre Gasquet (br). **Getty Images:** Corbis / Robbie Jack / Choreography: Frederick Ashton © Jean-Pierre Gasquet (cl); ullstein bild / Binder / Choreography: Frederick Ashton © Jean-Pierre Gasquet (cr). **238-239 ArenaPAL:** Roger-Viollet / Colette Masson / Choreography: Frederick Ashton © Jean-Pierre Gasquet. **240 Alamy Stock Photo:** Keystone Pictures

USA (tr). **Lebrecht Music and Arts:** Rue des Archives (cl). **241 ArenaPAL:** Mander and Mitchenson / University of Bristol (crb); SCRSS - Society for Co-operation in Russian & Soviet Studies (l). **242-243 Getty Images:** Gamma-Keystone / Keystone-France. **244 ArenaPAL:** Nigel Norrington (b). **245 Magnum Photos:** Eve Arnold. **246 ArenaPAL:** TopFoto (cl); Roger Wood / Royal Opera House (tr). **247 Getty Images:** Silver Screen Collection (crb); Baron / Stringer. **248 Alamy Stock Photo:** V&A Images (tr). **ArenaPAL:** Royal Opera House (b). **249 ArenaPAL:** Royal Opera House. **250 Getty Images:** Reg Innell / Toronto Star (tr); adoc-photos / Corbis (cl). **Mirrorpix:** (l). **251 Alamy Stock Photo:** Everett Collection, Inc. (br). **252 ArenaPAL:** Nigel Norrington / Choreography by George Balanchine © The George Balanchine Trust (b). **The New York Public Library:** UNK, "New York City Ballet production of movie version of "A Midsummer Night's Dream". / Choreography by George Balanchine © The George Balanchine Trust (cr). **253 ArenaPAL:** Johan Persson (bl). **Getty Images:** Erich Auerbach (br). **254 ArenaPAL:** Buhs / Remmler / ullstein bild (cl); John Timbers (tr). **255 ArenaPAL:** TopFoto / Choreography: Frederick Ashton © Anthony Russell-Roberts CBE (crb). **The Round Company:** Photo: © Roy Round (l). **256 Getty Images:** A. Jones. **257 ArenaPAL:** Nigel Norrington (br); Royal Opera House (cla). **258 ArenaPAL:** Bill Cooper / Choreography: Sir Peter Wright (cl); Royal Academy of Dance / Choreography: Sir Peter Wright (tr). **259 ArenaPAL:** Donald Southern / Royal Opera House / Choreography: Sir Peter Wright. **Oberon Books:** © Pieter Kooistra; Wrights & Wrongs published by Oberon Books / Choreography: Sir Peter Wright (br). **260 ArenaPAL:** Royal Opera House (cr). **Getty Images:** ullstein bild (bl). **261 ArenaPAL:** Nigel Norrington. **262 Getty Images:** Hulton-Deutsch Collection / CORBIS (tr); Rudolf Dietrich / ullstein bild (cl). **263 ArenaPAL:** Roger-Viollet (br); Roger Wood / Royal Opera House (l). **264-265 4Corners:** Richard Taylor. **266 ArenaPAL:** Nigel Norrington / Choreography by George Balanchine © The George Balanchine Trust. **267 ArenaPAL:** Nigel Norrington / Choreography by George Balanchine © The George Balanchine Trust (br). **The New York Public Library:** Martha Swope / Billy Rose Theatre Division,"New York City Ballet "Jewels". / Choreography by George Balanchine © The George Balanchine Trust (c). **268 ArenaPAL:** Bill Cooper (b); Royal Academy of Dance (cr). **269 ArenaPAL:** Henrietta Butler. **270 ArenaPAL:** ITAR-TASS (bl); Sputnik Images (cra). **271 ArenaPAL:** Sputnik Images. **272 ArenaPAL:** Clive Barda (tr); Roger Wood / Royal Opera House (bl). **273 AF Fotografie:** (cr). **V&A Images / Victoria and Albert Museum, London:** Anthony Crickmay. **274-275 Getty Images:** iStock / RugliG. **276 ArenaPAL:** Henrietta Butler (cr); Nobby Clark (bl). **277 Getty Images:** Sven Creutzmann / Mambo Photo. **278 ArenaPAL:** Sputnik Images. **279 ArenaPAL:** Sputnik Images (cla). **Bolshoi Theatre:** Bolshoi Ballet / Damir Yusupov (br). **282 Getty Images:** Corbis / Robbie Jack. **284 ArenaPAL:** Johan Persson (bl). **V&A Images / Victoria and Albert Museum, London:** Anthony Crickmay (cra). **285 ArenaPAL:** Elliott Franks. **286 Getty Images:** The Washington Post / Katherine Frey. **287 ArenaPAL:** Johan Persson (cl, b). **288 Getty Images:** Robbie Jack / Corbis (cl); Jerome De Perlinghi (tr). **289 Getty Images:** Anne-Christine Poujoulat / AFP; Pascal Guyot / Afp (br). **290 Front Row Posters:** (br). **The Round Company:** Photo: © Roy Round (bl). **291 ArenaPAL:** Bill Cooper. **292 Alamy Stock Photo:** PBS / Everett Collection Inc (cl). **Magnum Photos:** Ferdinando Scianna (tr). **293 Alamy Stock Photo:** Everett Collection, Inc. © Columbia Pictures (br). **Getty Images:** Joan Adlen Photography. **294-295 ArenaPAL:** Pete Jones. **296 Getty Images:** Gamma-Rapho / Alain Benainous / Dancer: Sylvie Guillem (cl). **Kiyonori Hasegawa:** Dancer: Sylvie Guillem (tr). **297 ArenaPAL:** Bill Cooper / Dancer: Sylvie Guillem. **298 ArenaPAL:** Mark Ellidge. **299 ArenaPAL:** Roger-Viollet / Colette Masson / Dancer: Sylvie Guillem (cl). **Getty Images:** LightRocket / Pacific Press / Hugh Peterswald (br). **300 ArenaPAL:** Bill Cooper / Choreography by George Balanchine © The George Balanchine Trust (cl). **John Garrett:** (tr). **301 ArenaPAL:** Bill Cooper (crb). **Camera Press:** Photograph by Anthony Crickmay (l). **302 Getty Images:** AFP / Boris Horvat (bl); Corbis / NurPhoto / Oscar Gonzalez (tr). **303 Getty Images:** AFP / Francois Guillot (cla, br). **304 ArenaPAL:** Roger-Viollet / Colette Masson (cl). **Maria Austria Instituut | MAI:** Dirk Buwalda (tr). **305 ArenaPAL:** Johan Persson. **Kristina Hruska:** (br). **306 Getty Images:** Split Second. **307 Getty Images:** Boston Globe (cr); Split Second (bl). **308 ArenaPAL:** Bill Cooper (bl). **Getty Images:** Gemma Levine (tr). **309 Front Row Posters:** (br). **Getty Images:** Corbis / Robbie Jack (l). **310 ArenaPAL:** Bill Cooper (bl); Royal Opera House (cr). **311 ArenaPAL:** Leslie E. Spatt. **312 ArenaPAL:** John Garrett (tr). **Getty Images:** United News / Popperfoto (cl). **313 ArenaPAL:** Bill Cooper (c, br). **314 ArenaPAL:** Nigel Norrington. **315 Getty Images:** Bertrand Rindoff Petroff (clb). **Hugo Glendinning:** Dancer: Richard Windsor (br). **316 ArenaPAL:** Vladimir Vyatkin / Sputnik Images (cl). **Getty Images:** Bertrand Guay / AFP (tr). **317 Getty Images:** Jack Mitchell. **Rex by Shutterstock:** Daniel Bockwoldt / Epa (crb). **318-319 4Corners:** Claudio Cassaro. **320 ArenaPAL:** Nobby Clark (tr). **Getty Images:** Robbie Jack / Corbis (cl). **321 ArenaPAL:** Andrej Uspenski / Royal Opera House. **Getty Images:** Robbie Jack / Corbis (crb). **322 ArenaPAL:** Nigel Norrington (bl). **323 ArenaPAL:** Nigel Norrington (cl). **Getty Images:** AFP / Dmitry Kostyukov (br). **324 ArenaPAL:** Johan Persson (tr). **Getty Images:** Robbie Jack / Corbis (cl). **325 Alamy Stock Photo:** Metrodome / Everett Collection Inc (br). **ArenaPAL:** Johan Persson / Choreography by George Balanchine © The George Balanchine Trust. **326-327 Getty Images:** Moment / Nutexzles. **328 ArenaPAL:** Bill Cooper (bl); Royal Opera House (cr). **329 ArenaPAL:** Royal Opera House. **330 ArenaPAL:** Marilyn Kingwill (cl); Johan Persson (tr). **331 ArenaPAL:** Clive Barda (cra); Johan Persson (l). **332 ArenaPAL:** Nigel Norrington (bl); Johan Persson (br). **333 Getty Images:** Corbis / Robbie Jack. **334 ArenaPAL:** Bill Cooper (tr); Johan Persson (cl). **335 Getty Images:** Robbie Jack / Corbis (br); Wendy Maeda / The Boston Globe. **336-337 Laurent Liotardo Photography**. **338 Getty Images:** Apic (bl). **339 ArenaPAL:** Topfoto / The Granger Collection. **340 Getty Images:** Jack Mitchell. **341 ArenaPAL:** Alan Bergman (br); Topfoto / TASS / Alexander Konkov (tc). **342 ArenaPAL:** The Royal Academyof Dance / G.B.L. Wilson (tl). **Getty Images:** Jack Mitchell (b). **343 ArenaPAL:** N.B.C. / Boosey and Hawkes Collection. **344 ArenaPAL:** Francis Loney (tc). **345 Getty Images:** Corbis / Robbie Jack (bl); The Washington Post / Yana Paskova (tr). **346 ArenaPAL:** Johan Persson (br). **Getty Images:** Photo12 / UIG (cl). **347 ArenaPAL:** Clive Barda (tl). **348 ArenaPAL:** Johan Persson (tr); Royal Opera House / Johan Persson (tl); Royal Academy of Dance / G.B.L. Wilson (tc). **349 ArenaPAL:** Nigel Norrington (tl); Johan Persson (tc, tr). **360 Mirrorpix.**

Endpaper image: Rudolf Nureyev and Margot Fonteyn, c.1963 (gelatin silver print), Beaton Cecil, (1904-80) **/ Private Collection / Photo © Christie's Images / Bridgeman Images / © The Cecil Beaton Studio Archive at Sotheby's**

BALANCHINE is a Trademark of The George Balanchine Trust.
All photos of ballets by George Balanchine, Choreography by George Balanchine © The George Balanchine Trust, with the exception of Symphony in C, Choreography by George Balanchine © School of American Ballet

All other images © Dorling Kindersley
For further information see: www.dkimages.com